THE EUROPEAN PARLIAMENT

The European Parliament

by
FRANCIS JACOBS
and
RICHARD CORBETT
with
Michael Shackleton

Westview Press

BOULDER & SAN FRANCISCO

THE EUROPEAN PARLIAMENT

Published by Longman Group UK Limited, Westgate House,
The High, Harlow, Essex, CM20 1YR, United Kingdom.
Telephone (0279) 442601
Telex 81491 Padlog
Facsimile (0279) 444501

Published in 1990 in the United States by Westview Press,
5500 Central Avenue, Boulder, Colorado 80301, USA.

ISBN 0-582-06269-1 (Longman)
ISBN 0-8133-1210-8 (Westview)

British Library Cataloguing in Publication Data
Jacobs, Francis. (Francis Brendan), 1951
    The European Parliament.
    1. European. Parliament
    I. Title   II. Corbett, Richard
    341.2424

ISBN 0-582-06269-1 (Longman)

Library of Congress Cataloging–in–Publication Data
Jacobs, Francis Brendan, 1951–
    The European Parliament / by Francis Jacobs and Richard Corbett.
        p. cm.
    ISBN 0–8133–1210–8
1. European Parliament.   I. Corbett, Richard
II. Title.
JN36. J33 1990
341. 24'24— do20   90–44535
                                                                         CIP

Produced by Longman Group (FE) Ltd
Printed in Hong Kong

Dedication

To Susan and Anne

TABLE OF CONTENTS

I: THE FRAMEWORK

II: THE ACTORS AND WORKING STRUCTURES

IV: CONCLUSION

V: APPENDICES

TABLES AND FIGURES

FOREWORD

As the two British Vice-Presidents of the European Parliament we welcome the appearance of this excellent and timely book, the first comprehensive survey for many years in the English language of the structure, working methods and evolving powers of the European Parliament.

Most Member States now recognize that they can achieve political and economic results through the European Community which even the most powerful of them could never achieve alone. This has been the motivating force with the 1992 programme and the further pooling of sovereignty which was necessary to bring it about. But every successful step forward brings a demand for more and already the Council, Commission and Parliament are looking forward to Economic and Monetary Union and to the further constitutional changes which that will need.

The structures, procedures and decision-taking mechanisms laid down as a result of these debates will be part of the constitutional system of a European Union by the next century.

The Parliament is the political dynamo in this process since the Council has no power of initiative and the Commission has no political base. And the Parliament wants in law as well as in practice proper powers of legislation and scrutiny and powers of appointment or confirmation of key administrative posts. It wants to eliminate the "democratic deficit", to recover at European level the powers of national parliaments which have disappeared into a bureaucratic black hole.

This book explains the state of the art in the European Parliament. It is eminently readable, having avoided an overly academic or legalistic approach, and enables the reader to get a "flavour" of the Parliament. It is up to date with the most recent developments in the fascinating evolution of this unique institution.

Sir Fred Catherwood, MEP
(Conservative)
Vice President
European Parliament

David Martin, MEP
(Labour)
Vice President
European Parliament

ACKNOWLEDGEMENTS

The authors' main acknowledgement as regards the content of this book is to Mike Shackleton, who not only drafted the chapter on the budget, and redrafted the first and last chapters of the book, but read through the rest of the text and made valuable suggestions throughout. At editing sessions he was a fully-fledged member of the team.

A number of other colleagues and friends made helpful comments on individual sections of the book. Particular thanks to Kieran Bradley, who read large sections of the text, and to Benoit Woringer and Roger Glass, who contributed their specific expertise. Any errors, of course, are the co-authors' responsibility alone.

Our other main acknowledgements are to Georgina Packer, Caroline Wood, Margaret Buchanan and Majella McCone who typed (and retyped) the text rapidly and efficiently, an achievement whose true significance can only be appreciated by those who have endured the illegible scrawl and hieroglyphics passed off as writing by the co-authors.

A word of thanks to Michel Beiger and his hospital staff at the café-restaurant "La Vignette" in Strasbourg, at which many of the final editing sessions took place, with papers and notes strewn among the delicious food and bottles of Pinot Noir.

An additional plea for indulgence from Hannah and Sophie, our respective daughters, both of whom were born during the project, and who were deprived of more of their fathers' company and attention than they should have been!

Finally, the co-authors would like to emphasize that the views expressed in this book are theirs alone, and do not necessarily reflect those of the Parliament or of its members.

The publishers are grateful to the UK Press and Information Office of the European Parliament for providing the seating plan of the Parliament on p. xxi and the maps on pp. xx and 270.

INTRODUCTION

The European Parliament is the first, and so far the only experiment in transnational democracy. No other institution in the world brings together under one roof representatives from different states (at present 518 from 12 states), who have been directly elected to that institution and who have been given a range of legally-entrenched powers. Nowhere is there an equivalent body, eager both to exercise its powers beyond the reach of individual governments and to extend its influence over the decisions that are taken above the national level.

At the same time, the importance of the European Community as a whole is growing. Particularly since the mid-1980s when the aim of creating a Single Market by 1992 was agreed by the Member States, there has been increasing debate about the broader consequences of such a market and a general willingness to go beyond it to economic and monetary union. What role will the Parliament play as the Community moves towards a higher level of integration? Many argue that there is already a severe "democratic deficit" in the Community with too many decisions taken behind closed doors, often without the express approval of the Parliament. The broader and the more controversial the decisions to be taken, the more critical it will be to reassess the position of the Parliament.

But what kind of institution is the Parliament? How does it work and what sort of powers does it possess? This book will explore the answers to these questions. Three introductory chapters sketch out the institutional and historical context of the institution and explain how the Parliament is elected, where and when it meets and the languages that it uses. Two main sections follow: one considers the structure and operation of the Parliament, the other examines the range of its powers.

The first of these (Part II) describes the work of individual members of the European Parliament, its organization into Political Groups, and how it is led. It then examines the Parliament's committee structure, how its plenaries are run, and reviews the unfamiliar but growing phenomenon of intergroups. It concludes with a brief description of Parliament's secretariat.

In the next section (Part III) attention switches to examine Parliament's powers and how they have developed as well as the various ways in which Parliament exercises influence. It considers these matters in terms of the traditional functions of parliaments: participation in the legislative process, the authorisation of expenditure, control of the executive and the articulation of public concerns. It concludes with a look at the special interest of the European Parliament in further changing the Community's constitutional system.

The Parliament has evolved in several different ways since the first direct elections in 1979, but the question remains: where does the Parliament go from here? There is no question that it has made significant progress, as the remaining chapters of this book make clear, but it will not be easy for the Parliament to achieve the momentum necessary to gain a stronger role within the Community system. Nearly 20 years ago, Andrew Shonfield spoke of the European Community as engaged in a journey to an unknown destination, and this remains true today. No-one can predict with any degree of confidence what the Community will look like in 10 years' time, just as few could have guessed 10 years ago what it is like today. And what is true for the Community as a whole is equally true, if not more so, for the European Parliament. The final chapter in the book thus considers the future options available to the Parliament and the kinds of reform that it is likely to seek.

ABOUT THE AUTHORS

Francis Jacobs is Principal Administrator on the European Parliament secretariat, currently working on its Economic Committee and on its temporary committee on the impact of German unification. He is the editor and principal author of *Western European Political Parties: A Comprehensive Guide* (also published by Longman), and has contributed various articles and chapters on the work of the Parliament and its Political Groups.

Richard Corbett is an official of the European Parliament, currently on detachment to the secretariat of the Socialist Group of the Parliament where he is political advisor on constitutional questions. He has previously worked in Parliament as a clerk to various parliamentary committees and on relations with national parliaments. He has written widely on European affairs.

Michael Shackleton is Principal Administrator on the European Parliament's Committee on Budgets. He has written widely on community policies, notably on the Common Fisheries Policy and on Budgetary Policy. His latest publication is "Financing the European Community", prepared for the Royal Institute of International Affairs.

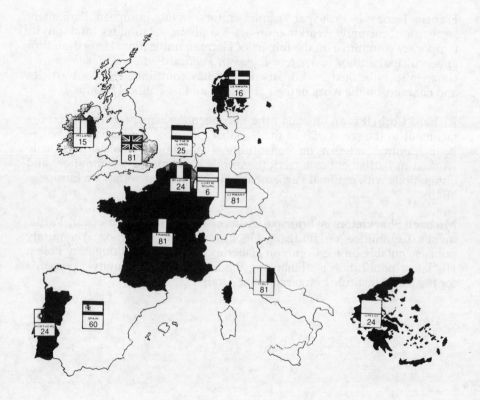

The European Community with number of MEPs per country

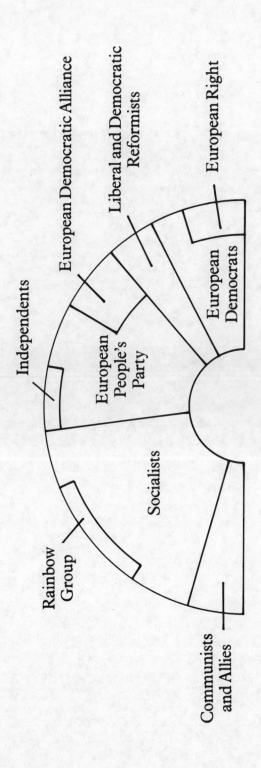

Independents

European Democratic Alliance

Liberal and Democratic Reformists

European Right

European People's Party

European Democrats

Rainbow Group

Socialists

Communists and Allies

Seating plan of Political Groups in the Strasbourg Parliament

I: THE FRAMEWORK

1. The Parliament in context

The institutional context

The European Parliament remains remote and unfamiliar to the majority of the European electorate. In part, this is because the amount of information about the Parliament is relatively limited. In the British context those who read newspapers, listen to the radio or watch television have an opportunity to follow what goes on in Parliament in London but they have to search hard to find the equivalent coverage of what happens in Strasbourg, Luxembourg and Brussels, the three working places of the European Parliament.

More important, however, Parliament operates within the broader framework of the European Community whose institutions have no exact counterpart in national political systems. Yet the European Community is not a traditional international organization; rather it enjoys certain features of supranationality, which effectively establish a tier of government above that of the Member States. It is a structure with a special purpose, namely the establishment of "an ever closer union among the peoples of Europe" and with law-making powers designed with that objective in mind. It can adopt binding legislation which does not have to pass through, still less be approved by national parliaments. Indeed this very fact formed part of the rationale for establishing a parliamentary institution at the European level.

The reasons for establishing this Community structure were twofold. First, there was the idealistic desire to bring together former enemies and to establish a lasting framework which would ensure stability. Second, there was the intensely practical concern to manage the growing interdependence of the European economies. The former idea was particularly important in the early years of the Community with the establishment of the European Coal and Steel Community (ECSC) in 1951, whereas the latter assumed greater weight in the 1960s after the setting-up of the European Economic Community. (The institutions of these two Communities along with the European Atomic Energy — EURATOM — were merged in 1965 and are referred to in this book as the European Community.) However, both elements have always been present, and indeed recent events in Eastern Europe have drawn attention once again to the argument that the Community can act as a framework for stability and for managing old enmities.

Probably the most familiar face of the Community structure is the *European Council*, the six-monthly gatherings at which the Heads of State and Government of the Community meet to resolve outstanding issues which their ministers have been unable to sort out or simply to discuss issues of common concern. However, the day-to-day work is carried out by a set of institutions, whose complex interrelationship is not matched by any traditional international body. The institutions are four in number: the *European Parliament*, the *Council* (generally referred to as the Council of Ministers), the *Commission* and the *Court of Justice*. The Court has the task of interpreting Community law in cases brought by individuals or firms or Member States against the Community institutions, by one Community institution against another or by the Commission against a Member State. The Court's role is of great and often underestimated importance in determining the direction of the Community. However, in this book, it is the relationships between the other three institutions which is central. Together they constitute a triangle, within which the Parliament has until now enjoyed a weaker position than either Commission or Council.

The Commission

The term Commission has a double meaning. In principle, it refers to the college of 17 Commissioners, who are nominated by the Member States to form the Community's executive. Two come from each of the larger states, France, Germany, Italy, United Kingdom and Spain, and one each from the others. They serve a four-year term and are headed by a President, also nominated by Member States but only for a two-year period. The present incumbent is the Frenchman Jacques Delors, who first took office in 1985 but was confirmed as President in 1987 and 1989. It is his job to distribute portfolios amongst the other Commissioners. In practice, the term Commission is used to refer to all the civil servants of the institution which the Commissioners are responsible for. They number some 13,000, working principally in Brussels but with a sizeable minority in Luxembourg. They are divided into Directorates-General, at present 22 in number, which cover the whole range of Community activity.

The Commission has the general task of acting as the guardian of the Treaties but it also has certain specific rights. It has the sole right of initiative to make proposals, the right to mediate between the competing claims of the other institutions and the right to implement decisions taken. Each of these rights have been the source of regular conflict with the Parliament. As the Parliament does not at present enjoy the right of initiative, it is eager to oblige the Commission to take over its proposals and has enjoyed a measure of success. Any mediation raises the issue of the willingness of the Commission to stand by the Parliament when it knows that final decisions rest with the Council. And the right to implement poses the traditional problems of the control of the executive by a parliamentary body, where the Parliament has developed certain important mechanisms of scrutiny.

The Council

The Council of Ministers brings together the ministers of the Twelve Member States, responsible for different areas of policy. Thus when agriculture is discussed, it is agriculture ministers who are present around the table; when the budget is discussed, budget ministers are there and so on. A special arrangement exists for Foreign Ministers who technically meet within a separate framework known as European Political Co-operation (EPC) when dealing with the political aspects of foreign policy as opposed to the commercial and trade aspects. Ministers usually meet in Brussels where the 2,900-strong secretariat is based, but three months a year (April, June and September) meetings take place in Luxembourg. The chairman-ship of meetings rotates with each country exercising the Presidency of the Council for six months before handing over to the next country in alphabetical order. In 1990, for example, Ireland held the Presidency for the first six months before handing over to Italy.

Under the existing Treaties the Council enjoys the last word on the amendment or adoption of legislative acts. In some areas, unanimity is necessary to get a decision (for example, the harmonization of taxation); more often a qualified majority will suffice to approve a Commission proposal (but unanimity to change it). In the second case, the Treaty lays down the weight that is accorded to each state. Germany, France, Italy and the United Kingdom all have 10 votes, Spain has eight, Belgium, Greece, the Netherlands and Portugal each have five, Denmark and Ireland each have three and Luxembourg has two. For a qualified majority 54 votes are required, with 23 votes from at least four states constituting a blocking minority.

Whichever decision-making process applies, the influence of the Parliament is limited. Although the Parliament is consulted on practically all proposals, if the Council can muster the requisite majority, then the legislation will pass. As we shall see, this statement considerably simplifies a much more complex reality and one which has not remained static. In particular, the Single European Act, a revision of the original Treaties agreed in 1986 which came into force in July 1987, has introduced a system of two readings by both Council and Parliament of certain categories of legislation, linked to the creation of a single market. Under this system, the Parliament has to muster 260 votes, i.e. half its membership, to amend proposed legislation in second reading. However, if it obtains this majority and if it obtains the support of the Commission for the amendments, then the Council can only override the Parliament by unanimity, which is far from easy to obtain. The psychological impact of this new procedure on the triangular relation between the three institutions has been very great indeed and within the Parliament it has prompted organizational change as well as encouraging the quest for wider involvement in the legislative process.

Other Community bodies

Outside the inner circle of institutions, there are other Community bodies which should be mentioned. The *Court of Auditors*, established in 1977 and based in Luxembourg, acts as a financial watchdog supervising the way that all the institutions spend their money. The *Economic and Social Committee*, based in Brussels, acts in an advisory capacity bringing together representatives from employers and employee organizations as well as from broader organizations, such as consumer groups. In Luxembourg, there is the *European Investment Bank* which acts as a borrower and lender for projects of Community interest both inside Europe and outside: it has a rather separate status, which exempts it, for example, from any form of parliamentary scrutiny.

The European Parliament and national parliaments

The workings of this array of institutions which make up the Community structure are difficult to understand in part because they are unfamiliar and are not replicated at the national level. However, the lack of understanding of the European Parliament is compounded by the fact that all the Member States of the Community have parliamentary bodies and everybody has some expectation as to what a parliament should be. Parliaments are seen as performing certain functions and inevitably the European Parliament is viewed against this background. One obvious function is that of legislation. The UK parliament, for example, is described as a legislative body, something which the European Parliament is only to a limited extent, although it is striving to strengthen its powers in this area. Hence, the tendency of some in Britain to suggest that the European Parliament is not a real parliament but rather a body that could be more reasonably described as an Assembly with less determinate powers.

But it is not useful to take one particular aspect as defining what it is that constitutes a parliament. To do so can lead to very perverse conclusions. For instance, the European Parliament is able to amend the budget to increase expenditure, something which the French parliament is not able to do under the French Constitution. But no one would want to say that the French parliament is not a real parliament. Rather their powers are different. Furthermore, it ignores the wider framework in which legislation in any political system is produced. Whereas in Britain, the government is in parliament and passes its legislation through parliament, this is not the case in the Community where there is a separation of powers between the three central institutions: legislation originates with the Commission, the Parliament gives its opinion and the Council of Ministers has the last word. The Council and the Commission do come to the Parliament, but as outsiders, explaining their positions: they are not operating *through* the Parliament in the way that the executive does in Britain.

What makes the European Parliament of interest is that it is a unique institution with an involvement in all the roles associated with parliaments. As Chapters 11 to 14 will show, it is concerned with influencing legislation, in drawing up a budget, in scrutinizing the executive, in making appointments and in providing a forum for discussions of political importance. The balance between these activities can certainly vary over time and between issues. Indeed, within the Parliament itself there are differences of view as to which activities are most important. For some, particularly those from northern European countries, it is vital to get involved in the fine-print of legislative detail; for others, the Parliament should seek to adopt a more broad-brush approach, concentrating on overall political priorities.

However, the important point is that the various roles are fulfilled in a very different way than that which applies in a national environment, particularly the British one. The distribution of members in Political

Groups cutting across nationality and the less clearly defined boundaries between left and right on the ideological spectrum contribute to an environment which is *sui generis* and not directly comparable with any national parliament.

Moreover, the Parliament has a further role which makes it distinctive from national parliaments, namely that it is interested in system change, i.e. in modifying the nature of the relationships that exist between it and the other Community institutions. Indeed, it is not possible to understand the workings of the Parliament without realizing that it is an institution concerned to alter the institutional *status quo*. To understand this point more fully, it is useful to review briefly its historical development from its first meeting in 1952 to the present day. Table 1 offers an overview of the Parliament's history in a nutshell.

The historical context

The establishment of a Parliamentary body among the institutions of the European Community was not only a gesture towards democratic scrutiny of the Community's supranational law-making powers, but also symbolic of the aspiration for that Community to develop into a closer form of union or federation. Indeed, it made little sense to provide for the eventual direct election of a common assembly responsible merely for debating coal and steel policy, as was the case with the original ECSC Treaty, unless such a body were to evolve into something more far reaching. An early indication of these aspirations was the decision of the Foreign Ministers of the Six to invite the ECSC assembly to transform itself into an ad hoc assembly to draft a constitution for a European Political Community. Although this fell with the demise of the European Defence Community in 1954, the provision for an Assembly and ultimately an elected one was later repeated in the EEC Treaty.

Having created a Parliamentary assembly, however, the Member States were extremely cautious about giving it any powers, even with regard to those areas in which their own national parliaments were asked to relinquish responsibility in favour of the Community institutions. Initially, the Assembly, as it was then designated, was given the power only to debate the activities of the High Authority (later the Commission) and to adopt, for good reason, a motion of censure by a two-thirds majority which would force the executive to resign. The Treaties also provided for Parliament to be consulted on certain categories of draft legislation.

These powers were, not surprisingly, considered to be too limited, especially by those called upon to serve in the European Parliament, but there were few significant developments of the Parliament's powers in the 1950s and 1960s. By contrast, the 1970s and 1980s have seen five important steps forward.

First, the budget treaties of 1970 and 1975 created what amounts to a bi-cameral "budgetary authority" composed of Council and Parliament which jointly thrash out the Community budget within the limits of the Community's resources. Although the budget procedures are complicated (they are described more fully in Chapter 12 below) they are significant.

Table 1:	*Main events in the Parliament's history*
Sept. 10, 1952	European Coal and Steel Community Common Assembly with 78 members holds its first meeting
March 19, 1958	Meeting of Parliamentary Assembly common to the three communities (ECSC, EEC and EURATOM). Now with 142 members
March 30, 1962	European Assembly decides to describe itself as European Parliament
Jan. 16, 1973	First meeting of enlarged Parliament of 198 members following accession of the UK, Ireland and Denmark
Jan. 14, 1975	Patijn Report adopted by European Parliament on direct elections to the European Parliament
March 4, 1975	Joint Declaration by Parliament, Council and Commission on conciliation procedure
July 22, 1975	Treaty changes signed consolidating new budgetary powers for the Parliament
Sept. 20, 1976	Adoption by Council of Act providing for direct elections
June 7–10, 1979	First direct elections to the European Parliament
July 17, 1979	First meeting of directly elected European Parliament of 410 members
June 1, 1981	European Parliament increases its membership to 434 after Greek accession to the Community and nomination of 24 Greek members
Oct. 18, 1981	First direct elections of 24 Greek members
Feb. 14, 1984	European Parliament adopts Spinelli Draft Treaty on European Union
June 14–17, 1984	Second direct elections
Jan. 1, 1986	European Parliament increases its members to 518 after appointment of 60 Spanish members and 24 Portuguese members following Spanish and Portuguese access to the Community
June 10, 1987	First direct elections of 60 Spanish members
July 1, 1987	Entry into force of Single European Act allocating new powers to the Parliament and giving Treaty status to the title European Parliament
July 19, 1987	First direct elections of 24 Portuguese members
June 15–18, 1989	Third direct elections

They allow Parliament to amend — and over the years, reshape — the budget. Although the budget is relatively small, less than 4 per cent of public expenditure, Parliament has managed, by using its powers, to allocate expenditure in areas other than agriculture and thereby to develop Community policies in new areas.

Second, in 1975 the conciliation procedure was introduced. This procedure applies to legislation with budgetary consequences where there is a need to avoid potential conflict between Council's legislative powers and Parliament's budgetary powers. The procedure was established by a Joint Declaration — a sort of constitutional convention — between the institutions. It laid down that should Council wish to diverge from the opinion of the European Parliament, the matter should first be referred to a conciliation committee composed of the members of Council and an equal number of MEPs.

The procedure is almost identical to that of the "Conciliation Committee" (*Vermittlungsausschuss*) in the Federal Republic of Germany, where one Minister for each *Land* from the *Bundesrat* meets with an equivalent sized delegation from the *Bundestag* to thrash out compromises where the positions of the two chambers diverge. The difference is that in the Community, at the end of the negotiations, whatever the result, it is up to one side, namely the Council, to adopt the act in question. The procedure is therefore more like an appeal for clemency in which MEPs ask the national ministers in Council to think again.

Third, in 1979 the Parliament was elected by universal suffrage for the first time. This is not only important for the obvious reasons of greater democratic legitimacy and more public debate on European issues. It also provided Parliament with full-time members, and more of them. The nominated Parliament had 198 members, the elected Parliament 410 (now 518 following the accessions of Greece, Spain and Portugal).

Fourth, in 1980 the "isoglucose" ruling of the Court of Justice struck down a piece of Community legislation because Council had adopted it before Parliament had given its opinion. This ruling gave Parliament a *de facto* delaying power. Parliament changed its internal rules to take advantage of this. It now first votes on amendments to Commission proposals and then, before voting on the resolution as a whole which formally constitutes its "opinion", seeks an undertaking from the Commission that its amendments will be incorporated into the proposal. If this undertaking is not forthcoming, Parliament can delay its final vote thereby preventing a decision in Council. In such cases, the matter is referred back to the relevant parliamentary committee while compromises are sought. Clearly, Parliament's bargaining position is stronger when there is pressure for a rapid decision. This is the case, for instance, for much of the 1992 programme where all the institutions are trying to work to a strict timetable.

Fifth, in 1987, as mentioned above, the Single European Act came into force, introducing two new procedures for the adoption of Community Acts.

One is the *co-operation* procedure which applies to only 10 Treaty Articles, but they cover most legislation necessary for the completion of the internal market as well as individual research programmes and regional fund decisions. This procedure in effect adds on a second reading to the traditional consultation procedure. Council's decision, now known as a "common position" is referred back to Parliament which has three months to approve it, reject it (in which case it falls unless Council then overrules Parliament by unanimity within three months) or press for amendments (which, if supported by the Commission, can only be rejected unanimously in Council, whereas a qualified majority can approve).

The Single Act also gives Parliament equal rights of co-decision with Council by requiring its *assent* for the ratification of Accession Treaties and Association Agreements. The former do not arise every month, but the growing list of possible applicants is a reminder that before long, Parliament will be in a position to block accession if certain conditions it feels are important are not met. It is more frequently able to use its powers concerning Association Agreements. It is possible that Member States, in signing the Single Act, did not realize that this power would apply not only to the basic agreements but also to additional protocols including annual financial protocols, etc. In the first year of the Act, Parliament dealt with 26 such protocols.

These five steps forward have significantly changed the Parliament's position in the Community system but they have not eliminated the democratic deficit. Three major hurdles remain before direct parliamentary control of EC decisions can be achieved. The first concerns the balance of powers between the Community institutions. The existing imbalance in the triangular relationship between Commission, Council and Parliament has not been eliminated by the Single European Act. One could begin to suggest that this was occurring when the Parliament acquired a right of *co-decision* with the Council of Ministers, i.e. its formal approval would be necessary for any legislation to come into force. Such a right would not necessarily reduce the powers of the Council but would certainly strengthen the position of the Parliament in the Community system.

The second hurdle concerns the relationship between the European Parliament and national institutions, particularly national parliaments. The relationship will have to be clarified as increases in the powers of the Community necessarily touch on the question of national sovereignty. The less the Council has the final word over Community questions, the smaller the remaining role of national parliaments. The Council is itself composed of national ministers who are, in theory at least, answerable to their respective Parliaments, but this link to the national system is perhaps challenged by majority voting and wider powers for the European Parliament. The Parliament will not be able to solve this problem on its own and will need to pursue its attempts to establish closer links with national parliaments. These efforts have so far met with relatively limited success and one can anticipate a degree of greater tension between MEPs and MPs in the years ahead as both sides seek to tackle this aspect of the democratic deficit.

The third and final hurdle, which is also perhaps the most difficult, is the relationship of the Parliament to the individual citizens of the Community. Here, there is a major issue of loyalties and of the willingness of citizens of national states to cede more powers to a body outside and above the national context. Attitudes vary from one Member State to another but there is some evidence that the Parliament's image has changed for the better over the last 10 years and that there is a greater willingness to accept a wider role for the Parliament. However, it is less clear that people are prepared to accept the precise consequences of such a wider role, for example the ability of the Parliament to impose additional taxation, or, indeed, to take decisions which could override strongly held national priorities.

As long as these uncertainties continue, it will not be easy for the Parliament to achieve the momentum necessary to gain a stronger role within the Community system. Nevertheless, there is no question that it has made significant progress, particularly in the past 10 years, as the remaining chapters of this book will make clear.

2. How it is elected

The European Parliament enjoys the unique status of being the world's only elected supranational assembly. Other international Parliamentary assemblies consist of representatives nominated by and from among members of national Parliaments, as the European Parliament itself was up to 1979.

The mere fact of direct elections in 12 European countries to one Parliamentary body is in itself remarkable, and has undoubtedly given greater legitimacy to the institution (although to what extent is a matter of dispute among politicians and political scientists). Nevertheless there is still no uniform electoral system for all the participating countries, as foreseen when direct elections were decided upon and the Member States have been allowed to retain their own national systems until a common system can be devised. The result is a great variety of national systems.

The procedures for drawing up a uniform system to replace the current hotchpotch are also unique. Unlike other areas of Community law where it is the Commission which has the right of initiative, in this case it is the European Parliament itself which enjoys this right. Its proposal must then be adopted by the Council by a unanimous vote.

Progress on these issues, firstly in moving to direct elections and secondly on devising a uniform electoral system, has been very slow. It was not until 1976 that the Council finally agreed on the form of direct elections, 16 years after the European Parliament had first submitted proposals for such elections. Moreover 10 years have now gone by since the first direct elections in 1979 without a uniform electoral system having been devised. The 1979–1984 Parliament submitted a proposal but this was never adopted by the Council. The 1984–1989 Parliament considered whether to submit a new proposal, but did not manage to agree on one.

The present chapter is divided into four sections. The first deals briefly with the period preceding direct elections, and with the Council Decision which finally enacted them. The second examines the variety of national systems in force, and the main differences between them. The third looks at the consequences of the current diversity, and at the main issues that have to be tackled in drawing up a uniform electoral system. The final section examines the efforts that have been made so far to draw up such a system. A brief postscript mentions the three sets of elections held so far.

1.   The run-up to direct elections

Direct elections to a European Assembly were already envisaged in the Treaties which established the European Community Institutions (138(3) EEC, 121(3) ECSC, 108(3) EAEC). Article 138 of the Treaty of Rome, for example, stated that "the Assembly shall draw up proposals for elections by direct universal suffrage in accordance with a uniform procedure in all Member States. The Council shall, acting unanimously, lay down the appropriate procedures which it shall recommend to the Member States for adoption in accordance with their respective constitutional requirements".

The European Parliament put forward its first proposals to this effect on May 17, 1961 (in the Dehousse report), and further resolutions on this subject were adopted in 1963 and 1969, but to no avail (although some national parliaments such as Italy considered bills unilaterally to elect their own MEPs by universal suffrage).

In 1973 the European Parliament decided to prepare new proposals and appointed Dutch Socialist, Schelto Patijn, as rapporteur. The following year, the Paris Summit of Heads of Government decided to institutionalize their meetings in the form of the "European Council", and to meet three times per year. To balance this reinforcement of the intergovernmental side of the Community the Heads of Government also agreed that direct elections of the Parliament "should be achieved as soon as possible" and stated that they awaited Parliament's new proposals, on which they expected Council to act in 1976 with a view to holding direct elections in or after 1978.

Parliament's new proposals (which took the form of a Draft Convention) were adopted in January 1976. One of the main stumbling blocks had been the treaty requirement for a *uniform* electoral procedure. Patijn's strategy was to overcome this stumbling block by allowing each country to use its own procedure for the first elections, and providing for the elected Parliament to make new proposals thereafter.

The Draft Convention put forward by the European Parliament in January 1975 suggested many of the key elements of a future directly elected Parliament, notably a five-year term of office. The Draft Convention also provided for members to vote on an individual and personal basis and that they should not be bound by any instructions or mandate. The office of representative in the European Parliament was held to be compatible with membership of the Parliament of a Member State, but a list of incompatibilities was suggested, such as membership of a national government or of the European Commission.

The European Parliament would have 355 members, ranging from six in Luxembourg and 13 in Ireland, up to 67 in the United Kingdom and 71 in West Germany. Direct elections were to be held in principle on the same day in all Member States, although individual Member States could have them a day earlier or later than the fixed date or spread them over two consecutive days. Other elements of the electoral system, and the method of filling seats which became vacant, were provisionally left to individual Member States until a uniform electoral system was adopted.

In spite of Parliament's action (no less than four resolutions adopted in 1976) and the adoption of a formal act in 1976, it still took a further three years before the first direct elections were held (they were originally scheduled for May/June 1978, but had to be postponed for a year).

Council Decision 76/787 (OJ 278 of 8.10.1976) was accompanied by an "Act Concerning the Election of the Representatives of the Assembly by Direct Universal Suffrage". It laid down a number of basic guidelines for the future conduct of direct elections, but left a number of other important issues to the discretion of individual Member States, pending the future adoption of a more comprehensive uniform electoral system.

The Council's 1976 Act followed the Parliament's proposal in most respects. The most important difference concerned the number of members in the directly elected Parliament and the sensitive issue of their distribution between the individual Member States. The Parliament was now to have 410 members. Compared to Parliament's Draft, the less populated Member States were generally to be relatively less well represented (although the smallest Member State, Luxembourg, was still given the disproportionate total of six Members), and the more populous Member States were given higher representation. Moreover, the four largest Member States, West Germany, the United Kingdom, Italy and France, were given the same total of 81 members each, although the population of West Germany, for example, was significantly higher than that of the others, especially France.

Another difference from Parliament's draft was that the elections would now take place over a four-day period, starting on a Thursday morning and ending on the following Sunday.

As in the Parliament's Draft, the electoral system, and the method for filling vacancies, was not tackled by the Council's Act pending a uniform system. The Act also added a new clause to the procedures for developing a uniform system when it stated that the Council would take its unanimous decision on a proposal from the Parliament only after "endeavouring to reach agreement with the European Parliament in a Conciliation Committee consisting of the Council and representatives of the European Parliament" (Article 13).

2. The variety of national systems in force and the main differences between them

The first direct elections in 1979 were thus fought under differing principles of individual national legislation. For the reasons explored in greater detail below, the second and third set of direct elections in 1984 and 1989 were fought under similarly divergent rules. The temporary rules have become increasingly entrenched and have even been compounded by the fact that three new Member States have joined the Community since 1979 and have devised their own national rules. This meant that there were 12 different national electoral systems in force for the 1989 European election (13 if the two separate systems in Great Britain and in Northern Ireland are taken account of).

However, the systems used by individual Member States for the European Parliament elections have not necessarily been identical to those used for national elections. A striking example of this has been in France, which devised a proportional system for the European elections with the whole country as one constituency and with a 5 per cent threshold, rather than the majority system in two rounds within single member constituencies which has been the traditional system for French domestic elections. West Germany too created a unitary proportional system for the European elections (although retaining the traditional 5 per cent threshold) and with three nominated seats for West Berlin (provided for in the 1976 Act) rather than the mixed constituency-list system used in national elections. Greece, Spain and Portugal, and to a lesser extent Denmark and Luxembourg, also made substantial breaks with national practice by having only one national constituency for the European elections rather than the smaller units used for national elections, although they all maintained a form of proportional representation. Belgium and Italy greatly reduced the number of constituencies for the European elections compared to national elections, as did Ireland and the United Kingdom. The latter two countries retained, however, their distinctive national electoral systems, the single transferable vote (STV) in the case of Ireland and the majority "first past the post system" in individual constituencies in the case of Great Britain (after the House of Commons had rejected the Labour government's alternative proposal for a regional list system). The United Kingdom did make an exception to its normal practice, however, by permitting the three Northern Ireland seats to be contested under the much more proportional system of the single transferable vote. Finally, the Netherlands made the least change of all, with one national constituency with fully proportional results being the norm for both European and national elections.

Any differences, however, between a country's European and national electoral regulations have been due more to reasons of national convenience than to any systematic attempt to make initial steps towards uniformity at European level.

The differences between national regulations for the European elections have thus remained very great. It is true that only the United Kingdom retains a purely majority-based system (with the above-mentioned exception of Northern Ireland), and the other 11 Member States all have systems with some kind of proportional outcome (although Ireland to a lesser degree). Most of them also use the d'Hondt system of proportional representation. Nevertheless even between these proportional systems there are considerable differences, for example between those countries which have one national constituency and those with several regional constituencies. Moreover some countries have *de jure* electoral thresholds (5 per cent in France and West Germany) below which no seats can be won, while some countries' electoral laws provide for closed party lists, whose order cannot be changed by the voter (Germany, Greece, France, Spain, Portugal); others for preferential voting in which the order of candidates can be modified by the voter. Irish and Luxembourgish voters can even vote for individual candidates from different lists.

Rules for the representation of candidates also vary greatly. In most cases they must be a national of the Member State in which they wish to stand (although Italy now permits candidates from any European Community country), but in some countries they must also be domiciled in that country. Age limits for eligibility vary between 18 (Denmark, West Germany, Spain, Portugal), 21 (Greece, Belgium, Ireland, Luxembourg,

United Kingdom), 23 (France) and 25 (Netherlands and Italy). Nine countries permit the dual mandate (membership of both the national and European Parliaments) but three do not (Belgium, Greece and Spain), all apparently in breach of Article 5 of the 1976 Act (which stated that "the office of representative in the European Parliament shall be compatible with membership of the Parliament of a Member State"). In some countries candidates must be nominated by political parties, in others independents can also stand. Some countries require deposits (e.g. a party standing in all United Kingdom constituencies would have to put up over £78,000), others lists of signatures. There are differing rules on the length of campaign and on election expenses, and on whether public money is available to meet certain party expenses.

Another important set of differences is on methods of filling vacancies, for example by the next candidate on the list (Denmark, Greece, Spain, France, Italy, Luxembourg, Netherlands, Portugal), by designated substitutes (Belgium and, optionally, West Germany) or through special by-elections, (United Kingdom). Ireland got into particular trouble in this regard, as it had a system of nomination by the party holding the vacant seat which cut out the voter completely. This has now been replaced by a not very transparent system of designated substitutes.

Rights to vote in elections are very different from one Member State to another. In some countries the right to vote has followed the nationality principle without qualifications, so that all citizens of that country can vote in the European Parliament elections irrespective of where they live. In others, they are also eligible if they are resident in another Community Member State, but not elsewhere. In other countries, voters lose their rights if they have lived outside their country for more than a certain limit of time. In other countries (e.g. Ireland), a voter must also be resident in his or her country. On the other hand, Ireland has given the vote in European Parliament elections to citizens of other European Community countries resident in Ireland. Similar rights have been granted in Belgium and the Netherlands, provided that a foreign resident's home country has not given them the right to vote. The United Kingdom also permits resident Irish citizens to vote, unlike certain British citizens resident abroad (even in European Community countries). Another British anomaly is that while some British citizens resident abroad cannot vote in European elections, they may stand as candidates!

Age limits for voting are more uniform; 18 in all countries except Greece (20). In two countries, however, voting is compulsory (Belgium and Luxembourg), where in others it is not.

A final set of differences is over the polling day for European elections, Sunday in most countries but Thursday in four others (i.e. Ireland, United Kingdom, Denmark and the Netherlands).

3. Main issues in drawing up a uniform electoral system

The above survey of the main differences in the national regulations for the European elections has indicated the range of issues that will have to be tackled in drawing up a uniform electoral system. Before tackling the specific issues, however, one preliminary set of questions must first be answered. How important is uniformity as an overall objective? What is the meaning of uniformity? Should it mean uniformity of detail or only broad equivalence of national systems in line with certain common principles?

Quite apart from the legal requirement for a uniform system in the Treaties and the 1976 Act, the practical case for greater uniformity than at present is extremely strong. The present set of national regulations does not give equal weight to European citizens' votes, and the overall balance within the European Parliament is potentially distorted as a result. Moreover the existing regulations ensure that not all European Community citizens are given the right to stand for election or even to vote in European Parliament elections. These are felt to be important failings in the current system that need to be redressed in the future.

On the other hand, certain other differences in national regulations are less fundamental. While it would be a symbolic gesture, for example, to hold the European Parliament elections on the same day in every Member State, it is not of vital importance.

The consensus within the European Parliament, therefore, has been that certain uniform principles must be established, but that full uniformity of the details is not required, at least not at present.

There is, however, less consensus over which principles should be applied; for example the extent to which the need for proportionality in the overall outcome should be balanced against other factors (such as the need for a constituency element or to protect regional or other minorities); whether the nationality or residence principles should be of greater weight in determining a citizen's right to vote and to stand as a candidate; or whether voters should have the right to choose between candidates as well as between parties. These issues are also discussed in more detail below.

A final preliminary point that should be mentioned is that of political feasibility and timing. Should a uniform electoral system be introduced at one go, or on a step-by-step basis? To what extent should special cases be taken account of and derogations be granted? Again there seems to be wide agreement that the main principles need to be established as soon as possible, that a certain amount of flexibility will be required, but that too much flexibility should also be avoided. National political realities and traditions should be taken account of, but should not be allowed to block all progress.

Specific issues

(i) The nature of the electoral system

A first and fundamental issue is whether there should be an obligation to have a system of proportional representation in all countries. The main exception in this regard is the majority system in use in the United Kingdom, which can alter the entire political balance in the European Parliament. A small swing in votes can produce a magnified swing in seats in a "first past the post" system. This is all the more so in the large constituencies used for European elections with relatively fewer "safe seats". As a result the overall balance in the European Parliament may depend on the result in some 20 to 25 marginal seats in Britain. In 1979, the British Conservatives won 60 of the 78 seats available in Britain (excluding Northern Ireland), with 50 per cent of the vote, thus obtaining 21 more seats than they would have obtained by a completely proportional system. In 1984 the European Democratic Group, of which they were the main component, obtained 50 seats with six million votes compared to the 32 seats obtained by the Liberal Group with 10 million votes (and with the Alliance parties unrepresented on 19.5 per cent of the United Kingdom vote). In 1989, on the other hand, the Socialist Group was "over represented" as a result of the British electoral system and with the Greens as the largest single losers (with the UK Greens obtaining 14 per cent of the vote and no seats).

The British electoral system is thus not only a British problem, but also a matter of concern for everyone else in the European Parliament as well.

The other system which is not inherently proportional in its outcome is that in Ireland, where the Labour Party, for example, could be said to have been over represented in 1979 with four seats on 14.5 per cent of the vote but under represented in 1984 with none on over 8 per cent. Nevertheless the distorting impact of the Irish electoral system is much less than that of the United Kingdom, partly because there are far fewer Irish MEPs but also because the outcome is more closely related to the votes cast.

As pointed out above there is a wide range of electoral systems used in the other 10 Community countries, but whatever their other shortcomings they are all broadly proportional in their effects, and have little or no distorting impact on the political balance of the European Parliament.

There is, thus, broad support within the European Parliament for the principle of proportional representation to be introduced as a central element of a uniform electoral system. With the exception of most current British members, there is very little support for a simple majority voting system. This is generally felt to be especially inappropriate for European Parliament elections, where the objective is more to achieve representation of all major currents of public opinion than to form a stable government majority.

Besides proportional representation, a second important issue is whether an element of constituency representation should be built into a uniform electoral system.

There is considerable recognition of the advantages of constituency representation in terms, in particular, of strengthening links between the electors and the elected, and of bringing local or regional concerns more to the forefront. Only a few countries have systems with an explicit element of constituency representation (the United Kingdom and Ireland, in particular, Belgium and Italy to a lesser extent, the Federal Republic of Germany also to some extent with its possibility for *Land* lists). In other countries it is implicit in some cases, in that individuals on party lists may well represent particular regions or interest groups, but there is no guarantee of this nor any open accountability. The most purely proportional systems, those where the entire country is the electoral area, are those where the constituency element is inevitably weakest. On the other hand, the more constituencies there are, and the smaller the electoral areas, the less proportional is the overall result.

There has been considerable discussion as to possible ways of combining proportional representation with a constituency element. Two main alternatives have been suggested, firstly proportional representation in multi-member constituencies (for example with a minimum of five and a maximum of 15 members), and secondly a mixed system on the lines of that used in German Federal elections, in which a number of members are directly elected in individual constituencies and others are elected on national lists to provide a more proportional overall outcome. Both systems have had their supporters in the European Parliament, but neither has yet prevailed, although there is clearly wider support for the former. A third possibility, the single transferable vote system used in Ireland (and Northern Ireland), also has advantages, but appears to be too complicated and to be too unknown in most European countries to win widespread support.

On the other hand, there is still considerable support for national list systems, whether for reasons of political tradition and practice, or for other reasons. Certain central governments, for example, such as that of Spain, are worried about the advantages more constituency-based systems might have for regional parties such as those in Catalonia and the Basque country, who might use such systems to further their case for greater regional autonomy or independence.

Another contentious issue with regard to a future uniform system is whether preferential voting should be allowed. There is considerable criticism of closed lists, especially those at national level, where the voters have no possibility of altering the order of the list or of expressing a preference between individual candidates. This is felt to give too much power to central party bureaucracies, and to weaken accountability to the voters. There is thus widespread support for allowing voters to express a preference for certain candidates within one party list. There is less support for a system based even more on preference for individual candidates, such as STV in Ireland, or the system of *panachage* in Luxembourg, where the voters can express preferences between candidates on several lists. One likely outcome is a uniform electoral system is for preferential voting within one list on an optional basis.

Another issue which must be tackled is whether minimum legal thresholds, such as the 5 per cent provisions in Germany and France, should be allowed in the future. The main argument against *de jure* thresholds (there will always be *de facto* thresholds, especially in more constituency-based systems) is that they reduce the degree of representativeness of the European Parliament, and exclude significant elements of public opinion. The argument in their favour is that they can help to prevent extremist parties being given a political platform, though they have not prevented protest parties of the right such as the *Front National* in France and the *Republikaner* in Germany from winning seats in the European Parliament.

A final issue is whether allowances should be made for specific geographical or regional circumstances.

(ii)   The choice of candidates

The main issues at stake here are whether the nationality or residence principles should apply as regards the eligibility of candidates, and whether any other conditions should be laid down regarding eligibility.

On the first issue, there appears to be strong support within the European Parliament in favour of the application of the nationality principle, with nationals of one Community country being able to stand for election in that country, irrespective of their place of residence within the European Community. The residence principle does not yet appear to have majority support if it is to be on a mandatory basis, but there is strong support for it developing on an optional basis. Member States would thus be encouraged to grant residents of other Community countries (especially those resident for more than a certain length of time, such as five years) the right to stand for election in their countries.

In the longer term, however, there appears to be a strong case for emulating the Italian example in the 1989 elections, and allowing any European Community citizen to stand anywhere in the European Parliament elections irrespective of nationality or residence (especially since they will generally be at a practical disadvantage compared to local candidates).

Among the other issues which will have to be looked at in the choice of candidates are whether individuals or only parties can stand and whether deposits or only signatures should be called for. As some feel strongly about both issues there has emerged no consensus as yet to include common rules on these subjects in the first version of a uniform electoral system.

There is more widespread concern, however, about the dual mandate. As mentioned above, the Council's 1976 Act expressly permitted members of national Parliaments also to be members of the European Parliament, but a number of Member States have (possibly illegally) forbidden it in their national legislation. Moreover, a large number of political parties, even from countries which permit the dual mandate, either forbid it formally in their statutes or informally in practice.

In 1988 the European Parliament adopted a report by its Committee on Legal Affairs and Citizen Rights (DOC A2-0065/88) prepared by the British Labour MEP, Geoffrey Hoon, which came out in favour of prohibiting dual membership of the European Parliament and national parliaments, although not of the European Parliament and regional assemblies. A minority of the Committee, however, dissented, on the grounds that this issue should not be treated separately but only as part of the uniform electoral system.

The main argument against the dual mandate is that membership of the European Parliament is now a very demanding full-time job, and cannot be combined with another such job without the member's performance and attendance being undercut in both Parliaments. The main arguments in favour are that the dual mandate, if used sparingly, permits a number of very well known national politicians to stand for, and hence give publicity to, the European Parliament, and also because it can enable stronger links to be maintained between the European Parliament and national parliaments. There is already a tendency for them to treat each other as rivals, and to fail to understand each other's political culture. This would be accentuated if the dual mandate were to be abolished entirely.

At present there is clear agreement on the need to restrict the dual mandate to the greatest possible extent, but not on abolishing it completely. There would be particular opposition from Italy and France, the two countries which account for the large majority of members with a dual mandate (but tellingly also the countries with the lowest degree of continuity of membership of the European Parliament).

Another controversial issue has been that posed by candidates who have given undertakings to their political parties to give up their seats after a certain time to other candidates on the list. This was first posed on a major scale by the French Gaullist party (the RPR) in 1979, whose candidates were meant to stand down after one year, so that in theory about 70 of their candidates would have entered the European Parliament in the course of the Parliament's five-year term.

This so-called "tourniquet" or "turnstile" system was challenged by some Members of the European Parliament who considered that it violated the terms of the 1976 Act which stipulated that members were elected for five-year terms, and were not to receive any binding instructions from outside.

The issue was twice examined by Parliament's Committee on the Verification of Credentials (first and second Sieglerschmidt reports, Doc. 1-398/82 and Doc. 1-1078/82), which concluded that the "tourniquet" system was legally acceptable, though politically objectionable. This was reinforced by the fact that the "tourniquet" system did not work smoothly in practice, with some RPR members refusing to leave the European Parliament.

The RPR subsequently abandoned the "tourniquet" for the next European Parliament elections. Rotation of members has only been very sparingly used by other parties, mainly Green alternative parties (e.g. the Greens in Germany from 1984 to 1989 and the Greens in France, and the Green Rainbow list in Italy in the 1989 elections: the former are meant to stand down after two-and-a-half years to make way for another Group, whereas the latter have devised a more complicated system of rotation). This no longer seems to be a major political issue.

(iii) The right to vote

Again the main issue is whether this should be based on the nationality or residence principle. The residence principle is considered by many to be the more "European" option and has considerable support, although it is opposed by a country like Luxembourg which feels that it would be swamped by what would be 30 per cent foreign voters, and would also not be greeted with enthusiasm by many foreign resident voters who still often tend to have much more interest in and understanding of the political system of their country of origin than that of their country of residence. It might also require constitutional changes in some countries (e.g. France). A minority of governments are also not keen on the nationality principle unless it is also linked to residence in the home country.

Within the European Parliament, however, there is overwhelming consensus on the need for all European Community citizens to be able to vote somewhere in the European Parliament elections, since at present a considerable number of them fall between two stools. The best solution in the short term would appear to be based on the criterion of nationality as a mandatory requirement, and with the criterion of residence as an option (with the appropriate safeguards to prevent dual voting).

(iv)   Finance

One of the most controversial sets of issues to deal with will be that of finance, whether there should be public financing of parties' election campaigns for the European Parliament and, if so, the extent to which it should be granted before election day on the basis of a party or group's size, or else afterwards on the basis of results actually achieved. This is a matter of great sensitivity, not only because some Community countries provide for public funding of elections, whereas others do not, but also because of the extent to which the system chosen might favour established parties at the expense of new ones.

The above issues first came to the fore when the French Greens challenged the European Parliament's budgetary allocations for information campaigns (item 3708 of the budget) which were distributed to individual political parties through the Political Groups (the issue is discussed in detail in Chapter 5). The sums involved were very substantial, and the whole system was felt by many parties with few or no members in the European Parliament to discriminate strongly against their interests.

The European Court of Justice eventually found in favour of the French Greens, primarily on the grounds that it was *"ultra vires"* for the European Parliament to have developed what amounted to public financial support for parties in the absence of a uniform electoral system. Since then the Parliament's information funds have not been discontinued, but have been modified to conform to the Court's judgement. They are now disbursed directly by the Political Groups and have had to stop several months before election day. This is clearly an issue which will have to be tackled in any future uniform electoral system.

(v)   The number of seats per country

In theory one of the central elements of a uniform electoral system should be approximate equality between the number of people per seat in each European Community country. However, this is balanced by the need to ensure that smaller countries have adequate representation. These two divergent concerns are often met in bi-cameral systems with one chamber elected proportionally to population and another representing the component states equally or more equally (e.g. US Congress: House and Senate; German *Bundestag* and *Bundesrat*). In the Community, it is in the Council that the Member States are represented as such. However, both the Council and the Parliament have weighted representation according to Member State. In the case of Council, the scale ranges from 10 votes each for the "big four" down to two for Luxembourg. In Parliament, the weighting is more proportional to population, but still with an advantage to small countries and with equality for the "big four" whose populations do diverge slightly. The result is that Luxembourg has one MEP per 60,000 population, whereas West Germany has one per 759,000 (though apart from Luxembourg the discrepancies are not quite so huge). Thus, in the Community, neither is Council based on full equality nor is Parliament based on full proportionality.

Apart from a possible adjustment to cater for German unification this situation is not likely to change in the short or medium term. In the longer term a new distribution may have to be found, especially if the European Community continues to expand and the number of total members in the Parliament becomes too unwieldy (the European Parliament already has 518 members, and no European national parliament has more than 650 if the UK House of Lords is excepted). Alternatively, if a bi-cameral parliament were ever created, including, for example, a Senate of the Regions and Nationalities, this could be based on the principle of minimum representation for each unit, whereas a Lower House could have seats distributed more on the basis of population. At the present moment, however, this is all in the realm of speculation.

4.   The attempts that have been made so far in drawing up a uniform electoral system

Responsibility for drawing up a uniform electoral system within the European Parliament was vested from 1979–1989 in its Political Affairs Committee, which in 1979 established a special sub-committee to deal with the issue.

Its rapporteur in the 1979–1984 Parliament was Jean Seitlinger, a Christian Democrat from Lorraine. In his first draft, presented in October 1980, he put forward two main options on the key issue of the type of electoral system. In his option A, he attempted to reconcile proportionality with a strong constituency element (and also to win over the then 60-strong British Conservative contingent) by suggesting a mixed system on the lines of that used for German *Bundestag* elections. Each voter would have two votes, one cast for candidates who would be elected by an absolute majority of the votes in single ballots in single-member constituencies, the other for national lists in order to ensure proportional representation of each list. Option B consisted, instead, of proportional representation within multi-member constituencies of between three and nine members.

In June 1981, the Political Affairs Committee, by majority vote, chose Seitlinger's option A as its preferred system. Difficulties immediately arose, however, as to how a mixed system could be implemented, with particular problems being posed by the respective percentage of constituency seats and list seats, and the linked problem of *überhangsmandate* (literally "overhang seats"). In the German *Bundestag* system a potential problem arises if a party is entitled to, say, 40 per cent of the seats on a proportional basis, but wins more than 40 per cent of all the individual constituencies. This is resolved not by surrendering its surplus constituencies, but by creating extra seats in the parliament. Such a solution would be impossible in the European Parliament which has a fixed, rather than flexible, total number of seats.

As a result of these problems the Political Affairs Committee reversed its decision in December 1981, and opted for proportional representation in regional constituencies. In February 1982 a report on these lines was adopted by the Political Affairs Committee and in March 1982 by the full Parliament by 158 votes in favour to 77 against with 27 abstentions. The

Parliament's text called for proportional representation in multi-member constituencies of between three and 15 seats. The d'Hondt system would be used and there would be the option of preferential voting (but within one list only). Member States were also allowed a certain amount of flexibility in order to take account of special geographical or ethnic factors recognized by the Constitution of a Member State. The text also gave nationals of a Community Member State the right to vote and to stand for election irrespective of the place of residence. One anomalous feature of the text, however, was that it conferred the right to stand for election to those who had been resident in a country for at least five years, but did not similarly confer the right to vote.

The adopted text was then submitted to the Council, which examined it within a Working Party for the next year, but without finding the necessary unanimity, with the British posing the main, but by no means the only, obstacle. Eventually the Council abandoned any attempt to agree on a system for the 1984 European elections, but undertook to continue this work with a view to the 1989 elections.

After the impasse in the first directly elected Parliament, the newly elected 1984 Parliament decided to draw up another report and chose another Christian Democrat, the German CSU Member, Reinhold Bocklet, as its new rapporteur.

Bocklet's draft report pointed out the need for a cautious step-by-step approach towards a uniform electoral system, with agreement on a few essential issues rather than uniformity in the details. He put a greater emphasis on flexibility than had Seitlinger. While only suggesting a proportional system rather than a mixed system he was prepared to allow either multi-member constituencies or a single national constituency. Thresholds could be maintained as long as they did not exceed 5 per cent. The nationality principle would be compulsory as regards the right to vote and to stand, and the residence principle would be optional only. In an annex to his report he even mooted the idea of Member States being granted an exemption from applying the agreed system for a limited period of time.

The report was eventually adopted by the Political Affairs Committee, but only by the unconvincing majority of 16 in favour to eight opposed, with 13 abstentions. This was considered insufficiently strong support to bring the report to the plenary, and it was referred back to a special working party under the chairmanship of the rapporteur.

This intergroup eventually came out in favour (in December 1986) of a modified version of the Bocklet report. Among the main differences were that multi-member constituencies of between five and 15 seats were again made mandatory, and the single national constituency was not permitted. Compulsory preferential voting was introduced, and thresholds were no longer allowed. The Hare/Niemeyer system of proportional representation was preferred to the d'Hondt system. A greater emphasis was placed on uniformity.

In view of continuing disagreements, however, a text on these lines was not brought before the plenary, and the 1984–1989 Parliament eventually failed to adopt any text. The Council was not, therefore, forced to consider any new proposal.

Table 2:   *Electorate and turnout
in EC States in the 1979, 1984 and 1989 European elections*

Country		Electorate	Turnout	Valid votes
Belgium	1989	7,096,273	90.7	5,899,285
	1984	6,975,677	92.2	5,725,837
	1979	6,800,584	91.4	5,442,867
Denmark	1989	3,923,549	46.2	1,789,395
	1984	3,878,600	52.4	2,001,875
	1979	3,754,423	47.8	1,754,850
France	1989	38,348,191	48.7	18,145,588
	1984	36,880,688	56.7	20,180,934
	1979	35,180,531	60.7	20,242,347
Germany	1989	45,773,179	62.3	28,206,690
	1984	44,451,981	56.8	24,851,371
	1979	42,751,940	65.7	27,847,109
Greece	1989	8,347,387	79.9	6,544,669
	1984	7,790,309	77.2	5,956,060
	1981	7,319,070	78.6	5,753,478
Ireland	1989	2,453,451	68.3	1,632,728
	1984	2,413,404	47.6	1,120,416
	1979	2,188,798	63.6	1,339,072
Italy	1989	46,566,688	81.0	34,829,128
	1984	44,438,303	83.4	35,098,046
	1979	42,193,369	84.9	35,042,601
Luxembourg	1989	218,940	87.4	174,421
	1984	215,792	88.8	173,888
	1979	212,740	88.9	170,759
The Netherlands	1989	11,121,477	47.2	5,241,883
	1984	10,476,000	50.6	5,297,621
	1979	9,808,176	58.1	5,667,303
Portugal	1989	8,107,694	51.2	4,016,756
	1987	7,787,603	72.4	5,496,935
Spain	1989	29,283,982	54.6	15,623,320
	1987	28,437,306	68.9	19,173,642
United Kingdom	1989	43,710,568	36.2	15,829,054
	1984	42,984,998	32.6	13,998,190
	1979	41,573,897	32.3	13,446,091
TOTAL	1989	244,951,379	57.2	137,932,917
	1984	200,505,752	59.0	114,044,238
	1979	191,783,528	62.5	110,952,477

Source: European Parliament Summary of Results.

The 1989–1994 Parliament began by transferring responsibility of drawing up a uniform electoral system from the Political Affairs Committee to that on Institutional Affairs. On Jan. 23, 1990, Karel de Gucht (Flemish Liberal) was chosen as the Committee's new rapporteur.

The European elections so far

Three sets of European elections have been held so far, in 1979, 1984 and 1989. (See Table 2 for electorate and turnout. For a more detailed analysis of results by country, see the tables in Appendix 1.) A few brief general observations can also usefully be made.

Firstly, the European elections that have been held so far can still more accurately be characterized as a set of 12 different national elections than as co-ordinated European-wide campaigns. The issues have still tended to be primarily domestic ones, and to be used to test governments' (and oppositions') popularity or unpopularity. In several countries the European elections have even been combined with national election campaigns, making it even more difficult to separate the issues, and to provide a distinctly European identity to the European Parliament elections in those countries.

Nevertheless, in certain countries European issues have gradually come more to the forefront. The positive and negative aspects of the 1992 internal market came under considerable scrutiny, for example, in the 1989 European elections, as did the need for European economic and political integration.

Moreover, certain Political Groups have campaigned on common manifestos throughout Europe, such as the European People's Party, the European Liberals and the Socialists (although with one or two reservations from individual national parties in the latter case).

The turnout in the elections has varied greatly from country to country (with the UK providing consistently the lowest figures, see Table 2), but the average turnout through the Community as a whole has slowly declined in the three elections, from 62.5 per cent in 1979 to 59 per cent in 1984 to only 57.2 per cent in 1989. These are disappointingly low figures, although it should also be borne in mind that they are still higher than those for national elections in the United States.

The European Community is clearly still a distant entity for many European voters, and the distinct role of the European Parliament itself is not yet fully grasped. This situation must change if turnout in subsequent European elections is to rise above present levels.

3.   Where, when and in *quale lingua*

The seat issue: where the Parliament meets

It is a hazardous business, on the Friday before plenary sessions in Strasbourg, to walk in the corridors of the European Parliament's buildings in Luxembourg and Brussels, blocked as they are by large metallic trunks stuffed with files and office equipment about to be transported by the Parliament's in-house delivery men to other offices in Strasbourg. This is one of the most visible signs that the European Parliament still has no permanent home. Often referred to as the Strasbourg Parliament, the reality is in fact much more complex. The plenary sessions do indeed currently take place in Strasbourg, although further efforts are likely to be made to transfer some of these to Brussels in the future. The Political Group and committee meetings, on the other hand, generally take place in Brussels. Finally, the secretariat is based in Luxembourg, although there is a growing number of staff in Brussels and even a tiny "antenna" in Strasbourg. The secretariat of the Political Groups, however, is now mainly in Brussels, although a minority of staff are still in Luxembourg.

As a result, the European Parliament has facilities in all three cities. In theory there are no less than three debating chambers (or "hemicycles"); the one which is actually used in Strasbourg (but belongs to the Council of Europe), the one which used to seat the former nominated Parliament when in Luxembourg (which is too small for the present Parliament but is used for accommodating visitors' groups, etc.) and another purpose-built chamber in Luxembourg, which can accommodate the present Parliament but is no longer in use. In coming years a chamber may also be available in Brussels, and the possibility has now also been put forward of a new and larger one in Strasbourg, where the European Parliament would no longer have to use the Council of Europe's buildings.

The duplication continues: Members of the European Parliament have their own offices in Strasbourg, and in Brussels. Members of the secretariat have their separate offices in Luxembourg, and tend to share offices in Strasbourg and to a much greater and more cramped degree in Brussels.

The European Parliament now sprawls over 13 buildings (four in Luxembourg, three in Strasbourg and no less than six in Brussels), two others being planned in Brussels and one in Strasbourg. Luxembourg, which is the main home of the secretariat, only contains 42 per cent of the total surface area rented by the Parliament, and a little over 1,850 of the 4,500 offices.

The lack of a single fixed seat is costly not just in terms of construction maintenance and rents (all of its main buildings are rented) but also in terms of unnecessary travel, with staff "commuting" from Luxembourg to Brussels and Strasbourg, and members from their constituencies to Brussels, Strasbourg and elsewhere. The costs to the Parliament of its geographical dispersion have been estimated in 1990 as around three million pounds sterling.

This waste of resources must be put in perspective. The figures quoted above only constitute a tiny percentage of the Community budget and only 10 per cent of the Parliament's own budget. Parliament's staff is relatively small and only a minority have to travel regularly to Strasbourg and a smaller minority to Brussels or Luxembourg. The Members of the European Parliament and the Group staff would have to travel greatly even if there was a single seat. In absolute terms the money spent is not vast. Such waste is, however, still unnecessary, and could be eliminated if there were a single seat. An even more fundamental argument is that the Parliament undoubtedly loses influence, access to power and effectiveness by being dispersed in three cities. One week a month is a limited period within which plenary decisions can be taken. The Parliament's image is also harmed with the public. All this is clearly unsatisfactory. How did the present situation come about, what has been done to remedy it, and what are the prospects for a solution in the future?

Article 77 of the European Coal and Steel Community Treaty (ECSC) laid down that the seat of the institutions of the Community would have to be determined by common accord of the governments of the Member States. This formula was repeated in the later EEC Treaty (in its Article 216) and in the Euratom Treaty (Article 189). No such common accord has been reached and the current working places of the European Community institutions and bodies are provisional only. Most are in one city (e.g. the Council and the Economic and Social Committee in Brussels, the European Court of Justice, European Investment Bank and Court of Auditors in Luxembourg). Although it has offices in Luxembourg, most of the European Commission's services and top decision-makers are in Brussels. Only the European Parliament is split between three cities.

The Parliamentary Assembly of the European Coal and Steel Community met in Strasbourg (with only two extraordinary sessions being held elsewhere), and after 1958 Strasbourg became the provisional site of the plenary sessions of the European Parliamentary Assembly which came into being after the signing of the EEC and Euratom Treaties. From 1959 the Assembly's Committees began meeting on a regular basis in Brussels where the bulk of the new Community institutions were now based. The staff was based in Luxembourg.

The 1965 Merger Treaty, whereby the three separate communities (ECSC, EEC and Euratom) were given a common Council and Commission, did not come up with a permanent solution for the seat of the Community. An accompanying decision by representatives of the governments of the Member States confirmed (in its Article 1) that Luxembourg, Brussels and Strasbourg would remain the provisional places of work of the Community institutions. Article 4 stated that the General Secretariat of the Assembly and its departments would remain in Luxembourg. No mention was made of the Assembly's plenary sittings or Committee meetings, and the *status quo* (plenaries in Strasbourg, Committee meetings in Brussels) was left untouched.

From 1967 onwards, however, and on its own initiative, the European Parliament began to hold occasional plenary sittings in Luxembourg as well as in Strasbourg. Only one meeting was held in Luxembourg in 1967 but from 1968 to direct elections in 1979, 58 sittings took place in Luxembourg compared to 77 in Strasbourg. In 1976 and 1977 more sittings were held in Luxembourg than in Strasbourg. One important practical reason for this development was the convenience of holding the sittings at the working place of the secretariat.

The situation changed rapidly after direct elections in 1979. For the first few months after the elections only Strasbourg had a hemicycle large enough to seat the greatly enlarged Parliament, and by the time Luxembourg had completed its own new hemicycle the members had got used to going to Strasbourg only. Another important factor was that members were given their own offices in Strasbourg, and these facilities were not available in Luxembourg when the Parliament again began to meet there on an occasional basis. By then, however, the majority of members had come around to the belief that it was preferable to have to travel regularly to only two cities, Brussels and Strasbourg, than to three. This evolution was of great concern for the Luxembourg-based staff who called a brief strike over the issue.

The ideal solution, however, was a single seat for the Parliament, and the directly elected members began to call more insistently on the national governments to take a decision on this matter. Nevertheless in March 1981, the European Council meeting at Maastricht in the Netherlands only decided to reiterate the *status quo*.

On July 7, 1981, the European Parliament adopted a resolution (based on a report by an Italian Socialist, Mario Zagari) by 187 votes to 118 with seven abstentions, in which it again called for a decision on a single working place but, pending such a decision, for plenary sessions to be held in Strasbourg and for committee meetings as a general rule in Brussels. The workings of the Parliament's secretariat would have to be reviewed to meet these new requirements, although there was no explicit call for a major transfer of staff. In August 1981 the Luxembourg government challenged this resolution (Case 230/81) but in February 1983 the European Court of Justice found in the Parliament's favour and stated that Luxembourg could not prevent the Parliament giving up the practice of meeting in Luxembourg, which it had only introduced on its own initiative and was not an integral part of the *status quo*.

Another important development in February 1983 was that the European Parliament voted by 130 to 99 with 11 abstentions that an additional part-session to be held on the problems of employment, which could not be held in Strasbourg, would take place in Brussels (at the Palais de Congrès) rather than in Luxembourg. To date, this is still the only full sitting that has taken place in Brussels, apart from one ECSC Assembly meeting in 1956.

In July 1983, the European Parliament decided to go a step further by adopting a resolution (by a written declaration of over half its members rather than by a formal vote in plenary) to divide up the secretariat in the most rational manner between the effective places of work, with services concerned with the functioning of part-sessions in Strasbourg and with those of the parliamentary committees in Brussels. This resolution was again challenged by the Luxembourg government (Case 108/83), on this occasion successfully, when the European Court of Justice annulled the Parliament's resolution as a violation of the *status quo*.

The next major area of controversy was over the Parliament's meeting facilities in Brussels. On Oct 24, 1985, a resolution was adopted by the Parliament by 132 votes to 113 with 13 abstentions which called for the construction of a new Parliament building in Brussels, including a chamber with seating for no less than 600 people. The resolution stated that Parliament needed a large meeting room in Brussels for many of its routine meetings (such as those of the larger Political Groups) but also for any supplementary plenary sittings that might be held in Brussels. The resolution's opponents argued that this was the opening step in a process that would lead to the abandonment of Strasbourg in favour of Brussels. The French government called for the resolution to be declared null and void (Case 258/85). The Advocate-General of the European Court found in the French government's favour, but the full Court rejected the request in September 1988, effectively acknowledging that the European Parliament would be within its rights to hold exceptional sessions outside Strasbourg.

A very recent, and one of the more bitter moments in the long saga over the "seat" came in January 1989, when the European Parliament adopted a new resolution on its working place (based on a report by Derek Prag, a British Conservative). It called for a major reorganization of the Parliament and for a reduction in the current dispersal of its work and staff between three working places. It again called for a final decision on a single seat but expressed pessimism that such a decision would be taken after over 30 years of failure to do so. It thus called for staff dealing with certain activities, such as committee and information work, to be based in Brussels. It also declared that it was now necessary to hold additional plenary sessions to coincide with one or more of the weeks devoted to committee or Political Group meetings.

Although the resolution appeared of more immediate concern to Luxembourg and did not explicitly challenge Strasbourg's position (indeed it recalled Strasbourg's historic importance in the history of the Community) its adoption was contested by the French government and by all the French members present in the Parliament, who found a considerable number of allies among other nationalities and groups.

The resolution was adopted by 222 in favour to 176 against with four abstentions. The Belgian members were, unsurprisingly, overwhelmingly in favour (23 out of the 24 members voted for the resolution) but so were the members from the Netherlands (18 out of 25, with not all present), from the United Kingdom and Northern Ireland (65 out of 81) and from Spain (42 out of 60 members). Other major support came from the German Social Democrats and the Italian Communists.

Opposition to the resolution was led by the French and Luxembourgish members. The vast majority of the European People's Party (Christian

Democrats) members were also opposed, with the exception of its Belgian and Dutch members. Eight of the 15 Irish members were opposed, compared to only two in favour.

In early 1990 the "seat" issue again sprang to life, over the proposed renting of new buildings in Brussels, and with a counter-attack by French members, in particular, calling for a guarantee with regard to plenary sessions in Strasbourg, and for negotiations over the construction of a new hemicycle in the city. In March 1990 a compromise on these lines was adopted by Parliament's Bureau, but was challenged by backbench supporters of Brussels. At the April 1990 plenary a bitter debate culminated in a final vote in which the Parliament supported the Bureau's text.

The question of the Parliament's seat is likely to continue to prove a controversial issue throughout the life of the 1989–94 Parliament and probably well beyond. For France defence of Strasbourg has become a matter of national prestige. Luxembourg is unlikely to see further plenary sessions at least on a regular basis but considers that maintenance of the bulk of the secretariat in Luxembourg is a major national interest, and is even prepared to challenge individual transfers of staff.

Strasbourg also has defenders from other countries, who see it among other things as a symbol of Franco-German reconciliation or emphasize that it is the only city of the three challengers that is not a national capital. Some see its detachment from the Commission and Council in Brussels as a guarantee of its greater independence.

The defenders of Brussels, on the other hand, primarily emphasize its logistical convenience, with its excellent air connections, in particular, and its proximity to the key centres of European Community decision making, to the Commission and Council, to the permanent representatives of the Member States, to the trade associations and lobbyists and to the European press corps.

It is this very proximity that is of concern to a considerable number of people, who are opposed to Brussels becoming, to an even greater extent than at present, the *de facto* capital of the European Community. Some do not even want the European Parliament to become a more effective threat to national parliaments and national centres of powers, and prefer the European Parliament to remain dispersed.

Others have argued for a purpose-built capital for the European Community. The Italian Radical member of the European Parliament, Marco Pannella, has called for an extensive European federal district including parts of several European countries.

Certain members (especially Greens and defenders of Strasbourg and Luxembourg) have also argued for "polycentrism", on the grounds that a decentralized European Community needs a decentralized Parliament.

There is thus no easy solution to the problem. Two possible alternatives are for the three countries most concerned to come to some form of package agreement between them for presentation to the other governments, (with a related factor being the future location of the proposed new European organizations, such as the Trade Mark office, the European Environmental Agency, the Bank for Reconstruction and Development, and the possible European Central Bank), or else for the uncomfortable *status quo* to continue, with a slow drift of staff, and perhaps also certain plenary sessions, to Brussels within Court-defined limits.

When: Parliament's cycle of activities

The European Parliament's timetable follows the same monthly pattern for most of the year. The plenary week in Strasbourg is followed by two "Committee weeks", during which the individual committees meet in Brussels or elsewhere. The cycle is then completed by the "Group" week when the Political Groups meet, in particular to prepare their stance at the next plenary session and other business.

There are only few exceptions to this normal pattern. In October there has traditionally been an extra plenary week, to deal with budgetary matters in particular, and there is thus only one week between two plenaries. (In the past there has occasionally been an extra plenary in March to deal with agricultural prices, but this has not been necessary in recent years). There is also a short Parliamentary recess in August but in 1989 the Parliament's legislative responsibilities under the Single European Act meant that a number of committees had to meet in late August. The final regular exception is during election year, when the outgoing Parliament winds up its activities by May, and the new one assembles in late July. (One can note in passing that in 1989 the pressure of business was such that one or two of the 1984–89 committees met again in late June).

This timetable is in fact less simple in practice than it looks. The committees and especially Political Groups also need to meet during plenary weeks. The reasons for these meetings are examined in greater detail in the sections on Political Groups and on committees below, and the conduct of plenary weeks is also discussed in greater length below.

What is worth mentioning, however, in this general section on Parliament's cycle of activities, is that there is now a certain pressure to change it.

The first problem is that it is inflexible. At the beginning of the five-year term, and at certain times of the year, one week a month is more than enough to handle the plenary business, whereas, at other times, and especially towards the end of the legislature, it is completely inadequate. Parliament is perfectly entitled to hold additional part-sessions but they would clash with Committee and Group weeks, and this has up to now been avoided. As Parliament's legislative, control and other activities build up in the future, there will be potentially conflicting pressures to hold both longer part-sessions and more committee meetings.

A second source of complaint has come from another quarter, from members who feel that the rhythm of Brussels and Strasbourg meetings is such as to give them inadequate time to cultivate their home political base or constituency.

There have thus been numerous proposals for reform, such as the suggestion to move to two-week long plenary sessions, with committees meeting at the same time, thus providing both greater plenary and committee flexibility, and more time to spend in the constituency. The continuing absence of a single seat, however, makes such a proposal particularly hard to implement.

Other suggestions have included the use of additional short part-sessions of one or two days to deal with urgent business, use of committees of the whole House to adopt legislation (as at Westminster), (both the above suggestions being especially popular with the supporters of Brussels for seat of the Parliament), or else cutting down on the reports to be brought to the plenaries, for example by greater delegation of the powers of decision to committees. These suggestions are discussed in greater detail in other chapters.

There is no easy solution to this problem, but it will have to be dealt with in the near future.

In *quale lingua:* languages within the European Parliament

The European Parliament is unique amongst parliaments in the number of its working languages, English, French, German, Italian, Dutch, Danish, Spanish, Portuguese and Greek.

Why does the European Parliament have to have more working languages than the United Nations or other international organizations? Unlike these it is a Parliament. Its elected members, unlike career diplomats, cannot automatically be expected to be competent linguists, although many are. The electorate should be free to choose a popular trade unionist from Germany or farmer from Portugal even if he or she cannot speak or understand a foreign language.

There is also another issue of principle involved. Many members, especially from the smaller Community countries, feel that they are there to defend their country's culture and language. At formal meetings, certain Danish members, for example, have insisted on Danish interpretation, even if they are fluent in English or another Community language.

It is thus extremely difficult to cut back on simultaneous interpretation at any Parliament meeting, although this is attempted where possible for meetings where only few members are involved. More informal meetings (such as meetings of committee co-ordinators) are often carried out in English or French, but this must depend on the agreement of all concerned.

The same is true to an even greater extent as regards translation of documents into all languages. The range of documents which must be translated according to Parliament's own rules of procedure goes well beyond the main documents for the committees and the plenaries to include resolutions tabled by individual members (Rule 63 motions), requests for debates on topical and urgent subjects of major importance, members' written declarations, amendments to plenary texts, censure motions on the Commission, the verbatim report of plenary proceedings and so on. Moreover the Parliament will only accept that it has received a common position on a Community legislative proposal when the common position and the Council's justification and the Commission's reaction have been transmitted to the Parliament in all languages.

Parliament's Rules of Procedure provide only very limited scope for flexibility as regards translation. For example, amendments in plenary should be put to the vote only after they have been printed and distributed in all the official languages, but Parliament may decide otherwise. Even in these circumstances individual untranslated amendments may not be put to a vote if at least 10 members object.

In committee meetings the practice is more informal. Oral amendments or untranslated written amendments are often put to the vote, with members who do not understand them having to rely on the interpretation into their own language. Even here, however, an oral amendment may not be put to the vote if a member objects.

In Political Groups, a less rigid system applies. Some Groups do not have a membership requiring all languages anyway, but even the Socialist Group, which, with the Christian Democrats, are the only ones with MEPs from all Member States, only uses four languages (English, French, German and Spanish) for most internal documents and for most Group meetings. Their MEPs may use any language, but will only be translated into these four. This, however, is only feasible (just!) in the context of non-public meetings among colleagues of the same political family. Another feature of Groups is that their secretariats often do a lot of their own translation because of time constraints.

Translation requirements are only less stringent for internal documents within the Parliament. French is not the main internal working language of Parliament's secretariat to the same extent as it is in certain other Community institutions (for example as in the European Court of Justice), but French is certainly the most used language in Parliament's administration, followed to a lesser extent by English. Meetings of Parliament's staff are normally conducted in French or English.

Certain attempts have been made to cut down on the volume of documents requiring translation, for example by trying to eliminate translation of the verbatim debates or to restrict translation of individual members' resolutions, but these have not been successful. One reform, however, has been that length limits have been imposed on certain types of document. Motions for a resolution, for example, are not meant to exceed two pages, nor explanatory statements more than 10 pages. Documents exceeding these limits have to obtain a special derogation if they are to be translated.

The consequences of this policy of multilingualism can easily be imagined, although the actual figures are still impressive. In 1988, for example, there were 2,022 session documents, of which 1,739 were Parliament documents (reports or motions) requiring translation in all languages. Almost a third of Parliament's staff are in its linguistic services (966 out of 3,349 is the figure cited in the 1989 version of "Forging Ahead"). Since 1989 there has been a separate Directorate-General for Translation with 485 LA grade translators (1990 figures). Parliament directly employs 179 interpreters, and also relies on a considerable number of freelance interpreters. Parliament thus employed 664 Linguistic Administrators (LA) in 1990, compared to only 344 other Administrators (A grades) outside the Political Groups.

The constraints on Parliament's working methods are also considerable. The need to restrict the length of Parliament documents has already been mentioned. Moreover, certain potentially useful documents cannot be translated at all. Whereas transcripts of US Congressional Hearings or

House of Lords inquiries are extremely valuable documents, translation of the full proceedings of European Parliament Hearings would be impossibly costly in terms of time and money.

A second and even more important constraint is that on reaction time by the Parliament. The policy of multilingualism clearly imposes severe delays. For example in 1989 a text prepared by a committee rapporteur had to be handed in to translation at least 10 working days before the meeting at which it was to be considered if it was to be ready in all languages. Any subsequent modifications by the rapporteur, or amendments submitted by other members of the committee when they have seen the rapporteur's text, all require several working days to be translated. Even when the text is ready in most languages one or two may still be missing. If there is good will by the Members affected this may not further delay adoption of the report in question, but it can hand a new weapon into the arms of a filibuster, who can use translation gaps to delay progress further.

The constraints provided by interpretation in meetings are of a different nature. However excellent the interpretation (and in the Parliament it is of a very high standard) it is a brake on spontaneity and comprehension at Parliament meetings of all kinds. The indirect irony or criticism of an Italian Member may well be completely lost in interpretation whereas the directness of a Dutch or Danish Member may only seem like rudeness. Words can be successfully interpreted but cultural differences may not. A joke told by a member in committee may well result in laughter from some Members and perplexed silence from others. As a result when a member wishes to direct a point to a specific Member they sometimes address them in the latter's language.

One constraint, however, for which the interpreters are primarily responsible, is regarded as beneficial by many members. This is the limitation on Parliament's working hours, with plenary and committee meetings needing to have special permission to go past certain fixed hours. Committee meetings, for example, cannot exceed seven hours a day (9–12:30 in the morning, 3–6:30 in the afternoon) and if the Committee wishes to go on past the closing hour without prior authorization it has to do so without interpretation. This is because of agreed limits to interpreters' working hours, and longer hours require costly additional teams of interpreters.

The costs of multilingualism for the European Parliament as a whole are very considerable. In 1990 these have been estimated at the equivalent of £11 million, or around 35 per cent of the total Parliament budget. Together with the 10 per cent of the budget due to the geographical dispersion of the Parliament these two cost centres alone amount to not far short of half the Parliament's budget.

The prospects for reduction in the number of working languages are extremely slim. If anything they are likely to increase if the Community expands. There is also pressure from groups such as the Catalans to have documents translated into their language. Every additional language used creates a large number of additional language combinations which will impose a major new burden on the Parliament. Before Spanish and Portuguese accession there were already 42 such combinations. There are currently 72 such combinations with the existing nine working languages, and this would increase to 110 if only two new languages were added (the formula is $n \times (n-1)$ where n equals the number of working languages). The tension between the conflicting criteria of democratic fairness and logistical practicality is likely to become even greater.

II: THE ACTORS AND WORKING STRUCTURES

4. The individual members

Any examination of Parliament's key "actors" must begin with its 518 individual members. The following section first looks at the position of individual members within the European Parliament system, their rights and their obligations, and the status and role of their assistants.

The second part examines the background of the individual members elected in 1989, such as their length of service in the European Parliament, their national and political background, the numbers holding a dual mandate and the number of women elected.

The final part looks more generally at the role of the individual member within the Parliament, his or her capacity for independent action, and the position of backbenchers.

1. Rights and obligations of individual members within the European Parliamentary system

Just as there is still no uniform electoral system for the European Parliament there is still no uniform statute for its members, and attempts to provide such a statute have not been successful.

Incompatibilities and verification of credentials

A few common principles were established, however, in the 1976 Act adopted by the Council concerning the election of the representatives of the Assembly by direct universal suffrage, which laid down, for example, a list of posts which were held to be incompatible with the job of MEP, such as membership of a government of a Member State, membership of the European Commission, being a Member, Advocate General or Registrar of the Court of Justice or an active official (e.g. not on leave) of a European Community institution. Even as regards incompatibilities, Member States were permitted to lay down additional national rules, pending the entry into force of a uniform electoral procedure.

The 1976 Act also provided for the Assembly to verify the credentials of representatives. This is done on the election of every new member, and is carried out by the Parliament's Committee on Rules of Procedure, the Verification of Credentials and Immunities which can only take note of the results, and has no decision-making competence. Even before this is finalised, newly elected members have the same rights as other members, and verification is almost invariably a simple formality. (One exception being the challenge, which was ultimately unsuccessful, to the credentials of the Irish Labour members nominated in 1981 to replace colleagues who had become Ministers: no criteria had been established for the replacement of elected Irish MEPs, and one of the individuals in question was not even a member of the national parliament.) Moreover, only one member has actually had her election invalidated, and had to stand again (successfully) for election, Dame Shelagh Roberts, who had been deemed to have occupied a post of profit under the Crown which was incompatible with being an MEP under the relevant UK rules.

Facilities

Once elected, new members are given an initial background briefing, receive a voting card for use in electronic votes at the plenary sessions, and also a special *laisser-passer*, which allows them to travel freely around the Community without any other documents.

The newly elected member is also given offices. In Strasbourg each member now has an individual office within the building known as IPE 1.

Members now have their own offices in Brussels as well. In Brussels they are more dispersed, although essentially in two buildings, the Belliard and Van Maerlant Buildings. (In Luxembourg, however, they were never given any office space, which undoubtedly harmed Luxembourg's case to continue to hold plenary sessions after direct elections.) Members also have a certain amount of working space available to them in the European Parliament's offices in their own national capital. Members' offices are broadly comparable in size and facilities, with only Parliament Presidents and Vice-Presidents, Quaestors and Committee Chairmen getting larger offices.

In certain other respects the failure to have a common statute for members has led to major differences in the treatment of members.

One such respect is a MEP's basic salary. This is still paid from the budgets of the Member States and is linked to the salary paid to national Parliamentarians from the members' own country. This results in very great diversity, with Luxembourgish or Irish members, for example, being paid far less than their German equivalents doing the same job. This is clearly an anomaly, and yet it is also a matter of great sensitivity in individual Member States where members of Parliament are paid less. In these countries a sharp rise in MEPs' salaries could have a negative effect on public opinion at large and on relations with lower paid national parliamentarians.

One way in which MEPs from different countries are treated equally, however, is in the size of the expense allowances. They receive daily allowances for the amount of time they spend in Brussels, or elsewhere, on Committee business, in Strasbourg for plenary sessions, and in Brussels or elsewhere for group meetings. To prove that they have actually attended they must sign a register. In the case of Strasbourg sessions their allowances are docked if they attend less than 50 per cent of the sessions. Once they have signed in, however, they have no obligation actually to sit in on the meetings. Members also receive allowances for travel to and from their constituencies or Member States, as well as a 2,500 ECU per annum allowance for other travel on Parliament business within the European Community. In certain special circumstances (such as research by rapporteurs) members may have other travel authorised by the Parliament's Bureau, (which has set certain criteria for such authorisation). On the other hand, members do not have any special funding for travel on Parliament business within their constituency beyond their general allowance. This has been of particular consequence for MEPs with large constituencies such as Winnie Ewing, who represents a constituency (Highlands and Islands) stretching from the Mull of Kintyre to the Shetlands.

Members also receive allowances to maintain offices in their constituencies, for stationery and office equipment and for secretaries and assistants (see discussion below). A number of selected members (such as Vice-Presidents, Quaestors and Committee Chairmen) have had computer terminals installed in their offices, in order to receive, for example, Parliament's in-house teletext system (OVIDE). More recently, the French government has offered telecopiers to all members in their offices in Strasbourg (and a matching offer may be made for Brussels by the Belgian government). Parliament cars are also available for members in Brussels and Strasbourg.

Members' allowances, and their working conditions in general, are regularly reviewed by the Quaestors who are those primarily responsible for such issues within Parliament's leadership structure (see Chapter 6 on this latter topic).

Members' allowances and privileges are considerable, and have aroused resentment among certain circles, and also accusations of abuse. While it would be hard to prevent unscrupulous individuals abusing the system it should also be borne in mind that the costs of being an MEP, notably of travel and telecommunications, are also very high. Moreover, if MEPs' office facilities are good (although no better than in certain national parliaments like the *Bundestag*), this is surely more conducive to effectiveness than the antiquated and cramped conditions in places like the UK House of Commons.

Two other issues concerning the status of members should be mentioned.

Immunities

The first is the issue of parliamentary immunity, another area where the lack of uniform statute for members has led to considerable diversity of national treatment. Members' immunity is still covered by the protocol on the privileges and immunities of the European Community, which provides for MEPs to enjoy the same immunities in their own country as national parliamentarians while in their home country. In other countries of the Community, they are immune from any measure of detention and from legal proceedings, and they are also immune while travelling to and from the Parliament, except when members are caught in the act of committing a criminal offence. Immunity can also be waived by the European Parliament, upon application of the legal authorities in the Member States, thus allowing the MEP in question to appear before Court.

The European Parliament called in 1983 for the protocol to be amended, and the Commission subsequently tabled a proposal to this effect, which would have provided uniform rules. This has still not been adopted.

Requests by the national authorities of the Member States for a members' immunity to be waived are a regular feature at most plenary sessions. Such requests are transmitted to the Committee on the Rules of Procedure, Verification of Credentials and Immunities which submits its report recommending in favour of or against the waiving of immunity, but not pronouncing on or even examining the Members' guilt. These reports are considered under Parliament's Rules as the first substantive item on the plenary agenda on Monday afternoons, and the vote immediately follows the debate. Parliament has established a tradition of having long-standing rapporteurs on immunity questions. In the 1979–84 and 1984–89 Parliaments, Georges Donnez (French Liberal) was the rapporteur, and after the 1989 elections he was succeeded by Jean Defraigne (Belgian Liberal).

In its many reports on requests for the waiving of immunity the Parliament has established a number of basic principles, the most important of which is not to waive immunity if the acts of which a member is accused form part of his political activities.

In the majority of cases, therefore, Parliament has not acceded to requests to waive immunity. A recent exception (December 1989) was when Jean Marie Le Pen's immunity was waived by a large majority after a long and passionate debate on whether the particularly obnoxious nature of his remarks justified abandonment of Parliament's customary concern to protect members' expression of political opinions. Parliament thus overruled its relevant Committee's narrow decision (10 to nine with two abstentions) not to waive Le Pen's immunity. Le Pen's immunity was again waived in similar circumstances on another charge at the March 1990 plenary.

Declaration of financial interests

Another issue which should be mentioned is that of declaration of members' financial interests.

Rule 8 of Parliament's Rules of Procedure states that Parliament may lay down a code of conduct for its members. The only implementing provision so far is that contained in Annex I of the Rules providing for such a declaration of financial interests. National traditions on this issue vary greatly, with some countries such as the UK and Germany having fairly rigid rules, others much weaker rules, and some none at all.

Parliament adopted a report in March 1983 on the issues involved, drawn up by Hans Nord (Dutch Liberal, former Parliament Secretary-General), which opted for brief general provisions rather than a set of very detailed rules. As a result, Annex I merely provides that each member shall be required to make a detailed declaration of his or her professional activities, and shall list any other paid functions or activities in so far as these are relevant (Article 2). Members are also meant to disclose orally any direct financial interest in a subject under discussion in Parliament or in one of its bodies, unless it is obvious from his or her written declaration

(Article 1). Finally members' declarations are to be contained in a register, which is open for public inspection.

Annex I is now being implemented, and members are now given a form with which to declare their financial interests. The register is kept for inspection in an office in Luxembourg and is brought to another office in Strasbourg during plenary sessions. Certain members have put down motions for a resolution on this issue, complaining about the lack of detailed information provided by many members, and lack of sanctions against members not in compliance, and also called for greater public accessibility of the register.

The members' assistants

In carrying out their Parliamentary work members need not only rely on the non-partisan permanent officials of the Parliament and the officials of the political groups, but also have their own personal staff and assistants. Members are given a secretarial allowance for such purposes.

In practice, members are allowed very considerable freedom as to the use they make of these funds, for example whether they wish to have one better paid full-time assistant or several less well paid or part-time assistants. In some cases members prefer to have their main assistant in Brussels, in others in their national capitals or in their own constituencies. While some have help in all three locations, others make little use of assistants.

The role of assistants also varies greatly, with some given considerable political responsibilities, and other concentrating more on office tasks, such as typing, booking tickets or running other errands. A typical task is to arrange meetings with Commission officials, or representatives of trade associations, or to carry out background research for reports. Some assistants help to draft reports when their boss becomes a rapporteur, but this still tends to be exceptional. Brussels-based assistants also often attend the relevant committee meetings when the member is absent, and brief the member on what took place. Some help service the intergroups in which their member is active.

Assistants based in the members' home country tend to have much more of a liaison function with the party at home, or with national or regional interests, a matter of considerable importance in view of the great amount of travelling of an average MEP. In some members' home bases their assistants act practically as constituency agents.

Members' assistants tend to be much less well paid than Parliament's full-time or political group staff, and there is a much higher turnover among them. They tend to be much younger (often just out of university), and take on the job for a short period to gain experience. A minority, however, remain assistants for several years, and when they leave the employment of one member may then start working for another. Some work for two or more members at once. In at least one case assistants have formed a business consortium with a number of MEPs on its books, as well as members from the respective national parliament. In other cases several members have pooled some of their resources and run a joint secretariat (e.g. Dutch Socialist members and some German SPD members with a trade union background).

A few assistants have their own successful careers (in consultancy, for example) and have a part-time role as assistants in order primarily to widen their range of contacts. A number have gone on to political careers in their own right, such as the current Labour MEPs Stephen Hughes (who worked for Roland Boyes), Anita Pollack (who worked for Barbara Castle), and Gary Titley (who worked for Terry Pitt and then John Bird).

The working conditions and status of members' assistants remains on a rather *ad hoc* and variable basis. They rarely have their own office, and tend normally to work from the members' offices in Brussels and Strasbourg, a constituency office or the European Parliament's office in their national capital, or even from their own home. A considerable number come regularly to Strasbourg plenary sessions, but many remain in Brussels or in their national base. On the other hand, their conditions of access to parliamentary meetings, which was once restricted in certain committees and Groups, has improved.

There is now discussion as to whether and how to reinforce the role and status of assistants, by increasing their numbers and by providing them with a proper statute.

Any strengthening of the role of the assistants will clearly change the relationship between individual members, their parties and Groups, and Parliament's full-time staff. For this reason alone it is a very sensitive topic. If it does come about, however, the likelihood is not that the role of Groups or of Parliament's full-time staff will diminish, but that they might become more specialized as Parliament's working methods are modified.

2. Background of the individual members elected in 1989

Length of service

One of the more remarkable features of the European Parliament is the high turnover in its membership at each election, and to a lesser extent even between elections. Of the 518 members elected in 1989, only 267 were outgoing members. Most of the other 251 were completely new members, although a small number had previously served in the Parliament.

Those with more than five years' experience of the Parliament are even fewer in number. Only 83 of the current MEPs have served continuously since 1979, and only 11 of these have been members continuously since before 1979.

Taking new and former members together, the current group of MEPs has an average of under three-and-a-half years' membership of the Parliament, an unusually low figure by parliamentary standards (although of course influenced by the fact that we are writing soon after an election, and only four years after Spain and Portugal joined the Community).

Nevertheless, there are clear variations in length of service between the different national delegations. The United Kingdom with its system of individual constituencies provides the delegation with the longest service. Thirty of its members have been in the Parliament since 1979, and the average length of service is five-and-a-half years. On the other hand West Germany, with a list system of election, is not far behind, with 26 of its

MEPs having been members since 1979, and with an average length of service of around four-and-a-half years. Fifty-six of the 83 MEPs who have been members since 1979 thus come from only two countries.

Another indication that the length of service is not necessarily linked to the electoral system but more to a country's political culture is that the Dutch MEPs also have an average of over four-and-a-half years' membership in the Parliament. Other countries with above average length of membership are Luxembourg, Belgium, Denmark and Ireland.

The first Greek members only joined the Parliament in 1981, and the first Spaniards and Portuguese in 1986. So it is unsurprising that members from these countries have short average lengths of service (although 47 of the outgoing Spanish members were re-elected in 1989). What is more remarkable, however, is the high turnover and low average length of service among French and Italian MEPs. Fifty-five of the 1989 intake of French members are new, and only seven French members have served continually since 1979. The average length of service of French MEPs is only two-and-a-half years.

Fifty-eight of the 81 Italian members are new, and only six have served since 1979. The average length of service of Italian MEPs is only just over two years, and has already been caught up with by the Spanish MEPs after only three years of Spanish participation in the Parliament.

Balance between men and women

There are currently 100 women MEPs, 19.3 per cent of the total. This compares to 69 women (16.8 per cent) elected in the first direct elections in 1979. The current figure is nevertheless higher than that in most national parliaments within the Member States and only lower than the Danish *Folketing* and the First and Second Chambers in the Netherlands.

Again there is considerable variation in these figures between the different national delegations. Twenty-six of the 81 German members are women (up from only 12 in 1979), compared to 18 in France, 12 in the United Kingdom and 10 in Italy. The highest proportion is from Luxembourg (three out of six), the lowest in Greece (one out of 24).

National parliamentary and ministerial experience

While so many of the current MEPs are newcomers and their average length of service in the European Parliament is so limited, many of them have nevertheless had considerable experience in their own national parliaments, and many have held office in their national governments or in their own party.

Although the dual mandate is not permitted in six Member States (see section on electoral systems above), 34 of the current MEPs are still members of their national parliaments as well. Eighteen of the 81 Italian members are in this position as well as 7 French members. The only two UK members with a dual mandate, in both the European Parliament and the House of Commons, are John Hume and Ian Paisley from Northern Ireland, although there are also four members of the House of Lords.

There are also many other former members of national parliaments among the current intake of MEPs. In all there are 150 former national parliamentarians, including all six Luxembourg members, 19 of the 24 Portuguese, 10 of the 15 Irish members and 39 out of the 60 Spaniards. On the other hand, only 11 Germans and 11 British MEPs have been in their national parliaments. Apart from the three Northern Irish members, and four members of the House of Lords, only four of the remaining 74 British members have been in the Commons.

No less than 73 MEPs have held ministerial office of one kind or another, many of them very senior office. The record is held by France with no less than 16 former Ministers and one Secretary of State, followed by Italy with eight former Ministers and four under-Secretaries of State. Other experienced delegations include Spain (eight former Ministers and one Secretary of State), Belgium (six former Ministers), Ireland (five former Ministers and three Ministers of State), Portugal (four Ministers and four Secretaries of State), Greece and Denmark (four former Ministers each).

The Germans, British and Dutch present a sharp contrast. The Dutch delegation has only one former Secretary of State and the British one former Junior Foreign Minister (John Tomlinson). The German delegation now has no former Federal ministers at all.

At the higher level of all there is one former Head of State among the MEPs (Valery Giscard d'Estaing) and six former Prime Ministers (Leo Tindemans of Belgium, Laurent Fabius of France and Emilio Colombo, Arnaldo Forlani, Giovanni Goria and Bettino Craxi of Italy). Other former Heads of Government who have also been members since direct elections have included Willy Brandt, Mariano Rumor, Giulio Andreotti, Jacques Chirac, Francisco Balsemão and Maria de Lourdes Pintasilgo. Not all of these former leaders have been particularly active in the European Parliament but some have held important office (Colombo as President of the European Parliament just before direct elections, Rumor and now Goria as Chairmen of the Political Affairs Committee, Tindemans as current Co-Chairman of the ACP Assembly, Giscard d'Estaing as current Chairman of the Liberal Group).

Among the current MEPs there are also two former members of the European Commission, Claude Cheysson (who has also served as French Foreign Minister) and Willy de Clercq (who went from being Commissioner responsible for External Relations to being Chairman of Parliament's External Economic Relations Committee).

Another significant group among the current MEPs are those holding leadership positions in their national parties, with around 24 MEPs being Chairman, Secretary-General or National Secretary of their party. (Six in Italy, five in France, four in Spain, two in Portugal, and one each in Belgium, Denmark, Germany and the Netherlands.) There are also two UK MEPs in this position (John Hume of the SDLP and the Reverend Ian Paisley of the Democratic Unionist Party) and one Irish MEP (Proinsias de Rossa of the Workers' Party). In Italy the leaders of the six largest Italian parties are all MEPs.

Other political experience

A considerable number of the current MEPs have held important posts in regional or local government. In general these members come from those delegations with the most national parliamentary and governmental experience, France, Italy and Spain. The French delegation, for example, includes two Presidents of Regional Councils and 10 current Mayors. The Italian delegation is even stronger in this respect, with no less than 19 former or current Regional Councillors, and nine former or present mayors of large towns.

The German delegation includes a considerable number of members with experience in *Land* Assemblies (and a smaller number of former *Land* Ministers), and also a number of former and present mayors (but only four of these from large towns). The Spanish delegation too includes a considerable number of former members of regional governments.

Certain other national delegations, however, have few members with local government experience, such as the Dutch and Danish delegations. Only a minority of the UK delegation have been local councillors (a higher percentage of these being Labour rather than Conservative members), and even fewer have held major posts in local government.

3. The role of individual members within the European Parliamentary system

As in any Parliament there are significant constraints on the freedom of action of individual members within the European Parliament. The agenda of plenary sessions, the distribution of speaking time and of rapporteur-ships, and other important decisions, are, of course, decided primarily by the leaders of the Political Groups. Backbench members of the Groups, and, even more, the non-attached MEPs find it difficult to have a direct say. Nevertheless individual members do play a considerable role in the life of the European Parliament, especially compared to their equivalents in national parliaments like the House of Commons where the need to maintain government majorities leads to much tighter whipping systems, and to less freedom of manoeuvre for individual members.

Lesser pressures for strict voting discipline within Political Groups (because there is no executive that must be backed) is one reason for the considerable independence permitted to individual members of the European Parliament. A second reason is the sheer variety of interests represented, of a party, sectoral, regional and national nature, which cannot all be expressed by one political Group spokesman. While attempts are made by the Groups to permit a variety of points of view to be expressed within a debate (the Socialist Group, for example, may have five or more speakers in a major debate), not all members who wish to speak may be given time to do so, and other members may feel that they must dissent from the Group line. On some issues, coalitions are formed between individual members from different Groups, a practice which is certainly being encouraged by the development of intergroups (see Chapter 9).

Another factor which encourages independence is the relative weakness of leadership structures within the European Parliament as a whole, and also within the Political Groups. Very few effective sanctions can be exercised against a rebel MEP. Expulsion or even suspension from a Political Group are practically unheard of events, assignments in a committee once made are almost always maintained (unless a member wishes to change), and withdrawal of a rapporteurship from an individual member by his or her Political Group is also extremely difficult. Gaullist members of the 1979–84 Parliament who refused to leave the Parliament when asked to do so by their party (see dispute over the turnstile system in Chapter 2) could not be forced to do so. The only practical sanctions lie in withdrawal of future patronage, such as not renominating a member in the next European elections (only valid when there is a rigid list system), not giving them rapporteurships, and so on. The non-attached members have even greater independence.

There are thus a number of maverick or "outsider" members who have made a considerable impact within the Parliament by effective use of the relevant Rules of Procedure (see below).

Another phenomenon worth mentioning is that of backbench revolts against Group leaderships, especially when such members from different Groups are angered by what they see as a cosy deal cooked up by the Group chairmen behind closed doors. A striking example of such a revolt is when the Group leaders decided in 1983 that a supplementary plenary session that could not be held in Strasbourg should be held in Luxembourg: they were forced by backbenchers to hold it in the Palais de Congrès in Brussels instead. Another example, but with an unsuccessful outcome, was over the seat issue in April 1990 (see Chapter 3).

Parliament's Rules of Procedure provide for numerous rights for individual members, or for several members acting together outside the normal Political Group or committee framework.

The independence of individual MEPs is emphasized at the very beginning in Rule 2-2 which states that "they shall vote on an individual and personal basis", "shall not be bound by any instructions, and shall not receive a binding mandate".

The rights of individual members include the right to put questions to the Commission, Council or Foreign Ministers meeting in European Political Co-operation for oral answer without debate (Rule 59); in the context of Question Time (Rule 60); or for written answer (Rule 61); the right to table a motion for a resolution on any Community issue (Rule 63) or a written declaration (Rule 65); the right to table a proposal to reject a common position of the Council (Rule 50) or table amendments to any text in committee or in plenary (Rules 69 and 123); the right to make explanations of vote (Rule 98); the right to ask questions related to the work of Parliament's leadership (Bureau, Enlarged Bureau and Quaestors, Rule 25-2); and the right to table amendments to the Rules of Procedure (Rule 132). Individual members may also raise points of order (Rule 101), or move a procedural motion, e.g. moving inadmissibility of a matter (Rule 102), referral back to committee (Rule 103), or adjournment of a debate (Rule 105). All such points of order or procedural motions have a prior claim over other plenary business (Rule 100). Individual members may also make personal statements (Rule 85), notably when derogatory comments have been made about them by other speakers.

The use of some of these powers is described in greater detail elsewhere in this book. A few additional comments, however, can be made at this stage, in terms of the use made of these powers by individual members, and their value for them.

The value of Question Time in plenary, for example, which was initiated before British entry into the Community, but which has been dominated by British members, has often been questioned in the European Parliamentary context, in that it has little of the cut and thrust of its original model, is often very poorly attended, and yet takes up valuable plenary time. Nevertheless, all attempts to shift it to a time other than that originally planned, or to reduce its duration, are met with strong resistance from certain MEPs (often but by no means exclusively British), who claim that it is of great importance for individual MEPs, and must always be given high priority.

Written questions too can be of considerable value, sometimes in terms of the information elicited, but even more often in enabling an individual member to put down a marker on an issue of constituency or other importance, especially in view of the requirement for questions to be published in the Community's Official Journal, even before a final answer has been given, after a certain time has elapsed. Certain individual members have made particular use of written questions, such as Henk Vredeling or Lord O'Hagan before direct elections, or Dieter Rogalla (German SPD) in recent years in the context of his fierce campaign to remove internal frontiers within the Community (Rogalla is one of the most instantly recognizable individual members in that he almost always wears an anti-customs post T-shirt, and carries a miniature customs barrier onto his desk in plenary or committee).

Another device for putting down a marker on a specific issue is through individual motions for a resolution tabled pursuant to Rule 63. These are the equivalent in certain respects of "early day motions" at Westminster, and are referred to Parliament's relevant specialized committee. Occasionally they are made the subject of specific reports, or else included within a wider report (in both cases the motion is annexed to the final committee report submitted to plenary). In most cases, however, the committee decides not to follow up the motion, and informs its sponsor accordingly. Members can, nevertheless, (as in the UK House of Commons where Early Day Motions are not normally followed up) still gain publicity from their initiative, and show their constituents or other Groups that they have played an active role on their behalf.

A very useful individual right is that to make explanations of vote in plenary. They are often unpopular with other members at the end of a long and tiring voting session, in that they precede the final vote on a text and can, although limited to three minutes per member, cumulatively delay it by up to half an hour or more. Considerable pressure is often exerted for them not to be made orally in the plenary, but converted into written explanations (cheers often greet members' calls of "in writing" and groans when they actually start to speak!). Members often do assert their right to an oral statement, however, especially if they have not had a chance to express their point of view during the general plenary debate. Moreover, these statements are often more concise and passionate than those made in the preceding debate, and they are also made before a much fuller, if often noisy, house. They thus often give more of a flavour of the real issues at stake.

As in any Parliament, points of order and procedural motions are often used (and sometimes abused) by individual members. They are particularly frequent at the beginning of plenary sessions (when they can go on for half an hour or more), after controversial rulings have been made by the President, or in order to continue a terminated debate by other means. They are also often used to make isolated points of constituency or sectoral concern. The French Communists and British members in general (especially Labour members) have been particularly active in this regard. In this context, however, the most well-known member of all has been Marco Pannella, who has made a particular crusade of defending the rights of backbenchers, the non-attached members or of small Groups, and also of baiting Parliament's leadership. The President of Parliament recently pointed out that Pannella had spoken on 31 different occasions during the September 1989 plenary, for a total speaking time of 56 minutes!

Besides these rights granted to individual members, Parliament's Rules of Procedure also grant rights to members acting together with a certain specified number of other members. This is done wherever the Rules confer such rights on Political Groups, and even in a few cases where Political Groups have no such rights (such as a request for a quorum to be ascertained by 13 or more members). The actual number of members required to assert such rights, however, varies from case to case, with 23 members (the minimum number to form a Political Group with members from only one country) being by far the most common figure, but with seven, 10, 13, one tenth, one fifth, one quarter, or one third of MEPs being required in certain circumstances. The higher the number, of course, the more likely it is to be used only by a Political Group or combination of Groups (e.g. either the Socialists or the European People's Party acting alone could successfully call for a secret ballot, which can be requested by one-fifth of all MEPs, or the Socialists acting alone could succeed in setting up a special committee of inquiry, which can be requested by one-quarter of all MEPs). The Rules, however, do give considerable scope for dissident members within a Political Group, or coalitions of individual members across Group divides, to request that certain action be taken. The situation can be summarised as follows:

7 members	May table question for oral answer with debate to Commission, Council or Foreign Ministers within European Political Co-operation (Rule 58) May request debate on an answer given by Commission, Council or Foreign Ministers in Question Time (Rule 61)
10 members	May prevent amendments which have not been printed or distributed in all official languages from being put to the vote (Rule 69-6)

13 members	May nominate candidates for President, Vice-Presidents or Quaestors (Rule 12)
	May prevent a report being taken in plenary without debate (Rule 38-2)
	May propose one change to plenary draft agenda (Rule 74)
	May request that quorum be checked in plenary (Rule 89-3)
	May request closure of a debate (Rule 104), or suspension or closure of a sitting (Rule 108)
	May nominate members of a committee (Rule 110) or suggest amendments to the Bureau's proposals
23 members	May propose that Commission and Council take part in a debate before negotiations with an applicant state (Rule 32-2) or on the proposed terms before the final signing of an agreement (Rule 32-4)
	May propose that Council be asked to consult Parliament on negotiating mandate for an association agreement (Rule 33-1) or significant international agreement (Rule 34-2) or that the Commission be requested to take part in a debate on its negotiating mandate for such agreements (Rule 33-2) or for a trade and co-operation agreement (Rule 35-2)
	May request that an amendment be put to the vote in plenary even if it received fewer than five votes in committee (Rule 36-6)
	May request application of Rule 37 (adoption of a report in committee)
	May propose reconsultation of European Parliament (Rule 43)
	May table amendments to a Common position (Rule 51)
	May request debate on statement by Commission or Council or Foreign Minister within EPC, and may table motion for a resolution to wind up debate (Rule 56)
	May table motion to wind up debate on oral question with debate (Rule 58-5)
	May request topical and urgent debate (Rule 64)
	May propose amendments to plenary agenda (Rule 74)
	May request urgency for a particular legislative report (Rule 75)
	May oppose any changes in normal voting order (Rule 92)
	May request roll-call vote (Rule 95-1)

one tenth members	May put down motion of censure on Commission (Rule 30)
	May oppose delegation of the power of decision to one of Parliament's committees (Rule 37-2)
one fifth members	May request secret ballot (Rule 97-2)
one quarter members	May call for establishment of committee of inquiry (Rule 109-3)
one third members	May request convening of Parliament on special occasion (Rule 9)

Besides the rights listed above, which mainly affect the conduct of plenary business, there are also a number of others applicable within committees.

The practical scope for use of these rights should not be exaggerated, and the Political Groups do, of course, play the leading role within the Parliament. The rights, mentioned above, however, do provide certain minimum safeguards against complete domination of Parliament by the Political Groups.

4.   The work of an individual MEP: choice of priorities

So far this chapter has examined the formal rights and obligations of individual MEPs, their political background and the techniques and procedures that they can use to make an impact as individuals. The final section looks at the wider choices that must be made by all individual members of the European Parliament, namely how best to spend his or her time.

The pressure on a member's time is extremely great. Consider the four-weekly cycle of activities. One week a month is taken up by the plenary session in Strasbourg, and much of the next two weeks by committee meetings in Brussels, especially if an MEP is on two committees or is an active substitute on another committee. Much of the fourth week is taken up by his or her Political Group meeting, in Brussels or elsewhere. The week after members must again return to Strasbourg!

This pressure is compounded by the amount of time it takes to travel between these various locations and the member's home country. In addition to all this a member is expected to keep in touch with his or her own political base at home, even if, like most members (with the major exception of the British and Irish members) they do not actually have a geographical constituency to nurse. Nevertheless, they may be responsible for keeping in touch with party members in a certain region of the country, or have sectoral (e.g. trade union) or specific policy responsibilities within their party.

Even when they are in one location there are further conflicting pressures on their time. The meeting of their full committee may coincide with a hearing or debate in another committee which is of greater political importance to them. Intergroup meetings (of which more in Chapter 9) are taking up more and more time. A member may also have to speak to visitors groups from their constituency, region or home country in Brussels or Strasbourg. At home they are often called upon to participate in seminars and conferences in their capacity as specialists on European Community affairs, or to be involved in their own party committees or working groups. Lobbyists are increasingly active, and wish to meet members, and to invite them to presentations and receptions. The member will also have many requests for interviews from the Brussels press corps, or from journalists from his or her home country, and will anyway wish to cultivate these contacts on a regular basis.

The pressure on certain members is even greater. The Parliament's President, the leaders of the Political Groups, committee chairmen and increasingly even committee co-ordinators, together with rapporteurs on controversial policy issues are all likely to have fuller agendas because of their specific role in the institution. Those members who have established a reputation in a particular field, such as the environment, tax harmonization or media policy, are also in particular demand, especially if they are proficient linguists.

In spite of these pressures, members do not have large personal staffs to help them to respond (in contrast especially with the United States Congress).

Being an MEP is thus an increasingly tough full-time job. Nevertheless, as we have seen, there are still a few who have dual mandates in their national parliament, or have important domestic, political or other responsibilities. While in certain circumstances this can lead to such members spending little time in the European Parliament, their other activities may also have benefits, in terms of maintaining links between the European Parliament and the national political party and so on.

All this shows that an individual MEP is faced with tough choices. An active member of a committee or of a Political Group may well gain greater influence within the Parliament, with prestigious rapporteurships, and so on. On the other hand, a member can be extremely active within the Parliament, and yet lose touch with his or her own political base at home, and risk not being re-elected. While the choice is not usually as stark as this (e.g. members who have built up their reputations within the Parliament may well gain domestically as well), a member must, nevertheless, select an appropriate balance of priorities. How much time should they spend in Brussels, Strasbourg and at home? Should they remain generalists or seek to become policy specialists? What activities should they concentrate on?

A number of factors condition these choices. Geographical proximity to the working places of the Parliament make it easy for certain members to come and go frequently, whereas this is more difficult for other members, such as those from Ireland, Southern Italy or Spain, Portugal or Greece.

Secondly, a constituency-based electoral system may put more pressure on a member to spend a lengthy period of time at his or her home base than a list system would do, especially if the latter is nationally rather than regionally based, and if there is no preferential element. Nevertheless, as pointed out above, list systems do not preclude regional or local responsibilities being put on a member, and list members must also spend time cultivating their national base if they want to ensure that they remain on the list the next time around.

Another factor is the nature of a member's interests and responsibilities. Moreover, while individual members cannot be mandated, some of them, nevertheless, have close links with the particular sectors or interest groups which will help to condition their choice of priorities.

Degree of access to positions of responsibility within the European Parliament is yet another factor. Members from small Groups, or non-attached members, may well find it easier, for example, to make an impact in plenary where they can make a well publicized speech, than in committee where they will find it hard to get major rapporteurships.

Differences in national culture also play a role, with different emphasis being put on different aspects of a parliamentarians' role, and even on the importance attached to attendance at meetings.

Examples of differences in national culture abound. Members from Northern European countries have generally been more prepared to spend time, for example, on the details of technical legislation than many members from Southern Europe; British members have traditionally put more of an emphasis on Question Time in plenary, and so on.

As a result of all these factors, the priorities of individual members are indeed very different, as are their profiles within the European Parliament. Some become known as men or women of the House, and are constantly present in plenary and elsewhere. Others are more effective within committee, or in their Group, whereas others concentrate more on their national or regional political image. Some members remain generalists, whereas others become specialists, and are always allocated reports or opinions within a particular policy area. Some members even develop functional rather than policy specialities (e.g. the Rules of Procedure, etc.). Some members only pay short visits to Brussels or Strasbourg, whereas others are always present, and have even bought accommodation there.

However, if Members of the European Parliament thus enjoy considerable freedom to choose their priorities, there are certain constraints on this freedom. One of these consists of the internal rules and priorities of the Political Groups to which they belong. It is to these that we now turn.

5. The Political Groups

Their importance in the work of the Parliament

The rules of the European Parliament permit a Political Group to be founded by 23 members from one Member State, by 18 members from two Member States or by only 12 members from three or more Member States.

In the past there has been considerable academic and other speculation as to whether these Political Groups would evolve into truly transnational political parties. While some of the groups are more cohesive than others, none of them has fully evolved in this direction, and the national delegations within each Group still play an important role. Nevertheless the Groups are of central importance in the work of the Parliament.

It is the Groups who play the decisive role in changing the Parliament's leaders, the President, Vice-Presidents and Quaestors, the committee chairmen and vice-chairmen and the interparliamentary delegations chairmen. The Groups also set the parliamentary agenda, choose the rapporteurs and decide on the allocation of speaking time. They have their own large and growing staff, receive considerable funds from the Parliament and often have an important say in the choice of the Parliament's own top officials. The power of the Groups is also shown by the powerlessness of those non-attached members who are not in Political Groups, who are highly unlikely, for example, ever to hold a powerful post within the Parliament, nor be a major rapporteur.

There are now 10 Political Groups within the Parliament, some with familiar names, others whose titles do not immediately indicate the nature of their membership or even their position in the ideological spectrum.

The next section of the book briefly examines the historical evolution of the Groups within the Parliament, and then the Groups as they are today. It surveys the structures and working methods of the Groups, and concludes with a review of their degree of cohesion and the emerging balance of power between them.

Their historical evolution

The Groups have been gradually evolving since 1953, when they were first formally recognized by the Common Assembly of the European Coal and Steel Community, which established the minimum membership for such a Group as nine. This was the first international assembly whose members sat according to political affiliation (e.g. this was first introduced in the Parliamentary Assembly of the Council of Europe in 1964).

The first three groups to be founded, all in June 1953, were those representing the traditional European political families, the Liberals, Christian Democrats and Socialists. From 1953 to 1965 these remained the only three Political Groups. The largest of the three Groups were the Christian Democrats, who were often close to but never attained an absolute majority of the Assembly's members, 38 out of 77 in 1953, 39 out of 78 in 1955 and 1956, 67 out of 142 after the Assembly was enlarged in 1958). The Socialists were generally the second largest Group, and the Liberals the third, apart from the years 1959/60 to 1961/62 when the Liberals overtook the Socialists (43 Liberals to 33 Socialists in 1961/62).

After the enlargement of the Assembly in 1958 the rules for forming Groups were also changed, with the minimum required membership being raised to 17, but this was subsequently again lowered to 14 in 1965.

In 1965 the first new Group was founded when the French Gaullists broke away from the Liberals and formed the European Democratic Union. From 1965 to 1973 the Christian Democrats remained by far the largest Group, with the Socialists in second place, the Liberals third and the European Democratic Union fourth.

British, Irish and Danish entry into the Community in 1973 led to a considerable change in the political balance. The arrival of the British Conservatives led to the founding of a completely new Group, the European Conservatives with 20 members. The European Democratic Union was also modified, when the French Gaullists were joined by members from the Irish party, *Fianna Fáil*, and the name of the Group was also changed to that of the European Progressive Democrats. The other major change was the reinforcement of the Socialist Group, which now had practically as many members as the Christian Democrats. It would have become the largest Group if the British Labour Party had not refused to nominate the members to which it was entitled, until after the 1975 referendum on UK membership of the Community. After it eventually did so in 1975 the Socialist Group became easily the largest Group, and it has remained so ever since.

In 1973 there was also another rule change. A Group could now be formed by as few as 10 members, if they were from three or more Member States.

The final change in the old nominated Parliament came with the foundation, in October 1973, of the Communist Group. This began with only 14 members, and remained the smallest of the six Groups in existence before direct elections. In February 1978 there were 63 Socialists, 52 Christian Democrats, 24 Liberals (since 1976 called the Liberal and Democratic Group rather than Liberals and Allies), 19 Progressive Democrats, 18 Conservatives and 17 Communists, as well as three non-attached members.

The advent of direct elections in 1979 saw further changes. As the number of members had more than doubled from 198 to 410 an attempt was immediately made to raise the minimum threshold for the creation of Groups. This would have prevented the formation of a proposed Group for the Technical Co-ordination and Defence of Independent Groups and Members, consisting of a heterogeneous mixture of small parties and individuals (the Italian Radicals and two small Italian parties of the Left, the Belgian Regionalists, the Danish anti-marketeers and an Irish independent, Neil Blaney), with no common platform, but sharing the recognition that it was much more advantageous to be in a Group than to be non-attached. Filibustering techniques were then successfully used to stop any rule change, with the main protagonist being Marco Pannella of the Italian Radicals. The Technical Group was able to survive, with 12 and later with 11 members. Unlike the other Groups it did not have one leader but three co-presidents who took turns to represent the Group at the meetings of Parliament's Enlarged Bureau.

While no other new Groups were created immediately after direct elections there was a considerable change in the balance between the existing groups. The Christian Democrats (who also changed their name to the Group of the European People's Party, EPP) did well in the elections, (advancing from 52 to 107 seats) but remained narrowly second to the Socialists (63 to 113 seats). The European Conservatives moved from being the fifth largest group with 18 seats to the third largest with 64 seats, due to the British Conservatives winning 60 of the 81 UK seats on 50 per cent of the vote. The European Conservatives also changed their name to that of the European Democratic Group. Besides the British Conservatives (and for a while also an Ulster Unionist) they included three members from the Danish Conservatives and one from the Danish Centre Democrats, but the latter subsequently joined the Group of the European People's Party.

The Communists also did well, advancing from being the sixth largest Group, with 17 seats, to being the fourth largest with 44. Their full name was the Communist and Allies Group. Besides the French, Italian and Greek Communists, they also included the non-Communist Socialist People's Party from Denmark and a number of left-wing independents elected on Communist lists.

The Liberal and Democratic Group advanced from 24 to 40 members, but slipped from being the third to only the fifth largest Group. Their membership included the traditional Liberal parties from Belgium (both Flanders and Wallonia), Denmark, Germany, Italy, Luxembourg and the Netherlands, as well as Italian Republicans, the majority of UDF members from France (Republicans, Radicals, Social Democrats and Independents elected on the UFE list) and also an Irish independent (T.J. Maher).

The European Progressive Democrats only advanced from 19 to 22 members. They again included the Gaullists elected on the DIFE list in France and the *Fianna Fail* members from Ireland but also recruited a Dane from the anti-tax Progress Party, and Winnie Ewing of the Scottish National Party, who had previously sat as an independent.

Greek accession in 1981 (and the subsequent special European elections in Greece) did not lead to major alterations in the political balance, the major beneficiaries being the Socialist Group, who were joined by *PASOK* members, and the Group of the European People's Party, who recruited members from the Greek centre-right Party, New Democracy. The Communists also gained three new members.

The second set of direct elections in 1984 led to the creation of an eighth Group, that of the European Right, with members from Le Pen's *Front*

National in France and from the Italian Social Movement (MSI) in Italy, as well as one member from the Greek right-wing party, *EPEN*.

Another significant change was the transformation of the almost completely heterogeneous Technical Group into a larger and slightly more structured Rainbow Group, consisting of the first set of Greens to be elected to the Parliament (from *Die Grünen* in Germany and *Agalev* and *Ecolo* in Belgium), left alternative parties (such as *Democrazia Proletaria* in Italy and those linked together in the *Groen Progressief Akkoord* in the Netherlands), regionalist parties of the European Free Alliance (such as the Flemish *Volksunie* and the Italian alliance of *Union Valdôtaine–Partito Sardo d'Azione*), and the anti-market Danes in the Danish People's Movement. The Italian Radicals did not participate in the new Rainbow Group, partly because of the latter's suspicion of what they saw as the overpowering personality of Marco Pannella.

The other Groups remained unchanged in structure, with the Socialists and European Progressive Democrats gaining seats and the others all losing some. Spanish and Portuguese accession was of greatest advantage to the Socialist Group, which gained 42 new members. The European Democrats recruited the main Spanish party of the centre-right (*Alianza Popular*). Significant gains were also made by the Liberals, in particular through the adhesion of the Portuguese Social Democrats (for whom the Group changed their name yet again to Liberal, Democratic and Reformist Group). The Group of the European People's Party, the European Progressive Democrats, the Communists and the Rainbow Group all made lesser gains. These first Iberian members were all nominated, and after the first Iberian direct elections in June and July 1987 the balance was again slightly altered.

One of the main parties that entered the Parliament as a result of these elections was the Social Democratic Centre (CDS) of Adolfo Suárez who remained non-attached. In late 1987 an attempt was made to create a new Technical Group within the Parliament, based on the CDS members, the Italian Radicals and one or two other non-attached members. The group had only 12 members but quickly lost its Dutch Calvinist member, who decided, in particular, not to be associated with the Radical party of Pannella and "Cicciolina" (the porno star, Ilona Staller, elected to the Italian parliament on the radical list). An attempt was made to "lend" two Italians from the Socialist Group to keep the new Group in existence, but this failed, and the new Group collapsed after a few days.

A final development that took place in the second directly elected Parliament was that the Group of the European Progressive Democrats renamed itself as the Group of the European Democratic Alliance.

The Groups after the third direct elections in 1989

The Political Group structure within the European Parliament was again significantly modified as a result of the elections in June 1989. The two major trends were, firstly, the reinforcement of the two largest Groups, the Socialist Group and the Group of the European People's Party (which between them now contain 301 or over 58 per cent of the 518 members compared to 280 or 54 per cent before the elections); and secondly, the fragmentation of the smaller groups, which have fewer members in all and which are now eight in number instead of six as a result of the creation of two completely new Groups. An explicitly Green Group has been formed for the first time, and the divided Communist and Allies Group has finally split into two separate Groups, one dominated by the Italians and the other by the French Communists, but neither calling itself Communist (see Table 3).

Table 3:　*Overall membership of each Political Group and its distribution by country*

	B	DK	FRG	GR	SP	F	IRL	I	L	NL	P	UK	EUR12
Socialists (SOC)	8	4	31	9	27	22	1	14	2	8	8	46	180
Group of the EPP	7	2	32	10	16	6	4	27	3	10	3	1	121
Liberals, Democrats & Reformists (LDR)	4	3	4		6	13	2	3	1	4	9		49
European Democrats (ED)		2										32	34
Greens	3		7		1	8		7		2	1		29
Group of the United European Left		1		1	4			22					28
European Democratic Alliance				1	2	13	6						22
Technical Group of the Right	1		6			10							17
Left Unity				3		7	1				3		14
Rainbow	1	4	1		2	1	1	3				1	14
Non-attached members					2	1		5		1		1	10
TOTAL	24	26	81	24	60	81	15	81	6	25	24	81	518

Note: B–Belgium, DK–Denmark, FRG–Federal Republic of Germany, GR–Greece, SP–Spain, F–France, IRL–Ireland, I–Italy, L–Luxembourg, NL–The Netherlands, P–Portugal, UK–United Kingdom, EUR12–total EC.

Socialist Group (SOC)

Chairman	Jean Pierre Cot	
Secretary-General	Julian Priestley	
Current membership	180	
Current Parliament posts	1 President	Enrique Barón Crespo
	5 Vice-Presidents	Nicole Pery
		Hans Peters
		David Martin,
		Georgios Romeos
		João Cravinho
	1 Quaestor	Ernest Glinne
	8 Chairmen of Committees	
	–Agriculture	Juan Colino Salamanca
	–Budgets	Thomas von der Vring
	–Energy	Antonio la Pergola
	–Social	Wim Van Velzen
	–Environment	Ken Collins
	–Development	Henri Saby
	–Rules of Procedure	Marc Galle
	–Women's Rights	Christine Crawley
	7 1st Vice-Chairmen of Committees	
	6 2nd Vice-Chairmen of Committees	
	6 3rd Vice-Chairmen of Committees	

Group founded: June 23, 1953

Member parties (1989–1994 Parliament) with number of members

Belgium	Parti Socialiste (5), Socialistische Partij (3)
Denmark	Socialdemokratiet (4)
France	Parti Socialiste (22)
FRG	Sozialdemokratische Partei Deutschlands (SPD) (31)
Greece	PASOK (9)
Ireland	Labour party (1)
Italy	Partito Socialista Italiano (PSI) (12)
	Partito Socialista Democratico Italiano (PSDI) (2)
Luxembourg	Letzeburger Sozialistesch Arbechterpartei (LSAP) (2)
Netherlands	Partij van de Arbeid (PvdA) (8)
Portugal	Partido Socialista (8)
Spain	Partido Socialista Obrero Español (PSOE) (27)

UK   Labour Party (45)
                           Social Democratic and Labour Party (SDLP) (1)

The Socialist Group is now by far the largest Group within the Parliament, with 180 members compared to 165 before. The increase in the Group's membership is mainly due to the 13 extra seats gained by the British Labour party. The Socialist Group again has members from every European Community country (as it did from 1979 to 1984), now that the Irish Labour Party has managed to win a seat in the Dublin constituency.

The composition of the Group is straightforward, consisting of the mainstream Socialist and Social Democratic parties in the Member States. The only anomalies worth pointing out are in Italy and Portugal. The group's Italian representatives come from two separate parties, the Socialists and the Social Democrats. The Portuguese members include a representative of the Democratic Renewal Party (PRD), which fought the European elections in alliance with the Socialist Party.

The Socialist Group is linked with the Confederation of the Socialist Parties of the European Community, which has had its headquarters in the Group's offices in Brussels. Unlike the European People's Party the Confederation does not see itself as a supranational party, and its statutes call for its decisions to be taken on the basis of consensus.

The Socialist Group has had one president of the Common Assembly (Paul Spaak, Belgian Socialist 1953–54) and four presidents of the European Parliament (Walter Behrendt, German SPD, 1971–73, Georges Spénale, French Socialist, 1975–77, Piet Dankert, Netherlands PvdA, 1982–84 and Enrique Barón Crespo, Spanish Socialist, 1989–).

Since direct elections, the Socialist Group has had three chairmen, Ernest Glinne (Belgian Socialist, 1979–84), Rudi Arndt (German SPD, 1984–89) and Jean-Pierre Cot (French Socialist, 1989–).

Group of the European People's Party (EPP)

Chairman	Egon Klepsch	
Secretary-General	Sergio Guccione	
Current membership	121	
Current Parliament posts	4 Vice-Presidents	Siegbert Alber
		Georgios Anastassopoulos
		Nicole Fontaine
		Roberto Formigoni
	1 Quaestor	Gerardo Gaibisso
	5 Chairmen of Committees	
	–Political	Giovanni Goria
	–Economic	Bouke Beumer
	–Legal	Franz Stauffenberg
	–Institutional	Marcelino Oreja
	–Petitions	Viviane Reding

> 7 1st Vice-Chairmen
>   of Committees
> 4 2nd Vice-Chairmen
>   of Committees
> 2 3rd Vice-Chairmen
>   of Committees

Group founded: June 23, 1953 (Christian Democratic Group until 1979)

Current member parties (1989–94 Parliament) with number of members

Belgium	Christelijke Volkspartij (CVP) (5)
	Parti Social Chrétien (PSC) (2)
Denmark	Centrum-Demokraterne (2)
France	Centre des Démocrates Sociaux, other UDF (6)
FRG	Christlich Demokratische Union (CDU) (25)
	Christlich Soziale Union (CSU) (7)
Greece	Nea Dimokratia (ND) (10)
Ireland	Fine Gael (4)
Italy	Democrazia Cristiana (CD) (26)
	Südtiroler Volkspartei (SVP) (1)
Luxembourg	Christlich Soziale Volkspartei (CSV) (3)
Netherlands	Christen Demokratisch Appel (CDA) (10)
Portugal	Centro Democratico Social (CDS) (3)
Spain	Unió Democràtica de Catalunya (1)
	Partido Popular (15)
UK	Official Ulster Unionists (1)

The Group of the European People's Party is the second major Group in the new Parliament, although well behind the Socialists. The Group has 121 members, compared to 115 in the old Parliament. This increase is due to the 15 seats brought by *Partido Popular* (see below). Without these the Group of the EPP would have had a net loss of nine seats, attributable in large measure to the losses of the CDU/CSU in Germany. The Group of the EPP now has members from every Community country for the first time, as a result of recruiting its first United Kingdom member (see below).

In terms of its composition a clear distinction must be made between those of its member parties who are full members of the European People's Party (EPP) and those who are not.

The European People's Party is the federation of Christian Democratic parties in the European Community, but it also sees itself as an embryonic European political party in its own right with its own federalist programme, although not yet with its own direct membership. It is linked to the European Union of Christian Democrats (which also includes Christian Democratic parties from non-Community countries) with which it has a joint secretariat.

Most of the member parties of the Group of the EPP in the European Parliament are also members of the EPP, but there are a few exceptions. The most important such exception is in Spain. The EPP Group has included three Spanish parties, Christian Democracy, the Democratic Union of Catalonia (Unió), (which takes part in elections as part of the wider coalition of *Convergència i Unió*), and the Basque National Party. Of these three parties only Unío had a seat at the end of the last European Parliament.

Early in 1989 Christian Democracy lost its separate identity as it achieved a rapprochement with the main Spanish party of the centre-right, *Alianza Popular*, which was relaunched as *Partido Popular*. In the 1989 elections *Partido Popular*'s European list was led by a man of Christian Democratic orientation, Marcelino Oreja, and the party subsequently decided to abandon its former membership of the European Democratic Group and to join up with the Group of the EPP (although not yet with the full EPP). The *Partido Popular*'s decision to join the Group of the EPP cost the group the one elected member from the Basque National Party, a party with a long Christian Democratic tradition but which did not want to be associated with *Partido Popular*. The re-elected member from the Catalan party, Unío, however, decided to remain with the EPP.

Another party whose elected members have joined the Group of the EPP, but are not members of the EPP, is the Centre Democratic party from Denmark (although it contests European elections in an alliance with the Christian People's Party, this latter is itself not yet a member of the EPP). The long-serving MEP from the South Tyrol People's Party (Joachim Dalsass) is also in the Group, but his party is not in the full EPP.

Jim Nicholson, from the official Ulster Unionists, also joined the Group in 1989, although his party has no links with the EPP and he is sitting in a personal capacity. His predecessor, John Taylor, had been first a European Democrat (Conservative) and then a member of the Group of the European Right.

The situation as regards the Group's six French members should also be mentioned. Five of these were elected on the list led by Simone Veil, of which three were from the Christian Democratic-oriented Centre of Social Democrats (CDS), which is a member party of the EPP. The final member in the Group (Marc Reymann) stood on the list led by Giscard d'Estaing but is also a member of the CDS.

The Group of the European People's Party has provided over half of the Presidents of the Parliament, Alcide de Gasperi (Italian DC, 1954), Giuseppe Pella (Italian DC, 1954–56), Hans Furler (German CDU, 1956–58 and 1960–62), Robert Schuman (MRP France, 1958–60), Jean Duvieusart (PSC Belgium, 1964–65), Victor Leemans (CVP Belgium, 1965–66), Alain Poher (MRP France, 1966–69), Mario Scelba (Italian DC, 1969–71), Emilio Colombo (Italian DC, 1977–79) and Pierre Pflimlin (CDS France, 1984–86). Apart from the years 1982–84, when the Group was chaired by Paolo Barbi (Italian DC), the Group has been led by Egon Klepsch (German CDU) since 1977. Klepsch was re-elected as Chairman in July 1989.

Liberal, Democratic and Reformist Group (LDR)

Chairman	Valéry Giscard d'Estaing
Secretary-General	Dominique Cattet
Current membership	49

Current Parliament posts	2	Vice-Presidents	Yves Galland
			Antonio Capucho
	2	Chairmen of Committees	
		–External Economic Relations	Willy de Clercq
		–Transport	Rui Amaral
	2	1st Vice-Chairmen of Committees	
	1	2nd Vice-Chairman of Committees	
	2	3rd Vice-Chairmen of Committees	

Group founded: June 23, 1953 (as Liberal Group, became Liberal and Democratic Group in November 1976, and Liberal, Democratic, and Reformist Group in 1986)

Member parties (1989–94 Parliament) with number of members

Belgium	Parti des Reformes et de la Liberte (PRL) (2)
	Partij voor Vrijheid en Vooruitgang (PVV) (2)
Denmark	Venstre (Danmarks Liberale Parti) (3)
France	Union pour la Démocratie Française (UDF), and associated parties (13)
	(Parti Républicain, Parti Radical, Parti Social Démocrate)
FRG	Freie Demokratische Partei (4)
Ireland	Progressive Democrats (1)
	Independent MEP (T.J. Maher) (1)
Italy	Partito Repubblicano Italiano (PRI) (3)
Luxembourg	Demokratesch Partei (DP) (1)
Netherlands	Volkspartij voor Vrijheid en Democratie (VVD) (3) D66 (1)
Portugal	Partido Social Democrata (PSD) (9)
Spain	Convergència Democràtica de Catalunya (CDC) (1)
	Centro Democratico y Social (CDS) (5)

The Liberal, Democratic and Reformist Group (LDR) is the third largest Group in the new Parliament, and is easily the largest of the smaller Groups. The Group has 49 members (compared to 44 before) from 10 countries, with no members from Greece or the United Kingdom.

During the constituent plenary of the new Parliament in July 1989 the group lost one of its members, the individualistic Marco Pannella (who had been elected on a joint "lay list" with Liberals and Republicans, but who finally preferred to return to the ranks of the non-attached members); but gained another, when the elected member from the Dutch party, D66, (Willem Bertens) decided to join the Group. While often classified as a party in the left-liberal tradition D66 has in the past distanced itself from the main Dutch Liberal Party, the VVD, and D66's former members of the European Parliament (it had two members in the 1979–84 Parliament) were not attached to any Group. D66 has not been a member of the Federation of Liberal, Democratic and Reformist Parties (see below).

The Italian situation is now also anomalous. The Italian Liberal Party (PLI) has been the traditional member of the Group, but it was subsequently joined by the Italian Republican Party (PRI), and the two parties have been together in the Liberal Group since well before direct elections. In the 1989 elections they participated in the joint "lay list" (*polo laico*) with Marco Pannella of the Radical Party (two other Radicals besides Pannella were subsequently elected to the European Parliament but on two completely separate lists — see section on Green Group below). The "lay list" (on which David Steel of the UK Social and Liberal Democrats was also a candidate) had a poor result in the elections and, due to the way in which the votes were distributed, three Republicans were elected but no members of the Liberal Party.

The biggest change in the composition of the Group was due to the decision of the five members of the Spanish Social Democratic Centre Party (CDS) of Adolfo Suárez to join up with it. In the previous Parliament the CDS members had sat as independents after trying unsuccessfully to set up a technical co-ordination group. Before joining the group the CDS had also joined the Liberal International. The other Spanish member of the Liberal group is a representative of the Catalan party *Convergència Democràtica de Catalunya* which fights elections with the Christian Democratic *Unió* party in the coalition of *Convergencia i Unió*.

The other major change in the Group was the return of the German Free Democrats with four members, who had been in the 1979–84 Parliament but had fallen below the 5 per cent threshold for representation in 1984.

The largest component within the Liberal Group are its 13 French members, who come from a variety of parties from two separate lists, including the heads of both lists, Giscard d'Estaing and Simone Veil. Veil is the only one from her list to join the Group (five of the others are in the Group of the EPP, and one is independent) although Veil was the previous leader of the Liberal Group in the European Parliament from 1984-89. Twelve of Giscard's list are from the Union for French Democracy (UDF) and its associated parties. Three are direct UDF members, one from the Social Democrats, two from the Radical party and six from the Republican Party. One is independent.

The Group now has a member from the Irish party, the Progressive Democrats. The Group's longstanding independent Irish member (T.J. Maher), who joined it in 1979, has also decided to remain. Another major component within the Group are the Portuguese Social Democrats, who joined it when Portugal entered the Community, and at whose behest the Group added the extra label "Reformist".

The other parties within the Group come from the traditional Liberal family. All the parties within the Group, however, are now also members of the Federation of Liberal, Democratic and Reformist parties of the European Community (ELDR), with the exception of D66.

There have been three Liberal presidents of the European Parliament, Gaetano Martino (PLI Italy, 1962–64), Cornelis Berkhouwer (VVD Netherlands, 1973–75) and Simone Veil (UDF France, 1979–82). The Group has had three chairmen since the first direct elections, Martin Bangemann (FDP Germany, 1979–84), Simone Veil (UDF France, 1984–89) and Valéry

Giscard d'Estaing (UDF France, 1989–).

European Democratic Group (EDG)

Chairman	Sir Christopher Prout
Secretary-General	Harald Romer
Current membership	34

Current Parliament posts			
	1	Vice-President	Sir Fred Catherwood
	1	Quaestor	Anthony Simpson
	1	Chairman of Committee –Budgetary Control	Peter Price
	1	1st Vice-Chairman of Committee	
	2	2nd Vice-Chairmen of Committees	
	2	3rd Vice-Chairmen of Committees	

Group founded (as European Conservative Group): January 1973 (name changed to European Democratic Group in July 1979)

Member parties (1989–94 Parliament) with number of members

Denmark	*Det Konservative Folkeparti (2)*
UK	Conservative Party (32)

The European Democratic Group suffered the heaviest losses of all the existing Political Groups in 1989. After being the third largest Group with 66 members in the 1984–89 Parliament it is now the fourth largest Group with only 34 members, and would have been in sixth place if the Communist and Rainbow Groups had not fragmented. Its decline was due to the electoral reverses suffered by both its remaining component parties, and by the decision of its former Spanish member party, *Partido Popular* (formerly *Alianza Popular*) to leave the group and to join up with the Group of the European People's Party.

The main component of the European Democratic Group remains the Conservative Party from the United Kingdom. In the 1979–84 Parliament this provided by far the largest delegation from any one party, with 60 members, but after the 1984 elections this fell to 45, and it now consists of only 32 members. Its one remaining ally is the Danish Conservative Party which itself fell from the four seats that it held from 1984–89 to its current total of two.

After the departure of its Spanish allies, and its setback in the 1989 elections, the members of the European Democratic Group subsequently sought to be admitted within the Group of the European People's Party. The application was not accepted, with two of the main problems being the intention of the European People's Party to develop into a truer supranational party, and its strong commitment to European Union. While these aspirations are supported by many Conservative MEPs they run counter to the positions adopted by Margaret Thatcher within the United Kingdom.

Certain of the Conservative MEPs from the United Kingdom, however, have established close links with Christian Democrats, especially with those from West Germany, and there will clearly be considerable co-operation between the two Groups in the future. Both Groups, for instance, seek to ensure that the timing and venue of their Group meetings coincide.

The European Democratic Group has provided one President of the European Parliament, Lord Plumb, who was President from 1987 to 1989.

Since direct elections in 1979 the Group has always been led by a British Conservative, Sir James Scott-Hopkins (1979–81), Sir Henry (later Lord) Plumb (1981–86) and Sir Christopher Prout (1989–).

The Greens

Co-Chairmen	Alexander Langer and Maria Santos
Secretary-General	Hans Nikolaus (Juan) Behrend
Current membership	29

Current Parliament posts			
	1	Vice-President	Wilfried Telkämper
	1	Chairman of Committee –Regional Policy and Planning	Antoine Waechter
	3	2nd Vice-Chairmen of Committees	
	1	3rd Vice-Chairman of Committee	

Group founded: July 1989

Member parties (1989–94 Parliament) with number of members

Belgium	Agalev (1)
	Ecolo (2)
France	Les Verts (8)
FRG	Die Grünen (8)
Italy	Verdi Europa Lista Verde (3)
	Verdi Arcobaleno per l'Europa (2)
	Democrazia Proletaria (1)
	Lega Antiproibizionista (1)
Netherlands	Regenboog/Groen-Links (2)
Portugal	Os Verdes (1)
Spain	Izquierda de los pueblos (1)

The Greens are a new group that was created after the June 1989 elections. Green members in the 1984–89 Parliament formed part of the wider Rainbow Group (in a subgroup called *GRAEL* or Green Alternative European Link) which also included regionalists and anti-market Danes).

There had been some speculation that there might be a split between the ecologist parties which do not consider themselves to be of the left or the right and those green-alternative or radical socialist parties which clearly position themselves on the left of the political spectrum. As constituted, however, the Green Group contains parties of both types.

The largest components within the new Group are the eight members from *Die Grünen* in Germany (up from seven in the old Parliament) and eight members from *Les Verts* in France, who were elected to the European Parliament for the first time. In all, nine members were elected on the French Green list, but one of them, a Corsican regionalist, chose to become a member of the Rainbow Group instead. The French Greens have undertaken to stand down at the halfway point of the legislature in order to be replaced by the next eight on the list. The most well-known French Green member is Antoine Waechter, candidate in the 1988 French Presidential elections and who is currently the only Green committee chairman in the European Parliament.

There are also seven members of the Green Group from Italy, but these were elected on no less than four separate lists. Three of the seven were elected on the list *Verdi Europa Lista Verde* which is that associated with the ecologist *Lista Verde* in the Italian national parliament. Two others were elected on the rival list *Verdi Arcobaleno per i Europa* (Rainbow Greens for Europe) including Adelaide Aglietta, a former national secretary of the Italian Radical Party. Like the French Greens the *Verdi Arcobaleno* have also decided on a rotation system for their members. The other two Italian members are Marco Taradash (another member of the Italian Radical Party) for the *Lega Antiproibizionista* (the "decriminalize drug offences" movement) and Father Eugenio Melandri, a priest standing for the left socialist party *Democrazia Proletaria* (Proletarian Democracy).

The three Belgian members of the Green Group come from the Walloon and Flemish ecologist parties, *Ecolo* and *Agalev*. The two Dutch members, however, come from the left alternative coalition *Regenboog/Groen Links*. One of them is a member of the Dutch Communist Party and the other of the Dutch Radical Party (PPR); the latter will be replaced in 1992 by a member of the Pacifist Socialist Party (PSP).

The Portuguese member of the Group comes from the party *Os Verdes*, which currently contests elections in a coalition with the Portuguese Communist Party. Finally, the Spanish member, Juan María Bandrés, was elected at the head of a list of left-wing regionalist parties, *Izquierda de los Pueblos*. Bandrés is one of the leading members of the Basque party *Euskadiko Ezkerra*.

The Greens have decided on a rotation of the leadership posts on a 15-monthly basis. The two Co-Chairmen must include one woman, as must the two Vice-Chairmen. The Greens executive also includes a Treasurer and three "assessors".

Group of the United European Left

Chairman	Luigi Colajanni
Secretary-General	Angelo Oliva
Current membership	28

Current Parliament posts	1	Vice-President	Fernando Perez Royo
	1	Quaestor	Andrea Raggio
	1	Chairman of Committee –Youth, Culture Education, the Media and Sport	Robert Barzanti
	1	2nd Vice-Chairman of Committee	
	2	3rd Vice-Chairmen of Committees	

Group founded: July 1989

Member parties (1989–94 Parliament) with number of members

Denmark	Socialistisk Folkeparti (1)
Greece	Elliniki Aristera (1)
Italy	Partido Comunista Italiano (PCI) (22)
Spain	Izquierda Unida (4)

The Group of the United European Left stems from a historic split in the Communist and Allies Group, which had been founded in October 1973 but had long been divided between what, at the risk of oversimplification, could be described as its Eurocommunist and more traditional pro-Moscow wings. The former was dominated by the Italian Communist party, the largest single part within the Group and which always provided the President of the Group (Guido Amendola from 1973–80, Guido Fanti from 1980–84, Gianni Cervetti from 1984–89). The Italians were supported by the member from the Eurocommunist party in Greece (the smaller of the two Greek Communist parties, and which itself later split in two) by the members from the Danish Socialist People's Party, and later by the members from Spain.

The more orthodox faction was dominated by the French Communists, and also included the members from the larger and more orthodox of the two Greek Communist parties and later by the members from the Portuguese Communist party.

As a result of these divisions the Group hardly ever held common meetings, and seldom agreed on a common line in Committee or plenary meetings. Towards the end of the 1984–89 Parliament there were even persistent rumours that the Italian Communists might apply to join the Socialist Group in the new Parliament.

After the 1989 elections, the two factions formally divided and created two new Groups with confusingly similar names, the Italian Communist-led group taking on the name "United European Left" and the more hard-line group the name "Left Unity". Twenty-two of the 28 members of the United European Left were elected on the list of the Italian Communist party, although one of them is a non-Communist independent from France, the well-known political scientist, Maurice Duverger. All of the Italian Communist MEPs who had served two terms in the European Parliament were dropped so that only five of the 21 Italian Communist MEPs are former members of the Parliament.

The second largest contingent in the Group are the four members from the Spanish *Izquierda Unida*, a left-wing coalition including the mainstream Spanish Communist party but also including other Communist and non-Communist groupings. Two of the four members elected are from the Spanish Communist party, one from the Catalan Communist party and one from the left-wing Socialist party, the *Partido de Accion Socialista (PASOC)*.

The Group also contains one of the four members of the joint left Socialist–Communist list in Greece (*Synaspismos tis Aristeras Katis proodou* or "Coalition of the Left and of progress"), who is a member of *Elliniki Aristera* (the "Greek Left"), one of the two parties which emerged after the split within the Greek Eurocommunist party of the Interior.

The final member of the Group comes from the Socialist People's Party in Denmark, a party of left Socialist orientation.

The most striking feature of the Group of the United European Left is that it has clearly put a distance between itself and the traditional Communist movement, and places more emphasis on links with other European left-of-centre groups and with the wider socialist movement. It is seeking to establish a privileged relationship with the Socialist Group in the European Parliament, and came out in favour of the Socialist candidate for president.

It is also much more favourable than the Left Unity Group to the idea of European Union and to the granting of greater legislative powers to the European Parliament, arguing that it should also receive a constituent mandate to draw up a new Treaty (although these views are not shared by the Group's Danish member, who joined it on other grounds).

The Group has an Italian Communist Chairman, Luigi Colajanni, and a Catalan Communist Vice-Chairman, Antoni Gutierrez.

Group of the European Democratic Alliance (EDA)

Chairman	Christian de la Malène		
Secretary-General	Thomas Earlie		
Current membership	22		
Current Parliament posts	1	Quaestor	Paddy Lalor
	1	3rd Vice-Chairman of Committee	

Group founded: January 1965 (under the name European Democratic Union, name subsequently changed to that of European Progressive Democrats, and later to its present name)

Member parties (1989–94 Parliament) with number of members

France	Rassemblement pour la République (RPR) (13)
Greece	Dimogratiki Ananeossi (DIANA) (1)
Ireland	Fianna Fáil (6)
Spain	Ruiz Mateos (2)

The Group of the European Democratic Alliance has been essentially based in recent years on an alliance between the French Gaullist and Irish *Fianna Fáil* parties, but for varying periods of time has also had allies from Denmark (the Progress Party), Greece (Ioannis Boutos, an independent), Scotland (Winnie Ewing of the Scottish Nationalist Party) and Spain (Ruiz Mateos, and another colleague elected on his list).

During the 1989 campaign a potential threat to the Group's continuing existence appeared to be posed by the RPR's participation in a joint list with much of the UDF under Valéry Giscard d'Estaing, which spoke of sticking together after the elections. In the event the elected member of the joint list went into different Political Groups, and the RPR members of the list again joined the reconstituted (but smaller) Group of the European Democratic Alliance. They were joined by the members of *Fianna Fáil* and the one member from *DIANA* (a breakaway party from the right of centre New Democracy party in Greece), but not by the SNP's Winnie Ewing, who joined the Rainbow Group. They were later joined by the controversial Spanish financier, Ruiz Mateos, and one other member elected on his list.

The Group continues to be chaired by the durable Christian de la Malène of the RPR, who has now led the Group without a break since 1975.

Technical Group of the European Right (ER)

Chairman	Jean-Marie Le Pen
Secretary-General	Jean Marc Brissaud
Current membership	17
Current Parliament posts	None
Group founded:	1984

Member parties (1989–94 Parliament) with number of members

Belgium	Vlaams Blok (1)
France	Front National (10)
FRG	Die Republikaner (6)

The Italian Social Movement (MSI) had had members in the European Parliament since 1979, but the European Right was only able to form a European Parliament Group in 1984, after the success of Le Pen's *Front*

National in France. Besides the *Front National* and the MSI the group also
contained a member from a small Greek party of the far right, and later
John Taylor of the Official Ulster Unionist Party, who split with the British
Conservatives over the signing of the Anglo-Irish agreement and joined up
with the Group of the European Right on a personal rather than party
basis.

After the 1989 elections there was a considerable realignment on the far
right. The Group was reconstituted, again with Jean-Marie Le Pen's *Front
National* as its largest single component but this time with the newly elected
German Republican party as the second major component of the Group
instead of the Italian MSI. The MSI was not able to co-exist with the
Republicans, primarily because of differences over the political situation in
the South Tyrol, where the MSI have been the most vocal defenders of the
Italian-speaking minority, but also to a lesser extent because of differences
of emphasis over the issue of immigration, which is the single most
important issue for the *Front National* and the Republicans, but less
significant for the MSI. The four MSI members are thus now non-attached
in the new Parliament.

Of the Group's other former components, the new member from the
Official Ulster Unionists has joined the Group of the European People's
Party, and the Greek far right did not manage to elect a member to the new
Parliament. The Group of the European Right did, however, manage to
recruit the new member from the Belgian *Vlaams Blok*, a far right Flemish
Nationalist party. Differences of emphasis over the issue of regionalism
(with the French *Front National* being strongly centralist, and the *Vlaams
Blok* being fiercely regionalist) almost prevented the group being formed at
all, but in the end the acceptable compromise was to set it up as a
"Technical" Group, with permitted differences of opinion on issues such as
regionalism.

The Left Unity Group

Chairman   Réne-Emile Piquet

Co-Secretary-Generals   Gerard Laprat and Kratis Kyriazis

Current members   14

Current Parliament posts   1   2nd Vice-Chairman
                                of Committee
                            1   3rd Vice-Chairman
                                of Committee

Group founded: July 1989

Member parties (1989–94 Parliament) with number of members

France	Parti Communiste Français (PCF) (7)
Greece	Kommunistiko Komma Elladas (KKE) (3)
Ireland	The Workers' Party (1)
Portugal	Partido Comunista Português (3)

The Left Unity Group is a new group stemming from the split in the former Communist and Allies Group, (see above) and consists in the main of members from its more orthodox and traditional Communist faction.

By far its largest component are the seven members from the French Communist party. There are also three members from the Portuguese Communist party who took part in the elections in a wider coalition called the CDU (Unitary Democratic Coalition), whose fourth elected member, from the Portuguese Greens, has joined the Green Group. The three Greek members are from the orthodox Greek Communist party which also took part in a wider Coalition of the Left and of Progress, whose fourth elected member sits with the Italian Communists in the Group of the United European Left.

The Left Unity Group has also recruited the one elected member from the Irish Workers' Party, its leader, Proinsias de Rossa. It is generally hostile to further European integration, unlike the Group of the United European Left, and less closely linked to the Socialist Group.

Rainbow Group (RBW)

Co-Chairmen	Jaak Vandemeulebroucke and Birgit Bjørnvig
Secretary-General	Herman Verheirstraaten
Current members	14
Current Parliament posts	1 1st Vice-Chairman of Committee
	1 2nd Vice-Chairman of Committee

Group formed: 1979 (as Technical Co-ordination Group, in 1984 as Rainbow Group)

Member parties (1989–94 Parliament) with number of members

Belgium	Volksunie (1)
Denmark	Folkebevaegelsen Mod EF (4)
FRG	Die Grünen, on personal basis only (1)
France	Union du peuple Corse (1)
Ireland	Independent (1)
Italy	Lega Lombarda (2)
	Unione Valdostana–Partito Sardo d'Azione (1)
Spain	Coalición para la Europa de los Pueblos/Eusko Alkartasuna (1)
	Partido Andalucista (1)
UK	Scottish National Party (1)

After the first direct elections in 1979 a heterogeneous Group for the Technical Co-ordination and Defence of Independent Groups and Members was established. The name was self-explanatory and there was little ideological cohesion to the Group. The Rainbow Group that was set up in 1984 was already slightly more cohesive in that it had three main sub-groups, the anti-market Danes, the Green/Left Alternative parties of the *GRAEL* (Green Alternative European Link) and the regionalist/nationalist parties of the European Free Alliance.

The Green and alternative parties have now formed a new group in the European Parliament (see above) and the reconstituted Rainbow Group is now more than ever a federation of regionalist and nationalist parties, the majority of them associated with the European Free Alliance, and which seek a Europe of the Regions or much greater autonomy or independence for their own region. Eight of the 13 members of the new Rainbow Group fall within this category. This is, however, still not enough to form a Political Group within the European Parliament and the numbers are made up by four anti-market Danes and an independent from Ireland.

The Rainbow Group has representatives of no less than 10 parties or political groupings from eight different Community countries.

Starting with the regionalist parties, the Belgian representative came from the Flemish federalist party, *Volksunie*. Two of the three Italian members came from the Lombard regionalist party, the *Lega Lombarda*, which is resentful of the central government in Rome and of southern Italian immigration into northern Italy. The third Italian member is a representative of the list of Italian national minorities, whose largest components are the party defending Aostan interests (the *Unione Valdostano/Union Valdôtaine*) and the Sardinian party (the *Partito Sardo d'Azione*), but which also defends the interests of Friulians, Slavs, Occitans and others.

The currently elected representative of this list is a member of the *Partito Sardo d'Azione*.

One of the two Spanish members was the leader of a list called the Coalition of Europe of the Peoples, an alliance between Basque, Catalan and Galician regionalists. The elected member, Carlos Garaicoetxea, is the leader of the Basque party, *Eusko Alkartasuna*, which is a breakaway party from the Basque Nationalist party. The other Spanish member of the Rainbow Group is a representative of an Andalusian regionalist party.

The French member of the Group, Max Simeoni, is a representative of a Corsican regionalist party. He was elected on the list of the French Greens, but chose not to sit with them in the Green Group.

The UK member is Winnie Ewing of the Scottish National Party, who was a member of the French Gaullist-led European Democratic Alliance in the old Parliament, but decided to join up with the regionalists after the 1989 elections.

The four representatives of the Danish movement against the EEC comprise the largest single component of the Rainbow Group. As the name implies, the movement is not a party, and only puts up candidates in European elections. Its elected representatives include members of the Danish Communist party and the Danish Justice party.

Another member of the Group is Neil Blaney, an Irish independent, who was a former member of the *Fianna Fáil* but who split with the party after the 1970 arms trial. He was also a member of the European Parliament from

1979 to 1984. The Group has now also been joined by one dissident member of *Die Grünen* from Germany, Dorothee Piermont, who split with her former colleagues in the Green Group.

The non-attached members

The successful struggle led by Pannella and others at the beginning of the directly elected Parliament in 1979 prevented the numbers required for forming a Political Group from increasing significantly to reflect the much higher membership within the Parliament. As a result, and because of the great advantages accorded to membership of a Political Group, only a small number of members have chosen to remain non-attached. Those who do, tend to be members of small political parties or individual personalities who have little common political ground with any of the existing groups, or who positively prefer the complete freedom of movement conferred upon them by non-attached status.

Parliament's Rules (notably Rule 27) do lay down certain rights and safeguards for the non-attached members.

The non-attached members are provided with administrative facilities and a secretariat, in proportion to their overall numbers. They are entitled to send two of their members to represent them (but not vote) at the meetings of Parliament's Enlarged Bureau (which takes key logistical and organizational decisions, including the setting of Parliament's draft agenda) and one representative to the meeting of the President and Political Group Chairmen which sets the final agenda. They are also entitled to nominate members for Parliament's committees. There are also special provisions to ensure that they each get a minimum of speaking time based on the fractions previously allocated to the different Political Groups, and this overall time is then doubled, "in order to take account of the great diversity of political views among the non-attached members and enable, as far as possible, each such view to be expressed" (Rules 27-4 and 83-2). Each non-attached member is granted the same speaking time, but if he does not wish to use it, he may assign it to another such member.

The non-attached members are allocated seats at the very back of the hemicycle, currently behind the Christian Democrats and Socialists.

There are at present (1989–94 Parliament) only 10 non-attached members, four of whom are members from the Italian right-wing party, the MSI, which did not rejoin the Group of the European Right as a result of a dispute with the newly elected German Republicans over the Alto Adige/South Tyrol (the MSI have won their highest support in all of Italy among the Italian-speaking minority in this German-speaking majority province).

The other non-attached members are Marco Pannella (who was elected on the Italian lay block list, but after initial hesitation decided not to join the Liberal group), Ian Paisley of the Democratic Unionist Party (the only non-attached member who has had that status since 1979), a representative of the mainstream Basque Nationalist party (Jon Gangoiti Llaguno, whose party has been traditionally associated with the EPP, but decided not to join it in 1989 because of its decision to admit the Spanish Conservative *Partido*

Popular), a representative of the more extreme Basque nationalist party, (Herri Batasuna–Txema Montero Zabala), a representative of the coalition of small Dutch calvinist parties (Leen Van de Waal), and finally, Jean-Louis Borloo, a member of Simone Veil's Centrist list, who has initially refused to join either the Liberals or the EPP.

As a general rule the non-attached members have been able to make more of an impact in plenary than in committees, through participation in debates relevant to their parties, points of order (such as those continuously made by Pannella) or demonstrations (such as those made by Mario Capanna in the 1979–84 Parliament when he wore Mohawk head-dresses to protest at the Lake Placid Olympics taking place on Mohawk ancestral ground, or when he waved the Palestinian flag), and also by Ian Paisley on several occasions, notably in demonstrating against the Pope being allowed to address the plenary, or against Margaret Thatcher. Their protests are rarer in committee (though Capanna was once physically removed from the Rules Committee after attempting to interrupt the proceedings), and non-attached members are never allocated significant rapporteurships. At best they are given the occasional minor report or opinion.

Support provided by the European Parliament to the Political Groups

The powerful political position of the Groups within the European Parliament structure has already been alluded to. This is clearly reinforced by the financial advantages which accrue to the Groups.

The European Parliament's budget allocates a considerable sum to the Political Groups (15 per cent of the total budget in 1990). The funds which go to each Group are dependent upon its number of members.

The relevant budgetary headings are Item 3705 which concerns the contribution to the secretarial expenses of the Groups (and also of the non-attached members); Item 3706 which concerns other political activities; and Item 3708 which finances information activities by the Groups. This was the controversial item which was previously used for European election campaigns and was largely distributed by the Groups to the individual national parties within their Group. The majority of the funds were distributed ahead of the elections on the basis of the number of seats held by a party as a result of the preceding European elections, and the balance of the funds were distributed after the elections on the basis of the votes actually won by each party, with some funds going, therefore, to parties not winning any seats in the elections. The whole system, however, was challenged by certain parties, notably *Les Verts* in France, who felt that it discriminated against new parties or parties which had been weak in the previous elections. After the European Court of Justice found in favour of *Les Verts* (see section on uniform electoral system in Chapter 2) the system was changed, so that Item 3708 now funds the information activities of the Groups as a whole, and these activities are now discontinued at the end of February before the beginning of each European election campaign.

In addition to these three main items there are also certain other items in the Parliament's budget of interest to the Groups, such as Item 2240 which includes the purchase of data-processing and office automation equipment for Group secretariats, and Item 2242 which includes the hire and maintenance of equipment.

Structures of Groups

Each Political Group has its own internal structures, notably a Bureau composed of a Chairman, Vice-Chairman, Treasurer and, usually, others. Bureaux vary considerably in size and responsibilities, and are obviously more important in the larger Groups where they tend to include one or two members from each national component of the Group. Bureaux can play a role in proposing the political discussions and positions of the Group as a whole, and they normally also take the decisions regarding the administration and management of the Group and its secretariat (though the Socialist Group delegates many such tasks to a separate "administrative bureau" composed of its Chairman, Treasurer, Secretary-General and one Vice-Chairman).

Group Chairmen, who also play an important role in major debates and in Parliament's enlarged Bureau, are elected by the Group and in most cases remain in office for some years. The Green Group and the Rainbow Group, however, have rotating chairmanships. The longest standing chairman is Christian de la Malène of the RDE (Gaullist) Group who has been Chairman since 1975.

Political Group staffing

Very precise rules have been established regarding the funding of the Political Group staff. The most important criterion is the number of members in each Group, but the number of working languages within the Group also plays a role.

Each Group is entitled to a fixed total of two A grade (Administrative) posts, with a further such post for every 4 MEPs within the Group, and another A grade post is for each language up to three languages, two posts for four and five languages, three posts for six and seven languages and four posts for eight and nine languages.

The total number of A posts to which a Group is entitled then provides the key to the number of B (Assistant) and C (Secretarial) posts within each Group, with 1.33 B and C posts funded for each A grade post. The total number of posts per political Group may not exceed the number of members within that Group. There is thus a great difference in the size of Group staffs from only 14 in the smallest Groups (e.g. the Left Unity Group) up to the 135 officials in the Socialist Group (50 administrators and 85 assistants and secretaries).

The number of staff employed by the Groups has grown considerably in recent years. In 1990, 486 posts were budgeted (of which 189 As) — as compared to 338 (of which 135 As) in 1982. This represents an increase of 44 per cent (40 per cent for As), as compared to 23 per cent over the same period for Parliament's own staff (17 per cent for As). It should be emphasized that the great majority of these are temporary, not permanent officials, and do not have the job security enjoyed by the permanent officials. They are recruited directly by the Groups (with the national delegations within each Group playing an important role in the recruitment of individual Administrators, in particular), and do not have to pass the open competitions which Parliament's permanent officials have been through.

In practice, however, (and as mentioned in Chapter 10) these comments have to be qualified to a considerable extent. The vast majority of Group staff enjoy *de facto* if not *de jure* job security, and relatively few of them are made redundant as a result of election results. Furthermore there are a number of permanent officials working within the Groups who have passed an open external competition. These may be officials who passed an exam but then immediately went to work for a Group, or they may be seconded officials (like one of the co-authors of this book) at a later stage in their careers.

A further qualification concerns the methods of recruitment of staff within a Group. While these are sometimes based on political and personal contacts and patronage, more objective methods are now being used with both written and oral exams and language tests, though, of course, candidates must normally have a political affinity with the Group and political experience is taken into account.

Partly because the Group secretariats are relatively rarely directly involved in the drafting of committee reports and opinions there is a tendency for certain people to underestimate the role and workload of Group staff. In practice this has become increasingly heavy. Group staff have both general and sectoral responsibilities, examples of the former being administrative or press work, or responsibility for urgency debates in plenary. Some staff work directly in the "cabinet" of the Group Chairman, whereas others must follow particular policy areas. The larger Groups are able to have an official to follow each committee, whereas an official in a smaller Group may have to follow up to three or four committees at once. Group staff have to assist their co-ordinators within each committee, help to ensure as unified a Group line as possible within a committee, and follow votes and new developments within a committee. On some occasions they even have to round up Group members from other committees to help in tight votes in their committee. They must prepare the debates within their Group meetings, and help their members to formulate a Group position before the plenary session. They may also have to prepare studies for the Group. They help to draw up Group whips both in committee and in plenary. They must also try and provide other background information of interest to their members. They help maintain contacts with national parties and other organizations. They must often take into account the fact that national, sectoral, or constituency considerations are sometimes of greater importance to an individual member than his or her Group stance.

While this is still the exception rather than the rule, more Group staff have gone on to become Members of the European Parliament than either former members' assistants or permanent officials of the Parliament. Recent examples include Florus Wijsenbeek and Jessie Larive of the Dutch Liberals (formerly in the Federation of Liberal Parties and Liberal Groups respectively), Raymonde Dury of the Belgian Socialists and Carole Tongue of the British Labour Party (formerly in the Socialist Group secretariat) and Caroline Jackson and Anne McIntosh of the British Conservatives (formerly of the European Democratic Group secretariat).

Working methods within the Groups

The Groups generally convene on two main occasions a month, once during the "Group week", when there are no committee or plenary activities, and secondly, during the Strasbourg plenary sessions.

The meetings during Group week are usually held in Brussels (although on occasion they are also held in other locations, normally at the invitation of one of the member parties of the Group). These meetings last two or three days, and are primarily devoted to examining the next week's plenary agenda. They are also used for discussion of the Group's own activities (such as conferences, publications etc. of the Group), and for receiving visiting delegations or leaders of national parties or other personalities (Commissioners, Ministers or personalities from third countries). These meetings are both preceded and followed by a variety of Group working parties of both a political and technical nature, as well as meetings of national delegations.

The meetings in Strasbourg are held on several occasions during plenary week, generally before the beginning of the plenary on Monday, and on Thursday morning (when the plenary only begins at 10:00 am), and also for an hour or so at the close of the plenary on Tuesday and Wednesday evenings. Each Group has its own meeting room. Groups each have their own rules and practices concerning the confidentiality of their meetings.

The Groups do not meet during the Committee weeks, but the Group members within a committee (especially from the two largest groups, the Socialist and the PPE) often get together before the start of the meeting to discuss the position that they will adopt on a controversial item or items. These meetings are generally led by the Group's co-ordinator on the committee. A large Group like the Socialists will often also appoint a shadow rapporteur to follow sensitive issues on behalf of the Group.

Own activities of the Groups

Apart from their work directly related to Parliament, Groups have developed their own political activities. They form an important channel of communication between similar parties in different countries and also between the Community and national politics. In this, they complement Parliament's role as a forum and channel of communication described in Chapter 14.

Thus Groups receive a constant stream of visitors from national parties such as "front-bench" spokesmen in national parliaments. They also send delegations to national parties, and Group chairmen or vice-chairmen normally speak at the congress or conference of each national party in the Group. Groups also publish brochures, studies and even newsletters aimed in part at national parties. Groups organize seminars and conferences with national parties on European themes. Thus, for instance, the Socialist Group is planning 26 regional conferences on social aspects of the internal market during 1990, and a dozen international conferences on various subjects.

A particular effort may be made by a Group towards one of its national parties when that Member State takes on the Presidency of the Council, especially when that party is in government. Some Groups organize special meetings and briefings for the Ministers or Shadow Ministers concerned which provide a valuable alternative to those prepared by national civil servants. As a source of information such briefings are of particular assistance to parties in the smaller Member States.

The Socialists, Christian Democrats and Liberals organize "summits" of their Group Chairmen, national party leaders and Prime Ministers of the countries where they are in government, prior to meetings of the European Council.

National delegations

Members of a Group from a particular nationality (normally from one party) form national delegations, which play an important role within some Groups and which also serve as an important link to national parties. Most national delegations within each Group meet during a "group week" and even during plenaries. They will often take a collective decision and try to act as a block in Group discussions. On important issues, Groups will try to negotiate compromises among their national delegations before taking a decision. When Groups fail to vote cohesively, it is usually because one or more national delegations have decided to opt out of a Group position. Posts within the Group structures (Bureau of Group, co-ordinators, etc) are often shared among the delegations within a Group in the same proportional method as posts among Groups in Parliament. It is also through national delegations that the bulk of the "information money" (item 3708 mentioned above) is spent. In the Socialist Group, for instance, 70 per cent is allocated to the national delegations (15 per cent shared equally and 85 per cent in proportion to the number of MEPs). This does not mean that the delegations have absolute discretion: there are strict rules preventing the responsibility being delegated any further (e.g. to national parties) and all sums must be spent according to Socialist Group priorities and relate to the activities of the Group and its members. Any printed matter must specify that it is on behalf of the Group and any reference to a national party or an individual member must not be larger in size than the reference to the Group.

Most national delegations, especially those from large parties, have their own officers (chairman, treasurer, etc) and their own staff, partly financed from Group funds, but who can be employed in the national capitals (e.g. press officers, liaison officers with national parties). These staff are relatively small in number.

Delegations are normally represented within the structures of their national parties (e.g. national executive committees, backbench committees in the national parliamentary groups etc.) where they will be involved notably, but not exclusively, in discussions with a European dimension (often alerting them to that dimension). Some national party leaders have sat in the European Parliament instead of in the national Parliament, e.g. Deprez, leader of the PSC (Walloon Christian Democrats), Van Miert, SP (Flemish Socialist) or as well as in national parliaments (most Italian party leaders, several French and Belgian leaders). In other cases, the European Parliamentary leader will be in close contact with the national leader. In the UK, for instance, the leaders of the Conservatives, Sir Christopher Prout, meets Margaret Thatcher almost monthly, and Glyn Ford, the Labour leader, meets Neil Kinnock even more frequently. Both Conservative and Labour MEPs attend their party conferences as of right. Naturally, frequent contacts are not a guarantee for identity of views. MEPs and MPs will inevitably have different perspectives and, on occasion, will even accuse each other of, respectively, "having gone native" or "being parochial". However, this does not detract from the utility of such contacts.

Leadership of a national delegation is usually occupied for several years in a row by the same person, even when annual elections are held. The two main British parties are in different positions, as the Conservatives have always constituted a majority of their political Group (currently 32 out of 34) to the extent that their leader and the Group chairman are identical, whereas Labour members are part (currently the largest part) of the Socialist Group. Conservatives have been led in the European Parliament since direct elections by Sir James Scott-Hopkins (1979–81), Sir Henry (now Lord) Plumb (1982–1986, when he was elected President of the Parliament) and Sir Christopher Prout (1986 to date). Labour has been led by Barbara Castle (1979–1985), Alf Lomas (1985–87), David Martin (1987–88), Barry Seal (1988–89) and Glyn Ford (1989 to date). The high turnover of Labour leaders in the 1984–89 Parliament reflects hotly contested elections at a time when pro- and anti-marketeers were evenly divided.

Whipping

Groups issue "whips" or voting instructions to their members, both in terms of how to vote on each amendment and text as well as indicating which votes are important (where a number of Groups have taken up the British tradition of issuing one-, two- or three-line whips). Whipping is far less tight than in some national parliaments, though some Groups have appointed members as "whips" to keep a check on discipline and report on wayward members. Fines have been imposed by Groups on members absent without leave from important votes. Groups obviously have difficulty in imposing discipline where one or more national delegation decides not to follow the Group line. The national delegations are, in fact, through their own national party structures, far more likely to be in a position to impose strict discipline, especially where candidates are (re)selected by central party decisions.

Power balances and relationships between the Groups

After each European Parliament election much of the attention has focused on whether the Parliament has had a left-of-centre or right-of-centre majority. This final part of the section on Political Groups looks at whether this has much validity as a means of predicting how the European Parliament operates in practice, or whether other factors are more important. It concludes by examining the current relationships between the Groups.

Compared to the UK House of Commons, or a number of other national parliaments, the left–right cleavage within the European Parliament is less strong. There are a number of reasons for this. One of the most obvious is that no government is drawn from the European Parliament, and there is no parliamentary division between government and opposition. A second key factor is the much more heterogeneous nature of the European Parliament compared to national parliaments. A huge range of different national, regional and sectoral interests are represented, which means that voting patterns are sometimes more related to these factors than to ideological divisions. Coalitions, for example, of those representing agricultural areas, are often forged across Group boundaries. The division between pro- and anti-marketeers, and between federalists and more cautious Europeans also often override ideological differences.

A further factor is that many members come from countries with more of a consensus political tradition than say, the United Kingdom or France. Certain political situations also reinforce the search for consensus, such as the need for a common front to defend Parliament's institutional prerogatives against the Council, and above all the need to get 260 votes for certain votes in the co-operation, assent or budgetary procedures, as will be discussed in more detail in Chapter 11.

Finally, the range of political beliefs within the individual Groups is often wide, and the Groups are not always easy to place on the ideological spectrum.

The Socialist Group, for example, has traditionally covered a wide political spectrum from left to centre, and has frequently acted more as a federation of relatively autonomous national delegations. The British Labour group, in particular in the early 1980s when it was controlled by anti-marketeers, frequently voted differently from the mainstream of the Group as a whole. As pointed out above however, the Socialist group has now become somewhat more cohesive.

The Christian Democrats have also been far from ideologically homogeneous, ranging from Social Christian members from the Low Countries with strong trade union links and who are left-of-centre on certain social questions, to highly conservative CSU members from Bavaria. The Liberals have tended to cover a narrower spectrum, but there have, nevertheless, been considerable differences between them as well.

As we have seen, the Communist Group was so divided between the more moderate Communists of Italy and Spain, and the hard liners in France, Portugal and Greece that it formally split after the 1989 elections.

The Greens are also divided between those who see themselves as clearly on the left, and others who claim to be above traditional left–right divisions.

All the above factors have tended to undercut the importance of left–right divisions in the European Parliament, or at least have made them much more complex than a simplistic analysis of left- or right-wing majorities would suggest. This is not to say that such divisions are com-

pletely without significance. There are certain important issues, which tend
to divide the Parliament on traditional left-right lines. Group whips also
sometimes entrench divisions in that individual members do not have the
time or experience to take their own position on every amendment on
every issue and usually follow the Group line on the order paper prepared
by the Group staff, or the upturned or downturned thumb of their
specialist spokesman.

A complicating factor is the nature of the balance of power within the
European Parliament. The Socialist Group is now by far the largest Group,
but it is still 80 members short of an overall majority within the Parliament.
It can not achieve that majority in combination with any one of the other
left-of-centre groups. It can if all of them combine, but this assumes a
commonality of interest between Social Democrats, traditional
Communists, Greens and Regionalists. On certain issues, narrow majorities
can be forged on these lines, but on other issues they are very unlikely. At
any rate the sort of majorities required under the co-operation procedure
are, to all intents and purposes impossible to achieve on this basis. In these
circumstances the Socialists must negotiate with Groups on the centre or
the right of the political spectrum.

The only single group with which the Socialists can combine to obtain an
overall majority is the European People's Party. Their combined forces
represent 301 of the 518 members of the Parliament. In view of inevitable
absenteeism even this is not enough to ensure consistent co-operation
procedure majorities.

The relationship between the Socialist and the European People's Party
remains, however, of central importance within the Parliament.
Representatives of the two Groups often meet with each other to strike
deals over political or patronage issues without their allies to left or right
always being consulted. These latter may then be forced to conform on a
take-it or leave-it basis.

Certain general rules of operation can thus now be observed in the
Parliament that was elected in 1989. When consensus or special majorities
are not of prime importance the Socialist Group turns initially to its left, in
the first instance to the Group of the United European Left (the former
Eurocommunists who are now evolving into left-wing Socialists).
Relationships between these two Groups are now very close on many
issues. On certain other issues the Socialists also liaise with the more
orthodox Left Unity Group. On the other hand the Greens are often
regarded as unreliable allies by the Socialists, although their voting
patterns quite often coincide. In terms of deal-making, however, the Greens
are still in a marginal position within the Parliament. However, when
consensus is important, especially when special majorities are required, the
Socialists negotiate with the European People's Party.

The relationships between the European People's Party and the other
Groups of the centre-right are also quite complex. The European
Democratic Group has close relations with certain elements within the EPP
(notably the German CDU and CSU members), and may again pursue its
application to join the EPP. Liaison mechanisms have been established

between the two Groups. Links also exist with the RDE and Liberal Groups.

An interesting phenomenon of Group co-operation is when the application of the proportional sharing of posts leaves the small Groups without representation (e.g. on a committee of inquiry of 15 members or a conciliation delegation of 12). In such cases, the Socialist Group will sometimes cede one of its places to a Left Group which would otherwise be unrepresented, and the EPP may do likewise for the RDE. No such co-operation, however, is extended to the Group of the European Right, which has an outsider role within the Parliament.

6. Leadership structures

At the beginning of, and halfway through each term of office (i.e. every two-and-a-half years) the Parliament elects its formal political leaders, its President, 14 Vice-Presidents and five Quaestors. At the same time the opportunity is sometimes also taken to renew the leadership of the Political Groups. Although they are only elected from within their Group and not by the Parliament as a whole, they play a key role in its leadership structures (see Chapter 5).

The three main decision-making bodies within the Parliament (other than the full plenary of course) are the Bureau (consisting of the President and 14 Vice-Presidents), the Enlarged Bureau (consisting of the Bureau and the Political Group Chairmen) and the College of Quaestors.

The present section looks first at the role of the President, Vice-Presidents and Quaestors, and how they are elected. It then examines the different responsibilities of the Bureau, Enlarged Bureau and the College of Quaestors, their working methods, and the relationships between them.

The President

The President's formal duties are to direct all the activities of Parliament to open, preside over and close Parliament's sittings, to chair the meetings of the Bureau and Enlarged Bureau, and to represent the Parliament in external relations, on ceremonial occasions and in administrative, legal or financial matters. The President also signs (or chooses not to sign!) the Community budget.

In practice the President invariably chairs the opening session of the plenary on Monday evenings (and normally stays until the week's agenda has been finally set), all formal sittings (when visiting Heads of State or political leaders address the Parliament) and during the most important and controversial debates or votes. For the rest of the time he or she delegates the chairing of the plenary to one of the Vice-Presidents. On the other hand the President is always in the chair during Bureau and Enlarged Bureau meetings. The President's role in representing the Parliament *vis-à-vis* the other Community institutions has also developed (see more detailed discussion below). He or she leads Parliament's delegations in important conciliation meetings with the Council of Ministers, and now not only attends European Council meetings but may address them as well. Finally, and working with Parliament's Secretary-General, the President also has an important internal role within the Parliament, in overseeing its day-to-day running and administrative structures.

In carrying out his or her duty the President is (like Members of the Commission) assisted by a personal private office ("Cabinet"), with a head and deputy head, and with four or five other members carrying out other specific functions, such as relations with the press. These Cabinet members may be drawn from a civil service or other background from the President's home country, or may come from the Political Groups, or from Parliament's own civil servants (generally, but not invariably those with a link, even if only nominal, with the President's own political party or Group). Most Cabinets contain a mix of the above elements. The President may feel, for example, most at home with someone from his or her own political background and nationality, but may also recognize the need to consult someone with a longer experience of Parliament's working methods and traditions, who is most easily found from within Parliament's own staff. Other useful expertise, for example, consists of inside knowledge of one of the other Community institutions, such as the Commission or the Council.

A factor which varies from President to President is the emphasis he or she puts on the other functions and duties mentioned above. Some Presidents have attached a particular importance to their external functions, in terms of relationships with other Community institutions or their activities in the international sphere. Certain other Presidents, while not neglecting their other essential duties, have taken a greater interest in Parliament's internal administration. These differing emphases also have a bearing on the President's choice of members of his or her cabinet.

Finally the President's "style" of presiding has also varied greatly, with some setting a more direct leadership example, and others adopting a more consensual system.

Presidents of the Parliament

The first President of the Common Assembly of the Coal and Steel Community (in 1952) was Paul-Henri Spaak of Belgium, and the first President of the European Parliament (in 1958) was Robert Schuman of France. In all there were four Presidents of the Common Assembly (Spaak, De Gasperi, Pella and Furler), and 11 Presidents of the European Parliament before direct elections (Schuman, Furler again, Martino, Duvieusart, Leemans, Poher, Scelba, Behrendt, Berkhouwer, Spenale and Colombo).

Since direct elections in 1979 the European Parliament has had five Presidents from four different countries, Simone Veil, (French UDF, Liberal Groups from 1979–1982), Piet Dankert (Dutch PVDA, Socialist Group from 1982–1984), Pierre Pflimlin (French UDF, Group of the European People's Party from 1984–1987), Sir Henry Plumb (later Lord Plumb, British Conservative, European Democratic Group from 1987–1989), and Enrique Barón (Spanish PSOE, Socialist Group from 1989 to the present).

The Vice-Presidents

Parliament has 14 Vice-Presidents, whose order of precedence is determined by the number of votes they received at their initial election (see below).

The main formal role of the Vice-Presidents is three-fold, to preside over the plenary sessions when the President is not in the chair, to replace the President in conciliation or other meetings when the President can not be present, and to take part in the meetings of the Bureau and Enlarged Bureau.

In practice the numerical ranking of the Vice-Presidents is of little direct significance, and other factors play a greater role in determining a Vice-President's importance within Parliament's leadership structure. Vice-Presidents who have been former Presidents of the Parliament (e.g. Piet Dankert) can clearly have particular authority. Vice-Presidents may speak with the authority of their Political Group behind them, but may also reflect the point of view of their own nationality (they may be, for example, the only Greek MEP in Parliament's leadership structure). Finally, of course, personal factors can also play an important role, with a Vice-President who is a strong personality becoming influential in their own right.

There is normally no particular specialization among the 15 Vice-Presidents, although some have special aptitudes which are put to use. Certain Vice-Presidents, for example (such as Nicole Péry) have been well known for their particularly speedy handling of votes in plenary.

The Quaestors

The College of Quaestors was first established by the Parliament in 1977. At first they formed a sub-group of the Bureau, but have been separately and directly elected by the Parliament since direct elections in 1979. The five Quaestors have an important internal function within the Parliament, in that they are responsible for administrative and financial matters directly concerning members, although their decisions are subject to guidelines laid down by the Bureau. On the other hand the Quaestors also take part in the meetings of the Bureau and Enlarged Bureau in an advisory capacity. Although they have no right to vote in these organs, they can thus speak on a wide range of issues, and a strong Quaestor can have considerable influence even on matters outside the Quaestors' direct competence. At the beginning of their term of office each Quaestor is entrusted with a particular area of responsibility, such as buildings policy or financial questions.

The election of the President, Vice-Presidents and Quaestors

Before direct elections Parliament's President was elected annually, although the practice developed of the President being given a second year of office, with election in the second year being by acclamation (only Alain Poher of France was conceded three years in office). Parliament's officers are now elected every two and a half years, firstly in the July session immediately following the June direct elections. The mid-term elections then take place in the January session two-and-a-half years later.

Even before direct elections, the method of election of Parliament's officers was determined by the Parliament itself, which resisted any instructions from outside (as was attempted by the Member States in 1958).

The first to be elected is always the President. Until he or she has been elected the chair is taken by the oldest member among the MEPs (not the member with the longest service in the Parliament). Although no business is transacted while the oldest member is in the chair, a tradition has developed that the oldest member delivers an initial keynote speech. The first such speech after direct elections was given by Louise Weiss. In 1989, however, the oldest member was the film director Claude-Autant-Lara, a member of the far right French *Front National*. His speech was boycotted by a large number of members from the outset, and a large number of other members left as a result of his remarks. It has now been strongly suggested that Parliament's Rules of Procedure should be amended so that the oldest member should no longer be permitted to deliver an introductory speech, but should merely conduct the business in hand.

Nominations for the office of President are generally put forward by a Political Group or coalition of Political Groups, but may also be submitted by 13 or more members.

The ballot is secret, with members lining up to cast their vote in the centre of the Strasbourg hemicycle, and with the result announced an hour or two later. An absolute majority of the votes cast (not of the total number of MEPs) is required for election. If this is not achieved, second and, if necessary, third ballots are held, with no obligation on any of the first ballot candidates to stand down, and with the possibility of new candidates (compromise or other) entering the fray.

If, however, there is no result in the third ballot, a conclusive fourth ballot is held, in which only the two candidates with the highest votes in the third ballot take part, and in which a simple majority is enough to ensure election.

Five sets of direct elections have been held since 1979, and the circumstances and degree of suspense have varied greatly.

In 1979, Simone Veil was the clear front runner on the centre right, with support from the Liberals, Christian Democrats and Conservatives. The left was divided, with Socialist and Communist candidates in the field. Veil was only eight votes short of an absolute majority in the first ballot, and was duly elected on the second ballot.

In 1982, however, the Presidential election was much more dramatic. With a slight centre-right majority in the Parliament, the expectation was that the standard bearer of the centre-right would be the winner. The right was divided, however, with the European Democratic Group (Conservatives) considering that it was their turn for the Presidency. Not only were they unwilling to give a free run to the candidate of the European People's Party, but were also unenthusiastic about Egon Klepsch, the EPP's choice as Presidential candidate. The Socialist candidate, by contrast, Piet Dankert, had made a name as Parliament's Budgetary rapporteur and then as a Vice-President and enjoyed the sympathy of some members from outside the ranks of the left.

In the first round Klepsch was ahead with 140 votes, followed by Dankert, with 106 votes, Scott-Hopkins of the European Democratic Group with 63, Chambeiron of the Communists with 43, and the outsider candidate Pannella with 16. In the second ballot all five candidates stood again, but Dankert's vote went up slightly and that of Klepsch went down. In the third ballot there were only three candidates (Dankert, Klepsch and Scott-Hopkins) and Dankert overtook Klepsch for the first time. In the decisive fourth ballot Dankert won by 191 votes to 175, clearly gaining support (or abstentions) from certain Conservative members, and from a few other centre-right members as well.

In 1984, there were no less than seven candidates in the first ballot, but there was again a clear front runner from the centre right, Pierre Pflimlin of the European People's Party, a former French Prime Minister and the long standing Mayor of Strasbourg. Dankert was again the Socialist candidate, but Pflimlin was easily elected on the second ballot.

The 1987 elections were also very close. Sir Henry Plumb was the candidate of the centre-right and Enrique Barón (Spanish Socialist) of the left. There were two other outsider candidates, Pannella (who won support well beyond his intrinsic strength with 61 votes on the first ballot) and Paul Staes of the Rainbow Group. Barón was ahead by 206 to 199 on the first ballot but Plumb pulled ahead by 233 to 219 on the second ballot, when only Pannella was also left in the field. In the third ballot, with only Plumb and Barón standing, the former won by 241 votes to 236.

In 1989, on the other hand, there was a tacit agreement between the two largest Groups, the Socialists and the EPP, to share the two Presidencies of the current legislature. The EPP supported Barón, and although there were other candidates in the first ballot, Barón won an absolute majority on the first ballot.

The Presidential elections have thus alternated between being close and unpredictable, and more or less foregone conclusions. Once they have been settled, however, they then have a bearing on the elections for the Vice-Presidents, and Quaestors (and subsequently on the Committee chairmanships, and other posts within the Parliament). These posts are effectively divided between the Political Groups (and within them between the different national delegations) on the basis of their numerical strength after having taken into account which Political Group has obtained the Presidency. An attempt is also made to ensure that a broad variety of nationalities are represented among the Vice-Presidents and Quaestors, although certain smaller countries, such as Luxembourg or Ireland, cannot always have such a representative (but see below).

In order to be elected as Vice-President a candidate has to receive an absolute majority of the votes cast. If 14 candidates are not so elected on the first ballot there are provisions for a second ballot for the remaining places under the same rules, and finally for a third ballot in which a relative majority is sufficient. The official nominees of the Groups are almost inevitably elected in practice, although some of them only on the second ballot, and although some are outsider candidates (such as the popular Green candidate, Roelants de Vivier in 1987), they may obtain respectable scores. As mentioned above, the numerical order of election is more a matter of protocol than of practical significance.

Once the Vice-Presidents have been elected there is then a separate ballot for the Quaestors, in which there is also very little suspense.

The Bureau, Enlarged Bureau and College of Quaestors

Working methods and responsibilities

The Bureau and Enlarged Bureau normally have two meetings a month. The meetings of both bodies are held in close conjunction, with the Enlarged Bureau either meeting on the same day as the Bureau or the day after. Both bodies invariably meet on one occasion during each plenary session in Strasbourg, and normally hold an additional monthly meeting between the plenary sessions in Brussels. Occasionally there are other exceptional meetings to deal with specific political problems.

The Quaestors have a similar pattern of meetings, although on a slightly more frequent basis. Their meetings take place before those of the Bureau and Enlarged Bureau, since a number of the issues that they examine then have to be decided upon by the other bodies.

The meetings of these three bodies are held in camera. Attendance is limited to their direct membership (with Political Group leaders in the Enlarged Bureau being accompanied by their respective Secretaries-General) and two representatives of the non-attached members. In addition the practice has developed of permitting a representative of certain nationalities not included in the Bureau to take part in Enlarged Bureau meetings as an observer, with the right to speak on issues where they are concerned (most obviously the issue of the seat of the Parliament), but without the right to vote.

On the staff side, attendance is limited to the Secretary-General, the Bureau's own Secretariat (three or four Parliament officials) and that of the Quaestors, the various Directors-General of the Parliament, and the head of its Legal Service. The minutes of the meetings are drawn up by the Bureau's or College of Quaestors' Secretariat, and are then subject to very careful review in view of the sensitivity of some of the decisions that are taken, and the need to prevent conflicting interpretations of these decisions.

Decisions are taken by consensus where possible, but voting is used when necessary. The precise voting figures are usually not provided in the minutes. Meetings of the Bureau and Enlarged Bureau are chaired by the President. The College of Quaestors has a rotating chairmanship with one of the Quaestors taking the chair for a period of four months before handing over to another Quaestor.

The actual division of responsibilities between the Bureau and Enlarged Bureau is laid down in the Rules of Procedure but is not always as clear in practice as in theory. The Bureau has primary responsibility for certain categories of decisions, such as financial matters, members' expenses and allowances, and issues concerning Parliament's own staff (overall staff number and organizational structure, appointment of the top officials in the Parliament — Secretary General, Directors-General and Directors).

The Enlarged Bureau's formal responsibilities include relations with non-Community institutions and organizations and relations with the other institutions and bodies of the Communities, organizational matters concerned with plenary sessions (e.g. the drawing up of its draft agenda, or deciding on the treatment of oral questions with or without debate), and the annual legislative programme.

Formal responsibility for certain other matters, however, is divided between the Bureau and Enlarged Bureau. For example, the Bureau draws up Parliament's preliminary draft estimates, but these are adopted by the Enlarged Bureau, after consultation and discussion with the Budgets Committee. Organizational matters affecting committees are another example. The Bureau puts forward proposals for members of committees and committees of inquiry (and for filling vacancies), deals with conflicts of competence between committees, authorizes committee meetings away from Parliament's normal places of work, travel by rapporteurs, etc. It is to the Enlarged Bureau, however, that a committee has to turn for the setting up of sub-committees, for the prior authorization to draft own initiative reports or for approval for proposed Committee hearings.

In view of the increasing power of the Political Groups within the European Parliament, and of the Socialist and EPP Groups in particular, and also, perhaps, of the fact that it is more widely representative than the Bureau of the whole range of Political Groups within the Parliament, the Enlarged Bureau has become a generally more powerful body than the Bureau. It often reviews matters already examined by the Bureau, and has gradually got more involved in issues in which the lead role used to be played by the Bureau.

Nevertheless, the Bureau continues to have a considerable role to play, especially when there are a number of strong Vice-Presidents, possibly also taking an independent line from that of their Group leaders. Moreover the Bureau can also be a useful sounding-board for representatives of particular nationalities or interest groups.

The College of Quaestors, on the other hand, has a more clearly subordinate role, although there are a number of issues on which it can take final decisions, such as the implementation of administrative and financial rules directly affecting members (e.g. use of vehicles by members, members' office equipment, secretarial allowances, etc).

7.   The Parliamentary committees

Members of the European Parliament are all full members of at least one specialized standing committee, and sometimes of a second committee as well. They are also substitutes on one or more committees. Much of the detailed work of the Parliament is carried out within these committees.

The present section examines the structure and functioning of these committees. It first looks at the division of responsibilities between the different committees, at the way committee office-holders are chosen, and members allocated to individual committees, at decision-making structures within the committees, and then at how they are staffed. It examines where and when the committees meet, and their working methods and workload, notably how committee rapporteurs are chosen, and how reports and opinions progress through committees. It then reviews other committee techniques, such as hearings and question time. The final part of the section reviews the workings of subcommittees, special committees of inquiry and temporary committees, and lastly, the functioning of interparliamentary delegations.

Development of the committee system, and division of responsibilities between committees

Development of the committee system before 1979

The Common Assembly of the Coal and Steel Community had already set up seven committees by 1953.

With the establishment in 1958 of the EEC and EURATOM with a Parliamentary Assembly common to the three communities, 13 committees were established. By now the Committee structure was beginning much more closely to resemble that of today. From 1958 to 1979 the committee system gradually developed, with occasional changes of committee nomenclature and also of committee responsibility. By 1967, the Committee on Economic and Financial Affairs had merged with that on the Internal Market. The Social Affairs Committee briefly merged with that on Public Health, but in 1973 two separate committees were re-established, one for Social Affairs and Employment, and one for Public Health and the Environment (with consumer protection added to its title in 1976). By 1973 Regional Policy had also been added to the areas of responsibility of the long-standing Transport Committee. The Legal Affairs Committee was divested of its original responsibilities for Rules of Procedure and Petitions, for which a separate committee was established in 1975. The separate Committees on Energy Policy and on Research (to which latter the responsibility for culture had been added in 1960) had merged by 1967. By 1973 a separate Youth and Culture Committee had been established (but was discontinued in 1976).

The responsibilities of several other committees, however, remained basically unchanged throughout the period, those on Political Affairs, Agriculture, and External Economic Policy.

Developments since direct elections

After direct elections in 1979 a number of changes were made. The Committee on Regional Policy, Regional Planning and Transport was split into separate Regional and Transport Committees. The Youth and Culture Committee which had had a short existence in the early 1970s was re-established as the Committee on Youth, Culture, Education, Information and Sport. Besides the Budgets Committee a new Budgetary Control Committee was set up. An ad hoc Committee on Women's Rights was also created. It was originally set up on a temporary basis to produce a report on the whole range of problems related to women's rights within the Community, but was later confirmed as a permanent specialized committee.

In 1981, two further committees were established, one on Institutional Affairs (which was chaired by Altiero Spinelli, and whose initial *raison d'être* was the preparation of a Draft Treaty for European Union), and one on the Verification of Credentials. Since 1981 there has been only one further change of substance, in 1987, when a separate Committee on Petitions was established to deal with the ever expanding number of such petitions. At the same time responsibility for the Rules of Procedure, the Verification of Credentials and Immunities was combined within one committee.

Factors inhibiting further expansion in the number of committees

Two conflicting factors have been at work with regard to the evolution of the committee system since direct elections. The great increase in the number of members since 1979 (from 198 to the present 518), reinforced by the entry of members from Greece, Spain and Portugal, and the expansion of the European Community's (and European Parliament's) fields of responsibility, have led to pressure to create new committees, and new committee chairmenships and vice-chairmenships. On the other hand a number of members have also strongly resisted such an "inflation" of the committee system, and of the administrative burden that this would entail. Such resistance prevented the creation of new committees on Fisheries (for which there had been a particular demand) and on Human Rights.

This has been partially mitigated by the creation of subcommittees, of which four are currently in existence (see below). Even here, however, there has been a reluctance to allow the proliferation of permanent subcommittees, which are sometimes felt to duplicate or undercut the prerogatives of the full committees. The Economic Committee, for example, which had established a working party (the word "subcommittee" having been avoided) on technical barriers to trade during the first directly elected parliament, decided to discontinue this after 1984, although it had been authorised to establish a subcommittee on this topic if it so wished.

Rather than create new permanent committees or subcommittees the Parliament has tended to prefer temporary solutions, such as committee working parties, temporary special committees or committees of inquiry (on which more detail is provided below).

Division of responsibilities between committees

Another area in which there has been a reluctance to make major changes in the *status quo* has been that of the responsibility of individual committees for specific subject matters. These responsibilities tended to evolve in an *ad hoc* and cumulative fashion, and this resulted in an uneven distribution of work between committees, to considerable anomalies (e.g. the Economic Committee continued to be formally responsible until 1989 for much of Community coal policy rather than the Energy Committee, although the latter took the lead in practice on such matters), and also to overlaps of responsibility between committees. Telecommunications policy, for example, was split until 1989 between three committees (Transport, responsible for historical reasons for PTT regulation; Economic, responsible for industrial and standards matters; and Energy, responsible for research and certain aspects of technological development).The "television without frontiers initiative" was originally launched by the Youth and Culture Committee, but Parliament's report on the European Commission's subsequent proposals was eventually prepared within the Legal Affairs Committee. Responsibility for achievement of the internal market in specific sectors is split between different committees, with the Economic Committee, for example, being responsible for the free movement of goods, and the Legal Affairs Committee for the free movement of services and persons.

There are a number of reasons why it has proved so difficult to make major changes to this division of responsibilities between committees, and why, for example, such major reviews as that chaired by Marcel Albert van de Wiele, a Flemish Christian Democrat, in 1981, mainly recommended changes on the margin. The first is the desire to avoid unravelling carefully achieved balances of power within the Parliament. The best moment to make fundamental changes is between the terms of office of the old and new Parliament, but, in practice, this only leaves a four-week period between direct elections and the first plenary of the newly elected Parliament, when there are many new members unfamiliar with the workings of the old Parliament and when there are many other key decisions which need to be taken.

A second reason is that it is often genuinely difficult to draw up clear demarcations between policy areas or to decide into which category they should fall. Is media policy, for example, a cultural, economic, commercial or legal matter? A third reason is that certain existing committees have developed an identity and *esprit de corps* of their own with some members having served on them for 10 years or more.

The maintenance of a broadly unchanged committee structure, however, does not mean that they are roughly equal in strength and prestige. The Political Affairs Committee covers areas where the European Parliament has few formal powers, yet it has always included a high percentage of the more well-known members within the Parliament, who have welcomed the opportunity to discuss and comment on foreign policy and security matters and on topical issues of the day. The Budgets Committee has traditionally had a high profile in an area where the Parliament has real powers following the Treaty revisions of 1970 and 1975. The European Community's responsibilities in the area of agriculture has been reflected in a powerful position for the Parliament's Agriculture Committee.

The reinforcement of the Parliament's legislative role following the ratification of the Single European Act is also leading to a strengthened role for such committees as the Economic, Legal and Energy Committees, which have seen a great increase in their workload in recent years. Busiest of all has been the Committee on Environment, Public Health and Consumer Protection, responsible for some of the most topical and controversial areas on the Community's agenda.

A number of committees, however, have a less obviously powerful role. These typically have smaller memberships, far fewer legislative proposals to consider, and hold fewer meetings. They tend to concentrate instead on own – initiative reports on issues of their choice (e.g. Women's Committee or Youth Committee), or else have specialized tasks to carry out (e.g. Committee on Petitions and Committee on Rules of Procedure).

For further detail on committees and their members, see Table 4.

Developments since 1989

Only relatively minor changes were made to the Committee structure and range of responsibilities after the 1989 elections. The number of committees was maintained intact at the existing 18 and their numerical order was also unchanged. There were, however, a number of changes in nomenclature and shifts of responsibility from one committee to another. The Agriculture Committee changed its name from that of Agriculture, Fisheries and Food to Agriculture, Fisheries and Rural Development. The Environment Committee ceded its responsibilities for the protection of employees at work to the Social Affairs and Employment Committee which added the words "and the Working Environment" to its formal title. The Transport Committee lost its responsibility for telecommunications (which went primarily to the Economic Committee) but gained tourism from the Youth Committee, and renamed itself as the Transport and Tourism Committee in consequence. In its turn the Committee on Youth, Culture, Education, Information and Sport renamed itself as the Committee on Youth, Culture, Education, the Media and Sport.

Parliament also took the opportunity to change the description of certain Committees' responsibilities, but most of these were to ensure clarity and coherence rather than bring about major changes of substance. Among the more significant changes was that the Institutional Committee, instead of the Political Affairs Committee, was made responsible for the drawing up of a draft uniform electoral procedure for the European Parliament

Table 4: *Permanent committees, with number of members and chairmen (March 1990)*

	Name	Number of Members	Chairman
1.	Political Affairs Committee	56	Goria (Italian Christian Democrat,EPP)
2.	Agriculture, Fisheries and Rural Development	47	Colino Salamanca (Spain, PSOE, SOC)
3.	Budgets	32	Von der Vring (German SPD, SOC)
4.	Economic and Monetary Affairs and Industrial Policy	52	Beumer (Dutch Christian Democrat, EPP)
5.	Energy, Research and Technology	34	La Pergola (Italian PSI, SOC)
6.	External Economic Relations	29	De Clercq (Belgian Liberal, LDR)
7.	Legal Affairs and Citizens' Rights	34	Stauffenberg (German Christian Democrat, EPP)
8.	Social Affairs, Employment and the Working Environment	41	Van Velzen (Dutch PvDA, SOC)
9.	Regional Policy and Regional Planning	38	Waechter (French Les Verts, Green)
10.	Transport and Tourism	30	Amaral (Portuguese PSD, LDR)
11.	Environment, Public Health and Consumer Protection	51	Collins (British Labour, SOC)
12.	Youth, Culture, Education, Media and Sport	31	Barzanti (Italian Communist, United European Left)
13.	Development and Co-operation	43	Saby (French Socialist, SOC)
14.	Budgetary Control	28	Price (British Conservative, EDG)
15.	Institutional Affairs	38	Oreja (Spanish Popular Party, PPE)
16.	Rules of Procedure, Verification of Credentials and Immunities	27	Galle (Belgian Socialist, SOC)
17.	Women's Rights	33	Crawley (British Labour, SOC)
18.	Petitions	25	Reding (Luxembourg, Christian Democrats, EPP)

elections and for general relations with the other institutions or organs of the Community. A few previously existing anomalies were also cleared up, with the Energy Committee, for example, now being made fully responsible for all aspects of Community coal policy. Certain new tasks were also taken account of: the Legal Affairs Committee, for example, was given a new responsibility for overseeing the choice of legal base for Community acts.

What was perhaps more significant, however, were the changes in the number of full members on each committee. As a general rule there was upward movement, with 13 committees increasing in size and five decreasing. This was due to a marked tendency for more MEPs to be full members of more than one committee (with 518 members there are 670 full committee posts in the new Parliament, compared to only 604 previously). This can be attributed, in particular, to membership of the Institutional Committee being systematically combined with membership of another committee as well.

This general increase makes it all the more striking that the number of members of the Committee on Budgets has decreased from 46 to 32, an indication of the considerably lower attraction of this committee following the signing of an inter-institutional Agreement which established a financial framework for the Community up to the end of 1992, and hence made the annual budget procedure of less obvious political significance. Another committee which lost members was the Agriculture Committee (52 to 47), again perhaps a reflection of greater constraints on its future operations. The Committees on Development (49 to 43), Rules (28 to 17) and Petitions (28 to 25) also lost members.

The biggest single increase, on the other hand, was for the Environment Committee, which is associated with heightened concern both with environmental matters and the 1992 legislative programme, and which increased from 36 to 51 members. The other committees most linked with 1992 legislation also saw substantial increases in their membership; the Economic Committee (45 to 52 members), the Legal Affairs Committee (24 to 34) and the Social Affairs Committee (31 to 41). The Institutional Affairs Committee (28 to 38 members) and the Budgetary Control Committee (19 to 28) also had large gains in membership, as did the Youth Committee (22 to 31) and Transport Committee (23 to 30). The Energy, External Economic Relations and Women's Committees had lesser gains.

Selection of committee office-holders

Each committee has a chairman and three vice-chairmen, (who together constitute its Bureau), who are elected at the committee's constituent meeting, normally during the July plenary of a new Parliament. In practice, all these positions are divided by agreement among the Political Groups on the basis of the number of members within each Group.

The actual allocation is determined by the d'Hondt system of proportional representation, whereby groups choose which committees to chair in an order determined by the size of the group. In 1989, for example, the Socialist Group with 180 members had the right to the first, third, fifth and seventh choices etc., the Group of the European People's Party with 121 members to the second and fourth choices etc., the Liberals with 49 members to the sixth and sixteenth choices, etc.

The order in which committees are chosen is a function of a number of factors, of which the most important is the prestige of a committee, the scope to make political capital from it, and also the availability of a suitable candidate for a post from within the Political Group. The first committees to be chosen are usually the Political, Budgets and Agricultural Committees. In 1989 it was also clear that the Environment Committee was regarded as one of the top committees, and indeed, it was the first choice of all, going to the largest delegation (British Labour) within the largest Group, who also had an experienced candidate for the post (Ken Collins), a previous Chairman (from 1979–1984) of the Committee.

Once a chairmanship has been allocated to a particular Group the actual choice of chairman also depends on a number of factors, such as the need to take into account size of the national delegations within a Group, and the experience and expertise of their individual candidates. In contrast with the US Congress, seniority within the Parliament does not play a very great role, although there is a general reluctance immediately to appoint new MEPs as committee chairmen. Another key factor is the previous distribution of posts. If a national delegation within a Political Group has already provided a President, Vice-President or Quaestor of Parliament, or the chairmanship of their Political Group, their chances of gaining a major committee chairmanship may diminish since other delegations must also get their turn. Once chairmanships have been distributed, a similar process occurs for the first, second and third vice-chairmanship of the committees, although these are clearly of lesser importance. Although preliminary agreement on all these matters are taken by the Groups in the weeks before the first plenary session of a new parliament it is not until the actual plenary that the final decisions can be taken. Much stems from the choice of President of Parliament, which has been by no means a foregone conclusion in most recent elections.

Once the nominations of chairmen and vice-chairmen have been decided upon by the Political Groups, the formal decisions are then taken by the committees at their constituent meetings. In practice there have rarely been competing candidates, and election of the Political Groups' nominees is practically always a formality, and by acclamation rather than by vote. Occasionally a candidate has been the subject of controversy. In the first directly elected parliament, for example, the choice of the British Conservative, David Curry, to replace Sir Henry Plumb as chairman of the Agriculture Committee, was strongly contested. A British candidate was automatically regarded with suspicion by the defenders of the Common Agricultural Policy but Sir Henry Plumb had overcome this because of his strong farming credentials (at European as well as at national level), whereas David Curry did not have this background, and was perceived as more hostile to the CAP. Curry failed to get a majority on the first vote, but was eventually elected.

Even in these circumstances, however, there is seldom question of a candidate from another Political Group being put up to oppose the official nominee, as this would upset the carefully constructed political balance between Groups (and often nationalities) that had been previously agreed upon. In the unlikely event of a Group nominee being defeated it would be up to the Group to suggest a new candidate.

The rare exceptions to these general rules of practice have come in the less important votes for vice-chairmanships. In 1984 in the Youth Committee, for example, the secret ballot provided for in the Parliament's Rules of Procedure took place, and the official Group nominee for one of the vice-chairmanships was defeated by a candidate from another group. Another case was in the Youth Committee half-way through the 1984–1989 Parliament, when the third vice-chairmanship was supposed to go to a representative of the Group of the European Right. No nominee was put forward, and there were no representatives of the Group present at the constituent meeting of the Committee, which proceeded to elect an Italian Communist as third vice-chairman. The Group of the European Right protested strongly, but to no avail, a decisive factor being the "outsider" position that the Group has tended to have in the political decision-making structure of the Parliament.

After the 1989 elections the whole system of distribution of chairmanships and vice-chairmanships was subjected to a more funda-mental challenge by the Group of the European Right, which put up candidates against the other groups' nominees in the vast majority of committees (in one or two committees the Greens also challenged official candidates).

Not only were all these challenges unsuccessful (although prolonging the duration of the constituent meetings of the committees) but the one "official" nominee from the Group of the European Right, (Hans Günter Schodruch for the third vice-chairmanship of the Transport Committee) was himself challenged and defeated, and the Group remained without a single chairman or vice-chairman.

Once elected by the Committee, the chairmen and vice-chairmen have terms of office of two-and-a-half years. Half-way through the five-year term of the Parliament, and after the election of the new President of Parliament, the whole process is thus again repeated. There is, however, usually a greater reluctance on this occasion to make major changes to the distribution of Committees between Political Groups, especially because there has normally been no change in the numerical balance between these Groups (although the situation in both the 1979–1984 and 1984–1989 Parliaments was complicated by the arrival first of Greek, and then of Spanish and Portuguese members).

There is, however, often a change over of chairmen, so that political offices within the Parliament can be more widely distributed within the Political Group in question. A really long-serving chairman is the exception rather than the rule. Perhaps the most striking such exception was the German SPD member, Erwin Lange, who was chairman of the Economic and Monetary Committee for four years and then of the Budgets Committee for seven years (1977–1984). Other long-serving chairmen included the Italian Communist, Pancrazio de Pasquale (Chairman of the Regional Committee from 1979 to 1989) and Heinrich Aigner (Chairman of the Budgetary Control Committee from its creation in 1979 to his death, in 1988).

Membership of committees

As was seen in Table 4 committee membership varies greatly from the 25 of the Petitions Committee to the 56 of the Political Affairs Committee. The membership of each Committee is also decided upon during the first session of a new Parliament.

Traditionally, the Political Groups agree on appointments to membership of committees in such a way as to ensure that each committee reflects the overall political balance between the Groups in plenary. Only small exceptions to the rule — to the tune of one extra member perhaps — are normally accepted. (Following the 1989 elections, however, the Socialist Group, which had a large number of members interested in sitting on the Environment and Consumer Committee and the EPP Group, which had a large number interested in the Agriculture Committee, agreed to a trade-off, with the result that these two committees do not so accurately reflect the plenary balance.)

Each MEP normally serves on one committee as a full member and on another as a substitute (although, as pointed out above more MEPs are now full members of two committees). Members are chosen from within their Political Group on the basis of their wishes, expertise and whatever places are still left over, with some committees potentially over-subscribed and others much less popular. Less well-known backbenchers in their first term are clearly often at a disadvantage in this hand-out. Some nationalities and Groups have a strong preference for certain committees. Irish members, for example, have been keenest to sit on the Agricultural and Regional Committees. One safety mechanism for members who are not completely satisfied with their primary committee assignments as full members is their assignation to a second committee as a substitute. In some cases this is the committee on which they would have preferred to have served as a full member, and they may then spend more time at this committee than on their main one.

Substitutes in fact suffer very little disadvantage compared to full members. They have full speaking rights, in practice full voting rights (they are only prevented from voting on those limited occasions when all the full members of their Political Group are present and voting: otherwise they can vote in the place of a designated absent full member) and can even be rapporteurs and draftsmen, on occasion drawing up some of the major reports within a committee. Of the full reports drawn up within the Economic Committee in 1984–1989 almost one in seven were drawn up by substitutes.

One other point worth making is that, despite the balance generally achieved between Political Groups, committees do tend to develop a corporate identity, and do tend to attract members with a particular sympathy to the sector concerned. For example, the Agricultural Committee has been more sympathetic to CAP spending than the Budgets Committee.

Decision-making structures within the committees

The formal office-holders within each committee are its chairman and three vice-chairmen, with the four together collectively known as its "Bureau".

The chairman presides over the meetings of the committee, speaks for it in the plenary sessions at a time of sensitive votes or decisions (such as whether to accept or reject a demand for urgent treatment of a proposal by Commission or Council) and also represents it at the regular meetings of committee chairmen (see below). He or she can also have a powerful role in shaping the agenda of the committee, and in acting as its representative outside Parliament.

The vice-chairmen substitute for the chairman in time of absence. In some committees, regular bureau meetings are held, and the chairmen and vice-chairmen acting collectively can then have an important say.

Other powerful members within the committee are its co-ordinators. Each Political Group chooses a co-ordinator as its main spokesman. One of their most important functions is to meet during a committee meeting (normally immediately after the end of an afternoon session) and to agree which Group will take which report or opinion (see below). These meetings of co-ordinators can also be used by the chairman to discuss the committee's future agenda and outstanding political problems before full discussion in the committee. Co-ordinators' meetings are often held during the Strasbourg plenaries to discuss forthcoming votes affecting the committee, possible compromise amendments and so on.

Co-ordinators also have a vital role in the allocation of tasks among the members of their Group. Once a report has been allocated to a Group the co-ordinator often plays the decisive part in the choice of rapporteur from among the members of that Group.

The co-ordinators often act as "whips", convening meetings of the members of their Group before the start of the full committee meeting, maximizing their Group's presence during key votes, and helping to establish the full Group's voting line for the plenary sessions.

The balance of decision-making power between the chairman, the bureau and the co-ordinators differs considerably from committee to committee. The chairman is generally in the most powerful position, and can be dominant within the committee (Erwin Lange of the Budget Committee being a good example). Other chairmen operate through a more collective style of leadership, whether through the committee's bureau or in conjunction with the group co-ordinators. Styles of chairmanship also vary from country to country, and these differences are often reflected in Parliament's committee chairmen.

Staff

Compared to the US Congress, in particular , the full-time staff of Parliament's committees is miniscule, although admittedly greater than in some national parliaments of the Member States. In 1988, Parliament's committees had 109 A Administrators, 38 B Assistants, and 117 C staff of secretarial grade, with staff numbers hardly increased since the early 1980s. Committees normally have between four and six administrators presided over by a head of division. There is also a committee assistant to look after the logistics of the meetings, and a number of secretaries. In view of the relatively rapid turnover of members of the committee (typically half of the members leave after each election, and only a small minority of them stay in one committee for more than 10 years) the committee staff often have an important role in briefing members of the past activities and positions adopted within the committee. They often help in background research for rapporteurs, and in the actual drafting of texts. They frequently tend to be generalists rather than specialists, largely because there are so few of them to cover what is often a wide range of policy areas, but also because of language constraints. A French-speaking expert on a particular subject area may have to hand over to a German-speaking, but non-expert, colleague if the rapporteur he or she is meant to assist speaks only German. However, increased specialization of committee staff is likely to develop in the future as a result, in particular, of the Parliament's increased legislative responsibilities under the Single European Act, the need to follow up adopted legislation and to monitor Commission actions, and the consequent need to establish closer contacts with Commission and Council officials.

Besides the committee staff other officials frequently attend committee meetings. Parliament's Directorate-General for Research, which sometimes helps committees with more detailed research, also sends one or two of its administrators to keep track of committee developments within their field.

A Political Group also has one or sometimes more of its staff whose responsibilities include following the activities of an individual committee. The smaller Political Groups, however, tend to be more stretched in this regard, and their staff may have to follow more than one committee. (See section on Political Group staff in Chapter 5.)

Finally, there are members' personal assistants. (Also see discussion in Chapter 4 on individual members and their staff.) In the early days of the directly elected Parliament their presence at Committee meetings was disputed in certain committees, but this is much less the case today. Only a minority of the assistants, however, regularly attend committee meetings, although they are quite often used as the "eyes" and "ears" of a committee member at a meeting with items of interest to them when they cannot attend personally. Unlike the situation in the United States (where, of course, Congressmen's personal staff are far more numerous), members' personal assistants are not generally called upon for drafting of reports. More typical tasks would include preparation of members' speeches, background research, or the drafting of amendments to legislative texts and to reports being discussed within the committee. This may change if the Parliament becomes even more of a legislature, and if the number of assistants is augmented, but US experience would suggest that the increase in their legislative role will tend to rise in parallel with that of the committee's full-time staff, rather than in competition with them.

Where and when the committees meet

The committees' normal meetings are during the two so-called "Committee Weeks" which immediately follow the plenary session, and precede the Group week. Regular committee meetings almost invariably begin after lunch (to allow members to travel in the course of that morning if necessary) and end before lunch on a subsequent day. The normal working hours are 3 pm to 6:30 pm and 9 am to 12:30 pm. These are strictly enforced, with the main exception being the meetings of the Budgets Committee at peak budget time, when meetings often continue until late into the evenings.

The busier committees now meet on a regular basis at least twice a month for two or four half days on each occasion. Other committees may only meet once a month, although often for four half days.

The vast majority of these meetings take place at Parliament's buildings in Brussels. There is a well-observed rule that Parliament's committees may only meet once a year outside Parliament's "normal working places" (but within the European Community). This is felt to ensure a good balance between showing the flag outside Brussels (and learning about national and regional situations), and not indulging in wasteful extra travel. A committee seeking to take advantage of this rule must seek the approval of Parliament's Bureau for any such meetings outside Brussels.

There are a few limited exceptions to this rule. The Political Affairs Committee holds twice-yearly meetings in the countries holding the Council Presidency, and members of the Development Committee also travel more regularly. On the other hand, the Budgets Committee has rarely met outside Brussels. When a meeting outside Brussels is proposed in certain committees a vote is insisted upon as to whether such a visit should take place.

Committees may of course also meet in Luxembourg or Strasbourg as these are normal working places. Meetings now only rarely take place in Luxembourg, but short extra meetings during Strasbourg plenaries are becoming more and more frequent. For a long time they were actively discouraged in that they competed for scarce room space and interpreters, as well as further undercutting plenary attendance, but Parliament's new legislative responsibilities have made them inevitable. Parliament's Rules of Procedure now state that, when more than 25 amendments are tabled for plenary that have not been considered by the committee, the committee must meet to examine them. Even when this is not the case committees often meet in Strasbourg to take a position on particularly sensitive reports and the amendments tabled on them, or to discuss major new developments. Such meetings generally take place on Monday afternoon or as early as possible on Tuesday.

Emergency committee meetings sometimes take place for other reasons, such as when a report for plenary consideration is unexpectedly sent back to committee. In the plenary session in May 1989 an attempt to defer a report by the Environment Committee on radioactivity levels in foodstuffs by referring it back to Committee was foiled when the members of the committee who were present left the plenary chamber, met for five minutes outside and returned, having reconfirmed their original report.

From 1979 to 1984, little over 70 per cent of committee meetings took place in Brussels, 20 per cent in Strasbourg, (although, as pointed out above, much shorter in duration), under 3 per cent in Luxembourg and 5.5 per cent elsewhere (source: European Parliament, Forging Ahead).

How the committees function

In 1981, Parliament's meetings in Brussels were switched from a small building on Boulevard de l'Empereur in central Brussels to a larger purpose-built office on rue Belliard nearer the Commission and Council. In

Boulevard de l'Empereur, the committees used to sit around a long rectangular table, with the chairman at the head. The meetings were very cramped but informal with the Commission representatives also at the same table, and with Communists next to or facing Conservatives, Socialists and Liberals.

In the new meeting rooms at rue Belliard the Chairman sits up on a raised dais, with the vice-chairmen on his or her left and the committee secretariat to the right. The Political Groups sit in the central bloc of seats, facing the chairman rather than each other, with the Socialists in the front seats on the left, the Left Groups, Greens and Rainbow behind, the Christian Democrats in the front seats on the right, and Conservatives, Liberals, Gaullists and others at the back.

The secretariats of the Political Groups, members' assistants and other members of Parliament's staff sit in the block of seats on one side of the room, with representatives of the Commission or Council in the block of seats on the other side.

Compared to Boulevard de l'Empereur there has been a considerable change in atmosphere. The rooms are much more spacious, but the meetings are also more formal, and the distinction between the various Political Groups is sharper. Jacques Delors, now President of the Commission, but formerly Chairman of a Parliamentary Committee from 1979 to 1981, was one who regretted the less intimate atmosphere, which, he said, made him feel more like a teacher in a traditional school. The change was perhaps inevitable, however, with the increase in Parliament's membership.

Space is also provided for visitors at the back of the meeting rooms and in special rows of seats on the side. Before direct elections, committee meetings were closed to the public, but after 1979 a number of committees, such as the Social Affairs and later the Environment and Economic Committees, opened their doors.

Visitors generally fall into three categories: casual visitors, the press and lobbyists. There is an increasing number of casual visitors, brought by a University, by their MEP, and so on. There is not, however, the same informality as in Washington D.C. where Congressional committee meetings and their subject matter are listed in the daily press, so that political "tourists" can drop in on the committee of their choice.

To some extent there are also members of the press present at committee meetings, but normally for big hearings on controversial subjects rather than for routine committee meetings.

The most regular visitors, however, are lobbyists, especially those who are Brussels-based, and who sometimes specialise in particular committees or specific subjects. All seats are filled, for example, when the Commissioner responsible for fiscal harmonization makes progress reports to the Economic Committee.

Finally, a few words about the languages used in committee meetings. The situation is similar to that for all Parliamentary activities, with all the Community languages in use. There is, however, a slightly greater informality than in plenary sessions, with members more frequently responding to points made by other members in the latters' language rather than their own. For co-ordinators' meetings, there is sometimes no interpretation, with only English or French being used.

Committee business

The bulk of committee business is concerned with the consideration and adoption of draft reports and opinions, in fulfilment of Parliament's legislative, budgetary monitoring and agenda-setting roles. In addition, however, the committees of the European Parliament carry out a number of other related activities, such as public hearings, cross-examination of Commission and Council representatives on general or specific issues and meetings with delegations from national parliaments or other organizations. These various activities are described in more detail below.

Origin of draft reports and opinions

There are three main bases on which committees draw up reports or opinions; formal consultations of the Parliament (involving one or two readings) by the Council or Commission, resolutions tabled by individual members, and on its own initiative. Falling outside these three categories are a number of miscellaneous reports.

When Parliament receives a formal Commission or Council request for an opinion or advice on a particular proposal it is then referred to the appropriate committee as "the committee responsible", and to one or more other committees for their "opinions". The decision as to where to refer the proposal is taken by a civil servant within the Parliament's committee service, and the decision is then announced by the President of Parliament in the subsequent plenary session. In controversial cases, however, there may be considerable political involvement, with a chairman of a committee, for example, calling for a particular proposal to be referred to his or her committee, or else requesting that responsibility for a proposal be switched from another committee. In the most difficult cases, the controversy may be brought before the Bureau of Parliament. Recent examples of problem areas include telecommunications, where controversy over which committee was competent prevented an early Parliament response to the Commission's Green Book on telecommunications, and Commission proposals on ship-building. Occasionally, two or more committees end up preparing reports on different aspects of the same proposal. This is rare, and most likely to occur when Parliament has been informally rather than formally consulted on a proposal, such as Commission Green or White Books which are discussion documents rather than formal legislative texts.

Committees may also request that they be asked to give an opinion on a proposal or suggest that another committee give such an opinion.

Being able to draw up an opinion for another committee enables a committee with a particular interest in a proposal to express its views, but is less satisfactory than being fully responsible. Opinion-giving committees, for example, may table amendments to Commission proposals but are not meant to vote on the Commission proposal as a whole. There is no obligation for the committee primarily involved to take other committee's amendments on board, and while such amendments are sometimes put to the vote in the main committee, there is no automatic rule to this effect. Not only can other committees' opinions be ignored by the main committee, but the latter also sets the timetable for consideration of the proposals. It is thus a frequent occurrence for a proposal to have been adopted in the main committee before the other committees have given their opinion, and main reports and opinions are sometimes presented separately in the plenary. (Opinions are otherwise annexed to main committee reports.) Even more frequently, opinion-giving committees are given very little time to draw up their opinions, and these often have to take the form of a short letter from their chairman.

All these factors have led some members to suggest that opinions are of little value, and should be scrapped. This has not happened. In spite of these disadvantages some committee opinions are taken very seriously. More points are sometimes allocated for them than for major reports (see below on appointment of rapporteurs and draftsmen), and considerable time is spent discussing them in committee. Moreover, committees whose opinions are ignored can retable any amendments for the plenary. Draftsmen of committee opinions are given the opportunity to express the committee's views in plenary debates on the subject. Opinion-giving committees even have the opportunity to examine common positions in second reading, although they can generally only retable any of their own amendments which had been adopted by the Parliament in the first reading.

The number of consultations has increased considerably in recent years; 135 legislative resolutions were considered in plenary in 1986, but this had increased to 264 by 1989. Parliament's workload was accentuated as a result of the full implementation of the Single European Act through the co-operation and assent procedures. By 1989, the 264 legislative resolutions comprised 135 single reading consultations, 55 first readings within the co-operation procedure, as well as 71 second readings, and three assent procedures (Source: Commission Annual Report).

The second basis for committee reports and opinions are motions for a resolution tabled by individual members on a matter falling within the sphere of activities of the Communities (Rule 63 of the Rules of Procedure). In practice, this means that almost any subject can be raised. These are also referred to specific committees for their reports or opinions in a similar way to Commission proposals. The committee must then decide whether or not and by which procedure each such resolution should be considered and inform the president and the author or authors of its decision.

A list of such resolutions is normally considered by the committee co-ordinators at their regular meetings with the chairman to distribute committee reports and opinions. The recommendations of the co-ordinators are then submitted by the chairman to the full committee for ratification.

In practice only a minority of individual resolutions are made the subject of individual committee reports. Many of the resolutions raise constituency matters of specific national, regional or sectoral interest only and are not considered to be appropriate for detailed committee consideration. Some committees have informal rules that such resolutions will only be considered in a specific committee report when they raise an issue affecting more than one Member State, though this may be less strictly observed in committees with lesser work loads or when a determined member (especially a group co-ordinator) continues to insist on a report. No further action, however, is a very common fate for many resolutions.

Another common solution is to wait until there are a considerable number of resolutions on the same theme, and then to group them together within one report. In both this case and in that of an individual report the motion or motions for a resolution are annexed at the back of the report. On many occasions the reports do not respond directly to the motion, and depart quite significantly from its terms of reference. Similarly a committee may decide to consider a motion for a resolution in conjunction with a report that it is drawing up in another context (legislative or "own-initiative"), in which case it is annexed to the report in question.

On certain occasions a motion for a resolution is indirectly sponsored by a committee's leadership in order to provide an opportunity to draw up a committee report on a desired subject. This procedure has the advantage that a report can then immediately be prepared, thus avoiding the uncertainty and delay of requesting an own-initiative report.

The number of reports considered in plenary stemming from Rule 63 resolutions has increased greatly in recent years. Nevertheless there are also occasions when a committee wishes to consider a particular issue and decides to request authorisation from the Bureau of Parliament to draw up such an own-initiative report. The committee may thus wish to bring up a new issue on the policy agenda, to give a view on a Commission Communication on which Parliament has not been formally consulted, and so on.

Permission to draw up own-initiative reports is not automatically granted by the Bureau of Parliament, typical reasons for rejecting them being that the subject matter is too close to that of another committee's report, or that the issue has been recently handled by Parliament. Towards the end of the 1984–89 Parliament, with the plenary agenda getting more and more overloaded, a decision was taken not to authorise any more own-initiative reports for the remainder of the Parliament's term of office.

The number of own-initiative reports increased greatly between the 1979 –84 parliament and that of 1984–89, but in recent years has stabilised. The balance, however, between consultations, own-initiative reports and other reports has varied greatly from committee to committee. As a rule the committees with a heavy legislative burden rely much less heavily on own-initiative reports (e.g. the Economic Committee which only worked on a handful of such reports in the latter half of the 1984–89 Parliament) whereas certain other committees (e.g. Women's Affairs), with few Commission proposals to consider, depend largely upon them for their workload. One exception to these norms is the Environment Committee which has a heavy legislative burden (the heaviest of any committee in the second half of the 1984–89 Parliament), but has continued to draw up a considerable number of own-initiative reports. In 1989, Parliament adopted 129 resolutions based on Rule 63 and on own-initiative reports (*Source:* Commission Annual Report).

Besides these, there are a number of other reports produced in committee, such as reports on the budget or budgetary control, waivers of immunity, changes in the rules of procedure, petitions of particular policy interest, or any other procedural matters, such as when a proposal's legal base is contested. The total number of non-legislative resolutions adopted by Parliament rose from 179 in 1980 to 340 in 1986, but has since remained at around the latter level (i.e. 336 in 1988 and 341 in 1989) (*Source:* Commission Annual Report).

Nomination of rapporteurs and draftsmen

Once a proposal or resolution has been referred to a committee, or authorisation has been granted to draw up an own-initiative report, the next task for the committee is to nominate a rapporteur (when the committee is primarily responsible) or a draftsman (when it has to draw up an opinion for another committee).

Only in a few cases are rapporteurs not appointed, namely when a committee decides to apply the procedure without report (Rule 116 of the Rules of Procedure). This is normally applied to highly technical consultations where only minor issues are involved. It is then placed on the agenda of the next plenary session, and put to the vote unless there is a protest by a political group or 13 members, in which case it is referred back to the committee.

Draftsmen of opinions, on the other hand, are quite often not appointed, because the issue is felt to be of little interest to the committee or because the timetable of the committee primarily responsible leaves no possibility for adequate discussion. On many occasions the committee chairman sends an opinion in the form of a letter (which must, nevertheless, also be approved by the committee).

The system of rapporteurs stems initially from Continental parliamentary practice, and is unfamiliar to those, for example, with British or American parliamentary backgrounds. It is the job of the rapporteurs (and also the draftsman) to prepare initial discussion on his or her subject within the committee, to then present a draft text, and to amend it if necessary to take account of the committee's observations or of new developments. Once the report is adopted by the committee the rapporteur is given time to present it in plenary, and is asked to give a view on behalf of the committee on any plenary amendments that have been tabled (this is normally communicated to the president in advance in writing, although the rapporteur may take the floor on complicated points). After the amendments to a Commission proposal are adopted, the rapporteur may also ask for the Commission's view on these amendments before the final vote on the proposal. When the co-operation procedure is involved the rapporteur must also follow developments between the first and second Parliament readings, and must prepare a recommendation for the second reading. Certain other rapporteurships call for continuing follow-up, especially those of an annual nature, such as those on the budget or competition policy.

The choice of rapporteurs and draftsmen is normally decided upon within individual committees by a system whose broad lines are common to all committees (although the detailed practice varies somewhat).

Each Political Group receives a number of points according to its size.

---

108 — THE EUROPEAN PARLIAMENT

Reports and opinions to be distributed are then discussed by the committee co-ordinators who decide on the number of points each subject is worth, and then make bids on behalf of their Group. A controversial issue may be the subject of competing bids. Groups may then raise the bid up to a maximum level which is normally around five points. If two or more Groups are still in contention it is normally for the Groups concerned to come to an agreement between themselves, possibly in the form of a package deal whereby one Group receives one report and the other is promised a subsequent report, or another one on a controversial issue. Very occasionally, rapporteurships are divided between two individuals from different Groups (e.g. Moreau/von Wogau report on the internal market in 1984, von Wogau and Patterson on VAT on second-hand goods in 1989).

Once the co-ordinators have decided on the number of points and the allocation of reports and opinions between Groups the latter is then submitted to the full committee for a final decision, although the co-ordinators' decisions are only rarely challenged. The co-ordinators must also decide which member of their Groups is to be the rapporteur or draftsman. The amount of points that have been used up by each Group are then added to their running total. These lists are sometimes subdivided into separate points lists for reports and for opinions.

There are certain features which are characteristic of this "auction" system for reports. One is the tendency for Groups not especially interested in a report to try and raise the bids, in order to make other Groups "pay" more for them. A second is that it is often advantageous for a Group to submit the name of a proposed rapporteur as early as possible. If the suggested rapporteur is recognized as a specialist on the issue it is easier to get agreement on his or her nomination. Certain technical issues on which there is little political controversy but on which a committee member is a specialist are again and again referred to that same specialist, often for very few points. A third feature is the general informality of the system. Trade-offs are common between Groups and there are very few formal votes to decide on rapporteurships. If a Group exceeds its total number of points a relaxed attitude is often taken by the other Groups. It is generally only for the most politically important issues that a more rigid and partisan stance is taken.

For certain major and regularly recurring reports a rotation system is sometimes developed between the Political Groups. This is especially the case for Parliament's most obviously prominent rapporteurship, that on the annual budget, which goes to the major Political Groups in turn. Similar rotations are arranged within individual committees for certain other annual reports, such as those within the Economic Committee on competition policy or the annual economic situation.

The progress of reports and opinions through a committee

Once a rapporteur is appointed he or she may proceed in a number of ways. The first element to consider is that of timing. Some legislative reports may be presented very quickly indeed, especially in such cases where the Commission or Council Presidency has indicated that the matter is an immediate priority (or even formally requested urgent treatment by the plenary), or where the Parliament itself has undertaken (which it now does to an increasing extent in the context of the annual legislative programme) to give its opinion within a certain time frame. On the other hand other reports, especially those on individual motions for a resolution, or own-initiative reports, are often less pressing, and in certain cases such a report may not be presented for a year or more.

All rapporteurships lapse at the end of the Parliamentary term of five years. Legislative consultations lapse (although this is a formality in practice: all such consultations in 1989 were re-presented by the Council immediately after direct elections), and new rapporteurs have to be appointed (or former rapporteurs reconfirmed).

Occasionally inactive rapporteurships are discontinued, where a rapporteur shows no sign of producing a text, and where the issue is no longer considered to be of political importance. This option is, of course, not available for legislative consultations where a report must be produced. Nevertheless, Parliament's Rules of Procedure lay down the possibility (Rule 119–4) for a committee to set a time limit within which a rapporteur must submit his or her draft report. Once the time limit (which may be extended) has elapsed, the committee may instruct its chairman to ask for the matter to be placed on a subsequent plenary agenda, with debates being conducted on the basis of an oral report by the committee concerned. For obvious reasons recourse to this procedure has been avoided, although there have been threats to use it within committee, and there have been clashes between rapporteurs and committee chairmen in certain cases.

Besides timing, the rapporteur must decide what assistance to obtain. Some rapporteurs rely heavily on the committee's permanent staff, who may be asked to draft a text on the basis of certain guidelines, or be given even wider latitude. Other rapporteurs (a minority) write all their reports themselves. Other possibilities include assistance from a member's research assistant, or Group, from his or her party at home, or from other organizations (such as research institutes). Background information may also be obtained from a wide range of sources, including not only the committee staff but that of Parliament's studies (research) directorate, from national governments, from employers or trade unions, from other trade associations and public interest groups, and so on. The rapporteur will in most cases also consult the Commission.

It is again worth pointing out that the resources available to rapporteurs are not very great when compared with a parliament like the US Congress. The rapporteurs and those helping them must often rely heavily on the services of the European Commission.

They must also make considerable use of information provided by lobbyists. The latter play a very valuable role in this respect, although the problem is also frequently posed as to whether a rapporteur is gaining a balanced overall picture. (These issues posed by the need for independent access to information are also discussed in Chapter 13 on scrutiny and control.)

In the course of his or her research a rapporteur may decide to consult people outside Brussels, in another country or countries of the Community or even in third countries. As pointed out in Chapter 4, each member has an allowance of 2,500 ECU per annum to be used for travel within the

Community. While this is often used by rapporteurs, they may seek to gain additional financial support from the Parliament.

A committee generally requests such support on behalf of its rapporteur, but this must then be authorised by the Bureau, which frequently rejects the requests. Requests by draftsmen of opinions are generally rejected, and rapporteurs on individual motions for a resolution are treated less generously than rapporteurs on authorised own – initiative reports or formal legislative consultations.

The actual structure of the rapporteur's text usually depends on whether it is of a legislative or non-legislative nature. A non-legislative text generally consists of a draft motion for a resolution and an explanatory statement. The motion for a resolution consists of a number of procedural citations (citing, for example, the resolution on which the report might be based, a relevant background Communication by the Commission, a list of committees drawing up the main report and any subsidiary opinions, etc.). It sometimes includes a number of factual recitals as well and concludes with a number of paragraphs giving draft conclusions on a particular problem, and calling for certain forms of action in response.

Certain phrases are used with great frequency such as "welcomes", "regrets", "deplores", "calls upon the Commission", etc. The final paragraph is again always procedural in that it calls for the resolution to be transmitted to the Commission, and Council, and sometimes to other bodies as well.

Accompanying the draft motion for a resolution ("Part A" of a report) is the explanatory statement ("Part B"), which provides the necessary background information on the problem, and outlines why certain recommendations were made. Unlike the draft motion this is not subsequently put to the vote in the committee, but is drafted by the rapporteur, who prepares it on his or her responsibility, although it is still supposed to reflect the opinion of a majority within the committee. Provision is also made in the Parliament's Rules for the addition of minority statements to an explanatory statement, although this provision is rarely used. In addition, any motion for a resolution serving as a basis for the report, or which was considered in conjunction with it, is annexed at the end.

Until the passing of the Single European Act, and Parliament's subsequent adoption of new internal rules of procedure (the Prout report, Doc. A2–131/86), all Parliament's reports followed the above model, even for legislative texts, except that these often included suggested amendments to Commission proposals before the motion for a resolution.

Parliament's new rules of procedure now provide for a different format for legislative texts. Any suggested amendments to the Commission's proposals are still put forward at the beginning of a report (in the form of a parallel text with the Commission's proposal on the left, and the Parliament's suggested amendment on the right) but the draft motion for a resolution is now of a procedural nature only, with two separate standard resolutions, the first for a proposal involving a single reading by the Parliament, the second for one involving two readings (the co-operation procedure). These standard resolutions only cover a limited number of points, such as whether Parliament approves the legal base of a proposal (this is normally a formality, but may be of considerable importance for the

Parliament, such as when it believes that a proposal should come under the co-operation procedure rather than involve a single reading only — see the discussion on this sensitive constitutional point below); approves the proposal with or without modifications, or rejects it. Other permissible procedural points include a request that Parliament be reconsulted in the event of a substantial change in a proposal or that the conciliation procedure be opened. Legislative motions for a resolution may not now include other comments of a non-procedural nature, and if so included they are now struck out. The idea is that comments must be as concrete as possible in the form of specific amendments to the draft legislation. This has proved controversial within Parliament, and some members have argued that legislative motions for a resolution should not be so rigidly limited to procedural points.

Explanatory statements to legislative reports are also prepared on the sole responsibility of the rapporteur, and not put to the vote.

Opinions are presented in a different form, beginning with the draftsman's comments (similar to but not called an explanatory statement) and finishing with a number of "conclusions". Only these conclusions are put to the vote within the committee. Suggestions may also be made to modify the Commission's proposals, often preceded by the words "calls upon the responsible committee to incorporate the following amendments to the Commission's proposal...". Once adopted, they are transmitted to the main committee, which may put its proposed amendments to the vote (but is not obliged to). Opinions are annexed to the main committee report, or else (if adopted too late), published separately.

While most reports and opinions fall into these standard patterns there are certain exceptions. Some rapporteurs are forced by time constraints to dispense with explanatory statements. This has happened quite frequently, for example, in the Agricultural Committee.

A more controversial exception has come when rapporteurs have prepared reports going beyond Parliament's traditional role, such as when they have tabled draft Community legislation rather than waiting for the Commission to do so. This has twice happened within the Legal Affairs Committee.

While many rapporteurs suggest Community legislation in their draft motions for a resolution, on these occasions a complete text was presented. These posed difficulties for the Commission, which has a monopoly over the presentation of formal Community proposals. At any rate there was no follow-up to the proposals. Another report which was exceptional in form was that of the Franz report on monetary integration, which included an annex with draft statutes for a European Central Bank.

It should also be pointed out that there are now length limits on parliamentary reports and opinions, which have been imposed because of the proliferation of such texts and consequent difficulties in ensuring translation. As a general rule motions for a resolution are not meant to exceed two pages, explanatory statements 10 pages and opinions five pages — special derogations are required to exceed these limits.

The most obvious constraint on a rapporteur, however, is that his or her report should be acceptable to a majority of members of the committee. Rapporteurs are not meant to express narrowly partisan views, whether from a national, sectoral or party political point of view. This is especially the case with regard to motions for a resolution on which the committee must formally vote. The rapporteur's own personal preferences can more easily be expressed in the explanatory statement, although even here highly partisan statements would be challenged within the committee. On several occasions rapporteurs have lost the confidence of the committee and been replaced by the chairman or another member, and on others rapporteurs have chosen to resign after their basic line has not been supported by the committee, or their basic text amended out of all recognition (as for example when Peter Beazley of the Economic Committee stood down as draftsman of an opinion on tobacco advertising in favour of Karel Pinxten after the latter's harder line anti-advertising stance had been adopted by the committee).

In spite of the near certainty of defeat within their committee, some rapporteurs nevertheless persist in expressing a minority point of view so that their position is clearly on the record. More common, however, is for a rapporteur to express a point of view which is controversial, but which still has a chance of winning a narrow majority within the committee, with the risk that this will be subsequently overturned in the plenary. As a rule committees do not have fixed majorities for left or right over the whole range of issues that they consider, but such majorities do exist for certain matters.

Whenever there is a need for a special majority in Parliament (for example assents, Second Readings, Budgets, etc.), there is more pressure on committees to try and achieve the widest possible consensus on an issue within the committee, so that the necessary majorities can be achieved in plenary.

There is clearly no one standard way in which a report goes through a committee. There are, however, a number of common stages for the majority of reports.

Unless there is particular urgency for a report, in which case these various stages are telescoped into one or two meetings (with a report sometimes being adopted at a special meeting during the plenary), there is normally a period provided for committee discussion before a draft text is produced. Typically the rapporteur will introduce the issue, and give an indication of his or her initial views, and there will then be a possibility for individual members to give their views. A representative (or representatives) of the Commission will be present, and will make a statement or answer questions about the Commission's proposals or position. This representative may be the actual specialist who drafted the proposal, or be someone higher up the Commission hierarchy. For more important issues the responsible Director-General or member of the Commission will often be present. A Commission representative will normally be present on all occasions when the issue is discussed, although problems are sometimes posed when the Committee agenda has to be changed at short notice. For a committee with a very full agenda there may be 10 to 15 Commission officials present at any one moment.

At the end of the initial discussion the rapporteur usually undertakes to produce a text by a particular time. It is also often clearer as to whether the issue is controversial within the committee or not.

Once ready the text is then sent for translation in all working languages (for which at least 10 working days is normally required), and then distributed to all members. There is then a new discussion, with committee members and the Commission commenting on the rapporteur's text. A deadline for amendments may then be set. The rapporteur may also decide to make modifications (in the form of a "corrigendum") to his or her text. Both amendments and corrigenda are sent to translation.

The committee then proceeds to vote at a subsequent meeting, first on the amendments and corrigenda, and then on the original paragraphs of the motion for a resolution as modified. Procedures are generally less formal than in the plenary session. Untranslated amendments are often permitted, especially if they have been presented in typed form, and even oral amendments are sometimes allowed, not just to permit minor improvements to a text but for major issues, especially when the chairman, rapporteur or co-ordinators put forward compromises. Voting is by show of hands, with the permitted option of standing and sitting being very rarely used. The plenary techniques of requesting roll call votes on sensitive issues, making explanations of vote, or calling for a quorum (one quarter of the members of the committee) are available to members, but are seldom used. The main reason for this is that it is felt by most members that committee meetings should retain a greater degree of informality than plenary sessions, and that procedural manoeuvres should be avoided where possible. There are, however, certain exceptions to this, such as in the Political Affairs Committee, where roll call votes are occasionally requested.

A proposal that electronic voting systems be installed in committees as well was rejected by the Bureau of Parliament, on the grounds both of cost and lack of necessity.

Once a report has been adopted within a committee it is then collated by the committee secretariat (including any opinions received from other committees) and sent for final translation in all the languages. It is then submitted to plenary as a sessional document (in the A series of documents).

The treatment of committee reports in plenary is described in Chapter 8 on plenary sessions. Legislative texts under the co-operation procedure are voted upon by the Wednesday of the plenary session, and other texts at any other moment of the week. Those non-controversial topics which are dealt with by the procedure without report (see above), by simplified procedure or without debate (in both cases see below), are adopted by the Parliament. The resolutions (and any legislative amendments) are forwarded to the Commission and Council (and often to Member States' governments and parliaments as well), as the opinion of the Parliament. These are published in the Official Journal of the Communities. The actual committee report with its explanatory statement is not re-issued.

For non-legislative texts, or for legislative texts involving only one reading, that is generally the end of the procedure as far as a committee is concerned. On the other hand, in reports involving the co-operation procedure, where there are two readings by the Parliament, the committee's rapporteur continues to follow developments between the two readings, and may bring the issue up again within the competent committee at any time. Once the Council has adopted a common position this is announced in the plenary, and is then placed on the next agenda of the competent committee. The committee then adopts a recommendation in second reading, which must be adopted by the plenary within a maximum of three months (or four months if the Council agrees) of the common position being announced.

The other ways in which a committee's involvement in a specific report can be maintained over a longer period are when a report is referred back from the plenary to the committee, or when reconsultation of the Parliament is requested.

Another device used by committees which wish to have Parliament pronounce on a certain issue, but do not want to produce a final report until a later date, is to come up with an interim report, which has proved to be another means of raising issues, and giving an interim Parliament view on an issue, without ending the committee's (and Parliament's) involvement in an issue.

Alternative committee procedures

Parliament has an increasingly full agenda. Every encouragement has thus been given to committees in recent years to adopt alternative procedures to the classic ones mentioned above, in order to lighten Parliament's agenda, and notably to deal with technical legislation.

The first such technique is the procedure without report, which was described above. A second technique is the so-called simplified procedure, where the committee chairman is appointed rapporteur (unless four members object to the procedure). A report is then drawn up and sent out the committee's members. Unless four members object within 14 days of the date of dispatch, the report is considered to be adopted, and is then sent to plenary without having been examined in committee. Both these techniques thus save committee and plenary time. A third technique is when a committee adopts a report and requests that it be adopted by the plenary without debate. This clearly only saves plenary rather than committee time. The procedure without report and the report without debate, are techniques which are frequently used by committees. The simplified procedure is much more rarely used.

The most controversial of all these techniques has been Rule 37 of Parliament's Rules of Procedure, which provides for a report to be adopted directly by a committee on behalf of the Parliament and without involving a vote in plenary. This rule was originally derived from legislative practice in the Italian Parliament.

A request for the power to take a decision on a particular issue to be delegated to the appropriate committee is normally made by the committee itself, but can also be made by the President of Parliament or by a minimum of twenty three members. The plenary must then decide on this request, and if one tenth of the Members of Parliament object to use of this procedure then the decision cannot be delegated to the committee concerned. Subsequently, its use can also be blocked in committee if one of its members call for the issue to be referred back to the plenary.

If the Rule 37 procedure is applied, the report then proceeds through the committee in the normal way, except that the committee meeting where the final decision is taken must be held in conditions akin to the plenary. The meeting must be open to the public, and the agenda must be published in the Parliament's own Bulletin. Any Member of Parliament can table amendments to the report, but only committee members and permanent substitutes can vote on these amendments.

Once adopted in committee, the report is then placed on the next plenary agenda and is considered to be adopted without a vote, unless there is an objection in writing from one tenth of the current members of Parliament belonging to at least three Political Groups.

Until late 1988 Rule 37 only applied to legislative reports, and was practically never used by committees. By the end of the 1984–89 Parliament, however, it was apparent that the plenary workload was becoming increasingly heavy, and it was decided to encourage much greater use of Rule 37. In October 1988 Parliament decided to extend the use of the Rule to non-legislative reports on members resolutions, and to own-initiative reports. A considerable number of reports were subsequently adopted in committee under this rule.

In the early part of the 1989–94 Parliament, the use of this rule again practically ceased, but it will almost certainly play a renewed role towards the end of the legislature.

Treatment of confidential documents in committee

The Parliament is generally a very open institution. Not only are many of its committee meetings open to the public, but even draft reports are rather freely available. As the Parliament becomes more powerful, however, and hence more closely involved in sensitive issues once restricted to Commission and Council, the need for confidentiality in certain cases has become more important.

The problem became particularly apparent in Parliament's Committee on Budgetary Control, which needed to consult confidential documents in the course of its duties. An agreement on handling these documents was then negotiated between the Commission and the Parliament, and adopted by Parliament in February 1989. As a result a new Annex VII was added to Parliament 's Rules of Procedure laying down criteria for the consideration of confidential documents communicated to the European Parliament. Individual members may also request application of these procedures to a particular document, but this request must then be accepted by a majority of two-thirds of the members present.

When the confidential procedure is to be applied, attendance at the relevant part of the committee meeting is restricted (to members of the committee, and only those officials and experts who have been designated in advance by the chairman and whose presence is strictly necessary). The relevant documents are distributed at the meeting, but collected again at the end, and no notes of their contents or photocopies may be taken. Procedures are laid down for breach of confidentiality, and the committee chairman can set down any penalties, which include reprimand, or a short-term or even permanent exclusion from a committee (with a possibility of appeal to a joint meeting of Parliament's Enlarged Bureau, and the Bureau of the relevant committee).

Since the introduction of these procedures confidential meetings have been held not only by the Committee on Budgetary Control, but also by the Committee on the Rules of Procedure, the Verification of Credentials and Immunities, when it has been dealing with issues of whether to waive a member's immunity.

Confidential meetings are now also likely to be held on a regular basis within the Economic Committee, as a result of an agreement reached between the Commission and Council in February 1990, when the Commission agreed to inform the Parliament on this basis of its work on surveillance of Member States' economies. This is in the context of increased co-ordination of Member States' economic policies, in the first phase of Economic and Monetary Union, and might include sensitive reports or recommendations aimed at a single Member State.

Another area where committees may apply these procedures more in the future is in the field of international agreements, for example, where sensitive political or commercial issues are being discussed.

Other activities of committees besides the preparation of reports

Committees have a number of other activities besides their bread and butter business of consideration and adoption of reports and opinions, such as meetings with members of the Commission and Council, representatives of national parliaments, or of other bodies and committee hearings. These are described in more detail in Chapter 13 below.

Certain committees have experimented with a number of other techniques and activities, such as the use of committee monitors on particular issues, who are meant to report back to the other members of the committee on the policy area within their responsibility.

A recent initiative of the Energy Committee has been to launch the STOA Project, which is described in Chapter 14 below.

Co-ordination of committee activities

As has been indicated on several occasions above, the committees of the European Parliament are by no means homogeneous in their activities and working methods. There is, however, a need for them to adopt a co-ordinated approach to certain common problems, to indicate their priorities for plenary agendas and the annual legislative programme and so on. The main way in which this is achieved is through the regular meetings of committee chairmen, which take place shortly after the plenary agenda has been finally set on the Monday evening of each plenary session. These meetings have taken place since 1981, and are chaired by a senior committee chairman. In the 1984-89 Parliament this task was carried out by Michel Poniatowski of the Energy Committee, and in the present Parliament by Henri Saby of the Development Committee. The chairman of the meeting of committee chairmen also attends the meeting of the Enlarged Bureau when it is setting the next plenary agenda.

The establishment of specific structures within or outside the existing committee framework to tackle particular policy problems

The committee structure is generally a flexible one, capable of responding to new policy problems that emerge. There are times, however, when strong pressure is exerted to create new structures, either within the existing committee framework (such as subcommittees or more informal working parties) or else outside it (such as Committees of Inquiry or Temporary Committees).

Within the standing committee framework

(i) Subcommittees

The European Parliament does not have the complex system of subcommittees that has been established within the US Congress, for example. As pointed out above, the Parliament has been reluctant to create too many new permanent bodies, in view of constraints of staff numbers and on members' time, as well as of other factors.

Nevertheless, a few subcommittees have been established, two within the Political Affairs Committee (on Human Rights and on Security and Disarmament), one within the Committee on Agriculture, Fisheries and Food (on Fisheries), and one within the Committee on Youth, Culture, Education, Information and Sport (on Information). These subcommittees all deal with longer-term problem areas. Their membership is drawn exclusively from the committee which set them up, and their meetings are held in conjunction with (normally immediately before or after) those of the parent committee.

(ii) Working parties

Far more working parties than subcommittees have been set up by Parliament's committees, the main reasons being that the former are easier to establish (they generally have no official status, and require no prior authorisation from Parliament's leadership) and also to discontinue, and because they enable committees to respond in a rapid and informal way not only to longer-term problems, but also to shorter-term issues.

While the majority of working parties have been established by individual committees, it is also possible for the Parliament as a whole to authorise the creation of a working party, as happened with the working party within the Agriculture Committee on the Monitoring of Milk Quotas. In such a case a working party can benefit from "official status", with the advantages of full interpretation, in particular.

Since direct elections in 1979, around 25 working parties have been established within no less than 11 committees of the Parliament. They have differed greatly in duration and public profile. Some have been of lengthy duration, e.g. Human Rights 1980–84; Fisheries 1977–85, both of which subsequently became subcommittees; Technical Barriers to Trade 1980–84; Milk Quotas 1984–89; while others have been linked instead to particular events (e.g. those on the Conference on Security and Co-operation in Europe 1979–80, on the Conference of the Regions 1982–84, on the 1986 Year of the Environment, on Lome III 1982–84). One of them has evolved into a different type of body (the STOA working party, see above). Another was primarily an exercise in the raising of public consciousness on a policy issue (the 1980 working party on Hunger in the World). Many others have been set up to help tackle a particular Community policy problem (e.g. several of the seven working parties set up within the Budgets Committee, such as those on Own Resources in 1979–80, the Financial Regulation in 1980, Budgetary Discipline in 1985–86 and Future Financing 1986–89).

Outside the standing committee framework

(i)   Committees of inquiry

Parliament's rules permit the establishment of committees of inquiry to investigate alleged contraventions of Community law or instances of maladministration with respect to Community responsibilities, though in practice they may have wider remits. Such a committee may consist of no more than 15 members and must conclude its work within a specified period not exceeding nine months. Such committees gather evidence, hold public hearings and publish the results which are submitted to Parliament. However, they may not submit any motion for a resolution to Parliament (thus putting them in a different position from temporary committees — see below). If Parliament wishes to take a stand on the issues concerned, it must do so in the context of its regular work or else engineer a resolution to wind up a debate on an oral question to the Commission and/or Council on the results of the work of the committee.

The establishment of a committee of inquiry is a minority right: one quarter of the members of Parliament may request such a committee to be set up. However, if the majority objects strongly to a committee of inquiry, it is always in a position to block its effective establishment by refusing to submit the nominations of members to sit on the committee or by blocking a decision in the Enlarged Bureau on the latter's proposal to plenary regarding the committee's composition. This fate befell an attempt in 1984 to create a committee of inquiry on the right to strike and the use of police force, requested by Labour members at the time of the UK miners' strike.

So far seven committees of inquiry have been set up by Parliament since direct elections. Their subject matter and the nature of their impacts is described in Chapter 14 below.

(ii)   Temporary committees

A rare device has been to set up a temporary committee on a matter of major topical concern. They are more powerful than committees of inquiry. Their powers, composition and term of office are more flexible. While their term of office is initially for 12 months, this can be prolonged. They can also submit interim and final reports on which Parliament formally vote.

The first use of this procedure was in 1983. Parliament had commissioned two prominent outside experts, Michel Albert and James Ball, to produce a report for the Parliament on ways to stimulate European economic development. The Parliament then set up a temporary special Committee on European Economic Recovery to provide the necessary follow-up to the Albert–Ball report. This exercise helped to launch the notion of the "cost of non-Europe" (i.e. the cost to the tax payer, consumer and businessman of the continuing fragmentation of the Community's internal market), which served to stimulate the 1992 internal market programme.

There was also an interim special Committee on Budgetary Affairs in 1984, and a further temporary Committee in 1987 to co-ordinate Parliament's view on the Commission's proposals on "Making a success of the Single Act". Lord Plumb, the President of Parliament at the time, chaired the committee which had two co-rapporteurs, Enrique Barón (the current President) from the Socialist Group and Karl von Wogau from the PPE Group.

The most recent example, however, is the Temporary Committee on the Impacts on the European Community of German Unification which was set up in February 1990, with 25 members, with Fernandez Albor (Spanish, PPE) as Chairman, and with Alan Donnelly (UK Labour Party) as its general rapporteur. The Committee is commissioning internal and external studies on the impacts, holding hearings in Brussels, Bonn and Berlin, and preparing interim and final reports.

Interparliamentary delegations

One of Parliament's chief ways of developing and maintaining close links with countries outside the European Community (apart from those within the ACP framework, for which special structures have been devised) is through its interparliamentary delegations (see Table 5).

Number and composition

The first of the interparliamentary delegations, that for relations with the USA, was established in 1972. The number of such delegations has grown considerably over the years, and by 1990 there were 26 delegations.

Some delegations — e.g. those for relations with the Maghreb and Mashrek countries, Cyprus and Malta — were set up as a direct result of the co-operation agreements between the EC and the countries concerned, which called for the "facilitation" of the "necessary co-operation and contacts" between the Parliament and the parliamentary bodies of the partner countries. Others resulted from initiatives taken by bodies like the Japanese Diet, which itself proposed a regular parliamentary exchange following a visit to Tokyo in 1978 of Parliament's President Colombo. Korea mounted a major diplomatic effort in 1985 and 1986 with a view to having its parliament accepted as a "partner" in the Parliament's system of inter-parliamentary delegations (it succeeded).

In other cases, it has been Parliament itself that has proposed the establishment of interparliamentary links. Following the 1979 direct elec-

Table 5:   *Delegations, with number of members and chairmen (March 1990)*

Delegation	*Membership*	*Chairman*
Europe		
Sweden, Finland, Iceland and Nordic Council	10	C. Rovsing (Danish Conservative, EDG)
Norway	10	H. McMahon British Labour, SOC)
Switzerland	8	G. Topmann (German SPD, SOC)
Austria	10	K. H. Mihr (German SPD, SOC)
Yugoslavia	10	P. Avgerinos (Greek PASOK, SOC)
GDR and Czechoslovakia	10	K. Jensen (Danish Social Democrat, SOC)
South-Eastern Europe	9	M. Aglietta (Italian, Green)
Soviet Union	22	M. Hoff (German SPD, SOC)
Malta	8	A. Michelini (Italian DC, EPP)
Cyprus	10	Sir James Scott-Hopkins (British Conservative, EDG)
Poland	11	E. Punset I. Casals (Spanish CDS, LDR)
Hungary	11	O. Habsburg (German CSU, EPP)
North Africa and Middle East		
Maghreb countries (Algeria, Morocco and Tunisia)	12	C. Cheysson (French Socialist, SOC)
Mashreq countries (Egypt, Jordan, Lebanon and Syria)	11	D. Nianias (Greek DIANA, RDE)
Israel	13	R. Imbeni (Italian Communists — United European Left)
Gulf States	10	A. Bonetti (Italian DC, EPP)
The Americas		
USA	26	G. Hoon (British Labour, SOC)
Canada	13	G. de Vries (Dutch VVD, LDR)
South America	25	M. Medina Ortega (Spanish PSOE, SOC)
Central America and Mexico	25	F. Suárez (Spanish Popular Party, EPP)
Asia and Australia		
South Asia (and South Asian Association for Regional Cooperation)	14	G. Stevenson (British Labour, SOC)
Members States of ASEAN and the ASEAN Interparliamentary Organization (AIPO) and the Republic of Korea	20	G. Rinsche (German CDU, EPP)
People's Republic of China	18	E. Bettiza (Italian PSI, SOC)
Japan	18	B. Sälzer (German CDU, EPP)
Australia and New Zealand	14	P. Lambrias (Green ND, EPP)
International Organizations		
United Nations	9	J. Gawronski (Italian PRI, LDR)

Besides the above committees there is also a delegation to Turkey, which has a separate status from the above interparliamentary delegations, in that it is an EEC–Turkey Joint Parliamentary Committee set up under the Association Agreement between Turkey and the Community. It has 18 members, and is chaired by Alman Metten (Dutch PvDA, Socialist Group).

tions, Parliament began setting up its delegations at the same time as its committees, by way of formal decisions taken after the elections and again at mid-term. These decisions lay down the total number of and areas of responsibility of delegations. On the basis of proposals put forward by the Group leaders, Parliament also establishes the number of members within each delegation, which can vary considerably from delegation to delegation (the current range is from eight members for the delegations to Malta and Switzerland up to 26 members for the delegation to the United States). There are currently 375 places available for members on all the delegations.

The composition of each delegation is meant to ensure a spread of representation of both Member States and of political views. Members are elected during the first part-session following the re-election of Parliament, and again two-and-a-half years later. They can be nominated to serve on the delegations by the political groups, the Non-Attached Members, or at least 13 members.

Unlike for committees, members who have been elected to delegations cannot be replaced by substitutes. If they are prevented from regular attendance they are meant to stand down and a new member chosen to take their place on a permanent basis.

Leadership

Each delegation is led by a chairman and two vice-chairmen. The procedure for choosing these officers used to differ from that for Parliament's standing committees in that they were appointed by the Political Groups on a proportional basis (using the d'Hondt system) rather than being elected by the committee members (although since the latter were normally elected by acclamation there was little difference in practice).

In 1989, however, there was intense controversy over this system of appointment of delegation chairmen and vice-chairmen, after members of the Technical Group of the Right were chosen to be chairman of the delegation to Switzerland and vice-chairman of the delegation to Israel (with the Technical Group of the Right itself putting forward a German *Republikaner* nominee for the latter post). These nominations were unpopular with the countries concerned, and were also successfully challenged from within the Parliament itself, to the anger of the Technical Group of the Right (see section on Order of the Chamber in Chapter 8).

Parliament has now amended its Rules to provide for election of the chairmen and vice-chairmen of the delegations by the delegations' own members rather than by appointment.

Role of delegations

The delegations have a range of tasks. The most obvious of these is to ensure dialogue with parliamentary bodies in third countries or in regional organizations such as ASEAN or the Andean Pact (with a new precedent being set in 1989 with the establishment of a delegation for relations with the United Nations). The delegations' other formally defined tasks are to exchange information on topical issues and research of special interest, and to provide parliamentary backing for the Community's external policies.

Besides contacts with parliaments they also have contacts with third country governments and other representatives.

The delegations also serve to provide a network of contacts for members of the European Parliament among parliamentarians from other countries. Particular friendships, for example, have been forged between MEPs and their equivalents in the US Congress.

Another particularly valuable function of delegations is to examine the situation in a third country prior to developments of particular importance to the Community, such as a possible accession of a third country to the Community, or conclusion of an association agreement, or simply prior to the discussion of the political situation in a country or region within the Parliament. The European Parliament delegations, for example, have regularly monitored the situation as regards observance of human rights in Turkey, an applicant country to the Community, and have also observed the conduct of elections in numerous countries in the world after democracy has been re-established in those countries. The delegations have been very active, for example, in Latin America (where ad hoc delegations have also been sent, such as one to Uruguay in1984 or to Bolivia), and now in Eastern Europe, for which no less than four delegations were established in 1989 (five if the Soviet Union is also counted). The Parliament delegation, for example, to the GDR and Czechoslovakia, observed the GDR's first democratic election on March 18, 1990.

Delegations have also been able to play a role in resolving problems between the Community and third countries. A recent example was over visas with the United States, where visitors from Europe had to have such visas, whereas Americans in Europe normally did not. The Parliament's US delegation had a major role in persuading the US Justice Department to set up a pilot scheme aimed at ending this anomaly.

In the past there have even been joint legislative initiatives between European parliamentarians and those in a third country. The most striking of these initiatives came before direct elections, with the development of the so-called Lange-Gibbons code for Multinational Corporations, named after the respective chairmen of the European Parliament's delegation to the United States (Erwin Lange of the German SPD) and the US Congress delegation to the Parliament (Sam Gibbons, a Florida Democrat). The contents of the proposed code of conduct for Multinational Corporations were developed and discussed by the two delegations. The European Parliament later adopted a resolution noting the proposed code (which was annexed to the resolution), and it was directly submitted as draft legislation within the US Congress (although it did not subsequently make any progress).

Working methods

Each delegation generally has a once-yearly meeting in the country or countries for which it is responsible. Parliamentarians or other representatives of that country reciprocate by visiting the Parliament in Strasbourg or in Brussels. The US delegation has had twice-yearly meetings with the US Congress since 1972, alternatively in the United States and once within the European Community.

In addition to these regular visits of the entire delegation, preparatory meetings are also held in Brussels and Strasbourg, at which the agendas of the visits and the issues to be raised are discussed by the members of the delegation. Ambassadors of third countries accredited to the EC, as well as commissioners and other Commission officials, are often invited to these meetings to brief members on relations with the countries concerned and on specific economic or political problems. Finally, ad hoc delegations, or the chairmen and/or vice-chairmen of the delegations, may visit a particular country to respond to a particular political event. Unlike the delegations' regular visits, these latter meetings require special authorisation from Parliament's leadership.

Parliament has adopted strict rules to restrict attendance at delegations' meetings outside the Community, and to keep their costs down. Members from outside the delegation are only very rarely authorised to join in these meetings, and spouses do not form part of the official delegation. Staff members are kept down, and the number of working languages is restricted whenever possible. Finally, members of a delegation themselves may only attend an external meeting if they have been regular attenders at preparatory meetings or other meetings at Parliament's normal working places.

Attempts are also made to ensure co-ordination between the various delegations and Parliament's standing committees. A committee chairman or rapporteur may be authorised to join a delegation visit. Much more common, however, is for committees to be associated with delegation meetings within the Parliament's working places, and especially Strasbourg. When a group of parliamentarians from a third country visits Strasbourg, periods of an hour or more are often set aside for joint discussions between them and members of Parliament's relevant committees, to discuss, for example, agricultural or trade issues.

Parliament's delegations generally operate in an informal way, and are thus not subject to too many political constraints. They must, however, closely reflect the Parliament's resolutions and policy positions when they seek to make any formal declarations during interparliamentary meetings.

Working documents drawn up for delegations must also follow this same rule, as must those members who are appointed as lead speakers for the delegation on any particular policy issue. Delegations are thus foreclosed from issuing unilateral statements or bilateral communiques which might contradict Parliament's adopted policy positions. Members expressing a purely personal or Political Group point of view are meant to make this clear.

The delegations do not formally adopt reports for the attention of parliament as a whole. The delegation chairmen, however, report to

Parliament's leadership on the outcome of the delegation meetings, and may, if necessary, make a statement at the plenary. This latter is very rare. They may also appear in person before individual committees of the Parliament, to report on interparliamentary contacts they have had, or to be briefed by such committees prior to meetings with partner parliamentarians.

The work of the delegations is prepared by a small group of permanent officials from the Parliament (five A Administrators, three B Assistants and five C Secretaries), who work within the Directorate-General for Committees and Delegations.

Finally, as the role and number of delegations increases, their functioning has had to be subject to greater forward-planning, and to more formalised rules. The activities of the delegations are now co-ordinated by a Committee of Chairmen of Interparliamentary Delegations, among whose duties is to draw up a calendar of future interparliamentary meetings. Parliament has also drawn up a set of implementing rules for the functioning of delegations, building on and formalising the practices developed within the delegations over the last few years.

ACP–EEC Joint Assembly

Parliament's day-to-day relations with developing countries, including those within the ACP framework (African, Caribbean and Pacific countries with especially close links to the Community through the successive Lomé Conventions), are carried out by its permanent Committee on Development and Co-operation. In addition to these contacts, however, there is also a wider body, the ACP–EEC Joint Assembly that was established by the Lomé Convention. Since its twice-yearly meetings involve 136 participants, this is on a much larger scale than Parliament's committees or delegations, and is in a category of its own. Its workings are described in more detail in Chapter 13.

8. Plenary sessions

Parliament's plenaries (formally part-sessions of an annual session), are currently convened for a week each month in Strasbourg (see Chapter 3). The present chapter starts off by examining the setting for each plenary (what it looks like, the seating of members and participation of Commission and Council, staff, press and public) and then outlines the typical timetable of a session. It then looks in more detail at the conduct of plenary sessions, how the agenda is drawn up, the organization of debates, voting procedures, order in the chamber, common procedural manoeuvres, and how the session is recorded. It concludes by reviewing some common criticisms of the functioning of plenary sessions, and the possibilities for reform.

The background setting

The plenary sessions proper take place in the striking debating chamber or "hemicycle" of the Council of Europe (where the latter's Parliamentary Assembly also meets, although less often). The shape of the chamber is a compromise between the different national parliamentary traditions. In the UK House of Commons, government and "opposition" representing opposite extremes face each other across a central alley; in the German *Bundestag* members face the front in rows and speeches are made from a podium; while the French *Assemblee Nationale* sits in a semi-circle in the traditional continental model. In the European Parliament members sit in a horseshoe-shaped chamber, with 11 rows fanning out from a central hollow. The opposite ends of the political spectrum do indeed face each other, but the bulk of members face the front at various angles (see plan of the chamber on p. xxi). Each MEP is allocated a fixed numbered seat in the chamber with a desk, a place to keep documents, and slots to insert his or her voting card (see below).

The MEPs sit in the chamber according to their political Group (before 1958 they sat alphabetically). The Group chairmen sit in the front row allocated to the Group. Next to them or immediately behind them are the vice-chairmen and members of the bureau of the Group (normally the leaders of the national delegations within the group). Behind these are the other members of the Group, seated in alphabetical order. Five of the Groups have their chairmen sitting in the front row of the hemicycle (the Socialists with five in the front row, the European People's Party (EPP) with four, the Liberals with two, the European Democratic Group with two and the Group of the United European Left one. The other five groups are situated further back in the chamber, along with the members not attached to any Group.

The actual location of the Groups within the chamber is fairly straight forward, with the Left Unity Group and the Group of the United European Left on the far left of the hemicycle (from the perspective of the President on his dais), with the Socialists occupying the next block of seats (with the Greens and Rainbow Groups behind them). On the far right of the chamber is the European Democratic Group (conservatives), with the Technical Group of the European Right behind them. The next Group are the Liberals, followed by the EPP (who are thus next to the Socialists). Behind the EPP is the Group of the European Democratic Alliance. The non-attached members (Independents) are in the back row in the centre.

This seating plan has generally not proved to be too controversial. In the past, however, there was a problem with the seating of the Liberal Group (LDR), which used to be on the far right of the hemicycle beyond the European Democratic Group. The Group leadership protested, and some wanted the Group to be located between the EPP and the Socialists. In the end, however, the Group was moved just one place over, between the European Democratic Group and the EPP.

Besides the seats allocated to the members (more seats had to be put in after the enlargement of the Community, and further enlargement could pose real problems), there are a few other seats in the main body of the chamber. A row of seats on the left are allocated for the Council, with one seat for a representative from each of the Member States. The seats in the front row are allocated for the relevant Minister from the country currently holding the Council Presidency, and his or her advisers (although the Minister only attends in person for some of the time).

A row of seats on the right (and directly opposite the Council) are reserved for the members of the European Commission, with its President occupying one of the seats in the front. The Commissioners are there to reply to the debate, respond in question time, make declarations, and so on. While every effort is made to ensure that Commissioners are present to respond to debates affecting their own portfolio, this is not always the case, and in practice a rota of Commissioners is established (especially for night sessions and the end of the week), so that one Commissioner deals with all the business on that occasion.

At the back of the hemicycle a very limited number of other seats are reserved for the Political Group staff (one each), and for those Parliament officials whose duties (such as assisting rapporteurs, or following votes on their Committee's reports) require their presence in the chamber. (Staff and members can also listen to proceedings on monitors in their offices. There are screens at various locations throughout Parliament's buildings which show what debate is in progress, and who are the next speakers.)

Facing the members are a podium and two rows of seats. The podium is in practice only used for addresses to the Parliament by distinguished visitors (such as Heads of State), since MEPs and the representatives of the Commission and the Council speak from their allocated seats.

On the dais, on the higher of the two rows of seats, sits the presiding officer of the Parliament, the President of the Parliament (who opens the session on Monday afternoon, and is in the chair for the most important debates and ceremonial occasions), or one of the Vice-Presidents, who take it in turns to chair the sitting (the only exception being the first session following direct elections and before the election of the President, when the chair is taken by the oldest member).

The presiding officer is flanked by the Secretary-General of the Parliament (on all important occasions) and by other administrators from Parliament's Directorate-General for Sessional Services, who advise the President on difficult procedural points, and on matters concerned with the running of the session. Other officials in the top row of seats keep tallies on the number of speakers in each debate, and advise members as to how long a debate is scheduled to last, and roughly when they will be called upon to speak.

In the lower row of seats are those officials (from Parliament's linguistic services), who keep track of the proceedings for the minutes and daily record of events. On ceremonial occasions, these seats are occupied by the Vice-Presidents.

Access to the main chamber is not open to members of the public. Access is controlled by Parliament's ushers, who wear a special uniform, and who also carry out other tasks in the chamber, such as transmitting messages to or from members, or assisting the President if there is disorder in or immediately outside the chamber.

The public are entitled to follow the sessions, however, from a gallery which is also shared with the press. Seating is normally available, apart from on special occasions, such as when a Head of State is speaking. All Parliament's plenary sessions are held in public, unless Parliament decides otherwise by a two-thirds majority, which has never happened.

Even higher up are two smaller galleries, for television crews and technicians, and for those officials from Parliament's information services, whose job it is to follow the sessions.

As in national parliaments, members of the public looking down at the hemicycle may only see a handful of members and wonder where everyone else is (this issue is discussed in more detail later). The likelihood is that most of the members are present in Strasbourg (at least in mid-week) but are working in their offices or taking part in another meeting, of their Committee, a Bureau or Quaestors' meeting, a meeting of their Political Group or of an intergroup and ad hoc working parties. There are, thus, a number of other large and small meeting rooms scattered around the Parliament's premises in Strasbourg. The two largest, the rooms for the Socialist and EPP groups in the IPE I building, are like miniature hemicycles in their own right. Other large rooms are on the second floor of the Palais building (the "hemicycle" is on the first floor, at the top of a sweeping staircase from the main entrance), and in the IPE II building. Each Political Group has its own meeting room, but which can be allocated for other purposes when it is free.

A member may also be addressing a visitors' group, from his or her constituency or elsewhere, and there are also rooms available for that purpose. Members often drop in to the press room, which is on the ground floor of the Palais, although a purpose-built new building is about to be constructed.

Another frequently used space is the "lobby" immediately outside the hemicycle, which members must traverse when leaving the chamber en route to their offices or to the bar, or to pick up documents from their letter-boxes or from Parliament's distribution service. The benches on the edge of this space are often occupied by lobbyists, members of the usually Brussels-based trade associations, or the press, and are also used for meetings between Parliament officials and members. An increasing number of television interviews are conducted outside the hemicycle, and national news broadcasts have even been made there.

As in all parliaments the bars are also important meeting places, such as the conveniently located circular Members' Bar near the hemicycle, the so-called "Chauffeurs' bar" and the "Swan Bar".

The typical timetable of a session

Parliament business begins on Monday afternoon, generally with short meetings of the Political Groups, to discuss last-minute changes in the agenda, issues for that day's business, and so on.

The formal session in the hemicycle opens at 5:00 pm, when the President (who presides in person at this stage) makes a number of announcements (this is when the President would make important proce-dural statements, announcing the arrival of a new member or the death of another, or that he has sent a message of sympathy to victims of a disaster, or of congratulations, as, for example, on the release of Nelson Mandela, etc.). A number of other procedural declarations (such as which proposals for legislation have been referred to which Parliamentary Committee) are normally not read out in full, but are included instead in the minutes of that day's session.

At the beginning of the plenary agenda there are also often a number of points of order from individual members, about constituency or other matters. While these are limited to three minutes per member they can sometimes lead to a mini-debate being started, and cumulatively they can take up a considerable amount of time.

The next and also often lengthy task is the final fixing of the plenary agenda, with Political Groups or numbers of members sometimes trying to make further modifications. Only when this is completed does debate begin on individual committee reports. If there is a report on whether to lift a member's Parliamentary immunity (see Chapter 4), this is always taken on Monday. Monday's session is over by 8:00 pm.

Tuesday's session is now normally the longest of the week, running from 9:00 am to 1:00 pm, from 3:00 pm to 7:00 pm, and then from 9:00 pm to midnight. Until after direct elections there were no limits to the number or duration of night sittings, but experience with one or two extremely long sittings (e.g. when Pannella and others were filibustering on the issue of raising the number of members to form a Political Group) led to an agreement to limit the number of night sessions to one per week, and to finish them by midnight. From 1979 to 1987 these night sessions were generally held on Thursdays, but in 1987 they were moved forward to Tuesday, in order to allow debates on legislation requiring special majorities under the Single European Act to be taken earlier in the week, and thus to permit votes at a time when the maximum of members were present (only on very rare occasions when Parliament was trying to clear its agenda before direct elections have two night sittings been held).

Tuesday's agenda begins with votes on whether to accept Commission or Council requests for urgent procedure to be applied by Parliament on particular pieces of legislation. The chairman of the committee responsible is normally called upon to give his or her view, and there can be a speaker in favour, and one against. If urgency is then adopted by Parliament, the item is usually placed on the Friday's agenda, and if the relevant committee has not already presented its report on the subject, it will have to hold a special meeting in order to debate and adopt it in the course of the plenary week.

The rest of Tuesday's agenda has few particularly distinctive features, although as mentioned above, legislative reports are given priority. There is usually a voting time at 12:00 noon, but only on reports on which the debate has already closed, and which do not require special majorities.

Early on in the afternoon there is usually question time to the Council and to Foreign Ministers in the context of European Political Co-operation. This would typically last for one hour and a half.

Each Council presidency introduces its priorities at the beginning of its term of office, and sums up its achievements at the end. The Commission also presents its annual work programme at the beginning of each year. Debates on Commission and Council statements of this kind thus occur during at least five plenary sessions a year and usually take place on Tuesdays or Wednesdays.

Wednesday's agenda lasts from 9:00 am to 1:00 pm, and from 3:00 pm to 8:00 pm. It often begins with votes on any objections to the list of debates on topical and urgent subjects of major importance (this procedure is described in greater detail below). The agenda also includes a second one and a half-hour period of question time, this time addressed to the Commission. There is also sometimes a second period of voting time, at 12:00 noon (again on texts not requiring special majorities). The most important voting time, however, which can often last a considerable period of time, is that held at 5:00 pm. This includes the key second reading votes under the Co-operation procedure which require absolute majorities of Parliament's current members (260 votes) in order to amend or reject Council's position. This is thus the moment when the highest regular turn out of members must be achieved.

Thursday's agenda begins at 10:00 am to allow the Political Groups to meet at 9:00 am, and lasts till 1:00 pm, and from 3:00 pm to 8:00 pm. Although the debates on topical and urgent subjects of major importance have occasionally been held at other times, these are most typically held on Thursday morning, and take up the whole of the morning agenda. The votes on the individual topics are taken immediately after each debate.

The rest of Thursday's agenda often includes debates carried over from Wednesday or even Tuesday's agenda. There is one other long voting time on Thursday, beginning at 6:30 pm, and lasting until 8:00 pm or even beyond. Turnout of members is already often lower by this stage, especially if the subject matter is less controversial.

Friday's agenda again begins at 9:00 am and goes on as long as is necessary to finish the remaining items unless they are postponed to a subsequent plenary. Friday's agenda may thus last for only a short time, or go on until 1:00 pm or even later. Ironically many of the members present on the final morning are those from remote destinations, such as the United Kingdom or Ireland, whose most practical way of returning to their country is to take the special plane which only leaves at around 2:00 pm or at the end of the session.

The Friday session begins with votes on those legislative proposals which have been taken without report, and on reports without debate (see Chapter 7), followed by votes on other reports on which the debate has closed. Once this continuous voting time is over, the agenda continues with the remaining debates. Resolutions are then put to the vote at the end of each debate.

The typical week described above refers only to the activities in plenary. Parallel to this, and as mentioned above, are numerous meetings of the Political Groups, intergroups and of committees and delegations, etc.

How the plenary agenda is drawn up

Unlike some national Parliaments, the European Parliament is master of its own agenda. It may discuss (or not) what it likes, when it likes, and according to its own priorities. It co-operates, of course, with the other Community institutions in dealing with proposals for Community legislation, and they in turn have a vested interest in co-operating with Parliament in order to ensure smooth passage of proposals. Only in the second reading of the Co-operation procedure and in the budget is Parliament bound by a formal deadline.

The drawing up of the plenary agenda is therefore a long and elaborate process. Informal meetings are held between the officials of Parliament's committees to monitor progress on reports within committees, and to see which items are likely to be ready, or should be ready for forthcoming plenaries. The meeting of committee chairmen which is held early on the late Monday evening of every session provides a more formal opportunity for stock-taking as regards preparations for subsequent plenaries, and to discuss which reports are ready, and which reports will have to be accelerated or held back. The Political Groups also provide input.

Now that the European Parliament is more of a legislature than it was, there are increasing constraints on what can be included on an agenda. Parliament may undertake to give a legislative proposal priority, and where possible, to deal with it within a certain time-frame within the context of the annual legislative programme (see Chapter 11) established with the Commission and Council.

Parliament has other commitments of an even more formal nature imposed by the fact that it must consider Council common positions in the Co-operation procedure within three (or maximum of four) months of their official receipt. Legislative items are thus given priority on Parliament's agenda.

The Commission and the Council also try to influence Parliament's agenda, most obviously through the mechanism of requests for urgent treatment of a particular proposal. A majority of these requests are rejected by the Parliament unless the Committee concerned is in agreement with the request (usually when it is of a minor or technical nature).

Once all of the factors have been taken into account a draft agenda is then formally drawn up by the Enlarged Bureau. If the reports included are then not adopted in time in committee they are subsequently withdrawn from the agenda. The meetings of the Political Groups in the week before the plenary also subject the draft agenda to careful scrutiny, and decide whether to push for further changes to the agenda.

A further meeting is then held on the Monday of plenary week before the session has opened between the President and the chairmen of the Political Groups to see if any final modifications are needed. Twenty-three members may also propose changes (unlimited in number) in writing at least one hour before the opening of the session. Moreover, a Political Group, or at least 13 members, have the right to propose just one amendment to the agenda, also one hour before the session.

At the beginning of Monday's plenary agenda, the President then goes through the agenda for each day of the plenary week, and announces which changes have been suggested at the meeting with the Political Group chairmen, and which other changes have been requested. Each such request is moved by one member and there is one speaker for and one against, followed by a Parliament vote on the request.

The plenary agenda has then been formally adopted. In practice, however, it is often subsequently modified, either because urgent requests from Commission or Council are accepted by the Parliament on Tuesday morning, or because unexpected events (e.g. emergency debates on Commission declarations) or straightforward delays mean that items are carried over from one day to the next. There are also a number of other, procedural manoeuvres to modify the agenda, such as calling for a quorum (in the absence of which a report can not be voted), moving the inadmissibility of a matter, calling for a debate (or evening sitting) to be closed or adjourned, or for a report to be referred back to committee.

Topical and urgent debates

A special word is required on the subject of the topical and urgent debates, and on how they are chosen.

The Rules of Procedure (Rule 73.3) provide for one or two periods, together totalling a maximum of three hours, to be set aside in the plenary agenda for debates on topical and urgent subjects of major importance. In practice this now tends to be combined in one three-hour period, and as pointed out above, this takes place on Thursday mornings. These debates and the resolutions adopted allow Parliament to react quickly to current events. Rule 64 lays down the procedures for these topical and urgent debates. These procedures and their practical implementation have been modified on several occasions in the light of experience.

Rule 64 debates may be requested in writing by a Political Group or at least 23 members, and must be linked to a motion for a resolution. Among the many proposals made each session (for example 85 motions on 30 subjects were tabled in January 1990), Parliament selects five subjects (maximum) for debate. One of these is always Human Rights which follows a special procedure outlined below. Another is almost always natural disasters, usually taken last and after minimal debate, allowing Parliament to adopt resolutions calling on the Commission to provide aid following storms, floods, droughts etc. (The aid then provided by the Commission is listed in the annex to the minutes of the following part-session in which the Commission reports on action taken following Parliament's resolutions.) This then leaves, in practice, three subjects to be chosen from current political issues in order to complete the total of five.

The procedure for drawing up this list, for subsequently accepting which motions for resolution fall within the subjects chosen, and then proceeding to a debate and vote are as follows:

the Thursday before the part-session, 6.30 pm (following Group meetings)	deadline for proposals on the subjects to be selected, and meeting of Group representatives to try to negotiate an agreed list
the Monday of the part-session, 11.30 am	meeting between the President and the Group chairmen for an exchange of views on the subjects to be selected for topical and urgent debate
Monday, 5 pm	announcement by the President of the list of five subjects to be placed on the agenda for urgent debate in plenary
the Monday of the part-session, 8 pm	deadline for tabling motions for resolution
Tuesday, 11.30 am	meeting between the President and the Group chairmen to draw up the list of resolutions accepted as falling within the five subjects
Tuesday, 3 pm	announcement to the House of that list
Tuesday, 8 pm	deadline for lodging objections to the list (additions, deletions or substitutions), including possibility to substitute one subject by another. Objection must be by a Political Group or 23 members.
Wednesday, 9 am	vote on the objections lodged
Wednesday, 1 pm	deadline for tabling amendments to the accepted resolutions (these are usually in the form of compromise resolutions negotiated by Political Groups)
Thursday, from 10 am to 1 pm	debates on the five subjects, each one followed by an immediate vote.

The main criteria for selection of topics are laid down in Annex III of Parliament's Rules of Procedure, and include the need for Parliament to express a view before a particular event has taken place, for Parliament to express a rapid opinion, or on a major issue relating to the Community's powers. Resolutions can be directed to Council, the Commission, the Member States, third countries or international bodies.

Compared to normal plenary debates the debates on topical and urgent issues have several distinctive features. Firstly, there is much less speaking time, and there are no explanations of vote. Nor can there be requests for inadmissibility of a motion, or for them to be referred back to a Committee. Moreover no-one can call for a debate to be adjourned. (A quorum call can, however, be made.) Another feature is that the motions are put to the vote as soon as a debate is closed, and in the order in which they were tabled. A compromise motion is put to the vote in place of the first resolution which it is meant to replace. It is now the practice to adopt a single resolution on each issue (it being understood that several issues are covered under the Human Rights and Disaster debates). Another distinctive feature is that all motions not included in the final list of topics automatically lapse, as do resolutions on which there is no time left to vote. This latter is a relatively common occurrence.

The organization of plenary debates

Debates in plenary, whatever their origin (legislative or non-legislative reports, and questions with debate, or debates on statements by the President of the European Council, the Commission or the Council), have many similar features in the way they are structured. A first important decision is on the allocation of speaking time for the debates, on which the President makes proposals after consulting the Political Groups. These proposals are outlined in the draft agenda for the plenary, and are divided into speaking time for debates on Monday, Tuesday, Wednesday and Thursday (with topical and urgent debates subject to a separate procedure and thus excluded). Speaking time is allocated to Commission and Council, rapporteurs and draftsmen of opinions, authors of motions, and finally between Political Groups to allocate to their members. Rule 83 of Parliament's Rules of Procedure lays down the guidelines for distribution of speaking time between members, with a first fraction of speaking time being divided equally among all the Political Groups, and a further and more important fraction being divided among the Political Groups in proportion to the total number of their members. Non-attached members are then given an overall speaking time based on the percentage of time given to the other Political Groups, which is then doubled to take account of the great diversity of views among such members.

An illustration of what this allocation of speaking time means in practice can be seen in the agenda for the Tuesday of the January 1990 plenary in which there were seven hours and 52 minutes (472 minutes) of speaking time to be distributed. The Council was given 60 minutes (12.7 per cent, an untypically high percentage because it included the debate on the priorities of the Irish presidency, and of question time to the Council); the Commission 30 minutes (6.3 per cent); Parliament's rapporteurs 30 minutes (6.3 per cent, the figure of 30 minutes being reached by allocating five minutes to each of the six rapporteurs); draftsmen of opinions from other Committees 12 minutes (2.5 per cent); and authors of motions for a resolution 40 minutes (8.5 per cent, the figure being reached by giving five minutes to each of the eight sets of authors). Speaking time for other members demonstrated the powerful position of the Socialist Group, and to a slightly lesser extent of the EPP. The Socialists were allocated 96 minutes (20.3 per cent of the total), the EPP 65 minutes (13.8 per cent), the Liberals 28 minutes (5.9 per cent), the European Democrats 20 minutes (4.2 per cent), the Greens and the Group for the European Unitarian Left 17 minutes each (3.6 per cent each), the Group of the European Democratic Alliance 14 minutes (3 per cent), the Technical Group of the European Right 11 minutes (2.3 per cent) and the Left Unity and Rainbow Groups nine minutes each (1.9 per cent each). The non-attached members were left with 14 minutes (3 per cent). Once this daily allocation of speaking time has been made for the set debates, the Political Groups then indicate how much of their overall time they wish to use for each individual item. They also divide up their speaking time within their Group.

A typical debate would thus begin with a five-minute statement by the rapporteur from the committee responsible. Draftsmen of opinions from other committees will also often choose to speak, though for a shorter time. The main Group spokesman for the issue would then speak beginning with the spokesman of the Socialist Group, and then going from Group to Group according to their size. Some Groups may wish to allocate most of their speaking time to one member, while others may prefer to give smaller amounts to several members, especially when there is a great variety of points of view on a subject within the same Group. An electronic board shows how much of a member's speaking time has elapsed, and indicates when it has come to an end by means of flashing asterisks. The presiding officer will then request the speaker to stop, and if he or she fails to do so can cut off the speaker's microphone.

At the end of a debate the Commission will reply. This is the moment when, for legislative resolutions, the Commission will indicate its position on specific amendments tabled in the report before the Parliament. In some cases the Commission will give a very lengthy reply, which cuts into the time allocated for subsequent debates. The Commission's allocation of speaking time is purely indicative, as Parliament's rules give the Commission an unlimited right to intervene.

In certain major debates involving both Commission and Council their representatives will speak at an earlier stage during the debate, and then reply again at the very end. This can happen, for example, when the budget is discussed, and the Council wishes to present its own position, and later to respond to the points made in the debate.

Parliament's Rules and practice thus means that the time for debates is strictly curtailed, and the scope for spontaneity, cut and thrust argument between individual members, and filibustering is very limited. This is also reinforced by a tendency for many members to read out their speeches. Nevertheless certain members do try and continue debates through other means, such as attempted points of order, or in their explanations of vote.

These are often livelier occasions than the debates themselves, where set positions that have often already been aired in Committee, are presented again.

Voting procedures

Members of the public, lobbyists or journalists who attend Parliament's plenary sessions to follow a particular subject are often surprised to find that the vote on a particular report does not usually follow the debate, but only takes place a day or two later (the exceptions are votes on whether to raise a member's parliamentary immunity, votes after topical and urgent debates, and votes on Friday morning's agenda).

This separation between debate and final vote may seem illogical, but there are several reasons why this is done. One reason is because the duration of voting is very unpredictable, and would make it even more difficult to plan the organization of debates. Another reason is because of the variety of activities which take place during plenary sessions (which unlike most national parliaments only take place for one week a month), and which would have to be interrupted every time there was a vote. Voting times are thus grouped at certain fixed moments of the week. Among the most important such times are 5:00 pm on Wednesday when the main legislative votes are taken and 6:30 pm on Thursday when other important votes are often taken (including some on which the debate was concluded on Wednesday, or even Tuesday).

Although members thus have a good indication of when voting time will take place they are also reminded by division bells, which can be heard throughout the corridor of the Palais and IPE buildings, shortly before a vote will take place and 10 minutes before a sitting is to start, as well as when it does start.

Voting is a personal right in the European Parliament and no proxy voting is permitted. There are two main ways of voting in the European Parliament's plenaries, by a simple show of hands and by electronic voting. Secret ballots may also be used, but, in practice, are only required for election of the President, Vice-Presidents and Quaestors. One fifth of the current Members of Parliament may request voting to be by secret ballot, but this has never happened. The Rules of Procedure also permit voting by sitting and standing (when a vote by show of hands is unclear) and also by full roll call vote with members replying "yes", "no", or "I abstain" in alphabetical order. Both of these methods have been used in the past, and they have constituted excellent weapons for a filibusterer, especially oral roll call votes which can take a very long time to complete (an example of such use was during the successful Pannella-led filibuster to prevent the number of members required to form a Political Group from being raised). Electronic voting has now replaced both methods in practically all instances (the main exceptions being occasions when the electronic system has broken down).

Wherever possible, a simple show of hands is used for voting. There are two circumstances, however, when it must be replaced by electronic voting; firstly when the result of a vote is unclear, or secondly if a formal roll call vote has been requested in writing by a least 23 members for a Political Group before voting has begun. They are also used for quorum checks, and to see if the absolute majority of members (260 votes) has been obtained when required by the Treaties (Co-operation and Assent procedures, budget, etc.).

The electronic voting system was first installed in May 1980, and after initial teething problems, now generally works well. The members are given a voting card, which they must insert in the voting machine and press on a green button for a "yes" vote, red for a "no" vote, and yellow for an abstention. When the President announces an electronic vote, the text being voted (a paragraph, amendment or final text) is posted on the electronic scoreboard. Members out of their places must then rush back to them in time, creating a scramble at moments of close and tense voting. Sometimes before the result is finally announced certain members will catch the attention of the President to say that their voting machine was not working, and telling him or her how they voted. These are then added to the tally.

The final results (which appear after about half a minute) are posted on the electronic scoreboard. If electronic voting was merely used by the President to provide a precise result when the outcome by show of hands was uncertain this result is not recorded for posterity, and the minutes merely record that a text was adopted or rejected by electronic vote.

If, however, a roll call vote has been requested, the result is formally recorded, first in a special annex to the minutes which appears the next day, and later in the translated minutes which come out in the Official Journal of the European Communities about a month later.

Roll call votes tend to be called by Political Groups for three main reasons; firstly to put that Group's position on an issue firmly on record; secondly to embarrass another Group by forcing the latter to take a specific stance on an issue; and thirdly to keep a check on their own members' participation in a vote, and voting stance. The European Parliament has not generally had a very strong whipping system in the past (though this may be slowly changing in some Groups), but a recorded roll call vote does provide potential help in this task.

Whatever the reason for a recorded roll call vote, it provides a very valuable but currently underutilized source for assessing the political positions taken by a Political Group and by individual members. It could, for instance, be used by European interest groups the way American congressmen's voting records are assessed by the Washington-based lobbies. While a potentially valuable tool, however, it is one that must be used with caution. It is easiest, for example, to assess a roll call vote on the finally adopted text, whereas the most significant vote may have been on a specific amendment. Deciding which of these votes was really significant is one which requires considerable knowledge of the issue at stake.

The electronic voting system has also had the great advantage of ensuring that Parliament's votes are now comparatively rarely contested, except when only one or two votes separate the two sides, and members complain that their voting machines did not work, and that they did not catch the eye of the President.

There have been very occasional accusations that certain members have double voted by voting for absent colleagues. None of these has been proved.

Voting order

Another issue which should be mentioned as regards voting in the European Parliament is the order in which votes are taken, on which the Parliament has laid down standard procedures. A distinction must first be made here between non-legislative texts involving only one reading by the Parliament, and legislative texts requiring one or two readings.

When a non-legislative text is put to the vote, Parliament only votes on amendments to specific parts of a resolution (when there are several amendments, it normally begins by voting on that furthest removed from the original text), then on the unamended parts of a motion (but which may be taken *en bloc* to save time, or paragraph by paragraph if there is an objection), and finally on the motion for a resolution as a whole. If an amendment is adopted, then subsequent contradictory amendments or text fall. Requests may also be made for separate votes on an amendment or original paragraph, so that votes can be taken on its component parts. Such a request for a separate vote is an individual right of any member, as long as the President has not yet declared the vote to be open.

Once the voting on the separate amendments is concluded, an opportunity is then given for explanations of vote by individual members (orally or in writing, see Chapter 4) before the final vote is taken. Oral explanations are limited to one-and-half minutes for individual members and three minutes for an explanation of vote on behalf of a Group. Written explanations of vote are limited to 200 words, and are included in the verbatim record of proceedings. Explanations are not allowed on procedural matters.

Most votes on non-legislative resolutions require simple majorities only, with no requirements for a certain number of members to be present, and indeed unless a quorum call is made (see below) or a roll call vote taken there is no check on how many members are actually voting.

Certain non-legislative votes of a procedural or decision-making nature, however, do require special majorities, such as amendments to Parliament's Rules of Procedure, which require a majority of the total number of members, and censure votes on the Commission which require a two-thirds majority of the votes cast, representing a majority of the current members of Parliament.

Voting on legislative texts has many similar features with the above procedures, such as the order of voting on amendments, and the possibility of explanations of vote. The main difference is that a distinction is made between voting on the Commission or Council text (any amendment to it, on specific paragraphs or articles of the text, and on the proposal as a whole) and voting on the accompanying draft legislative resolution. After voting on the former is completed but before Parliament completes its procedure by voting on the draft legislative resolution the Commission may be asked to react to Parliament's rejection of the proposal or its amendments to it. If the Commission is not in a position to react immediately, or gives a negative or unsatisfactory response, the vote on the draft legislative resolution may then be postponed for a period sufficient to allow the responsible Committee the time to examine the situation. This period may not exceed two months unless the Parliament decides to extend it. Until Parliament finally votes on the draft legislative resolution it has not given its opinion.

This possibility for separation of the votes on a Commission proposal and on the accompanying draft legislative resolution represents an important procedural device developed by the Parliament in order to reinforce its role in the legislative process. Its significance is described in greater detail in the section on Parliament's powers in Chapter 11.

The above procedure applies to legislative resolutions involving either one or two readings by the Parliament. In cases, however, where there are two readings (e.g. those involving the Co-operation procedure on internal market matters under Article 100A of the Treaty) special procedures apply in the second reading. Whereas single readings or first readings require simple voting majorities, this is not the case in Parliament's second reading, when a "common position" has been transmitted by the Council. The first difference from normal procedure is that Parliament must give its opinion on the common position within three months of its receipt, with the possibility of a further extension of one month. Parliament has developed rules for determining the moment from which the three-month period is to run, namely when it has received the common position, the Council's explanation of how it was reached, and the Commission's reaction. The three documents must be transmitted in all the official languages. Only then does the President of Parliament announce receipt of the common position during the relevant plenary session.

In second reading Parliament may adopt the common position without amendment, reject it outright or adopt it with amendments. In the first case there need be no plenary vote at all (with the President of Parliament simply declaring it to be adopted in the absence of any other proposal). In the second and third cases, however, an absolute majority of the current members is required to reject a text or to amend it. The consequences of these procedures are again described in more detail in Chapter 11.

A final word should be added as regards the amendments that are voted upon in plenary. Amendments can be tabled by any member, (except to common positions in second reading) but are subject to certain rules. Firstly, they must meet the timetable set down for each report or resolution. For most reports this is mid-day on the Thursday of the week preceding the plenary session, but for more urgent topics the deadline is a set for a moment during the plenary itself, and it is announced by the President of Parliament.

Secondly, amendments are generally put to the vote only when they have been printed and distributed in all the official languages. Parliament may decide otherwise, but not if 10 members or more object. Inevitably the practice in plenaries is more formal in this respect than in Committee meetings.

Parliament has also laid down rules as regards the admissibility of amendments, such as whether they are directly related to the text which they seek to amend. Finally, if more than 20 amendments are tabled to a Commission proposal other than those tabled by the responsible Committee these may then be referred back to the Committee for its further consideration. This procedure is described in Chapter 7. At present it is only used for the most controversial cases, with a recent example being Parliament's examination of the "Television Without Frontiers" directive.

The only major exception to the rule that amendments tabled after the close of a debate may not be put to the vote is where compromise amendments are put forward by Political Groups, or Committee chairmen or rapporteurs. The President of Parliament must examine their admissibility, and must then obtain the agreement of Parliament before they are put to the vote.

Such compromise amendments would typically entail the withdrawal of amendments tabled by different Political Groups in favour of one composite text. For controversial issues where there are a large number of amendments, considerable efforts are made to try and reduce the number of such amendments. It is relatively difficult, however, to reach last-minute agreement on a compromise amendment which will satisfy most Political Groups, and they are often reached between two or three Groups only, notably when these Groups together constitute a majority. It is also common for Groups to agree to support each other's amendments without these being formally withdrawn.

Common procedural manoeuvres

Parliament's Rules provide considerable scope for procedural manoeuvres by individual members or by Groups. The most important of these are the right to make points of order, request whether there is a quorum and to request referral of matter back to committee. Other possibilities are to move the inadmissibility of a matter, the closure or adjournment of a debate or the suspension or closure of the sitting.

By far the most frequently used of these devices are points of order (Rule 101). They may last for three minutes and take precedence over other business. They are meant to cover the subject of the debate. They are, however, used (or abused) for a wide variety of reasons. Some of these are directly linked to the matter at hand, requesting clarification from the President of Parliament, a rapporteur or the Commission, pointing out that a text has not been translated into the speaker's language, and so on. Points of order are also used to bring totally different subjects onto the agenda, to respond to an event that has just taken place, to make a constituency point, to criticize another member, to criticize a ruling by the President, to participate in a debate when not due to do so or to continue a concluded debate by other means. On certain occasions, such as prior to the setting of the agenda on Monday afternoon, or after a controversial ruling by the presiding officer of the Parliament, they can lead to mini-debates lasting a considerable time.

The other procedural devices cited above are mainly used for one reason, to get a controversial item off the plenary agenda, and thus to try and block Parliament's decision on the matter. The most commonly used rule to achieve this is Rule 103, providing for referral of a matter back to committee. This is often done by the responsible committee itself, if difficulties have emerged during a debate, or if new developments or an unsatisfactory response by the Commission require reconsideration of the matter within the Committee.

A request for referral back, however, may be made by any member at any time during a debate, and at the latest before the final vote on the matter is agreed by the President. (This has now been interpreted to mean up to the final vote on the text as a whole, in other words even after there have been votes on the individual amendments to a text.) As on other procedural matters, the President, after having heard the mover of the motion, will then call for one speaker in favour and one against. The committee chairman, or rapporteur, may also speak. Parliament then proceeds to a vote on the request, and if it is adopted, the rest of the debate (if applicable) and the final vote are postponed to a future plenary. Requests for referral back are sometimes accompanied by requests that the matter be placed on the next plenary agenda, but this is by no means automatically accepted.

Another, and more controversial, device to get a matter taken off the agenda is through a request to ascertain the quorum. As pointed out above, most plenary decisions can be taken by simple majority, without any particular number of members being present (unlike committee decisions, where a quarter of the membership must be present).

At least 13 members, however, may request that the number of members be checked. A quorum call cannot be made on behalf of a Political Group. The President asks these members to stand up so that they can be counted. The President will then put a particular amendment or point to the vote, and announce whether or not the necessary quorum of one third of the current members of Parliament (173 members) has been attained. If is is not the vote is then placed on the agenda of the next sitting (e.g. in theory even the next day).

The 13 or more members who request whether a quorum is present are now automatically included in the number of members counted as being present in the chamber for the purpose of establishing the quorum. This new interpretation of the Rule was made after an incident when one particular group of members had made a quorum call, and subsequently walked out of the chamber to ensure that a quorum was indeed not present.

Quorum calls are not often made, especially because they tend to create a bitter atmosphere within the chamber. The situation can arise where a quorum call with a report not satisfactory to the right may be withdrawn from the agenda, only to be followed by a report not satisfactory to the left. Friday mornings, when plenary attendance is at its lowest, is the most frequent time for a quorum call to be made, although they can be requested throughout the week when the most controversial topics are being considered. Quorum calls may not be used for preventing debate, nor for preventing the adoption of the agenda or the minutes. In other words, they cannot bring Parliament itself to a halt.

The other procedural devices mentioned above are less frequently used. To find that a matter is inadmissible, for example, is relatively rare, since the range of issues debated by the Parliament is so vast. Motions to move closure or adjournments of a debate tend to be used only during the most controversial debates.

The most striking recent example of procedural moves being used to block a report was during Parliament's consideration of the Prag report on the working place of the Parliament in January 1989 (see Chapter 3), which was strongly opposed by a large number of members supporting Strasbourg and Luxembourg in particular. In consequence a number of procedural devices were used to try and get the issue off the agenda. Firstly, when the agenda was set, an unsuccessful attempt was made to remove the report from the agenda. When the debate started, a further unsuccessful attempt was made to refer it back to committee (Rule 103(1)). A request for the debate to be adjourned until Friday (Rule 105(1)) was adopted, but the sitting was then suspended, and the President used his discretion to reinstate the item at its original place on the Wednesday agenda, to which Parliament agreed. Finally, when the text was put to the vote (after a successful motion to close the debate prematurely) roll call votes were requested on each amendment, and a further unsuccessful attempt made to suspend the sitting (Rule 106).

Order in the chamber

Lack of order is only rarely a problem within the European Parliament, whose proceedings are usually rather calm, especially in comparison with certain national parliaments like the UK House of Commons. The variety of languages used, and also of national parliamentary traditions, means that there tends to be less spontaneous repartee between individual members, and fewer interruptions of members while they are speaking. Nevertheless the European Parliament is livelier than some of the national parliaments in the Member States. When Hanja Maij-Weggen, a long-serving MEP, was appointed as Minister in the Dutch government, and her aggressive debating style was commented upon in the Dutch Parliament, she claimed to have learnt the technique from British members of the European Parliament. The fact, however, that many of its debates are rather technical, and even more that no government's fate depends on the outcome of its deliberations, mean that there are relatively few moments of high drama within the European Parliament, although this does not mean that there are not occasionally very lively debates (e.g. on the use of rubber bullets in Northern Ireland), or periods of unrest in the chamber when a presiding officer's decision is contested or during a heated voting time.

There have, however, also been a number of individual demonstrations within the chamber, many by the Parliament's "outsider" members. Mario Capanna (of the Italian Party Proletarian Democracy) once held up a Palestinian flag in the Chamber during an address to Parliament by the late President Sadat of Egypt. Ian Paisley made a demonstration against the visit of the Pope to address the Parliament, and had to be removed from the chamber after having been warned by the President. Elected Green members of the European Parliament came into the Chamber wearing United Kingdom Green T-shirts to protest against the absence of UK Greens due to the British electoral system. There have been a few other incidents.

The major such incident in recent years, however, occurred in October 1989, and was orchestrated by members of the Technical Group of the Right in protest at their exclusion from leadership posts within Parliament's interparliamentary delegations that would have been allocated to them under the d'Hondt system used for dividing posts proportionally among the Groups (the chairmanship of the delegation to Switzerland, and even more controversially a vice-chairmanship of the delegation to Israel). After a speech by Bruno Gollnisch (French *Front National*), the members of his Group began a systematic demonstration, which eventually ended with a scuffle, with the suspension of the sitting and with the lights being switched off in the chamber.

As a result of this incident the Parliament reviewed those of its Rules of procedure dealing with order in the chamber, and some minor modifications were agreed in January 1990. Rule 86 provides for members to be called twice to order by the President if they create a disturbance in the chamber. On the second occasion their offence is recorded in the minutes. If there is a further repetition the President may exclude the offender from the chamber for the rest of the sitting. Parliament's security service is given the task of actually removing the member from the chamber if he or she refuses to leave. This rule has been applied on several occasions but it has now ben reinforced by adding a reference that the Secretariat-General of Parliament should see that a disciplinary measure is immediately carried out.

Rule 87 provides for the possibility for Parliament to pass a vote of censure in serious cases disorder, automatically involving immediate exclusion from the chamber, and suspension for two to five days. This rule too has been modified, to provide for greater flexibility as to when it can be applied, and to tighten up the rules in certain other respects. In practice Rule 87 has still not been used on any occasion.

The final such rule is Rule 88, which provides for closure or suspension of the sitting by the President when disturbances in Parliament threaten to obstruct the business of the house. This rule has only been used on one occasion, the incident mentioned above on Oct. 11, 1989.

Record of plenary sittings

Two documents are prepared on a daily basis. Firstly, there are the daily minutes of each session, recording the business that took place, who spoke in each debate, the procedural decisions and the overall results of voting on amendments and texts. In the second part of the minutes are the texts of each resolution as finally adopted by the Parliament, and the list of which members were present for the day's business (prepared on the basis of lists to be signed by members at one of two locations within the chamber). The minutes are translated into all the official languages for distribution at least half an hour before the opening of the next sitting (i.e. usually the following morning). They are approved on that occasion, unless objections are raised.

The minutes are subsequently published in the Official Journal of the European Communities, and Parliament also publishes a collection of all the resolutions adopted at a particular part session. These documents take a certain time to prepare, and anyone who wishes immediately to know the result of Parliament's deliberation should try to consult the minutes of the previous day's sitting.

When there are recorded roll-call votes, these are not published in the daily minutes, but in a special annex of the minutes listing the amendment or text which was the subject of the roll-call vote, including which members voted in favour, who were opposed, and who abstained. They are eventually added to the final version of the minutes as published in the Official Journal of the European Communities, and constitute the best source for analysing individual or group voting records within the Parliament (see discussion above).

The other publication which comes on a daily basis during plenary session is the verbatim report of the proceeding of each sitting, familiarly known as the "Rainbow" because it contains the members' speeches in the languages in which they were given. Members wishing to make comments or corrections to the transcripts of their speeches are required to do so not later than the day following that on which they received them. The "Rainbow" is eventually translated into all the official languages, and published as an annex to the Official Journal of the European Communities, which thus serves as full record of what was said on which subject at each plenary session. This is important not just in terms of recording for posterity the views of MEPs, but also as an official record of positions taken by the Commission, Council and Foreign Ministers on subjects not always of their own choosing.

Parliament's information service (its DG III) also provides a briefing for the press as to which issues are coming up at the next plenary, and also publishes a daily summary of events at the plenary. These come out in all the official languages. The monthly newsletters in each language also carry reports on the most important events in the preceding session.

Formal sittings

An increasingly frequent practice in recent years has been to allow Heads of State of the European Community countries or of third countries to address the members of Parliament during the plenary week in Strasbourg. These are often held on the Wednesday of the plenary week, typically at 12:00, and are not treated as part of the normal agenda.

Among the most prominent visitors in recent years have been Ronald Reagan (May 1985) and the Pope. The visit of Mikhail Gorbachev has also been mooted. Only Heads of State or heads of government of Community may address the full plenary session of Parliament. Certain other prominent visitors have been able to speak to special meetings of the Enlarged Bureau and the relevant committees (i.e. Shevardnadze and premier Mazowiecki of Poland). Alexander Dubcek and Nelson Mandela were able to speak to the Parliament session after having received the Sakharov Prize from the President of Parliament.

Concluding comments on plenary sessions

Some common criticisms, and some suggestions for reform

Certain criticisms of the functioning of plenary sessions have been alluded to in the text above, such as the apparent poor attendance, the lack of cut and thrust in some of the debates, and the separation between debates and concluding votes. Some answers to these criticisms have also been given.

The poor attendance at individual debates does not mean that there are few members present at Strasbourg, in view of the whole range of other meetings and activities which are taking place elsewhere in the buildings. While certain nationalities have consistently higher attendance than others, average attendance at plenary sessions, especially in mid-week, is now generally high, with absenteeism discouraged not merely by financial penalties but also by pressure from the Political Group leaders and whips. As for the lack of cut and thrust in debates, this results from constraints of language, but also from the fact that it is easier to interrupt and debate with political adversaries of your own nationality whose mentality you are more likely to understand (indeed many of the liveliest exchanges in the Parliament are between British Labour and Conservative MEPs), and finally by severe time constraints which impose tight restrictions on the length of debates and on individual speaking time. The separation between debates, and the votes to conclude the debate, are clearly frustrating for journalists and for others following a debate, but are extremely hard to avoid in present circumstances.

Nevertheless, certain other criticisms have also been made. One of these is that voting time has become too long. Certain votes, such as those on the budget or the agricultural prices review, or even controversial legislative texts, may last for two hours or more, and many members feel that they have become little more than voting machines. To remedy this, however, would require a curtailment of individual members' rights to table amendments. A second criticism is that the reinforcement of Parliament's work since the Single European Act, and with detailed internal market legislation, has made plenary sessions too technical, and caused the Parliament to lose sight of broad political priorities. Parliament should thus put more emphasis on debating the main political issues of the day — rather than debating and voting on issues better left to civil servants (although some other members have accused Parliament of spending too much time on issues outside the European Communities' formal competence).

There are no easy answers to these points. Parliament's work must inevitably consist of a mix of the technical (on which there would otherwise be inadequate Parliamentary accountability) and the more obviously political, of shorter-term detail and of longer-term principle. Moreover, the fact that members come from 12 different parliamentary and political traditions means that it is hard to decide on common priorities. To give one small example, members from the Northern European countries often appear to be generally more interested in the details of legislation and of

Parliamentary oversight than their Southern European colleagues, who are more eager to establish the general principles that should govern the Community's activities.

Nevertheless certain reforms have been suggested or even attempted. Committees have been encouraged, for example, to adopt certain reports themselves without passing through the plenary sessions (Rule 37 Procedures, described in more detail in Chapter 7), in order to spare debating and voting time in plenary. Committees have also been urged to sift through amendments more ruthlessly (Rule 71 Procedures). The idea of a "Plenary Committee" or Committee of the whole House has also been suggested, in order to release valuable plenary time. As suggested by the European Democratic Group, for instance, this would meet in Brussels and could deal with "non-decisional" matters, such as Question Time to the Commission or Council, Declarations from Commission or Council, or oral questions with debate. By meeting in committee weeks such a plenary committee could save six to eight hours of plenary time in Strasbourg.

For a while an attempt was also made to give each plenary a distinct theme, such as environmental policy, or social policy, in order to have a concentration of debates on the same subject and to attract media and public attention. In view of the unpredictable flow of legislation, and last-minute problems in committee and in the plenary, these so-called "grand thèmes" proved to be hard to organize in practice. Nevertheless, the reinforcement of legislative planning, by means of inter-institutional agreement on an annual legislative programme, may again facilitate such exercises in the future. Moreover a series of major debates have been held at each Session since the 1989 elections on the basis of oral questions with debate to the Commission and/or Council on an important issue currently facing the Community.

Perhaps the most radical reform of all would be permitted by the establishment of a single seat for the European Parliament, which would permit a different organization of its work, such as plenary sessions running for continuous two-week periods, and interspersed with Committee meetings.

Whatever the criticism, the fact remains that, despite having to blend 12 different parliamentary traditions, use nine languages and two alphabets, operate in three locations and cope with successive enlargements and modifications of its powers, the European Parliament continues, nevertheless, to handle complex issues and to play an important role in the Community's decision-making processes.

9. Intergroups

One of the most striking developments in the European Parliament's working methods since direct elections has been the creation of a large number of "intergroups", consisting of members from different Political Groups with a common interest in a particular political theme. This chapter briefly traces the evolution of the intergroup phenomenon, and gives an indication of its scale and diversity after the 1989 elections. It goes on to examine the advantages and disadvantages of the intergroups, and concludes by reviewing the activities of a few individual intergroups in summary form, and of one in greater detail.

Of the intergroups established shortly after the first direct elections the most well-known was the Crocodile Club.

At first the European Parliament's Bureau was prepared to give official recognition to certain intergroups. Such status is still enjoyed by the Intergroup of Local and Regional Representatives, which was founded in 1980. Official recognition means that the Parliament itself is prepared to provide the necessary logistics, such as a meeting room and interpretation. It was very quickly realized, however, that Parliament would not be able to provide facilities for all the possible intergroups, and no other intergroups were subsequently granted recognized status despite many requests. Intergroups, therefore, have to meet with only restricted facilities, or with facilities provided by sympathetic Political Groups (e.g. Socialist Group for the Trade Union Intergroup or by the Left Unity Group for the Disarmament Intergroup).

This did not prevent, however, a proliferation in the number of intergroups. Their actual numbers have been hard to gauge, since they have not been officially registered, but over 50 were holding meetings during plenary sessions by the middle of the 1984–89 Parliament, and a similar number appear to exist today (March 1990).

The importance of these intergroups varies greatly. Some hold regular meetings (e.g. the Animal Welfare Group which had already held 57 meetings by Spring 1989), have prominent visiting speakers, have large attendances at their meetings, and have their own secretariat, sometimes on a practically full–time basis. Other intergroups represent the hobby-horses of a small group of members and have few resources and infrequent meetings. Some, such as the Mountain Intergroup, which consists of MEPs and staff with an interest in mountains and mountain climbing, has had a strong social as well as political purpose.

Their structures and financing are also very varied, ranging from those supported by the Parliament or its Groups, to others which get support from the Commission's budget, to those whose main support (staffing and finance) is from industry (e.g. the Kangaroo Group) or from other groups external to the Parliament. Some have membership limited to MEPs, others, such as the Tourism Intergroup, also include trade association members or other external members. A new intergroup has even been founded (Global Legislators for a Balanced Environment) with members from the US Congress and Japanese Diet as well as from the European Parliament.

A few intergroups have had broad-focus political goals, such as the self-explanatory Federalist Intergroup for European Union (successor to the Crocodile Club) or the Kangaroo Group (the movement for free movement within the European Community), the Animal Welfare Group, Drugs, and the Minority Languages Intergroups. Others have less explicit political goals, but provide a focus for those interested in sharing their experiences (such as the Intergroup of Elected Local and Regional Representatives) or discussing a range of issues within a particular field (such as the Media Intergroup).

Others have had a narrower focus, and have concentrated more on promoting specific interests, be they industrial (e.g. Wings of Europe, concerned with the aeronautical industry, and the TGV or High Speed Train intergroup) regional (mining regions, mountainous regions, regions affected by large airports, Atlantic regions, islands and peripheral and maritime regions in the EEC) or particular national or political causes (Armenians, Baltic States, Central America, Chile, Euro-Arab, Friends of Israel, Friends of Poland, etc.).

The scale of all this intergroup activity has clearly had a considerable effect on the working methods of the European Parliament, especially during the plenary sessions in Strasbourg when their meetings are normally held.

Any visitor to the Strasbourg plenary session can have an idea of their significance by looking at the list of scheduled meetings on Parliament's notice boards, with several such meetings taking place each day, in meeting rooms often put at their disposal by individual Political Groups. There are fewer such meetings in Brussels. Members tend to be in Brussels more frequently but for shorter lengths of time. Strasbourg, which is more difficult to reach and leave, and where members come for longer, and where there is much more overlapping of attendance, is thus more suitable for intergroup activities.

Intergroups have developed because they have a number of major advantages. Unlike the plenary sessions, where there is a set menu with items of interest and others of no interest to an individual member, intergroups permit a member to focus his or her attention on a particular set of issues of specific national, constituency or personal concern. They permit members to specialize, make contacts with outside interest groups on a more informal basis than in committee meetings, and last but not least to make close political contacts outside their own Political Groups. The Political Groups tend to be very heterogeneous and a member may sometimes find that he or she has more in common with certain members in other Groups. Intergroups thus not only help to form cross-Group coalitions on specific issues, but to forge wider political friendships which can be useful in other circumstances, and can help to build that wider consensus which is essential in the European Parliament on certain issues.

Finally, intergroups can also provide new roles and responsibilities for members and their assistants.

The very success of intergroups, however, has meant that they now constitute a rival centre of attention to official parliamentary activities, and in certain circumstances may undercut the latter. They may lead to lower attendances at committee and especially plenary sessions. There have even been occasions when prominent outside speakers have been reluctant to address a committee meeting because they have already appeared before an unofficial intergroup.

There are thus certain concerns about their proliferation. The Bureau of the Socialist Group, for example, decided in November 1989 that the number of intergroups supported by the Group should be limited and more related to the Group's priorities. To avoid undercutting other activities, supported intergroups would be granted full interpretation facilities in nine languages in the Group's main meeting room only on Thursday afternoons and Friday mornings of Strasbourg plenary sessions. On other days they would have to use another meeting room and be limited to French and English interpretation.

The development of intergroups may thus be subject to certain constraints. There is wide agreement, however, that they will continue to play an important role in the future.

Specific intergroups

In view of the large number of intergroups, and of their very varying degrees of activity, no attempt is made in this chapter to give a comprehensive survey of individual intergroups, and of their objectives and working methods.

It is not even easy to compile an up-to-date list of intergroups, and Parliament itself does not attempt any official listing, as mentioned above. The list at the end of this chapter, therefore, of the intergroups which apparently existed in November 1989, is indicative only. It does not necessarily include all of the intergroups, and may also include some whose level of activity is very low or sporadic (see Table 6).

In addition to this list a brief description is given below of the objectives and working methods of a few selected intergroups, and finally a rather more detailed case study of the Animal Welfare Intergroup.

Intergroup of Local and Regional Representatives

This intergroup was first founded in 1980, and as mentioned above, still has official recognition from the European Parliament. Its membership is based on members of the European Parliament who currently hold, or have held, local or regional office. Its main objective is to act as a consultative forum on the problems faced by local and regional governments in Europe, and on what can be done to help them at European Community level. The intergroup also works closely with certain representative organizations of local and regional governments, in particular, the Council of European

Municipalities and Regions and the International Union of Local Authorities.

The main activities of the intergroup are its regular symposia in Brussels (averaging around three a year) on a wide range of topical issues. The Bureau of the intergroup meets every session in Strasbourg. The intergroup also sponsors draft resolutions of relevance to its activities.

Among the topics which have been considered in recent years are voting rights of Community nationals in Member States other than their own, local and regional structures in the Member States and their role in European integration, the problems of economically underprivileged and declining towns, cities and regions, poverty in large cities, and the impacts of the completion of the 1992 internal market on economically weak local and regional communities. The latest such symposium was held on 29–30 March 1990, in Brussels, on the economic role of large cities and conurbations within the European Community, and the competition between these cities.

The current Chairman of the intergroup is Catherine Trautmann (French Socialist), the Mayor of Strasbourg, and the five Vice-Chairmen are Pol Marck (Belgian, PPE), Renzo Imbeni (Italian Communist, Mayor of Bologna), Edward Kellett-Bowman (British Conservative) and Solange Fernex (French, Green).

Kangaroo Group

This is one of the most well-known intergroups within the European Parliament, and was founded in 1979 by the late Basil de Ferranti, the industrialist and former Chairman of the Economic and Social Committee as well as British Conservative MEP from 1979 to 1988. Its founder members included Kai Nyborg, Karl von Wogau (German Christian Democrat) and Dieter Rogalla (German Socialist), the latter two of whom are still Vice-Presidents of the Kangaroo Group. The main objective of the intergroup, which calls itself the Movement for Free Movement, is to eliminate all barriers obstructing the free movement of goods, services and people across the internal frontiers of the European Community. It thus seeks the development of common European standards, the reduction of red-tape and customs and statistical formalities prior to their complete abolition, and the full implementation of the 1992 internal market. The name "Kangaroo Group" was chosen to symbolize the Kangaroo's ability to "leap over barriers", and because it "has a good hard kick in its hind legs" (from the Kangaroo Group's own information brochure).

The intergroup is funded by a corporate membership scheme — and does not receive financial backing from the European Parliament or national governments. The Kangaroo Group has a number of regular activities. A lunch is held on the Tuesday of each plenary session in Strasbourg, at which a prominent speaker is often invited. In Brussels its members have traditionally met at the Gigotin Restaurant. An annual conference is also held.

The Kangaroo Group publishes a newspaper on its activities, which includes other articles related to its objectives. Kangaroo News appears on a bi-monthly basis, and a German version *Kangarüh Nachrichten* has also been published. The Group is supported by a large number of MEPs (around 200 is its current estimate), from a wide spectrum of Political Groups and nationalities within the Parliament (although the Left is generally less well represented).

Besides MEPs and its corporate sponsors, it also has supporters in individual national parliaments and governments and in the European Commission. One Member of the European Commission (Christiane Scrivener), an active member of the Kangaroo Group when she was an MEP, is still one of its Vice-Presidents (the others are all members of the Parliament).

The Kangaroo Group currently has eight Vice-Presidents from four Political Groups and seven different nationalities. It has never appointed a formal President. It has a Director (Pamela Entwhistle, who has been associated with the Group since its inception) and an Assistant Director (currently Arabella Price).

Media Intergroup

This has been an active intergroup, whose main activity has been regular meetings in Strasbourg. It played an important role in the European Parliament's review of the "Television Without Frontiers" Directive (and of the parallel European Council Convention) on which it invited numerous speakers to give their views on various topics. The intergroup has also had a particular interest in the development of Europe-wide television programming.

Land Use and Food Policy Intergroup

The main objectives of this intergroup, whose original initiator was the British Conservative MEP, Tom Spencer, are to discuss the needed trade-offs between the competing aims of low-cost food for consumers, European agricultural interests, conservation and ecology, social needs in rural areas, the needs of the third world and the expansion of international trade. It has had a particular interest in the reform of the Common Agricultural Policy, and the formulation of a wider Community Food Policy.

The intergroup has a relatively small number of participants, but these include the Chairman of the Socialist Group, and the Chairmen of the Parliament's Committees on Budgets, Environment and External Economic Relations. It is currently chaired by the British Conservative, Sir Fred Catherwood, and has a Steering Committee which meets regularly in Strasbourg.

Federalist Intergroup for European Union

This is the successor to the famed Crocodile Club. The Federalist Intergroup for European Union was set up in 1986, soon after the death of Altiero Spinelli, to continue his work for "achieving European Union through the effort of the European Parliament, the only democratically representative institution at Community level". In this sense, it was the direct successor of the Crocodile Club, an informal discussion group, named after the Strasbourg restaurant where it first met, created by Spinelli with the aim of getting Parliament to take the initiative in constitutional change in the Community by itself drafting a new treaty. The Crocodile Club was the initiator of the decision to create a special Committee on Institutional Affairs within Parliament, and it was this Committee which prepared Parliament's proposal for a "Treaty on European Union" in 1984, which in turn led to the negotiation of the Single European Act (see Chapter 15).

The Federalist Intergroup was set up by those who considered the Single Act to be an insufficient step towards European Union. It immediately attracted about 150 members, despite a hefty membership fee. These members covered all Political Groups (except the European Right) and all nationalities. Since then the intergroup has held monthly meetings during sessions in Strasbourg (and extra ones in Brussels), adopted a Political Declaration and detailed rules of procedure and set up a Bureau whose dozen members rotate monthly in the chairmanship. It has appointed a Secretary-General, Virgilio Dastoli, who is the former personal assistant of Spinelli, and is assisted by a volunteer Federalist Intergroup Support Group (FIGS) composed of students in Brussels in the Federalist Youth Movement.

The intergroup's activities are mainly directed outside Parliament, but it also co-ordinates the position of the more "maximalist" members of the Committee on Institutional Affairs. It has set up Federalist Intergroups in a number of national parliaments which hold joint meetings. It has sponsored several opinion polls in all the Member States (financed by selling exclusive rights to newspapers), the results of which showed clear majorities in all except two Member States (UK and Denmark) for such things as European governments accountable to the European Parliament, legislative powers for the European Parliament, and giving Parliament the task of drafting a constitution for European Union. The referendum held in Italy at the same time as the 1989 European elections on this last point was a direct result of the intergroup pressing for this, together with its counterpart in the Italian Parliament and the Federalist Movement in Italy.

Detailed case study: Intergroup on Animal Welfare

(i) Purpose

The Intergroup on Animal Welfare is aimed at mobilizing cross-party support within the European Parliament for the whole range of animal welfare issues, which overlap the remit of several of Parliament's standing committees, especially those on Agriculture and on the Environment. It exists to exchange information on topical issues, to put pressure on the Commission to come up with new legislative initiatives, and then to follow these through. It also takes an interest in related conservation and environmental issues.

(ii) History

A Eurogroup for Animal Welfare was first set up in 1980 as a co-ordinating group for the various national societies for the protection of animals (such as RSPCA). Its first director was Edward Seymour-Rouse. It had no special links with members of the European Parliament. In 1983, however, a British Conservative member, Stanley Johnson, established an Animal Welfare Intergroup. Members from all Political Groups took part in its work, and its secretariat was provided by the Eurogroup. Stanley Johnson was Chairman for the first few months, and was later succeeded by Lieselotte Seibel-Emmerling (German SPD) for around two-and-a-half years and then by Madron Seligman (British Conservative). After the 1989 elections a hotly contested election for the chairmanship between Hanja Maij-Weggen (Dutch Christian Democrat) and Hemmo Muntingh (Dutch Socialist) was won by the former, with around 90 MEPS taking part in the meeting, and even with party whips being applied. Shortly afterwards, however, Maij-Weggen was appointed as a member of the Dutch government, and was replaced as chairman by Mary Banotti (Irish *Fine Gael*).

Seymour-Rouse remained Director of the Eurogroup secretariat (and hence chief assistant to the Intergroup) until 1987, when he retired (although he is now Director of Global Legislators for a Balanced Environment) and was replaced by Ian Ferguson.

(ii)   Structure and membership

As pointed out above, the intergroup is staffed by the Eurogroup on Animal Welfare. Its Director (Ian Ferguson) spends around half his time with the intergroup, and the rest acting as a liaison officer between the different national animal welfare associations. A second member of the Eurogroup Staff (currently Anton Gazenbeek) works full-time for the intergroup, helps to draft its minutes and resolutions and provides other secretarial and political advice. The third member of the staff to come to Strasbourg for plenary sessions is the Eurogroup's Scientific Co-ordinator (currently David Wilkins), who either provides scientific advice directly, or through his contacts.

The intergroup does not have direct card-carrying members, and its meetings are open to all Members of the European Parliament. Turnout at its meetings has ranged between a tiny handful and 90, but the average attendance tends to be around 25 - 35.

The intergroup includes a number of members who attend practically all of its meetings, and others who come occasionally, or when a specific item of interest to them is on the agenda. Sometimes opponents (e.g. supporters of the fur trade, hunting or farming interests, etc.) turn up at intergroup meetings, which are thus considerably enlivened. The intergroup has occasionally even made common cause with the Hunting Intergroup, such as when both were in opposition (although for different reasons) to the proposed directive providing for animals to be killed only in slaughterhouses.

The most faithful members of the intergroup tend to be British and Irish MEPs, who often receive the most amount of constituency mail on animal welfare issues. There are also a good number of regular attenders from among the German and Dutch members.

As a general rule one can talk of a north–south divide in terms of national interest in the work of the intergroup. There are, however, certain exceptions in that Belgian and, perhaps more surprisingly, Danish members have been poor attenders, whereas the Italian members, who used not to be much involved, are now showing more interest. There are also a few faithful attenders from Portugal. On the other hand Spanish, French and Greek members have tended to be less involved.

In terms of political allegiance the intergroup has tried to achieve the widest possible spread. Five Political Groups are thus represented among the chairman and vice-chairmen.

(iv)   Working methods

The main working session of the intergroup is its monthly meeting in Strasbourg (apart from the Budget session in October). Invitations to this meeting are issued to all members of the Parliament at the beginning of the week. Press conferences are also often held in Strasbourg. Meetings are not held in Brussels. Ad hoc meetings of the intergroup's leadership are held more frequently.

As a general rule, only MEPs can speak at the meetings of the intergroup, although experts can be called upon to speak on the invitation of the Chair. The agenda for the meetings is drawn up jointly by the leadership of the intergroup and the secretariat.

A typical agenda would begin with a discussion of legislative strategy on current Commission initiatives having a bearing on animal welfare which are on the agenda of the current plenary session. There are then discussions of items of general interest, such as proposed future legislative initiatives, or issues which the intergroup would like the Commission to tackle. On all these items an individual member will introduce the discussion. Other issues are put on the agenda as a result of concern expressed by an individual member, or by a national animal welfare association, or simply as a matter of topical interest.

The intergroups' meetings are held in rooms provided by individual Political Groups, for example, by the European People's Party when the chairman is from that Group. Interpretation is provided in English, French and German, and in other languages where possible. The minutes, however, are drawn up in English and French alone. Wherever possible, the intergroup tries to work on a consensus basis, and not through simple majorities.

The intergroup drafts Rule 63 resolutions and seeks to have reports drawn up on them by the committees to which they are referred. It also seeks the direct adoption of written declarations under Rule 65 of Parliament's rules for which an absolute majority of Parliament's members are required. A total of 272 signatures was achieved, for example, on the fur labelling issue mentioned below. If and when the Commission responds to Parliament's pressure, the intergroup then tries to mobilize support within the Parliament, and to fend off counter-lobbies.

Another feature of the intergroup's working methods is that its secretariat will also help individual members in their correspondence on animal welfare issues. The Eurogroup has a permanent office in Brussels, but its secretariat comes every session to Strasbourg. Their "office" is a bench located just outside the hemicycle, and on the way to both the members' offices and the members' bar.

(v) Achievements

The intergroup has played a prominent role in a number of major animal welfare initiatives, and has been unusually successful in getting the Commission to take up legislative initiatives. Its best publicized initial success was in obtaining an initial ban on imports of baby seal products into the European Community, and later in getting the ban made permanent.

Other successes have been achieved on the issues of animal experimentation, and on animal welfare on farms. A current issue of topical concern is a ban on the import of certain furs made from animals caught in leghold traps. A written declaration on this topic was approved by the intergroup and then obtained 272 members' signatures. A report was later drawn up by the Environment Committee and was eventually adopted by the Parliament after successful lobbying by the intergroup in response to counter-lobbying from Inuit interests in particular. The Commission is now responding by proposing a ban on the import of certain furs by 1996, and this proposal is now going through the European Parliament. Yet another current initiative of the intergroup is opposition to high-seas drift netting.

The intergroup has been less successful on certain other issues where a consensus approach has proved hard to achieve, such as on wild birds and kangaroo products. A report on cruel sports also made little headway, with particular difficulties on the sensitive issue of Spanish bullfighting.

Table 6: *Indicative list of intergroups (end 1989)*

America — EC Associations : MEP section
Amnesty International
Armenians
Atlantic Regions
AWEPAA (Association of Western European Parliamentarians Against Apartheid)
Baltic States
Central America
Chile
Disarmament
Euro-Arab
Federalist Intergroup for European Union
Friends of Israel
Friends of Poland
Jewish Intergroup
Islands and Peripheral and Maritime Regions in the EC
Mountain Intergroup
Non-Food Uses of Agricultural Products
Rural Areas
Land Use and Food policy
European Monetary System/ECU
Kangaroo Group
Mining Regions
Small and Medium-Sized Undertakings
European Energy Foundation
Science and Society
Space Policy
Civil Protection
Local and Regional Representatives
Elderly People
Family Policies
Handicapped/Disabled
Professions
Trade Unions
Wings of Europe (Aeronautics, Airbus)
Regions Affected by Large Airports
TGV
Tourism
Animal Welfare
Consumers
Cycling
Drugs
Hunting
Vivisection
Media
Minority Languages
Afghanistan
Mediterranean Countries
Left Wing Women
Pyrenees
Intergroup on Co-operation with the Countries of the Eastern Bloc
Social Economy (Co-operatives)

---

10.   The Parliament secretariat

"Cut it out, whose stooge are you?" said the sceptical Canadian political staffer to one of the co-authors of this book when the latter tried to explain that he had been recruited through an open competition, and was not beholden to any one Political Group or national administration.

Parliament's permanent officials are European Civil servants and are recruited directly by the European Parliament through open external competitions. The Staff Regulations state that "an official shall carry out his duties and conduct himself solely with the interests of the Communities in mind", and "shall neither seek nor take instructions from any government, authority, organization or person outside his institution". The Staff Regulations also go on to specify that "no posts shall be reserved for nationals of any specific Member State", although in practice a strong attempt is made to ensure rough balance between the nationalities, especially for senior posts within the Parliament. The seven Directors-General, for example, come from six different nationalities, and certain Directorates-General tend to remain within the hands of the same nationality for long periods. Community enlargement has also led to the creation of new Directorates-General. Before 1973 these were only four but British accession was followed by the creation of a Directorate-General for Research. Two new ones have been added after the latest accession.

The external competitions are organized by language groups (e.g. for "English Language Administrators") rather than by nationality, although this in itself ensures that there will be a certain number of new recruits of each nationality. Certain countries, however, are considerably over represented among the staff as a whole and others under represented, for reasons which are often very difficult to rectify, such as a shortage of suitable candidates.

Language competence is one of the factors in candidate recruitment but is not necessarily decisive. The rules merely call for an official to have a "satisfactory" knowledge of one language in addition to his or her mother tongue.

The European Parliament's establishment plan now numbers 3,482 posts (1990 figures), of which 432 are for temporary agents in the Political Groups, who are recruited directly by the Groups, and whose separate role and status has been discussed above. There are also a small number of other temporary officials elsewhere in the Parliament, as well as short-term auxiliaries (whose posts are not in the Parliament's establishment plan), and a number of local staff.

There are four categories of officials; A administrators, B executive assistants, C clerical staff (mainly secretaries) and D manual or service staff. Language staff are LA. It is possible to move from one category to another (especially from C to B) , and this is done through internal competitions. When the Parliament was smaller and more informal some officials rose from one category to another through the system, but this has become much more difficult. Within each category there are a number of grades. Newly recruited administrators, for example, tend to come in at A7 level. An A1 is at Director-General level or above. Of Parliament's 3,482 posts in 1990, 344 were for its A administrators outside the Political Groups and 664 were for LA officials.

The number of Directorates-General within the Parliament has gradually increased and there are now seven of these; DG I (Sessional Services), DG II (Committees and Delegations), DG III (Information and Public Relations), DG IV (Research), DG V (Personnel, Budget and Finance), DG VI (Administration), and DG VII (Translation and General Services). Two additional services report directly to the Secretary-General, the Directorate for Data Processing and the Parliament's Legal Service (see Figure 1).

The Secretary-General is the highest official within the Parliament and is formally appointed by the Bureau. Enrico Vinci has been the Secretary-General since 1986 and his two immediate predecessors were Hans Joachim Opitz and Hans Nord, who was subsequently an elected Member of Parliament from 1979 to 1989.

Two issues deserve further discussion; the question of the overall size of the Secretariat and that of its relationship with the Political Groups.

Since the Assembly's beginning in 1952, there has clearly been an enormous rise in the Parliament's staff from the 37 posts in 1952–1953 to 1,995 by 1979, 2,966 by 1984 and 3,482 today. The rise has been due to a number of factors; the increase in Parliament's membership from 78 to 518, the increase in the number of working languages from four to nine (almost a third of Parliament's officials are now in its linguistic services), the rise in the number of nationalities from six to twelve (with each expansion of the Community necessitating recruitment of new officials), and finally the increased range of Parliament's tasks and responsibilities.

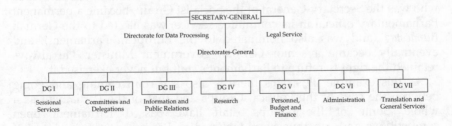

Figure 1: *The structure of Parliament's Secretariat*

In recent years, however, a determined attempt has been made to keep Parliament's overall numbers of permanent staff under check. In June 1983 Parliament voted that its establishment plan should not increase by the end of the subsequent four-year time span so that the establishment plan in 1989 should be back at its December 1985 level. This was not achieved, mainly as a result of the increase in staff numbers after Spanish and Portuguese accession. If the increase in the Political Groups' staff is not taken into account the increase in other Parliament staff has been very limited. Irrespective of whether Parliament's staffing levels are actually frozen or only undergo a slow increase it is clear that the days of rapid growth in the number of permanent officials are now over, and new tasks will have to be largely met through redeployment of the staff rather than through major new recruitment.

What has grown more rapidly, however, is the number of temporary agents in the Political Groups and the number of Member's personal assistants, as described elsewhere in the text. This changed balance between permanent officials recruited through open competitions and temporary agents owing their allegiance to a particular Political Group or Parliamentarian will clearly have considerable implications in the future, although it is less evident whether this will result in a lesser role for the permanent officials, or merely a redefinition of their role (e.g. greater specialization for Parliament's Committee staff than at present).

The relationship between the Political Groups and Parliament's permanent officials is a sensitive one. Parliament's officials have a truly independent status, and many are no more (or less!) politicized than their British civil service equivalents. Unlike the latter, however, they are not prevented from being open members of particular political parties, or standing as candidates in local, national or European elections (although they must take leave during national or European election campaigns and must take indefinite leave if elected to any office. They may, however, return to Parliament's staff if subsequently defeated or otherwise leave elective office).

In practice, few permanent Parliament officials have stood for national or European elections. The only present British MEP who is a former Parliament official (Deputy Head of its London Office) is Ben Patterson, although there have been a larger number of former Commission officials. A remarkable example from another country, however,is that of Hans Apel, who was the Secretary-General of the Socialist Group, became a permanent Parliamentary official in its committee service, was elected to the German *Bundestag* (and was also nominated to the European Parliament), and eventually became a senior German government Minister. He always retained the right to return to Parliament's staff but never exercised it.

As this example illustrates there is also a certain coming and going between the staff of the Political Groups and that of the Parliament as a whole. Some of the Groups' staff have passed Parliament open competitions and can thus be redeployed as Parliament permanent staff without difficulties. Moreover a number of long serving permanent officials have gone to work in the Political Groups, on a temporary or longer-term basis. (One such Parliament official, Julian Priestley, who had previously stood in Westminster elections as a Labour candidate against David Owen in Plymouth, recently became the Secretary-General of the Socialist Group; Sergio Guccione, Secretary-General of the EPP Group is another example.)

There are also some transfers of temporary group officials to permanent posts on Parliament's staff. In particular, there are a number of former Group Secretary-Generals who now hold senior posts within the Parliament.

There is little direct Political Group influence on appointments at lower levels within the Parliament (and where there is it is usually successfully resisted). At the highest levels, however, political factors do clearly play a key role in appointments although not exclusively so, and with factors such as nationality, seniority and outstanding ability also playing a role. Moreover Parliament's staff has been prevented from being dominated by any one political or national interest not only by those who have defended the concept of a continuing neutral European civil service, but also by the sheer variety and number of political forces and nationalities represented within the Parliament, which act as a counterweight to each other.

III: THE POWERS OF THE PARLIAMENT

11.   The Parliament and legislation

The Treaties did not assign to the European Parliament the full range of legislative powers enjoyed by the parliaments in typical Western European systems of government. The legislative power given to the Community was placed mainly in the hands of the Council (composed of ministers from the national governments). Although the first President in office of the Council, Adenauer, in his first speech to the Parliament asserted that it was a sovereign Assembly, and likened Council and Parliament to two chambers in a national Parliament, it was in fact given only consultative powers. Nonetheless, Parliament from outset sought to exploit and extend its powers to the maximum. As indicated in Chapter 1, this has been done both by making the most of whatever formal powers it had, and by constantly seeking to extend those formal powers. Parliament's participation in the Community's legislative procedure now goes well beyond its initial consultative role, and has been described as being that of a "co-legislature". How has this been achieved?

Making the most of consultation

Under the ECSC Treaty, Parliament merely exercised powers of control over the High Authority (Commission), and did not participate in the adoption of legislation. The EEC and Euratom Treaties, which entered into force in 1958, gave the Community a more wide-ranging power to adopt legislation and correspondingly provided for the participation of the European Parliament in legislative procedures. This was done by laying down in 22 articles in the EEC Treaty and 11 articles in the Euratom Treaty provisions obliging Council to consult the European Parliament on Commission proposals before their adoption.

The Treaties provided for Council to consult the Economic and Social Committee as well in certain cases, but in the case of this body, Council could lay down a deadline within which it must adopt its opinion. No such deadline was provided for in the case of the Parliament, and as we shall see this difference was to prove very important.

Over the years, through agreements with the other institutions and through interpretation of the Treaties, Parliament has sought to maximize the significance of this consultation procedure. Even before direct elections a number of important steps forward were achieved.

Extension of the scope of the procedure

In response to parliamentary pressure, Council undertook in March 1960 to extend the consultation procedure to all important problems, whether or not the Treaties specifically required the consultation of Parliament. These are known as "voluntary consultations" (*Consultations Facultatives*). Council agreed in February 1964 to extend these still further (i.e. beyond "important problems"), but without defining new limits. In practice, Council now consults Parliament on virtually all legislative proposals referred to it except those of a purely technical or temporary nature.

In November 1968, Council undertook to consult Parliament on non-legislative texts, as well. These include Commission memoranda and Council resolutions which, whilst not legally binding, nevertheless lay down guidelines, timetables and commitments which provide the framework for forthcoming legislative measures. At the same time, the Commission undertook to send to Parliament all memoranda and communications that it sends to Council. Parliament does not normally go so far as to draft its own report on these or adopt a resolution on them, but that option is available and the documents are in any case useful material.

Improving the quality of the procedure

In successive letters in November 1969, March 1970 and July 1970, Council committed itself to informing Parliament of the reasons for departing from Parliament's opinion when it does so in adopting Community legislation, initially for legislation with financial consequences and subsequently for all important questions. This information would be provided upon request either orally or in writing.

The Paris Summit of Heads of Government following the enlargement of the Community in 1973 invited the Council and the Commission "to put into effect without delay practical measures designed to achieve the reinforcement of the powers of control of the European Parliament and to improve the relations both of Council and of the Commission with the Assembly". As a result of this Declaration, Council agreed in October 1973:

- that it would consult the European Parliament on Commission proposals, in principle, within one week of receiving the proposal;
- that "except in cases of urgency when it will enter into contact with the Parliament, and subject to the fulfilment of its obligations, not to examine a proposal of the Commission on which the Parliament has been consulted until the opinion of the Parliament has been received, provided that such opinions are given by an appropriate date which may, in certain cases, be fixed by common agreement";
- to provide better information to Parliament as to the action taken by Council on its opinions and to this end, in addition to existing procedures, to have quarterly meetings of the Presidents of Parliament and Council;

Also pursuant to the 1973 Summit, the Commission agreed on May 30, 1973:

- to propose consulting Parliament on all proposals of any kind other than those of minor importance, or confidential matters;
- to express its opinion in Parliament's plenary on all amendments and to justify its opposition to any amendments in writing or orally in plenary;
- to amend its proposals to Council on the basis of Article 149(2) of the EEC Treaty in order to incorporate Parliament's amendments, even when these were only technical. (It should be recalled that Council can only amend the Commission's text unanimously whereas a qualified majority is often sufficient to adopt it.)
- to send directly to Parliament the proposals it sends to Council.

Also in 1973, the Commission and Council agreed that Parliament should be reconsulted whenever significant changes were made to the text on which Parliament initially delivered its opinion.

The result of all these developments was to provide the possibility for MEPs to be involved in all discussions on Community legislation and policy-making. The development of Parliament's committee system was, at least in part, an attempt to maximize these possibilities and in particular to provide for dialogue both with Commissioners and with their officials at all levels. Until direct elections and full-time MEPs as of 1979, the practical use made of these possibilities was necessarily limited, but the establishment of these procedures laid down a basis on which the elected Parliament could build.

However, no matter how extensive the possibilities for parliamentary involvement in the discussion of Community legislation, the bottom line of being able to block proposals or impose its will on the other institutions was lacking. Most national parliaments have such powers, even if they rarely make use of them. The European Parliament could make its opinion known at all stages, but it had no bargaining power if the other institutions failed to respond to its views. This situation changed dramatically following a ruling of the European Court of Justice in 1980.

Giving teeth to the procedure: The Court ruling of 1980

The "Isoglucose" ruling of the Court of Justice in 1980, which annulled a piece of Community legislation adopted by Council on the ground that Parliament had not yet given its opinion on it, made it clear that Council cannot adopt Community legislation before receiving Parliament's opinion, where this is required under the Treaties. In this ruling, the Court stated that the provisions in the Treaty requiring the consultation of Parliament are:

"the means which allows the Parliament to play an actual part in the legislative process of the Community. Such a power represents an essential factor in the institutional balance intended by the Treaty. Although limited, it reflects at Community level the fundamental principle that the peoples should take part in the exercise of power through the intermediary of a representative assembly. Due consultation of the Parliament in the cases provided for by the Treaty therefore constitutes an essential formality disregard of which means that the measure concerned is void".

It is important to note that this ruling was favourable to Parliament despite the fact that:

- Parliament had actually had a debate in plenary on the issue on the basis of the report from its committee, and had finished its consideration of its position on the proposal, but had not taken a final vote on the resolution as a whole, referring the text back to the relevant parliamentary committee.
- there was an objectively justifiable deadline for taking a quick decision in order to avoid a legal lacuna.
- Council maintained that, in the circumstances, it did try to get Parliament's opinion but that "Parliament, by its own conduct, made the observance of that requirement impossible".
- the Commission intervened on the side of Council.

Parliament included in the arguments on its side of the case the fact that Council had not exhausted all the possibilities of obtaining the opinion of Parliament in that it did not request the application of the emergency procedure provided for by the internal rules of Parliament nor did it make use of the possibility it had under Article 139 of the Treaty to ask for an extraordinary session of Parliament. In its judgement, the Court expressly avoided taking a position on what the situation would have been had Council availed of these procedures and had Parliament still not delivered its opinion. Some observers doubt whether, if Council were to exhaust its procedural possibilities to obtain Parliament's opinion, or if Parliament were to state openly that it was withholding its opinion in order deliberately to block decision-taking in the Community, the Court would rule the same way. The Court has, in other judgements, referred to the duty of loyal co-operation among the institutions, and it is possible that if Parliament were to block indefinitely, the Court might rule against it.

Taking advantage of the "Isoglucose" ruling

The isoglucose ruling coincided with the major overhaul of Parliament's Rules which it was carrying out following the first direct elections. Parliament sought to take advantage of the Court's ruling that its opinion was an indispensable part of the legislative procedure which Council must obtain. Notably, Parliament adopted new Rules whereby it could decide, on a proposal from the Chairman or Rapporteur of the committee responsible, to postpone the vote on the Commission's proposal until the Commission had taken a position on Parliament's amendments. Where the Commission refused to accept these, Parliament could refer the matter back to Committee for reconsideration, thereby exercising a *de facto* veto on the measure. Parliament generally avoids *explicitly* blocking decisions by withholding its opinion indefinitely and giving the impression that it is being entirely negative. Instead, if proposals are referred back to committee, or delayed in other ways, this is done in order to get further information, to investigate the social consequences, to pursue discussions with other institutions or interested parties, to hold public hearings, or to wait for related events. Parliament has also (even before the isoglucose ruling) used the device of an "interim report" such as on the Commission corporate taxation proposals, which it blocked for several years.

These procedures were used rather infrequently in the period from April 1981 to June 1987, and a number of weaknesses become apparent. Referral back was not automatic (the Chairman or rapporteur was not even forced to make a recommendation) and was sometimes not asked for when it should have been. The most serious difficulty for Parliament, however, arises where Council takes a decision "in principle" or "subject to Parliament's opinion" before this opinion has been delivered (11 times in 1986, eight in 1987, 12 in 1988, seven in 1989). This breaks Council's 1973 undertaking, and breaches the spirit and probably the letter of the isoglucose principle: it is unrealistic to think that in such circumstances Parliament's opinion will be taken into account or even examined by the Council, and it is therefore not surprising that Parliament experiences difficulty in obtaining formal information on when the Council resorts to such politically and legally reprehensible practices.

Notwithstanding these difficulties, the isoglucose ruling gave Parliament a potentially important device to fall back on if it is not satisfied with the response of the other institutions. This device is more significant for urgent matters where any delay can cause problems than for items that have been in the pipeline for 10 years and could equally well remain there for another 10. But even in the European Community, some matters are urgent and Parliament then has a strong bargaining position to fall back on.

A recent example was when Parliament considered the Commission's proposals for the first phase of Economic and Monetary Union, which had to be in place by July 1, 1990 if the timetable agreed at the Madrid Summit was to be respected. Parliament was keen to ensure a degree of accountability for the strengthened committee of Governors of Central Banks and the Economic Policy Committee and amended the Commission's proposals accordingly in December 1989 (Cox and Donnelly Reports Doc. A3–21/90 and A3–20/90). The Commission rejected key amendments, however, so Parliament referred the proposals back to committee, which jeopardized the whole timetable for EMU. By the February 1990 session, the Commission, anxious to avoid delay, made important concessions to Parliament, which then duly adopted its opinion.

The conciliation procedure

The conciliation procedure was instituted by a Joint Declaration of Parliament, Council and Commission on March 4, 1975. Such a Joint Declaration can be considered to be sort of constitutional convention between Council and Parliament, laying down procedures which they both undertake to follow. Whether such provisions are legally binding has not yet been tested, though the Court of Justice has referred to their existence.

Adoption and application of the procedure

The conciliation procedure resulted from a realization that the European Parliament might be in a position to use its new budgetary powers (see Chapter 12) to prevent the implementation of legislation with budgetary consequences. Council was therefore willing to negotiate and agree on a procedure aimed at reducing the risk of such conflicts by first seeking agreement with Parliament on the legislation.

The 1975 Declaration is as follows (our emphasis):

(i)   A conciliation procedure between the European Parliament and the Council with the active assistance of the Commission is hereby instituted.

(ii)   This procedure may be followed for Community acts of general application which have appreciable financial implications, and of which the adoption is not required by virtue of acts already in existence.

(iii)   When submitting its proposal the Commission shall indicate whether the act in question is, in its opinion, capable of being the subject of the conciliation procedure. The European Parliament, when giving its opinion, and the Council may request that this procedure be initiated.

(iv)   The procedure shall be initiated if the criteria laid down in paragraph (ii) are met and if the Council intends to depart from the opinion adopted by the European Parliament.

(v)   The conciliation procedure shall take place in a "Conciliation Committee" consisting of the Council and representatives of the European Parliament. The Commission shall participate in the work of the Conciliation Committee.

(vi)   *The aim of the procedure shall be to seek an agreement between the European Parliament and the Council.*
        The procedure should normally take place during a period not exceeding three months, unless the act in question has to be adopted before a specific date or if the matter is urgent, in which case the Council may fix an appropriate time limit.

(vii)   *When the positions of the two institutions are sufficiently close,* the European Parliament may give a new opinion, after which the Council shall take definitive action.

The Declaration thus uses terms that imply a certain number of obligations for Council, and its formal aim is to "seek agreement between the European Parliament and the Council". However, since Parliament is given little bargaining power, as the ultimate power to legislate has up to now been almost entirely in the hands of the Council, the procedure has in practice been merely an attempt by MEPs to beg Members of Council to think again. The parliamentary delegation has no bargaining position *vis-à-vis* Council other than, possibly, threatening not to vote the necessary credits when it comes to the following year's budget. Unless Parliament is totally opposed to the proposal, such a stance lacks credibility. Council has therefore had little in incentive to make major concessions to Parliament in the conciliation negotiations, especially when this would re-open nego-tiations within Council itself, and quite possibly endanger a compromise which Council may have reached only with the greatest difficulty. Only since the entry into force of the Single European Act has this situation changed (see below).

Nevertheless, there have been noticeably successful conciliations such as those on the Financial Regulation in 1977, which strengthened Parliament's budgetary powers; the Food Aid Regulation adopted in 1986; the New Community Instrument Regulation (NIC IV) of March 1987 extending the Community's borrowing and lending capacity to assist small- and medium-sized undertakings; the new regulation on agricultural structures of June 1987; the budgetary discipline provision of 1988; and the reform of the Regional and Social Funds in 1989; and the regulation on the collection of own resources of 1989 which strengthened the Commission's rights of inspection in Member States.

Furthermore, use of the procedure has increased over the years. Whereas only three procedures were completed between the signing of the Declaration and the first direct elections in 1979, and only two in the first three years of the directly elected Parliament, its use has risen to 18 in 1987 and 1988. In 1989, Parliament adopted a resolution aiming to improve the preparation and conduct of conciliation meetings (Prag Report), and some recent successes have led to the rehabilitation of the procedure.

The procedure does, after all, have the merit that:

- it is the only procedure permitting a direct confrontation between Parliament and Council as a whole. Ministers are confronted by the physical presence of MEPs, and it is possible to make a direct input to Council that has not previously been filtered by national officials or by the Commission;
- it would be difficult for Council systematically to refuse all Parliament requests;
- Council is not monolithic and it is sometimes possible to reopen discussions within Council;
- it helps Council get accustomed to negotiating with Parliament and to developing closer working relations with it.

Extension of the procedure

In 1981, the Commission started work on a second Joint Declaration and submitted a draft to Parliament. It proposed that the conciliation procedure should be applied to *all* important Community acts, as provided for by Article 58 of the Parliament's Rules of Procedure, and should be instituted at the request of any of the three institutions involved.

When it considered this proposal in 1983, (the De Pasquale report) Parliament substantially modified the Commission text but accepted its main points. It put forward three main demands:

- extending the field of application of the procedure;
- the possibility for the procedure to be initiated at the request of the Council or Parliament;
- the immediate holding of the first conciliation meeting between Parliament and the Council, with the active collaboration of the Commission, before they have adopted their respective positions on the proposal under discussion.

This question is still on the table. In the Stuttgart "Solemn Declaration" , the European Council undertook to "enter into talks with the European Parliament and the Commission with the aim, within the framework of a new agreement, of improving and extending the scope of the conciliation procedure". The Commission, the Parliament and all the Member States except Denmark have since agreed on the principle of extending it to include all significant Community legislation. Parliament is now returning to this question and trying to put pressure on Council to take a decision in an area in which it can, after all, act by a simple majority.

Meanwhile, Council has interpreted the concept of legislation "with appreciable financial implications" flexibly, allowing conciliations, in some cases, on proposals which do not obviously fall in this category. In addition, some "informal conciliations" have been held (such as on the proposals for the first stage of monetary union by means of a meeting between the Council Presidency, his successor, two Commissioners, and Parliament's rapporteurs and committee chairmen concerned). Council also agreed in 1989 to authorize its Presidents to hold preparatory meetings with the other institutions, prior to conciliation meetings. This enables detailed discussion to solve minor issues before the meeting.

The co-operation procedure

With the entry into force of the Single European Act in 1987, Parliament gained new powers. The co-operation procedure applies only to some 10 articles of the EEC Treaty but they include important areas, notably the bulk of legislative harmonization necessary for the single market, specific research programmes, regional fund decisions and some social policy matters. In volume, this is between one third and one half of the legislation Parliament considers. In these areas, the legislative procedure starts in the usual way: Commission proposal, Parliament opinion (possibly delayed to obtain concessions) and Council decision. However, the Council decision is not final. It is called a "common position" (even if it is adopted by qualified majority) and returns to Parliament for a second reading in which Parliament may do one of three things within a three-month deadline:

- explicitly *approve* the text, or by remaining silent approve it tacitly, in which case Council "shall definitively adopt the act in question in accordance with the common position" (Art. 149);
- *reject* the text, in which case it will fall unless Council unanimously agrees within three months and with the agreement of the Commission (which can always withdraw the proposal) to overrule Parliament;
- *propose amendments* which, if supported by the Commission are incorporated into a revised proposal which Council can only modify by unanimity whereas a qualified majority will suffice to adopt it. Council has three months to choose one of these options, failing which the proposal falls. Any amendments not supported by the Commission require unanimity to be adopted by Council.

In these last two cases, Parliament can only act by a majority of its members (currently 260 votes). The three-month deadline may be extended to four by joint agreement between Council and Parliament.

The consequences of the two readings procedure are ambiguous. On the one hand, parliamentary amendments not incorporated in the text in first reading seem likely to fare better in second reading, when Council positions have been fixed and where Parliament cannot act so easily (needing an absolute majority and unable to threaten to delay). Similarly, rejection is an unattractive option as Parliament is usually in the position of persuading a reluctant Council to act. On the other hand, as only legislation that Council *wants* will reach the stage of second reading, a Commission-

Parliament alliance could put a lot of pressure on Council, as it must choose within a short deadline whether to accept an amended proposal or lose it entirely. Unanimity would be required to change it back again. A single ally within Council can thus strengthen Parliament's position, and the threat of rejection if Parliament's views are not taken into account can strengthen the bargaining position within Council (already in first reading) of any state agreeing with Parliament. If it were to become unthinkable for a parliamentary rejection to be overridden (e.g. the Commission agreeing to withdraw any such proposal or just one Member State undertaking not to over rule Parliament for democratic reasons) then a position of co-decision would be achieved and Parliament could negotiate with Council (through the conciliation procedure or elsewhere) as an equal.

In any case, the second reading gives Parliament a chance to react to Council's position, gives some added scope to use public opinion, and provides for a more publicly visible way for dealing with parliamentary amendments. In view of future reforms, the ritual of two readings gives the impression of classic bi-cameral legislative procedure being followed at European level.

A good example of how Parliament can use these new powers was when it considered exhaust emission standards for small cars. Here, it was faced with a Council common position that fell below the standards it supported in its first reading. Parliament was keen on raising these standards to levels equivalent to those required in, for instance, the USA and Sweden, and it was known that some Member States shared Parliament's concern, but had been in a minority in Council. Parliament's committee on the environment therefore prepared second reading amendments that would restore the higher standards. In the debate, pressure was put on the Commission to accept these amendments before Parliament took its final vote. It was made clear that if the Commission did not do so, Parliament would instead reject the common position, and the legislation would fall as there was clearly no unanimity within Council to overrule Parliament. The Commission therefore accepted Parliament's amendments which were duly incorporated into a reviewed proposal. Council then had three months in which either to approve it by a qualified majority, or to amend it by unanimity (which it could not do as at least three Member States agreed with Parliament) or to see it fall (which it could not countenance, as this would have created havoc in the car industry with a divided internal market and uncertainty as to what standards to adapt to while the whole procedure started again). A reluctant majority in Council therefore adopted the reviewed text (which, incidentally, could cost every small car purchaser an extra £300 or so as a result, but will lead to a major improvement in the environment).

An analysis of the first two years of the co-operation procedure (July 1987–June 1989) shows that, for the 68 procedures that have gone through both readings in both institutions and, when adopted, been published in the Official Journal before June 14, 1989 (i.e. by the time of the last elections):

In first reading:
– Parliament approved 11 of them and amended the 57 others

- The Commission accepted 473 of the 712 amendments adopted by Parliament (i.e. 66 per cent) and modified its proposals to Council accordingly;
- Council approved 332 of the 712 parliamentary amendments (i.e. 47 per cent).

In second reading:
- Parliament approved without amendment over half (35) of the Council common positions;
- In 32 cases, Parliament adopted a total of 132 amendments to the common position, 70 of which (53 per cent) were supported by the Commission and 30 (23 per cent) by Council;
- In one case, Parliament rejected a common position and the text fell as Council was unable to overrule Parliament by unanimity within three months.

All these figures must be analysed cautiously. As crude arithmetic, they take no account of the importance of various amendments, nor, of course, of the discussion and bargaining that can lead to the withdrawal of amendments before they are voted on, or, conversely, the adoption of "no-hope" amendments merely to put pressure on for a compromise. Furthermore, the Commission or Council sometimes agree to take up Parliament's amendments in another way such as in another or a new directive, or simply give a political undertaking to Parliament. None of this can be reflected in the figures. What *is* clear is that Parliament is entering the traditional Commission-Council dialogue, is devoting time and energy to this, and is having a perceptible impact. The take-up rate for Parliamentary amendments by the Commission and by Council in first reading bears comparison to certain individual chambers in national parliaments. The EP is still some way from becoming an equal "chamber" with Council in a fully bi-cameral system, but some progress has been made in this direction. This is illustrated by Council's unwillingness to overrule Parliamentary rejection of a common position in second reading.

Developments resulting from the co-operation procedure

Determination of the legal base of proposals

Now that different procedures apply to different sectors of legislation, it is important for Parliament to ascertain that Commission proposals are put forward under the correct article of the Treaty. This "legal base" for proposals determines whether or not the co-operation procedure applies at all: Parliament has thus been vigilant to ensure that Treaty articles requiring the co-operation procedure are used in preference to those that do not, wherever there is scope for interpretation.

The Commission has usually been willing to co-operate closely with the Parliament on this. When the Single Act came into force, it immediately forwarded a list of some 145 proposals already before Council whose legal base would now be amended. Parliament and the Commission reached agreement on all but seven. Parliament also confirmed that the opinions it had already given on these proposals could be considered as its first reading under the co-operation procedure, except in the case of those 12 opinions predating the first direct elections to the Parliament in 1979, for which it insisted on renewed consultation (i.e. a new first reading).

For new proposals, the issue arises on a case-by-case basis, and a procedure for challenging the legal base has been provided for in Parliament's Rules (rule 36(3)), allowing the committee responsible, after consulting the Committee on Legal Affairs, to report straight back to the plenary on this point alone.

The more obvious areas that can be subject to divergent interpretations are those concerning emission standards for pollution (an environmental matter subject to Article 130 S or a harmonization necessary for fair competition in the Internal Market under Art. 100A?), and matters concerning the rights of workers that could come either under Article 100 or 118 A, or, indeed, 235. Parliament and Commission have disagreed on a number of these, but the Commission has accepted the Parliament's views that agricultural research should come under Article 130 H, and that mutual recognition of qualifications of doctors, nurses, vets and midwives should come under Article 57.

The most spectacular disagreement was on the Commission's proposal for a regulation laying down maximum permitted radioactivity levels for foodstuffs, where the limits agreed after Chernobyl needed to be replaced by a permanent measure to avoid separate national measures fragmenting the internal market for foodstuffs. Here, the Commission avoided Parliament's involvement under Article 100 A by using Article 31 of the Euratom Treaty as a legal base, requiring only the consultation of Parliament. Parliament first sought to amend the legal base, and then delayed giving its opinion when the Commission refused to change it. The delay forced Council to prolong the existing (temporary) regulation with its stringent limit values. Parliament then decided to give its opinion rejecting the Commission's proposal in the December 1987 plenary. In giving its opinion, it allowed Council to take a decision which it then attacked in the Court of Justice on the grounds of an incorrect legal base (case still pending).

The Commission and Parliament did agree on using 100 A as the basis for harmonizing environmental standards applicable to the Titanium Dioxide industry, but *Council* modified it to 130 S, which not only avoids the co-operation procedure but also requires unanimity in Council and therefore reduces the resultant legislation to the lowest common denominator acceptable to all Member States. The Commission, with Parliament support, has challenged Council's decision on this in the Court of Justice (this case is also still pending).

Reconsultation of Parliament

Where, in its common position Council departs markedly from the text on which Parliament deliberated in its first reading, and especially where new elements are incorporated into that text by Commission or Council, Parliament must be reconsulted (i.e. have a "second first-reading") in the same way as it is reconsulted in similar circumstances under the traditional consultation procedure. A second reading under the co-operation procedure is not sufficient if the changes made to the Commission's proposal are major ones (unless obviously, they are the changes proposed by Parliament). Council accepts this in principle, but difficulties sometimes arise, such as on the second directive on insurance other than life insurance, where the Council forwarded to Parliament a text that it regarded as its common position but which Parliament insisted on treating as a basic text on which it was being reconsulted on first reading. Clearly, however, Parliament is often reluctant to demand reconsultation when this would hold up a matter which it is keen for urgent action. Thus it let through some research programmes on which it could have insisted on reconsultation.

One special example of reconsultation is where Council amends the legal base to an article that eliminates the need for a second reading. Council has agreed to reconsult Parliament which gives a second opinion under the ordinary consultation procedure (first-reading procedure) on Council's "common orientation" (rather than "common position"). This is now being applied whenever Council seeks to make a change that would eliminate the second reading.

Information on Council's common position

Article 149, par. 2b of the Treaty now requires the Council and the Commission to inform the European Parliament fully of the reasons which led Council to adopt its common position. This is, of course, open to very wide interpretation. Council quickly agreed to present its justification to Parliament in writing. However, the first such justification received by Parliament merely referred in the covering letter to the preambles of the draft directives in question as constituting Council's justification. Not surprisingly, Parliament objected strongly to this, once its relevant committee (the Environmental Committee in this case) woke up to what had happened. Informal contacts were taken with Council, but President Plumb had to return to this subject again and make a formal statement to plenary on Oct. 28, 1987 on the unacceptability of Council's position. He stated that "as a minimum, the Council should provide a specific and explained reaction to each of Parliament's amendments".

The explanations provided by Council have now improved to the extent that they provide an account of Council's viewpoint on each of the substantive issues raised in the consideration of draft legislation. This is a considerable improvement, but still falls short of President Plumb's request. If Parliament were also to know what positions were taken by each Member of Council during votes, this would not only improve transparency but also enable Parliament to know what support might be forthcoming for possible second-reading amendments. Unfortunately, Council is still some way from providing such information on an official basis.

Contacts, negotiations and dialogue with the Council and Commission during the legislative procedure

The increase of its formal powers strengthens the European Parliament's position in the contacts and discussions with other institutions that inevitably accompany the consideration of legislative proposals.

The only formal procedure for negotiating with Council is the conciliation procedure mentioned above. Parliament's new powers could strengthen its bargaining position in this procedure, but the conciliation procedure can only be combined with the co-operation procedure in two areas (individual research programmes and regional fund decisions: the only two areas subject to the co-operation procedure which have budgetary consequences) and this has only been done so far for the regional fund decisions. Otherwise, Parliament has preferred to use informal contacts with Council between the two readings pending an extension of the conciliation procedure referred to above.

Dialogue with Council also takes place through the regular appearances of the Presidents-in-Office of the various specialized Councils before the responsible Parliamentary committees. Most appear twice during their six-month term. Since the entry into force of the co-operation procedure, these appearances have become an opportunity to discuss — formally in the meeting or informally in the corridor — the take-up of parliamentary amendments to legislative proposals still being considered by Council. The Commission also reports to Parliamentary committees on developments in Council.

Parliament is also exploring new forms of dialogue with Council. A provision to this effect was included in Parliament's new Rules (Rule 47, Point 5). Meetings and correspondence between committee chairman/rapporteurs and presidents-in-office have increased. On occasion, committee chairman have been invited to participate in relevant Council meetings. Contacts between officials in the committee secretariats and their counterparts in the Commission and Council are also being developed, and this has been facilitated by the transfer of a number of such officials from the isolation of Parliament's secretariat in Luxembourg to Brussels.

Change in balance of Parliament's activities

The increase in Parliament's legislative work, arising both from the introduction of two readings and from the growing volume of Community legislation generally in the run-up to 1992, has led to a shift of emphasis in Parliament's work. The number of legislative resolutions (opinions, second readings and assents) has doubled between 1985 (132) and 1989 (264), whereas the number of non-legislative resolutions has stagnated (392 in 1986, 341 in 1989) despite recourse to delegated adoption of such resolutions by committees (see Figure 2).

At the same time, Parliament tightened up its Rules to lay down that legislative resolutions deal only with procedural points and state whether Parliament approves, rejects or amends the text in front of it. They no longer contain lengthy comments on the proposal: any substantive points must be made by amending the Commission proposal or Council's common position directly.

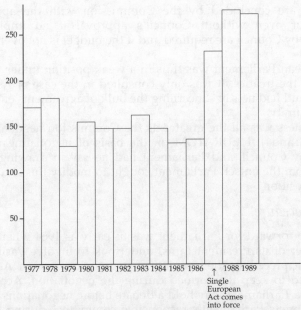

Figure 2 : *Legislative procedures (single reading, first and second readings, assent)*

Ratification of international treaties, and the assent procedure

The treaties allow the ·Community to be party to various sorts of international agreements. These agreements are always negotiated by the Commission (leaving aside accession agreements whereby new States join the Community, where the Member States negotiate after a decision in principle by Council). However, a variety of provisions were laid down in the treaties for authorising the Commission to open negotiations and for concluding (ratifying) the resulting agreement:

- under the ECSC treaty, no provisions were laid down for international agreements, but in practice the Commission, within the limits of its fields of responsibility, may negotiate and conclude agreements;
- under the EEC treaty, Art. 228 provided for the Commission to negotiate agreements which "shall be concluded by the Council after consulting the Parliament, where required by this treaty". Only Article 238 (Association agreements) provided, in fact, for such consultation of Parliament. The main instrument for international agreements, articles 113–114, (trade, commerce and tariffs) provided for no such consultation;
- under the EURATOM treaty, it is again only under Association agreements that Parliament is consulted (Art. 206). Ordinary agreements

(Art. 101) are concluded by the Commission with the approval of Council (or even without Council's approval if no implementing provisions by Council are required and if the budget is not overstepped).

The European Parliament was thus in a weak position under the initial provisions of the treaties. It was only consulted in the case of Association agreements, and had no say concerning the bulk of agreements entered into by the Community.

This weakness was all the greater as the Commission negotiates under Art. 113 EEC and 101 EURATOM on the basis of negotiating mandates decided on by Council, and Parliament had no say in drawing up such mandates. From the outset, Parliament sought to modify this situation and improve its position.

The Luns procedure

A first step forward for Parliament was as early as 1964 when Council, though a letter of its President Luns, undertook to involve Parliament in the discussion preceding the opening of negotiations for an Association agreement and to keep it informed during the negotiation. According to this procedure, Parliament may hold a debate before negotiations open, the Commission briefs Parliament's responsible committees during the negotiations, and when they have finished, Council's President or his representative appear before the same committees to brief them confidentially and informally, of the contents of the agreement.

The AETR ruling of the Court

In an important judgement in 1971 (case 22/70) the Court ruled that the Community as such is also responsible for the external aspects of its internal policies. This implies that the same treaty provisions would apply in approving external agreements as apply to the policy area in question. Where this provided for consultation of Parliament, Parliament would therefore also be consulted on the external agreements. This has been important notably in the areas of agriculture (Art. 43), transport (Art. 75) and for general economic co-operation agreements (Arts. 113 + 235).

The Luns–Westerterp procedure

Until the 1970s, Council had refused to give any rights such as those incorporated in the "Luns" procedure to Parliament for trade and commercial agreements, although these were more numerous and frequently more important (e.g. GATT) than Association agreements. The climate in Council changed somewhat in the early 1970s, partly as a result of the AETR ruling, partly because of the Paris Summit of 1973 agreeing to reinforce Parliament's powers (see above) and especially because of a realization that Parliament's new budgetary powers might enable it to cause problems for the implementation of agreements that have budgetary implications. First, the Commission agreed in its Memorandum to Parliament of the May 30, 1973, to participate in any debate that Parliament decided to organize in plenary or in committee on the negotiation of commercial agreements, and to brief Parliamentary committees during the negotiations (as in the Luns procedure). Then, in October 1973, Council President Westerterp undertook in a letter to Parliament on behalf of Council, to apply a modified version of the Luns procedure to commercial agreements. The text of Council's letter was virtually the same as that of 1964, except that it made no reference to the Commission briefing committees (covered already by the Commission's Memorandum) and it undertook to supplement the informal confidential briefing of Parliament's committees before signature of an agreement with a formal and public information to plenary after signature but before conclusion.

Improvement of the Luns–Westerterp procedures

The growing number of agreements entered into by the Community and the constant need to update and revise them led to further developments in 1977 when Council, through a letter of its President Crosland, agreed to distinguish between two types of agreement:

– Important agreements, where the Council's President's briefing of Parliament's committees would take place at a special meeting (normally in Brussels) instead of at the fringe of a plenary session, and where the President would submit a written aide-memoire in advance.
– Other agreements, where Council would simply inform Parliament in writing of the opening and the conclusion of negotiations, but where Parliament could, if it expressed the wish within two weeks, follow the procedure for important agreements instead.

At the same time, the Community was entering into more and more "co-operation agreements", a sort of half-way house between commercial agreements and association agreements involving such things as trade, technical co-operation, aid, loans, etc. These, not being specifically provided for under the treaty, required the use of Article 235 as a legal base and this in turn required consulting Parliament.

The Stuttgart "Solemn Declaration on European Union"

In this Declaration by the Heads of Government of the Twelve and the Commission, it was agreed that Parliament should be formally consulted on all "significant" international agreements before their conclusion, as well as on accession treaties. The Luns–Westerterp procedures were also extended to cover all important agreements (i.e. even those outside the scope of Article 113 and 238 EEC).

The assent procedure introduced by the Single European Act

The single European Act modified two articles of the EEC treaty in order to introduce a procedure whereby the assent of a majority of Members of the European Parliament is now required for the conclusion of association agreements (Art. 238) and for the accession of new Member States to the Community (Art. 237). Accession of new Member States is not something that arises every month, but the growing list of possible applicants to the Community is a reminder that, one day, Parliament will be in a position to block accession if certain conditions that it feels are important are not met. As accessions require changes to the Treaty, they would be an opportunity for Parliament to press for Treaty changes.

On the other hand, Parliament has dealt with a substantial number of association agreements with third countries or groups of countries. Indeed, this power has been far more significant than had been supposed by some of those involved in negotiating the Single European Act. The UK Permanent Representative, for instance, thought that there would be no such procedures "coming forward in the life of this Parliament". In fact, there were over 30 cases between the entry into force of the Single Act and the end of the 1984–89 Parliament. The large number arises in fact because of the need for parliamentary assent not just for the original agreement, but also for any revisions or additions to that agreement, such as financial protocols which may be adopted only for limited periods and require renewal.

Two examples show how Parliament can make use of this power. In December 1987, it simply postponed its vote on an agreement with Turkey in protest at the arrest of the leaders of two political parties upon their return to Turkey, accompanied by MEPs, for elections. It later approved the protocol in early 1988. More spectacular was Parliament's initial refusal to give its assent to three agreements with Israel. Parliament was unhappy with the conditions for exports to the Community for Palestinian producers in the occupied territories. The dispute occured at the time of the beginning of the *Intifada* in the West Bank and Gaza. Parliament therefore rejected three protocols to the EEC/Israel Association Agreement. Two were rejected by majorities and the third fell by virtue of failing to achieve the necessary support of a majority of members (it received 255 votes in favour instead of the 260 necessary, with 112 against). The agreements were referred back to Council. Council in turn referred them back to Parliament which agreed to put the proposals back on its agenda, but postponed consideration of them for several months. During this period the Commission, as well as MEPs from various Political Groups and Parliament's committee on external economic relations, had discussions with Israeli representatives which produced some concessions on West Bank exports. Parliament then approved the protocols.

The co-operation procedure and international agreements

The Single European Act also provided for the Community to adopt external agreements in the field of research and technology, and for such agreements to be approved by means of the co-operation procedure. This was a somewhat surprising provision, as the main purpose of the co-operation procedure, especially in first reading, is to enable Parliament to amend the texts before it. It is, however, difficult to amend either the texts of international agreements or even the legislative instruments bringing them into effect without reopening the whole negotiation, which would clearly be inappropriate except for important matters. Nonetheless, the procedure has been applied on a number of occasions, now, with Parliament approving the proposals in question without amendment in both readings.

If Parliament were to reject such an agreement, and to maintain its rejection by an absolute majority in second reading, then Council would need unanimity to adopt the agreement in question, whereas a qualified majority would normally suffice. This places the use of the co-operation procedure for the adoption of international agreements somewhere in between a simple consultation of Parliament (where a qualified majority in Council can adopt a proposal rejected by Parliament) and the assent procedure (where Council cannot adopt a text rejected by Parliament).

Recent developments

The application of the assent procedure to association agreements has led to a curious discrepancy in Parliament's powers. Whereas its assent is now necessary for what may frequently be only minor technical changes, to, for instance, financial protocols with Morocco or Malta, it is not even formally consulted under the Treaties for major agreements such as GATT or trade and co-operation agreements with the Soviet Union or other Eastern European countries.

Parliament has attempted to compensate for this discrepancy by providing in its Rules of Procedure (Rule 34) that significant international agreements (i.e. that category of agreements which the Stuttgart Solemn Declaration provided for Parliament to be consulted on) would be dealt with within Parliament by the same procedure as that applicable to association agreements. This means that Parliament will give its assent to their conclusion, renewal or amendment in the same way as it does for association agreements (though not requiring the same special majority, as this would not be a Treaty requirement in this case). Parliament would expect Council not to conclude an agreement that did not receive the assent of Parliament.

Parliament has also pressed the Commission and Council to make greater use of Article 238 (Association Agreements). Indeed, the criteria under which some agreements are deemed simply to be co-operation agreements (Article 113 + 235) and others are deemed to be association agreements are not always clear. Some "Association Agreements" are not even designated as such in their title. Parliament has therefore requested that significantly important agreements should be based on Article 238. This would apply in particular to the next generation of agreements with Eastern European countries, and the Commission has expressed sympathy with this viewpoint.

Indeed, the developments in Eastern Europe have raised the whole political profile of international agreements, and Parliament is now beginning to apply more systematically the various provisions at its disposal, and to request formal consultation on negotiating mandates and agreements, to press for Article 238 to be applied wherever possible, and to press for a clear definition of which agreements can be considered as "significant". The fact that the External Economic Relations Committee of Parliament is now chaired by Willy De Clercq, former Commissioner for external relations, has given added weight to this development. Discussions are now focusing, besides Eastern Europe, on the current

GATT (Uruguay Round) negotiations,. and the EC–EFTA, EC–Gulf States and EC–USA negotiations.

The Commission also undertook, following a statement made by Jacques Delors to Parliament in February 1990, to include MEPs as observers in its delegations, negotiating international agreements. This will greatly increase Parliament's access to information on such negotiations.

Parliament has thus come a long way from its initial position regarding international agreements, where it was merely consulted on a limited category of such agreements and received no information on their negotiations. Although its powers, apart from the assent procedure, still fall short of the right to authorise ratification that most national parliaments enjoy, its access to information on the conduct of such negotiations is actually better than most national parliaments.

Right to initiate legislation

The right to initiate legislative proposals is one that is traditionally associated with parliaments. But in practice, in most countries, this role has been taken over completely, or almost completely, by governments. In the UK, for example, MPs have to rely on a lottery system (the ballot for "private Members' bills") to introduce a limited category of legislative proposals themselves. In France, the government is given a virtual monopoly in this respect by the Constitution. Even in countries where there are no constitutional or regulatory limitations on Parliament in this respect, the detailed and technical nature of much modern legislation means that, in practice, most legislation is initiated by the Executive.

So it is in the European Community, where the Commission has a virtual monopoly of legislative initiative. The European Parliament itself has no formal right under the Treaty to initiate legislation, except for the purpose of adopting a uniform electoral procedure for European elections. Similarly, the Council cannot normally initiate Community legislation. Nevertheless, as in national situations, the formal provisions do not grant the Executive a monopoly on ideas nor the right to exercise these powers without due regard to the wishes of Council and Parliament. Council, indeed, was given the right under Article 152 EEC to request the Commission to undertake studies and to submit to it the appropriate proposals. Parliament, however, has had to fight for its rights in this regard itself.

Resolutions seeking to initiate legislation

Reference has already been made to Parliament's procedures governing the adoption of reports at its own initiative (either "own initiative" reports of parliamentary committees, or reports drawn up in response to Rule 63 motions for resolution tabled by MEPs, or indeed resolutions adopted through the urgency procedure or to wind up a debate). Being an independent institution, whose majority is not beholden to the Commission, Parliament frequently uses these opportunities to call on the Commission to take action of one sort of another, and this frequently includes calls for new legislative proposals. Naturally, individual MEPs or Political Groups or indeed parliamentary committees frequently make such proposals in their own right, but those carrying the most weight are own initiative reports drawn up after due consideration (possibly including public hearings) by the responsible parliamentary committee and adopted after due debate in plenary.

The Commission first responds to such initiatives in the debate in plenary. The Commission agreed in 1982 (in its "report on inter-institutional relations", the so-called Andriessen report, Bulletin EEC supplement 3/82) in principle to take up any parliamentary proposals to which it did not have any major objection. Where it had an objection, it undertook to explain its attitude in detail to Parliament. Since then, the Commission has submitted written reports every six months explaining how it has responded to Parliament's initiatives and what action it has taken.

Examples of how Parliament has initiated legislation in this way are not hard to find, but it is difficult to know in most cases whether Parliament can take exclusive credit or whether it has just played its part in a wider campaign. For instance, Parliament took the initiative in 1982 of pressing for a ban on the import of baby seal skins to the Community. In this, it was supported by a large amount of public campaigning including a petition with over a million signatures. These efforts resulted in a Commission proposals, then backed by Parliament in the legislative procedure, and the adoption of a Council regulation, despite initial reluctance by both the Commission and Council. Another example, this time without much support from public opinion, is the Community's directive on trans-frontier television broadcasts, laying down rules for such broadcasts. This can also be traced back to an own initiative report of Parliament's.

In the field of external relations too, parliamentary initiatives can lead to results. Thus the STABEX fund in the Lomé Convention which helps stabilize the exports earnings for certain products of the ACP countries, as well as the human rights clauses in that same Convention, owe their origin to parliamentary initiatives. Currently, the Community institutions are considering a directive on general product safety in the internal market which also owes its origin to an own initiative report on consumer protection.

Initiatives pursuant to the Joint Declaration of June 1982

The Parliament has used its budgetary powers to initiate new Community policies by means of creating new items in the budget and endowing them with funds. This procedure proved controversial, with Council taking the position that the creation of an item in the budget was an insufficient basis for the Commission to carry out the expenditure in question in the absence of a basic legislative act (normally a regulation) adopted by Council. Parliament considered that, as Article 205 EEC requires the Commission to execute the budget, the inclusion of an item in the budget itself provides a sufficient legal basis. In 1982, in the context of the inter-institutional agreement on the budget procedure described in more detail in Chapter 12, a compromise was reached on this issue on the basis of what had been the Commission's half-way house position. In this Joint Declaration of the institutions, it was agreed that legislation would be required where such a budget line created "significant" new Community action. When this was the case, the Commission would put forward the necessary proposal before the end of January, and Council and Parliament would use their best endeavours to adopt the necessary regulation before the end of May (failing which the Commission would propose transfers to other budget items).

This agreement thus opened the door for Parliament to initiate legislative proposals in areas that require Community expenditure by means of adopting appropriate items in the budget. This procedure has been used, for instance, to create the Community's food-aid policy, now a major component of the Community's development aid. At the same time, the creation of items in the budget that are not of "significant" character has continued, allowing one-off actions by the Community, studies, preparatory work for new initiatives and such like.

Cutting off budgetary funds

Parliament can also use its budgetary powers to cut certain items of non-obligatory expenditure, or to propose cuts in obligatory expenditure which Council can only overrule by a qualified majority. Theoretically, Parliament could use this technique to press for the revision of legislation governing the use of such expenditures, for instance, by reducing appropriations available to cover particular products under the Common Agricultural Policy. Until recently, the dilemma of whether a legal obligation arising out of agricultural regulations overrode the lack of provisions in the budget was always resolved in favour of the former interpretation. Nowadays, in the era of budgetary discipline, this is now no longer necessarily so, and Parliament has thereby gained extra leverage. These points will be discussed in more detail in Chapter 12.

Annual legislative programme

In the revision of its Rules of Procedure following the Single European Act, Parliament provided for its Enlarged Bureau and the Commission to agree on an annual legislative programme and timetable. Parliament's need to manage its workload and, no doubt, the fact that (unlike some national parliaments) it is master of its own agenda, persuaded the Commission of the advantages of negotiating an agreed programme. It has therefore accepted the procedure, and the first such programme was agreed in March 1988. Although this first experience consisted largely of determining a timetable for Commission proposals and parliamentary consideration thereof on a quarter-by-quarter basis, it did open the door for Parliament to influence the priorities in the Commission's programme and to press for the inclusion of new items (e.g. following-up parliamentary "initiative" reports) or even the exclusion of items.

The 1989 programme included a preamble in which the two institutions agreed to give priority to certain sectors (completion of internal market, social policy, environment policy and monetary integration) and to improve procedures by providing for trilateral meetings (Commissioner responsible, Council President and Parliament committee chairman and rapporteur).

In 1990, difficult discussions were held on re-scheduling various legislative proposals. Agreement was finally reached both on this and on a "code of conduct" in which the Commission undertook to improve its co-operation with Parliament.

Attempts are now being made to bring Council into legislative planning. This would be an opportunity to press for deadlines for finishing Council's first readings, which can still drag on for years. A useful step forward was initiated in November 1989 when the Irish Minister of Foreign Affairs, due to take up the Council presidency the following January, met the chairmen of Parliament's legislative committees to discuss the timetable of his presidency.

An inter-institutional working party of officials of all three institutions and the Economic and Social Committee meet every month to monitor progress in current legislative procedures and to try to anticipate difficulties.

Overall assessment

See Figure 3 for an overview of the stages in the legislative procedure.

The European Parliament's role in the Community's legislative procedure has increased from having, initially, no role whatsoever to play, to having a consultative role (the significance of which has developed considerably) to powers that are more than consultative in certain areas, even reaching the level of co-decision with Council.

Whatever their "bottom line" in terms of formal powers, MEPs also exert influence by their very presence in the discussions. Five hundred and eighteen politicians, with their own access to information, their own links to national, local and sectoral interests, with their own ideological perspectives and contacts, and with considerable facilities at their disposal, cannot fail to have an impact on the decision-making circuits of Brussels. The fact that their formal rights in the legislative procedure have increased can only reinforce their informal role.

The European Parliament is clearly not a sovereign Parliament in the sense of its word being final when it comes to the adoption of legislation in the areas for which it is competent. On the other hand, it is not a rubber-stamp Parliament whose real powers are in practice exercised merely to legitimize the Government's legislative wishes. The European Parliament is an independent institution whose members are not bound to support a particular governing majority, who do not have a permanent majority coalition within Parliament and whose party structures are not all pervasive. In this sense it resembles somewhat the United States Congress, with its own identity, independent legitimacy and separation from the executive, though seeking to interact intensely with the executive.

The European Parliament is part of an institutional triangle in which all three institutions have an important role to play in the adoption of Community legislation. It is still, perhaps, the weakest corner of the triangle but no longer as markedly so as it was 15 years ago. Indeed the very term institutional triangle was virtually unused two decades ago when most commentators referred to a bicephalous Community (Commission and Council).

184

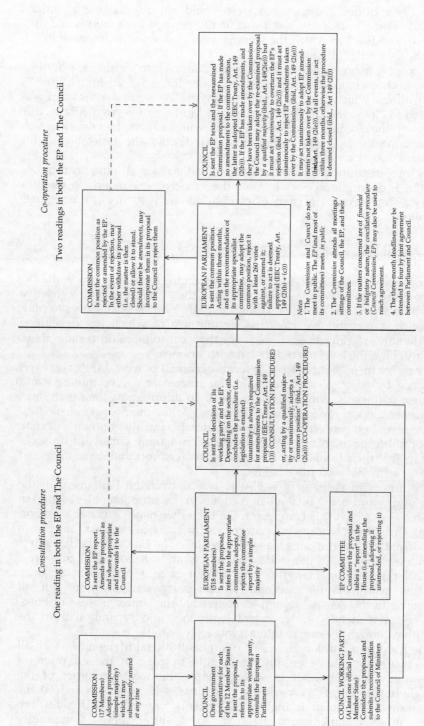

Figure 3: *Stages in the European Community legislative procedure*

The European Parliament has demonstrated its ability to initiate new legislation in areas of concern to the public (such as banning the import of baby seal skins), to force substantial amendments to major legislative proposals (e.g. the emission standards for cars) and to secure changes of detail (e.g. maximum decibel levels for small machinery) which, when cumulated, lead to a generally higher standard of protection for consumers, workers and other users. This direct impact on the life of Community citizens may well not be widely known. It is nonetheless real.

Table 7: *Which legislative procedure applies to what?*

The *assent procedure* applies to:
- accession of new Member States (Article 237)
- association agreements (Article 238)

The *co-operation procedure* applies to:
- Rules against discrimination on grounds of nationality (Article 7)
- Measures to bring about free movement of workers (Article 49)
- Freedom of establishment as regards a particular activity (Art. 54(2))
- Co-ordination of national provisions providing for special treatment of foreign nationals on grounds of public policy, public security or public health (Article 56(2))
- Mutual recognition of diplomas, certificates and other evidence of formal qualifications (Article 57(1))
- Co-ordination of national provisions on the activities of self-employed persons, except where existing principles laid down by law would be amended (Article 57(2))
- Harmonization measures to achieve the internal market (Article 100a)
- Equivalence of national provisions affecting the internal market (Article 100b)
- Improvements in the health and safety of workers (Article 118a(2))
- Economic and social cohesion as regards the ERDF (Article 130e)*
- Specific and supplementary programmes implementing the multiannual framework programme for research and development, Community participation in R & D programmes undertaken by several Member States, Community provision for co-operation with third countries or international organizations, and detailed arrangements for financing programmes (Article 130q(2))*.

The *consultation procedure* applies to:
- *common policies*: agriculture (Article 43)*, transport (Article 75)*, private sector competition (Article 87), certain social policy matters (Articles 126 and 127)*, co-ordination of structural funds (Article 130d), multi-annual framework programmes, for research and development policy and setting up of joint undertakings (Article 130q(1))* environmental policy (Article 130s)*, further measures to attain one of the Community's objectives (Article 235), abolition of restrictions on the freedom of establishment and on the provision of services (Articles 54(1) and 63(1)), directives to liberalize a specific service (Article 63(2)), taxation (Article 99) harmonization of national provisions which affect the common market (Article 100), and nuclear energy and radiation (11 articles in Euratom treaty);

- *institutional matters*: framework decision on implementing powers for the Commission (Article 145, third indent), setting-up of the Court of First Instance (Article 168a), amendments to Title III of the Statute of the Court of Justice (Article 188), appointment of the members of the Court of Auditors (Article 206(4)), adoption of the Staff Regulations (Article 212), and the calling of an intergovernmental conference to modify the Treaty (Article 236);
- *budgetary matters*: decision on the Community's own resources (Article 201)*, and Financial and other Regulations (Article 209)*.

*matters regarding which the *conciliation procedure* may also apply.

12.   The budgetary role

The role of the Parliament in the budgetary process can only be understood in the context of the distinctive way the Community is financed and the use to which that finance is put. Both in terms of revenue and in terms of expenditure, the EC is quite different from traditional international organizations. Such organizations, like the United Nations, are financed by national contributions calculated on the basis of the relative wealth of the Member States and devote by far the largest part of their revenue to administrative costs, including the upkeep of buildings, salary costs etc. By contrast, the EC has its own revenue, entitled "own resources", and uses it to finance the policies which the Commission implements, with running costs constituting a relatively modest element. In 1990, for example, of a total budget of 46.7 bn ECU, only 2.3 bn ECU or 5 per cent was set aside for the administrative expenditure of all the institutions.

The financing system has also been subject to important changes over time. Until 1970, the Community *was* financed by national contributions but it was then decided to replace them with "own resources", made up of customs duties and agricultural levies on imports from outside the EC as well as a proportion of national receipts from VAT. This change was not only important in making the resources collective Community property which Member States were legally obliged to make available but it also provided a debate about who should exercise control over the revenue collected and who should decide how it be allocated and used. The result of this debate was that the top limit on the revenue available to the EC is fixed by the Member States with any change requiring ratification at the national level, but that within this overall limit expenditure is determined jointly by Parliament and Council, often referred to in this context as the twin arms of the "budgetary authority".

This change in the position of the Parliament, as consolidated by treaty revision in 1975, established four major powers for the Parliament. The first three relate to the procedure for establishing the budget, the fourth concerns the implementation of the budget. The Parliament:

– first, acquired the right to increase Community expenditure, within certain defined limits, without having to obtain the approval of the Council;
– second, gained the opportunity to distribute the sums voted across the various sectors of the budget;
– third, gained the power to reject the whole budget; and
– fourth, was given the exclusive right to grant the discharge to the

Commission, i.e. to approve or not the way in which the Commission spends the money voted in the budget.

The mechanisms that give effect to the powers relating to the budgetary procedure, which are to be found in Article 203 of the EEC Treaty, are summarized as in Table 8 below:

Table 8: *The budget: rules of the game*

The budget procedure begins with the Commission preparing its estimates for Community policies (and adding each institution's estimates for its own administrative expenditure) in the form of a *preliminary draft budget* which it forwards to Council. Council, acting by a qualified majority, then prepares a *draft budget* which it must forward to Parliament by Oct. 5, Parliament then*:

- adopts "modifications" to "compulsory expenditure" (essentially agriculture, administrative refunds to Member States and expenditure arising out of agreements with third countries) by a simple majority of those voting;
- adopts "amendments" to "non-compulsory expenditure" (including the Regional and Social Funds, energy and research, transport, development aid, the environment, education and culture) by a majority of its Members (260 or more).

The Budget is then referred back to Council for a second reading. Concerning Parliament's "modifications" to compulsory expenditure, Council has 15 days to take a final decision, needing:

- a qualified majority to *approve* any modification that increases expenditure
- a qualified majority to *overrule* any modification that does not increase expenditure (cuts or transfers)

Concerning Parliament's "amendments" to non-compulsory expenditure, Council may modify them, but only by a qualified majority, and such modifications are referred back to Parliament for its second reading.

In its second reading, Parliament has 15 days to amend these latter modifications, which requires three-fifths of the vote cast and at least a majority of members. Parliament may also by a similar majority reject the draft budget as a whole, in which case the whole procedure must start again, Community expenditure in the meantime being frozen at the previous year's level on a month-by-month basis.

Council and Parliament may not increase non-compulsory expenditure beyond a "maximum rate" worked out (by the Commission) from economic indicators (GDP, inflation, government spending). However, they may jointly (by qualified majority in Council and majority of members and three-fifths of votes cast in Parliament) agree on a higher rate and Parliament anyway may always allocate an amount equal to half the maximum rate, even if Council has used more than half or all.

Finally, it is up to the President of Parliament to sign the budget into law when all the procedures have been completed.

*If it does not act within 45 days, or if it explicitly approves Council's draft, the budget is adopted as Council established it. This has never happened.

The procedures within Parliament

What, though, does all this mean in practice for the Parliament? How does the Parliament behave to take full advantage of its powers? To answer these questions, it is useful to follow the budget discussions through the year and to identify the variety of choices that face Parliament.

The first step is taken by the Committee in Budgets which nominates two rapporteurs, one with responsibility for the Commission's budget, the other for the other institutions, including the Parliament itself. Normally these appointments are made already in January of the year preceding the financial year under discussion. (In the Community, the financial year runs from January to December.) In the months leading up to the summer, it is the second of the rapporteurs who has the most to do because he or she is responsible for guiding the estimates of the Parliament itself through the plenary, usually in May. The discussions are not limited to the Budgets Committee — both the Bureau and the Enlarged Bureau are involved, the former having a decisive say on the number of new posts to be created in the establishment plan, with the Budgets Committee deciding whether to grant the related appropriations.

During the same period the rapporteur for the Commission budget steers through committee and plenary a set of guidelines laying down the Parliament's priorities with the aim of influencing the Commission's pre- liminary draft. The preliminary draft is made up of the consolidated estimates of revenue and expenditure of all institutions. It is divided into five sections:

Section I	Parliament
Section II	Council with an annex for the Economic and Social Committee
Section III	Commission
Section IV	Court of Justice, including the Court of First Instance
Section V	Court of Auditors

It is usually presented by the Commission to the Parliament in May or June, though officially in the Treaties it is not obliged to do so until July.

The role of the Commission in preparing the preliminary draft has a major bearing on the rest of the procedure. Its own budget constitutes around 94 per cent of the total and is the subject of the broadest discussion between Parliament and Council. Its initial shape is strongly influenced by the budget of the previous year but also serves as a reference point for the remainder of the procedure. It reflects the established spending priorities of the Community but also allows the Commission a major power of initia- tive, comparable to that which it exercises in the realm of legislation.

The presentation of the preliminary draft in June is usually followed by the adoption of the draft budget by the Council in July. The Treaties specify that the draft must be adopted by Oct. 5 but normally it proves possible for the Council to adopt before the summer holidays. However, respect for the Treaties is not guaranteed. In 1987, even the later October date could not be respected because of the severity of the revenue crisis at that time and the draft was not adopted until February of the following year. On that occasion both Parliament and Commission took the Council to court for failure to respect the Treaty. By the time the Court ruled, however, the procedure had been resumed and the only sanction applied to the Council was that it had to pay the costs of the case!

On the day that the Council meets to adopt the draft budget a *conciliation* meeting takes place between a delegation of the Parliament and the Ministers gathered for the budget first reading. Although the term "conciliation" is the same as that used for the meetings between Council and Parliament in the legislative procedure discussed in Chapter 11, its purpose is not the same. It is not designed to bring the positions of the two parties closer together nor does the Parliament have the option to decline to close the procedure, thereby blocking the adoption of the Council's first draft. Rather it gives the Parliament an opportunity to underline its priorities and to invite ministers to engage in a discussion with them. Such meetings can be very formal occasions with ministers reluctant to accept the invitation of the Council Presidency to comment on the Parliament's views in advance of the Council's own deliberations on the draft budget. However, at other times, lively discussions can take place, with ministers wishing either to underline their disagreement with the Parliament's position or to signal their basic sympathy with it. Once the conciliation meeting is at an end, the Council continues its meeting in closed session, adopts the draft budget and forwards it to the Parliament.

Normally the Council sees its role as reducing the preliminary budget presented by the Commission to what it considers more reasonable proportions. However, this is not always the case. Following the agreement made in February 1988 at the European Council meeting in Brussels to double the size of the structural funds by 1993, the Commission enters the amount required to reach this goal and the Council leaves it intact. Furthermore, in relation to the Parliament's budget, there is a gentleman's agreement that the Council will not alter the figures. By the same token, the Parliament does not amend those of the Council at its first reading. This mutual forbearance is viewed with some envy by the other institutions, none of which escape the Council's reductions. Within the Parliament, there are those who feel that the agreement stifles debate between the two institutions, but so far this view remains in a minority.

If adoption of the draft does not take place at the end of July, there is an informal agreement between Council and Parliament that it will not formally be forwarded until the end of August. The Parliament then has 45 days in accordance with the Treaty to respond to the Council's first reading. This is a period of intense activity, particularly within the Budgets Committee, which is the committee which co-ordinates the Parliament's response and mediates between the different interests within the Parliament.

It is the task of the rapporteurs to determine the main lines of the response to be given to the Council and of suggesting how the Budgets Committee should choose between the competing demands presented by the other spending committees of the Parliament. Both are the subject of considerable lobbying, particularly from within Community institutions.

The Commissioner responsible for the budget will be in close contact with the rapporteur for the Commission's budget, although this will not stop approaches from other parts of the Commission, including those who may have been disappointed by the decisions taken within the Commission. And, although the budgets of the other institutions are smaller than that of the Commission, contacts with the rapporteur responsible are usually very intense: the smaller institutions recognize that the Parliament's rapporteur offers them their best chance of improving on the results of the Council draft.

The ideas of the rapporteurs, based on their consultation, rarely go directly to the whole committee. There are usually meetings of the Political Group co-ordinators to discuss the general guidelines presented by the rapporteur and to seek some kind of agreement in advance of the discussions in committee. This is particularly important when it comes to discussing the amendments that are tabled by the other committees, individual members of the Parliament or Political Groups. As we have seen, the Treaty lays down that amendments require the support of at least a majority of the members of the Parliament, i.e. at present 260. There is therefore a high premium on gaining a consensus within the committee and thereafter in the Parliament as a whole. Failure to reach such a consensus can only endanger the chance of amendments being adopted in the plenary.

In the budgetary procedure, as in the co-operation procedure discussed in Chapter 11, there is particularly strong pressure on the two largest groups in the Parliament, namely the Socialists and the Christian Democrats, to reach agreement. If they can reach an agreement then it is most probable that the majorities needed will be gained. However, if either one of them is unwilling to go along with the particular amendment then it is highly unlikely that it will be adopted in plenary. The success of this process of mediation and consensus seeking in the Budgets Committee for the 1990 budget can be measured by the fact that at the first reading of the budget in October some 700 amendments were put to the vote, and only on two occasions were the positions taken by the Budgets Committee earlier on those amendments defeated.

Compulsory and non-compulsory expenditure

As explained above, the Parliament has the right to increase expenditure, but only within certain defined limits. First, the expenditure in the budget is not all subject to the same rules. A basic distinction is that between what is called "compulsory" and "non-compulsory" expenditure. The distinction is not a very helpful one to the outsider in that it does not tell him or her what kind of expenditure falls into one category or the other. Definitions have varied, but it is often argued that compulsory expenditure is unavoidable expenditure to which third parties have a legal claim, whether they be farmers benefiting from the Community's guaranteed prices or non-EEC countries linked to the Community by international agreements, with a financial component. On this basis, non-compulsory expenditure is defined as avoidable expenditure where the Community enjoys broad discretion as to the level of expenditure that it incurs.

Unfortunately, such definitions are far from foolproof. So although the salaries of the officials of the European Communities have to be paid, nevertheless the expenditure is classified as non-compulsory. At the same time, expenditure provided for the depreciation of agricultural stocks is classed as compulsory even if there are no stocks to depreciate.

The distinction is in fact much more of a political than a technical one. It serves to cordon off a large part of the budget and to reduce to a minimum the Parliament's involvement in shaping that part. Thus, rather than seeking to offer a coherent, objective basis for the distinction, one can offer a crude distinction in terms of compulsory expenditure applying to agricultural expenditure, refunds to Member States and expenditure arising from international agreements with third countries. Virtually all other expenditure is classified as non-compulsory.

However, the situation is far from static. Much of the activity of the Parliament has been geared to changing the frontiers between the two kinds of expenditure and considerable success has been enjoyed in this struggle. Fifteen years ago there was less than 10 per cent of the budget in the non-compulsory category, whereas now that category represents around 35 per cent of the total. The section of the budget where Parliament makes the final allocation (see section "The budget: rules of the game" above) has thus become a bigger proportion of a bigger budget.

This does not mean that Parliament has no influence in the field of compulsory expenditure. This is particularly true if it does not propose an increase in expenditure. If proposals for modification either involve a decrease in expenditure or compensate an increase by a reduction in another area, then it requires a qualified majority in the Council to *overrule* the proposed modification suggested. This is in contrast to proposed modifications for an increase in expenditure which require a qualified majority to be *accepted*.

Consider the example of the line that the Commission wished to create in the 1990 budget providing for rural development. It suggested expenditure totalling 200 mn ECUs which the Council eliminated from its draft budget. The Parliament then had the choice of re-entering the line with the 200 mn ECUs proposed by the Commission or it could simply put a p.m. against the line. The latter alternative would mean that there was no money available immediately but that funds could be transferred to it in the course of the year. Though the former course might look more adventurous from the outside, it was agreed that it was more important to establish the principle of such expenditure within the budget and to do so by entering a p.m. in the budget. This proved to be a sensible decision in that at second reading the Council was not able to find a qualified majority to overrule the proposed modification, which thereby stood adopted. Had Parliament re-entered the 200 mn ECUs, it would probably not have obtained the qualified majority in favour that would have been necessary.

The maximum rate of increase

Despite the fact that Parliament enjoys some scope for influencing compulsory expenditure, it is nevertheless true that the bulk of its activity is geared to discussing non-compulsory expenditure where it enjoys the last word. This last phrase should not be misunderstood. It does not mean that Parliament is free to enter in the budget any increase that it wishes to. At first reading it can certainly adopt amendments of any level but it knows that at second reading those increases will have to be reduced to the level permissible under the Treaties. The Treaties specify that non-compulsory expenditure can increase from one year to the next by no more than what is called the maximum rate of increase. This is a statistical measure calculated by the Commission which takes account of economic growth, government expenditure and the rates of inflation in the Member States.

Article 203 of the Treaty indicates that the Parliament can always enter amounts totalling at least half the maximum rate (i.e. if Council enters increases that account for all or most of the maximum rate, Parliament still retains the right to enter an amount equal to half the rate). This has generally meant in practice that the Council, at its first reading, has entered half the maximum rate, leaving it to Parliament to enter the other half. The amount involved inevitably varies depending on the maximum rate but has regularly been of the order of 600 to 700 mn ECUs. In other words, the Parliament has been given the opportunity to add and distribute expenditure of between 300 and 400 mn ECUs. (Any further distribution must be done by transfers from one item to another, which is inevitably more delicate politically.)

However, the situation is complicated by the fact that the Treaty also allows for the budgetary authority to decide to increase the maximum rate set by the Commission if it considers that Community activities require it. Hence, Parliament has often sought to persuade the Council to agree to a new maximum rate. Through most of the 1980s, up until 1988, this was not always easy as the total volume of expenditure was under severe pressure because of difficulty in controlling agricultural expenditure. The Parliament regularly argued that the Council was not making adequate provision for what was required. Thus, in 1985 Parliament maintained that in the draft budget for 1986 Council failed to provide adequate finance for 12 Member States with the prospect of Spanish and Portuguese membership, and ignored the problem of the "weight of the past", i.e. accumulated commitments from previous years which were liable for payment. At the end of the procedure, the Parliament's President signed a budget which went more than 600 mn ECUs beyond the maximum rate figure to which the Council could agree. The result was that the Council took the Parliament to court in Case 34/86 and won, in the sense that the Court ruled that any new maximum rate had to be *explicitly* agreed between the Council and the Parliament. However, the new budget that was agreed in July 1986 included virtually identical increases in the structural funds to those voted by the Parliament in December 1985 as well as important increases in the EAGGF Guarantee Section.

The debate about increases in the maximum rate has taken on a different form since February 1988. At that time, the Heads of State and Government agreed to a new framework for Community financing which allowed for a major expansion in the revenue available to the Community, as well as stricter controls on the development of expenditure, with particular

194   THE EUROPEAN PARLIAMENT

reference to agriculture. In relation to expenditure the European Council meeting went so far as to envisage what the budget of the Community should look like in 1992, not just in overall terms but by category of expenditure. Subsequently, in negotiations between the Council, the Parliament and the Commission, it proved possible to fill out the figures agreed by the Heads of Government and to provide a financial framework for each year leading up to 1992 and the creation of a single market. The three institutions signed what is called the "interinstitutional agreement on budgetary discipline and the improvement of the budgetary procedure". This agreement radically altered the argument about the maximum rate of increase. In particular, it provided for the very major increases in the structural funds that were agreed in 1988 so as to enable those funds to be doubled by 1993. Such doubling could not take place without the normal maximum rates being substantially exceeded. Hence, the interinstitutional agreement contained within it the effective agreement of the institutions in advance of the budgetary procedures to go beyond the traditional maximum rate. The Parliament has interpreted this agreement as allowing it to go up to the ceilings of expenditure in those areas which are of most interest to it and to assume that the maximum rates arising out of its actions were acceptable to the Council. So far the Council has not challenged this interpretation.

Parliament's objectives and strategy

What the Parliament has been always eager to do has been to use the budget to promote new Community policies. For many years, it devoted a large part of its margin for manoeuvre (i.e. at least half of the maximum rate allowed under the Treaties) to increase spending on the structural funds. However, with the agreement taken at the European Council in February 1988 it no longer has to do this. It now devotes more attention to other areas of policy which are not privileged in this way by the Council. One example is transport, where the Parliament has consistently entered substantial funds with the aim of inducing the Council to adopt a Community policy in this area. However, despite its best endeavours and despite a ruling of the Court of Justice that the Council was failing in its duties by not agreeing to such a policy, so far the money entered has not led to a real Community transport policy. This has not stopped Member States from using the money but they have done so by agreeing to ad hoc arrangements allowing the Community to finance particular projects put up by the Member States.

Another major area of interest is development aid. Although a very large part of the aid financed by the Community in this area falls under the European Development Fund which for the time being lies outside the Community budget, there is still a substantial volume of expenditure (about 1 bn ECU), including large appropriations for food aid, which does come before the Parliament. This section of the budget regularly receives between a third and a half of the Parliament's margin for manoeuvre with members eager to respond to the pressure from within their countries that the Community use its influence to act against food shortages in the third world. Similarly, there is considerable pressure to increase expenditure in the fields of social affairs, education, the environment, energy and industry.

The increases that the Parliament can vote on individual lines are necessarily small when set against the overall size of the budget. However, the importance of those increases should not be underestimated. First, even quite a small sum of money can help to generate a substantial level of activity. An example of small amounts having a substantial effect is the ERASMUS programme designed to encourage university students to spend part of their study time in another Community country. In the 1989 budget the Parliament voted for an amount which was 9.5 mn ECUs larger than the sum the Council was prepared to include and indeed, 7.5 mn ECUs more than the Commission itself had asked for. This was an increase of some 20 per cent in the budget of this programme and therefore enabled a very much more substantial level of activity than would otherwise have been possible.

Secondly, the effect of entering money can accumulate over a number of years so as to generate a very substantial level of activity. An example of this second process is the aid set aside for Latin American and Asian countries. This began in the middle 1970s with very minimal amounts of money but now there are nearly 300 mn ECUs in the budget provided for aid to these countries. The sum remains limited, but there has, nevertheless, been a substantial increase over the period of life of these appropriations.

The amendments voted to add appropriations are not created in a vacuum. Some derive from the encouragement of the Commission to reinstate the appropriations entered in the preliminary draft. Others may be in response to pressure from outside: in the 1990 procedure, for example, there was an amendment adopted to add 1.26 mn ECUs to the Community action programme to assist the handicapped. This amendment was the focal point of a "fair deal" campaign launched by the co-ordinating body of 10 different national disability organizations from the Member States and began life at a Social Affairs Committee meeting, where these organizations presented the proposal for increase. It witnessed a very effective cross-party and cross-nationality campaign which meant that the amount initially proposed was left unscathed as a result of the discussions, both in the Budgets Committee and the plenary. Others again may be proposals that the rapporteurs are eager to support. Such was the case, for example, of the amendment amounting to 24 mn ECU adopted in 1989 for the budget of the Court of Auditors which enabled the Court to buy its own building and to cease paying substantial rental charges. This suggestion was strongly backed by the rapporteur, eager to encourage all the institutions to review their buildings' policies.

Not all amendments are designed to increase expenditure. The budgetary rights of the Parliament allow it to redistribute expenditure between lines in the budget and this opportunity was taken in the 1990 budget by, for example, the Environment Committee which proposed that a consumer protection programme that the Commission wished to maintain be deleted by the cutting off of its funds. The committee felt that a new programme, with different priorities, needed to be established. In the budget, as finally adopted, the programme was duly deleted.

Amendments are also not restricted to expenditure. Next to every line of the budget there are remarks which specify the use to which appropriations are to be put. Many amendments are concerned to modify these remarks and to determine different criteria for the allocation of expenditure than those proposed by the Council. In the 1990 procedure, for example, it was agreed that certain aid provisions be modified to exclude the possibility of payments to China, following the events in Tiananmen in the summer of 1989. The Parliament considers that these remarks are binding and therefore follows, with great attention, the way in which the money is spent in the following year, eager to check that the Commission does indeed act as specified in the budget.

From first to second reading

When the Parliament votes the amendments before it at first reading it is essential to ensure that there are sufficient members present to obtain the 260 votes to adopt them. The Groups issue instructions to encourage all their members to be present and when the vote comes before any amendment is voted there is an electronic check to verify that enough members are in the chamber. Thereafter the vote proceeds at a considerable pace. If the work of the Budgets Committee has been successful, then the vote on individual amendments is usually clear. However, there are controversial points where it is necessary to have an electronic check on the way the votes were cast. At the end of the vote the amendments voted by the Parliament are collated and sent as forming the Parliament's first reading to the Council for its discussion at second reading. The Council, for its part, has 15 days in which to respond. At the end of this period it holds a meeting at ministerial level and before this meeting there is a second conciliation meeting with the Parliament's delegation, comparable to that held in July before the first reading. At this stage the positions of the two parties are much better known and the Parliament has an opportunity to make it clear what it anticipates the Council will do to enable it to proceed with its second reading.

In the 1990 procedure the conciliation meeting in November was dominated by the Parliament's calls for an increase in the volume of aid for the economic restructuring of Poland and Hungary. The whole Community was absorbed in discussions about how to respond to dramatic events in Eastern Europe and the Parliament considered that it was essential that the maximum effort be made out of the Community budget to respond to these unexpected circumstances. At first reading the Parliament voted for a level of aid of 300 mn ECUs, but this amount could not be provided within the existing ceiling for that category under the interinstitutional agreement referred to earlier. The Parliament's delegation urged the Council to agree to an upward revision of the ceiling to make this possible, arguing that there was a substantial volume of revenue available within the overall resource ceiling and that it was important for the Community to show its willingness to respond to events in Eastern Europe.

Both Commission, which had the responsibility to propose an increase in the expenditure ceiling, and Council were reluctant to move on this

question and the second reading of the Council did not give satisfaction to
the Parliament. This, therefore, generated an atmosphere of uncertainty as
to how the Parliament would act at second reading. The Parliament
representatives and in particular its rapporteur and the Committee on
Budgets made it clear that the Parliament intended to enter the 300 mn
ECUs in the budget whatever the Council might think and would challenge
the Council to take the Parliament to court if it did so. The result was that
there were very intense negotiations between the three institutions in
advance of the second reading of the Parliament at the December plenary.

There is provision for problems in the budgetary procedure to be
discussed by what is called the "trialogue", a meeting of the Presidents of
the three institutions. In fact, these negotiations took place between the
President-in-Office of the Council (the French Minister responsible for the
budget), the Commissioner with responsibility for the budget and the
rapporteur of the Budgets Committee. They met on the Monday of the
plenary session in December and held an eight-hour negotiating session in
the course of which the Parliament did gain the agreement of the other two
institutions for a proposal to revise upwards the level of expenditure
allowable to the Community, thus making it possible for 300 mn ECUs to
be made available to Poland and Hungary. In exchange, the Parliament
conceded on a number of other amendments that it wished to be included
in an upward revision of the expenditure ceiling, inviting the Commission
to take account of those proposals when that ceiling was reviewed in the
spring of 1990.

The result of the negotiations was endorsed by the Budgets Committee
and by the plenary at the vote two days later on the Wednesday. Indeed,
the negotiations were supported so widely that it was proposed that the
vote on the amendments be taken in one block, but this did not prove
possible. Such negotiations just in advance of the Parliament second
reading have been a regular feature of the budgetary procedure in recent
years. Indeed, it encouraged the use of the phrase "the night of the
crumpled suits". However, the importance of these negotiations is that they
underline the strong pressure that exists for the two arms of the budgetary
authority to use their maximum endeavours to find an agreement in
advance of the vote at second reading of the Parliament. Both sides wish to
have a budget which is closest to their conception but both also wish to
reach a conclusion.

The 1986 court case referred to above shows that the Parliament is not
able to act unilaterally and indeed, the following year the impact of the
court case was well illustrated. In December 1986 it voted amendments in
non-compulsory expenditure which went beyond the maximum rate of 8.1
per cent. However, the President of the Parliament whose job it is to sign
the budget into law recognized the force of the court ruling and did not
sign the budget on the grounds that there had not been an agreement
between the Council and Parliament on the new maximum rate. The
following February, agreement was reached following some movement on
the vexed question of agriculture expenditure in the Council and a face-
saving formula on non-compulsory expenditure was devised. The Council
agreed to an increase of 8.149 per cent in non-compulsory expenditure

arguing that the maximum rate only applied to the first decimal point. The
Parliament, for its part, was able to claim that the maximum rate had been
exceeded and honour was saved on both sides.

The option of rejection

The Treaty does provide for the option of the Parliament rejecting the
budget. This is what it did in December 1979 in the first budgetary
procedure that followed direct elections to the Parliament and in December
1984 following the second direct elections. In 1982, it also rejected a
supplementary budget, designed to finance the British rebate. On all three
occasions, the Parliament was dissatisfied with the budget that the Council
was prepared to accept and called for a new draft to be submitted to it. The
impact of such a decision is not to bring the whole Community to a
standstill. A complex arrangement comes into force on Jan. 1 if no budget is
voted by that time, whereby the Commission is only allowed to spend each
month the equivalent of one twelfth of the expenditure included in the
previous year's budget or in the draft budget under preparation before it
was rejected, whichever is the lower. This allows the Community to
function but it does not allow any new activity to take place. Take the
example of the 300 mn ECUs voted for Poland and Hungary in December
1989. As there was no budgetary line for such action provided in the 1989
budget, if the budget had not been agreed, it would not have been possible
to spend any of the money that the Parliament wished to spend at the
beginning of 1990. This was naturally a situation that both the Council and
the Parliament wished to avoid given the amount of attention that the
countries of Eastern Europe were devoting to the Community.

Implementation of the budget

Once the budget is voted, it is then the duty of the Commission, under
the Treaty, to implement it as it has been voted. This does not, however,
mean that the Parliament's involvement ceases.

First, in the course of the financial year the Commission has to come to
the budgetary authority with any request it has for transfers of
appropriations from one part of the budget to another. If, for example, the
budgetary authority has entered monies in the general reserve referred to
as Chapter 100, then the Commission has to ask for permission for that
money to be used. Where the money is compulsory then the Council has
the last word, with the Parliament only giving an opinion. However, where
the expenditure is non-compulsory the Parliament has the last word.
Hence, it can block the expenditure or delay its being released until certain
conditions are met. This is, in fact, an important instrument of
parliamentary control over the Commission which will be explored in
Chapter 13.

Second, the Commission may feel in the course of the year that there is
an imbalance between the ordinary chapters of the budget, other than the
general reserve, perhaps due to new circumstances. It may then come to the
budgetary authority with a request for transfer. In this case, the discussion

in the Parliament takes place in the Budgetary Control Committee, which again has the right to refuse or only partially approve the transfer requested.

The Parliament also follows the implementation of appropriations in general with great interest. A particular procedure, known as the "Notenboom Procedure" (after the MEP who first proposed it), has been established to invite the Commission to comment on the level of implementation of appropriations voted in the budget in the autumn of the financial year. This is designed to help the Parliament in its discussions on the appropriations to be voted for the following year. Since 1987 this procedure has been widened, in that now the Commission provides monthly reports on the use of appropriations as well as reports on agricultural spending, known as early warning reports and designed to indicate whether agricultural spending is likely to exceed the financial envelope provided for it. These mechanisms provide an opportunity for the Parliament to see whether its wishes are being adhered to, and if not, why not.

After the financial year in question all the institutions have the job of drawing up their audited accounts. At this stage the Court of Auditors enters the debate and draws up a report on the activities of each of the institutions in the financial year concerned. Its report appears in the December of the year following the relevant financial year. On the basis of this report the Committee on Budgetary Control discusses in the months following whether the Commission should be granted discharge, i.e. whether the Parliament should give its approval for the way in which the budget was implemented. This procedure enables the Parliament to look in some detail at the difficulties of implementation and to make recommendations for improvement.

To refuse to grant the discharge would be a very significant act. Indeed, the Commissioner has maintained that refusal to grant the discharge would be sufficient grounds for the whole Commission to resign. This has never really been put to the test as the only time Parliament refused discharge (in December 1984 for the 1982 budget) the Commission was anyway due to leave office a few days later. However, the Parliament has also been prepared to delay granting the discharge and to demand that certain improvements be agreed before approval of the accounts is given.

The importance of these discussions cannot be overlooked. Since 1975, as indicated at the beginning of the chapter, it is the sole responsibility of the Parliament to grant the discharge. The Council of Ministers discusses the Court of Auditors' report and gives its opinion to the Parliament but that opinion is generally couched in general terms and leaves the Parliament with considerable scope for defining its response. The debate is also one which casts considerable light on the difficulties that the Commission has in implementing appropriations in the most efficient way. In the last few years, for instance, there has been growing recognition of the threat of fraud to the Community budget. It is in the context of the discharge that considerable attention has been given to the rules governing the way agricultural expenditure is made. Here the Parliament has been able to play an important role in encouraging a review of those procedures to make them less prone to fraud. The extent of the problem was such that in 1989 the Council even added a specific statement on the problem of fraud in its opinion on the discharge and expressed its willingness to revise the existing legislation with urgency.

Relation between the budget and legislation

Finally, in this chapter it is important to stress that the budgetary role, despite its rather esoteric flavour, is intimately linked with the other areas of Parliament activity and in particular, legislative activity. Indeed, much of the tension that has been generated between Council and Parliament since the Treaties were revised in 1975 to extend Parliament's budgetary powers can be explained by the gap that has existed between the Parliament's legislative and its budgetary roles. The Parliament has found itself with a larger part to play in the budgetary area but, at the same time, has found that this increased role has to be exercised in an environment where the Council has the last word over legislative acts. The Single European Act has modified the situation in relation to some areas of legislation, as we have seen, but the basic contrast between the two areas remains.

The result has been that the Parliament has sought to make maximum use of its budgetary powers, frequently with the aim of influencing legislation. In the first years after the Treaty was amended, the Parliament argued that if money was entered in the budget then it had to be implemented by the Commission in accordance with the wishes of the budgetary authority. This point of view was strongly resisted by the Council which argued that the budget was not a sufficient legal base. It claimed that the Commission could only act if there was an agreed legislative framework, a framework within which, of course, the Council itself had the final word.

A temporary truce in this conflict was declared in 1982 when the Council, the Commission and the Parliament signed a Joint Declaration which specified that a legislative base was required for "*significant* new Community actions". For such action it was agreed that the three institutions would use their best endeavours to ensure that a decision on a new legislative framework was provided by May of the financial year concerned. This did not stop the argument, however. It left unclear what was to be considered a "significant" new Community action and the Parliament naturally tended to argue that much Community activity lay outside this definition. Such a tendency was only encouraged by the fact that the "best endeavours" of the institutions rarely did prove sufficient to agree basic legislation by the May deadline.

In the course of the 1980s the argument developed a different aspect in that the period was marked by constant difficulties in controlling expenditure, notably in the agricultural sector. The Parliament now found that not only was the budget not sufficient to *authorize* significant new Community actions but also that it could not prevent the amounts provided in the budget from being *exceeded* if the legislation adopted by the Council made extra budgetary provision necessary. Once again, therefore, the Parliament went on the offensive and succeeded in 1988 in gaining the agreement of the Council that where the financial provision for a legislative act was not available, then the implementation of the policy could not take place until the budget was suitably amended, a process in which of course the Parliament itself has a direct part to play.

It is this link between legislation and the budget which has been so strongly contested over many years that may be central to future developments. One can imagine that if the Parliament achieves stronger legislative rights, then it may place less stress on the use of its budgetary powers to influence the direction of the Community. If, on the other hand, such rights are not achieved, then one can suppose that Parliament will continue to use all its ingenuity to shape legislation through the decisions it takes on the budget. However, it would be wrong to suppose that the budget and legislation are the only channels that will be available to the Parliament in the years ahead. Its role has been and will continue to be a much wider one, as the next three chapters will underline.

13. Scrutiny and control

Scrutiny of the executive branch is one of the main traditional functions of parliaments. As the sheer size of bureaucracy and administration has grown, and as governments are given more and more powers to adopt secondary legislation or statutory instruments, so the importance of parliamentary oversight has grown in order to ensure democratic accountability.

In the Community, similar trends can be observed. The Commission, although not frequently referred to as the "government" of the Community, *is* the executive branch. Its power to adopt implementing measures independently is substantial (it adopted, 5,737 such instruments in 1989 as compared to 624 proposals for legislation forwarded by it to Council). The number of civil servants working for the Commission, whilst still fewer than for most small towns, has increased from 8,435 permanent administrative posts in 1980 to 12,334 in 1990. It also has a virtual monopoly in drafting and proposing new legislation to Council and Parliament.

Not surprisingly, Parliament has tried to build on the powers of control (or "supervisory powers") initially granted to it by the Treaties, namely the right to receive and debate an annual report of activities, the right to receive oral and written replies to parliamentary questions and the right to dismiss the Commission by a vote of censure. As we shall see, Parliament has tried, not without some success, to use its legislative and budgetary powers as vehicles for exerting pressure on the Commission and has also obtained a limited role in the appointment of the Commission.

In the Community system, as it is today, some scrutiny must also be exercised over the Council. Although the Council is, strictly speaking, a legislative authority (and has no right of initiative, no power to implement the budget and a relatively small staff — 2,183 in 1990) it may, in specific cases, reserve implementing powers to itself (Art. 145 EEC). Furthermore, the detailed nature of much EC legislation and the fact that it is composed of ministers (albeit *national* ministers) often leads to a public misperception that the Council is the "government" in the Community. This misperception is reinforced by the very name "Council of Ministers" which (like the "cabinet" in the UK) is the term used for the government in Italy and France. The fact that in a phase of development of the Community in which key decisions are about getting new policies off the ground, rather than managing existing policies, the Council is the "bottom line" institution, also reinforces this interpretation.

Parliament obviously cannot dismiss an organ whose function is to represent Member States via members of their national governments. Parliament instead aspires to sharing Council's legislative powers. On the other hand, Parliament has sought and obtained the right to question Council, to receive in committee the ministers holding the Council presidencies, and to obtain regular reports. The same applies to the Foreign Ministers meeting in Political Co-operation (strictly speaking, not the Council, and where the Commission does not play an executive role, but the Presidency acts as spokesman for the 12 Member States assisted by a special secretariat). The President of the European Council of heads of governments also reports to Parliament, normally after each meeting in the last month of each Council presidency.

Last but not least, Parliament has sought to play a role in the nomination of members of other Community institutions and organs.

The development of Parliaments' powers in these areas is described below.

The right of censure

The ECSC Treaty only allowed Parliament to censure the Commission ("High Authority" as it was then) when the latter presented its annual report. This limitation was not included in the EEC and Euratom Treaties and when a single Commission for these Communities was set up in 1965, the Treaty provided for a general right of censure which, if carried by a two-thirds majority comprising half the Members of Parliament, would force the Commission to resign. Indeed, only Parliament, and not the Council nor the national governments, can force a Commission to resign before the end of its four-year term.

Parliament has, in fact, never adopted a censure motion though a number have been threatened and five actually tabled in Parliament but rejected or withdrawn. Four of these five pre-date direct elections in 1979 and three motions of censure were all on behalf of smaller Political Groups seeking publicity and were all decisively defeated (Conservative Group in 1976 on milk powder, Gaullists in 1977 on butter sales, European Right in 1990 on the Commission's general policy). Parliament has in practice forged a close working relationship with the Commission, and has had growing influence on its proposals. When conflicts have broken out between the two institutions they have been resolved in other ways than by censure. It remains a reserve power, of limited practical significance in the day-to-day work of the Communities, but just as national parliaments only rarely make use of their power to dismiss governments, the fact that they *can* do so is enough to encourage the executive to pay some attention to their viewpoint.

This was illustrated in December 1989 and January 1990 when the Socialist Group considered a proposal from one of its members to table a censure motion in Parliament. Although this found little support, and was decisively turned down in the Group, it did provoke a flurry of extra meetings between Commissioners and Socialists Group leaders and greater attention being paid to the "social dimension" of the Commission's 1990 work programme then being prepared. An earlier example was in 1976 when a censure motion was tabled over the issue of Parliament's access to Commission documents, and then withdrawn when the Commission backed down. Similarly, in 1972, a motion was withdrawn when the Commission undertook to submit a proposal to increase Parliament's budgetary powers, which ultimately led to the 1975 revision of the Treaties and the increase of Parliament's budgetary powers, as described in Chapter 12.

It has been suggested that if Parliament were to censure a Commission there would be nothing to prevent national governments from re-appointing the same Commissioners. In fact, this is unlikely, as the European Parliament could dismiss them again, and some Commissioners would not want to come back under such circumstances. This would be especially true of the President. Furthermore, Parliament has now gained a small role in the appointment of the Commission, as we shall see.

A motion of censure can only be addressed to the Commission as a whole, reflecting the doctrine of collective accountability of the Commission for its actions. A vote of censure cannot be passed on an individual Commissioner, but two ways of meeting this difficulty can be envisaged. First, there is nothing to prevent Parliament adopting a resolution criticizing an individual Commissioner or, indeed, calling upon him or her to resign. Such a resolution would carry weight if it were implied that Parliament might move to censure the Commission as a whole if he/she did not resign.

Second, an attempt to introduce a less drastic means of calling the Commission to order was made in 1989 when the Rules Committee considered introducing a "reprimand motion". This would have enabled Parliament to adopt a special motion criticizing the Commission or an individual Commissioner for a particular action and calling upon the Commission to remedy the situation — in so far as possible — within one month. Failure to do so would lead to a full censure motion being placed upon the agenda of Parliament. The Rules Committee did not manage to finalize its report on this matter in time for a decision by Parliament before the elections, but it could resume consideration of this issue now. Such a procedure, more flexible than the full motion of censure, would enable Parliament to criticize the Commission in a way that would carry more weight and solemnity than routine criticism in an ordinary resolution, but without being as dramatic as a motion of censure.

Parliament and the appointment of the Commission

Under the Treaties the Commission is appointed collectively by the governments of the Member States for a four-year term of office. The Treaty specifies that there should be one or two per country and in practice, the UK, Germany, Italy, France and Spain supply two Commissioners each. The President of the Commission is, according to the Treaty, nominated for a two-year period from among the members of the Commission. In practice, the President is usually agreed on first by the Member States and is automatically reappointed midway through the term of office of a Commission.

Since the Stuttgart Solemn Declaration on European Union of 1983, the European Council consults the enlarged Bureau of the European Parliament before it nominates the President of the Commission. In 1984, the President-in-Office of the European Council (Irish Prime Minister, Garret Fitzgerald) actually came to a meeting of the enlarged Bureau to discuss the issue. In 1988, this consultation was done through the President of the European Parliament (who attended the relevant European Council meeting) acting in consultation with the Enlarged Bureau.

There could, however, be more than consultation. President Mitterrand proposed in his speech to the European Parliament on Oct. 25, 1989 that the procedure could be changed to allow Parliament to elect the President of the Commission. Such a change would not necessarily need a Treaty amendment — the Member States could simply agree to appoint the person chosen by Parliament. This would enable the President of the Commission to be the reflection of the majorities that emerge when the public votes on European issues in the European elections — indeed, it would give a greater significance to those elections. It would not prevent the balance of interests and nationalities achieved by the current system if the rest of the Commission continued to be appointed in the usual way by national governments, though hopefully in consultation with the president-elect.

Since 1982, Parliament has held a debate and a *vote of confidence* on an incoming Commission when it presents itself to Parliament for the first time with its programme. This has become an established practice and was recognized by national governments in the Stuttgart Solemn Declaration. The two Delors Commissions both waited until they had received the vote of confidence from Parliament before taking the oath at the Court of Justice. This was an important gesture and precedent, showing that the Commission accepted that without the confidence of the Parliament it should not take office. Of course, if it did so, Parliament would surely dismiss it through a motion of censure.

An alternative way for Parliament to be involved in the appointment of the Commission would be to follow an "advice and consent" procedure on the model of US Senate hearings of American Administration members. The individual Commissioners put forward by the governments would appear before a Parliament committee and Parliament would have to approve their appointment. Up to now, this model has not had majority support in Parliament.

Appointments to the Court of Auditors

The importance of even a consultative role in appointments can be seen by observing how the provisions laid down for the Court of Auditors have been applied.

The 1975 budget treaty which set up the Court of Auditors provided for Parliament to be consulted by Council on the appointments it makes to the Court of Auditors. This provision goes beyond the role allocated in the treaties to Parliament for appointments to the Commission (or the Court of Justice where Parliament plays no role at all).

The bottom line of such a consultative procedure is what happens when Parliament gives a negative opinion on a proposed candidate. Such a case first occurred in November 1989, when Parliament was consulted on the appointment or reappointment of six candidates. Parliament approved four of them but felt "unable to give a favourable opinion" in respect of two of them, the French and Greek candidates. The French government immediately responded by withdrawing the nominated candidate and putting forward a new candidate who, after he appeared before Parliament's Budgetary Control Committee, was approved by Parliament at its next part-session and duly appointed. The Greek government, which was in the middle of a government crisis and between two general elections in succession, claimed to be unable to find a more suitable candidate. Parliament chose not to fight, being pleased enough with the French reaction, and merely regretted the Greek government's position.

Control of expenditure and the right to grant discharge

Parliament carries out a careful *post facto* examination of Community expenditure. In this it is assisted by the Court of Auditors.

Granting discharge is a formal statement that the Parliament is satisfied with the implementation of the budget by the Commission. It is the political endorsement of the Commission's stewardship of the Communities' budget.

The Treaty of July 22, 1975, gave the right of discharge for the implementation of the European Communities' budget to the European Parliament alone (Article 16 amending Article 206 EEC). Prior to the 1975 Treaty, the Parliament had shared the power of discharge with the Council. Before the Treaty amendment of 1970, the decision lay with the Council and Parliament made a recommendation.

The right to grant discharge is the basis of the Parliament's powers of budgetary control. Discharge is the necessary final act in adopting the Communities' accounts.

The act of granting discharge can be considered as being more than mere endorsement. Article 90 of the financial Regulation, which lays down the detailed rules for preparing and executing the budget, requires all institutions to "take all appropriate steps to act on the comments appearing in the decisions giving discharge". The same Article also requires them to report on the measures taken in the light of these comments, if requested by the Parliament, and to include in an annex to the Revenue and Expenditure Account an account of these measures.

This is the basis of the procedure of "follow-up" to the Discharge by which the Commission gives an account of its consequential actions to Parliament.

Refusal to grant discharge represents a major political reprimand for the Commission. It is a public statement by the Parliament that either the Commission's management of the Communities' fund has been irregular or uneconomic and for that the Commission has failed to respect the political objectives set when the budget was adopted.

Neither the Treaties nor the Communities' Financial Regulation deal with the consequences of a refusal to grant discharge. However, on July 7, 1977, Budget Commissioner Tugendhat stated to Parliament that "refusal to grant discharge (....) is a political sanction (....) which would be extremely serious; the Commission thus censured would, I think, have to be replaced".

It is generally believed that the Parliament would feel bound to follow a refusal of discharge with a motion of censure should the Commission fail to resign. In November 1984, Parliament did refuse discharge for the 1982 financial year, but the Commission was anyway at the end of its term and due to leave office a few weeks later.

Parliament's position on these matters is prepared by a special Committee on Budgetary Control, which monitors implementation of the budget in different areas, prepares the draft discharge decision for adoption by Parliament, and reports on any necessary follow-up to the discharge decision. Its partner on these issues is the European Court of Auditors, whose Annual Report is examines.

The Court was set up by the 1975 Treaty and is responsible for examining the legality, regularity and sound financial management of all revenue and expenditure managed by the European Communities. It prepares a detailed annual report which includes its observations and replies by the Institutions. This Annual Report is submitted to Parliament and is examined by the Committee on Budgetary Control when the latter prepares the discharge decision.

The effectiveness of Parliament control is limited by the time gaps involved, and by the fact that many discharge decisions concern preceding Commissions. Parliament has therefore concentrated on extracting concessions and undertakings from the Commission through its "comments" on which the Commission is obliged to act, and, if necessary, by delaying discharge in order to extract extra information. The Budgetary Control Committee attempts to enhance continuity and consistency of its monitoring by allocating specific sectors to each of its members for them to specialize in for a number of years. It also works with the parliamentary committees responsible for the policy areas covered by Community spending policies. Some of these committees have themselves introduced systems whereby they are briefed every few months on the implementation of their areas of the budget by the Commission officials responsible.

Scrutiny of executive decisions and implementing measures: the issue of "comitology"

This aspect of democratic control has been the subject of much controversy over the last few years. At stake is, firstly, how implementing measures are adopted and who is accountable for them and, secondly, how best to ensure Parliamentary scrutiny of such decisions.

These issues are worth investigating in some detail, as they are likely to be of growing importance. This is because, as the Community adopts more and more basic legislation, the areas covered by the Commission's implementing powers will grow. For example, when the Community agrees through legislation on common rules for the single market, for, say, authorizing food additives or for labelling dangerous chemicals, it is frequently up to the Commission (subject to the procedure described below) to decide which new additives or chemicals can be allowed, banned or tolerated under certain conditions laid down in the rules. These decisions can frequently be controversial and often major commercial interests are at stake.

(a)   who adopts what: ensuring efficiency and transparency

Most Community legislation provides for its implementation, execution or the adaptation of its provisions by the Commission as the executive body of the European Community, just as national legislation allows governments to adopt statutory instruments. However, over the years, Council has subordinated the exercise of these powers by the Commission to the approval of committees of national civil servants. Such a variety of committees and procedures have been provided for in various items of Community legislation, that the name "comitology" has been invented to describe it. Parliament has consistently criticized this mish-mash, and sought to strengthen the Commission by giving it full executive powers, no longer subject to the approval of national civil servants, on the grounds that the Commission, which is accountable to Parliament, should be clearly responsible for such decisions.

In response, Member States agreed in the Single European Act to amend Article 145 of the EEC Treaty to lay down that Council:

"shall confer on the Commission, in the acts which the Council adopts, powers for the implementation of the rules which the Council lays down. The Council may impose certain requirements in respect of the exercise of these powers. The Council may also reserve the right, in specific cases, to exercise directly implementing powers itself. The procedures referred to above must be consonant with the principles and rules to be laid down in advance by the Council, acting unanimously on a proposal from the Commission and after obtaining the opinion of the European Parliament."

These provisions thus laid down an obligation on Council to confer executive powers on the Commission, except in specific cases to be defined in advance. Member States also agreed in a declaration contained in the Final Act annexed to the Single European Act that priority should be given to the "advisory committee procedure" for matters falling under Article 100 A of the EEC Treaty.

However, an implementing decision was required to lay down the principles and rules to be followed. The Commission put forward a proposal which would still allow committees of national civil servants to be set up, but which would rationalize them into three types: advisory, management (which would be able to block the Commission decision if it were *opposed* by a qualified majority in committee) and regulatory (where the decision would be blocked if it were not *approved* by a qualified majority in the committee). A blocked decision would go to Council which would have up to three months to adopt an alternative measure, failing which the Commission decision would stand. A decision was therefore guaranteed. In its opinion, Parliament sought to delete the regulatory committee formula.

The Council decision of July 13, 1987 took no account of Parliament's opinion and modified the Commission's initial proposal in order to increase the blocking powers of Member States. It provided for the following procedures:

Procedure I *(advisory committees)*	Commission listens to view of committee and then takes a decision taking account of the committee's opinion
Procedure II *(management committees)*	If the Commission is *opposed* by a qualified majority in the committee, then *either*; variant a) The Commission *may* delay the application of its decision for up to one month variant b) The Commission *shall* delay the application of its decision for a period up to three months and, within these deadlines, Council may, by a qualified majority, take a different decision
Procedure III *(regulatory committees)*	If the Commission is *not supported* by a qualified majority in the committee, the matter is referred to Council, which may take a decision on a Commission proposal within a deadline not exceeding three months. If it fails to adopt a decision then: variant a) The Commission shall adopt its proposal variant b) The Commission shall adopt its proposal unless a *simple* majority in Council votes against in which case no decision is taken.
Safeguard measures (mainly trade)	No committee, but any Member State may ask for a Commission decision to be referred to Council. In this case: variant a) Council has a deadline to take an alternative decision by a qualified majority variant b) Council must confirm, modify or annul the decision by a qualified majority. If it fails to act within a deadline, the decision is abrogated.

The Commission issued a declaration regretting that the Council had adopted procedures III (b) and Safeguard (b) which allow Council to block Commission decisions even where it cannot agree itself on an alternative. President Delors assured Parliament that the Commission would never put forward any proposals containing procedure III (b) or Safeguard (b). Parliament decided to take Council to the Court of Justice on the grounds that this decision did not conform to the intention of the Single Act which was to strengthen the Commission's executive powers. However, the Court ruled that Parliament does not have the right to bring proceedings for annulment before the Court under Article 173 EEC (see below).

The only way for Parliament to take any action in this important issue is to scrutinize closely and, if necessary, amend legislative proposals containing unacceptable "comitology" procedures. In order to avoid the various parliamentary committees adopting a divergent approach, the meeting of committee chairmen agreed on the following ·guidelines, subsequently endorsed by the Bureau of Parliament:

"1.   In first reading, Parliament should systematically delete any
        provisions for procedure III (a) or III (b) and replace it by
        procedure II (a) or (b), or, for proposals concerning the internal
        market put forward under Article 100 A of the EEC Treaty,
        procedure I. Alternatively, when the subject matter is particularly
        important or sensitive, Parliament could provide for decisions to be
        made by the legislative procedure instead.
2.   In second reading, Parliament should continue to oppose any
        provisions in a common position for procedure III (b), but III (a)
        could be accepted exceptionally, as a compromise, except for
        proposals concerning the internal market put forward under
        Article 100 A of the EEC Treaty, where II (b) should be the
        maximum acceptable compromise.
        Comitology provisions pursuant to Article 145 are unacceptable
        for taking decisions concerning expenditure, as Article 205 EEC
        specifies that the Commission *alone* should be responsible for
        implementing the budget approved by Parliament."

These guidelines have generally been followed. However, in a few cases,
notably in the sector of the environment and consumer protection, some
members have taken the view that it is undesirable to allow the
Commission too much autonomy, (for instance, because it tends to take a
too liberal line on allowing dangerous chemicals on to the Community
market). They have taken the view that national civil servants might at
least act as a break on this tendency. This view has remained a minority
viewpoint because:

– it is not reasonable to prejudice Parliament's general position because of
   a special situation in one sector;
– even in this sector, it is far from certain that national civil servants can be
   relied upon to have a more enlightened position than the Commission;
– in any case, the European Parliament has at least some influence over
   the Commission, but it has little if any influence over national civil
   servants;
– Parliament should first make efforts better to exploit the procedures
   agreed bilaterally with the Commission for parliamentary scrutiny of
   draft implementing proposals (see below).

Parliament has therefore generally stuck to these guidelines, although it
has sometimes approved Council common positions where they include
Procedure III (a) as part of a general compromise.
The results have been mixed. Despite pressure from the other
institutions, Council has not respected the Declaration annexed to the
Single European Act: from the entry into force of the Act until January 1990
it only introduced the advisory committee procedure into four Acts under
Article 100 A (while the Commission proposed it 14 times) and, for all
internal market measures, seven times (out of 24 proposed). On the other
hand, the use of Procedures III (b), Safeguards (b) or the reservation by
Council of executive powers to itself have been kept to a minimum.
Nevertheless, the bottom line is that, when it is determined to see its
implementing measures through, the Commission can do so easily under
Procedure I, relatively easily under Procedure II (generally the procedure

used in agriculture) where it needs only a blocking minority in the committee to support it and where, even if the measure is referred to Council, a blocking minority would also be sufficient to see the Commission decision stand. Under Procedure III (a), a Commission proposal to Council requires unanimity in Council to amend it. This is paradoxically more difficult than under Procedure II as it falls under the provision of Article 149 (1) EEC whereby Council may only depart from a Commission proposal by unanimity. Again, a determined Commission can see its position through at the end of the day unless the Member States are unanimous in wishing to modify it. Only under Procedure III (b) or Safeguard (b) can the Commission be blocked by a simple majority. Provided it has a simple majority with it, it can ultimately see its position through.

The main problem with the comitology procedures lies in their delaying power and the facilities which they provide for national civil servants to exert an unduly high influence over decisions. The Commission is not normally determined enough to force through proposals against their opposition, lest this provoke the retention of executive powers by Council in future decisions. Consequently, implementing decisions tend to be compromises thrashed out between the Commission and national civil servants. This makes democratic scrutiny and public accountability for decisions difficult, as neither the Commission nor any individual national civil servant carries full political responsibility for the decisions.

(b) Ensuring parliamentary scrutiny of executive decisions

As mentioned above, an increasingly large field of policy will be regulated henceforth by these Community executive decisions. The ability of Parliament to scrutinize and monitor such decisions will be of crucial importance in ensuring democratic accountability.

The Commission has agreed to keep Parliament fully informed of all proposals it submits to "comitology"-type committees. This undertaking was formalized in 1988 in an exchange of letters between the President of the Parliament and the President of the Commission. Henceforth, all draft implementing measures, with the exception of routine management documents with a limited period of validity and documents whose adoption is complicated by considerations of secrecy or urgency, will be forwarded to Parliament at the same time that they are forwarded to the "comitology"-type committees in question and in the same working languages.

Rule 53 of Parliament's Rules of Procedure requires these drafts to be referred by the President of Parliament to the various parliamentary committees responsible. The committee chairmen agreed that:

- given the volume of implementing measures that will be received, a staff member of DG II, accountable to the Director-General or one of his colleagues based in Brussels should sift the material concerned and draw the attention of the secretariat of the responsible committee to those items which raise important political questions. In addition, a list of items received should be circulated to members of each committee, and copies of the texts in question should be available in the secretariat for consultation by any member.

– when a committee is dissatisfied with a Commission proposal, the relevant member of the Commission should be invited to the committee to discuss the matter. In urgent situations, notably between meetings, the committee chairman should be able to contact the responsible Commissioner directly. If the committee remains dissatisfied, it may, if the importance of the matter warrants such action, take the matter up in plenary, using one of the existing instruments available under the rules (e.g. oral question with debate).

These procedures have been in place since May 1989, although it seems that some Commission departments have been slow in implementing these provisions. Nevertheless, the system should now offer the opportunity to committees to follow these matters. It will be up to members, and in particular chairmen, to ensure that committees and their secretariats apply these procedures properly.

There are, however, some areas where it is the Treaty itself and not legislation which gives executive powers to the Commission in certain fields. These areas include, most notably, competition policy, certain trade measures (e.g. anti-dumping), limitations on state aids to industry and coal and steel production. Parliament has taken a close interest in these areas. In competition policy, it has taken a close look at the block exemptions from the application of the competition rules to several types of agreement provided that certain criteria are met. Such block exemptions (e.g. motor vehicle distribution, tied-house arrangements for beer sales, patent licences, etc.) can have considerable economic importance for a particular sector, and the Council has delegated the powers to take the final decisions to the Commission. Parliament is not formally consulted, but has taken the initiative on several occasions to draw up specific reports on the Commission's proposals (e.g. motor vehicle distribution, exclusive distribution and purchasing, and on franchising and know-how licensing agreements) and it has insisted that all Commission proposals for block exemptions be forwarded to its responsible committee. On franchising licensing, the Commission made substantial amendments as a result of Parliament's observations. The Commission has also agreed to send annual reports to Parliament in a number of areas where it exercises its own powers (e.g. on anti-dumping measures in trade, on competition policy). While still not having any formal consultative role Parliament has thus been trying to fill this particular area of "democratic deficit".

However, within Parliament, an interesting cultural divide has meant that Parliament's scrutiny over such matters is not what it could be. Many members, notably from countries where the traditional view has been that detailed regulatory matters should be left to the government, consider that Parliament should concentrate on major political debates and primary legislation. Other members, notably from countries with a strong tradition of MPs being involved in the nuts and bolts of day-to-day issues, consider these procedures to be important and worthy of substantial effort.

Scrutiny within the Parliamentary committees

This takes a number of forms, including reports on implementation of particular Community policies, and regular questioning both of

Commissioners and of their civil servants. A more formalized question time to the Commission was introduced in certain committees (Legal and Economic Committees) but these did not prove to be effective, because the scope, as interpreted by the Commission, was too restrictive, and they were discontinued. A new experiment along these lines is now under way in the Environment and Consumer Protection Committee.

The presence of individual members of the Commission at committee meetings is now a routine event. A committee like the Economic Committee will typically have one or even two Commissioners speaking and answering questions for periods of up to two hours at its monthly meetings.

The increasing presence of ministers from the country currently holding the Council Presidency has been a striking trend over the last few years. During a six-month Council Presidency, there would normally be some 20 to 30 ministerial appearances in front of Parliamentary committees, and an important committee may be visited by two or three ministers, who will speak and answer questions on developments within their sphere of competence. The questions are often rather general in nature, but this is changing. Ministers have already been summoned to explain and justify Council's "common position" at the end of first readings in the co-operation procedure. It is now much more difficult for ministers to avoid coming to Parliament's committees.

The head of the new European Political Co-operation secretariat also frequently attends and speaks at meetings of Parliament's Political Affairs Committee. This committee holds a special "colloquy" four times a year with the President-in-Office on foreign policy matters, and its bureau meets in between with the chairman of the "Political directors" of national foreign ministries.

The Director of the European Investment Bank and the heads of various Community auxiliary organs (The Vocational Training Center in Berlin, the Foundation for the Improvement of Working and Living Conditions in Dublin, etc.) also appear on occasions before the relevant committees.

Scrutiny of implementation of international agreements through special organs

In a number of cases where association agreements entered into by the Community provide for joint decision-taking organs (usually called Joint Councils or Association Councils), those same agreements have set up a joint Parliamentary body whose main task is to serve as an organ of control (receiving reports from the joint Council, able to ask questions, etc.), but which can also be consulted on new proposals and serve as a forum for discussing bilateral issues.

The ACP – EEC Joint Assembly

The most important joint parliamentary body is the Joint Assembly established by the Lomé Convention with 68 African, Caribbean and Pacific (ACP) countries. Each ACP country sends one parliamentarian or repre-sentative (in practice, frequently their diplomatic representative to the Community) and an equivalent number is sent by the European

Parliament, which provides the administrative facilities. The Assembly meets twice a year — once in the EC and once in an ACP country. The meetings in ACP countries are supposed to rotate A-C-A-P-A-C-A-P etc., but in practice the Pacific turn is usually skipped as it is very expensive and MEPs are naturally very sensitive to criticisms about trips to far away places.

The Lomé Conventions, the fourth of which is due to enter into force after receiving Parliament's assent later this year, have set up a unique instrument of co-operation between a group of developed and a group of developing countries. Its main features are access to the Community for ACP products, financial co-operation and aid (including STABEX — an attempt to stabilize export earnings from commodities with fluctuating prices) and on-going dialogue about the ACP countries' economic policies and the EC's support for those policies.

Assembly meetings are attended by the Joint Council and the EC Commissioners responsible and the Council President. A Bureau (each side nominating a co-President and nine Vice-Presidents) is elected for a term of one year (frequently renewed) to manage day-to-day affairs. Parliament's co-President is currently Leo Tindemans, former Belgian Prime Minister. Ad hoc working parties may be set up (no more than three at any one time) to investigate particular problems in greater depth. Such working parties have dealt with, for example, technology and training, refugees, commodities, debt, human rights and environmental problems.

In a number of ways the working methods used by the Joint Assembly reflect those used elsewhere within the European Parliament. The main output consists of resolutions. Draft resolutions can be tabled by any member of the Joint Assembly, and are then examined by the full Assembly, which also examines a keynote report by a general rapporteur on the whole range of ACP issues. A large number of reports are examined by the Joint Assembly. For example, the 1989 meetings in Barbados adopted 29 resolutions and in Versailles 25.

Another technique familiar from plenaries is that of Question Time, when members can pose questions to the ACP–EEC Council of Ministers. Written questions are also possible. A technique used for the first time in 1989 in conjunction with a Joint Assembly was that of holding a hearing, with the subject being health.

The Assembly's current priorities are the local processing of commodities, the need to avoid adverse impacts of the 1992 internal market on ACP countries (and better to co-ordinate the Community's development policies with its other policies), the need to promote training in and technology transfer to the developing countries, and the situation in South Africa.

There are several ways in which feedback is provided from the ACP–EEC Joint Assembly meetings into Parliament's work as a whole. The main way is through the Parliament's Development and Co-operation Committee, which can draw up reports on specific problems identified at Joint Assembly meetings so that there can be a debate in plenary on what took place, and a resolution adopted on the principal recommendations that had emerged.

Joint Parliamentary Committees

Other Association Agreements have established "Joint Parliamentary Committees", which, whilst much smaller and dealing with only one third country, fulfil similar functions of control and scrutiny. The most notable one is with Turkey, the operation of which was suspended by the European Parliament for several years during and following the period of military government.

Interparliamentary delegations

Whilst primarily fulfilling a forum role (described in detail in Chapter 14), delegations can also be a useful vehicle for monitoring and discussing agreements with the country concerned.

Freezing items of the Commission's budget

One way which Parliament has found to put pressure on the Commission (and sometimes the other institutions, including the Council), is to use its budgetary powers for this purpose. As explained in Chapter 12, the budgetary authority can place individual items in Chapter 100 (Reserve) and then the Commission has to come to the budgetary authority if it subsequently wishes to use those appropriations. If those appropriations are compulsory, then it is the Council which has the last word on the release of the funds but if they are non-compulsory, then it is the Parliament which has the last word. The decision is effectively taken by the Committee on Budgets which can reject or approve (wholly or partially) the Commission's request or else invite the Commission to provide further information before taking its decision. Hence, the Parliament has the opportunity to exercise influence over the Commission by entering appropriations in Chapter 100 in the course of the budgetary procedure.

The most spectacular use of the power took place after Parliament had rejected a supplementary budget for 1982 designed to provide for refunds to Britain amounting to 850 mn ECU and obliged the Council to use the refund on specific infrastructure programmes in the UK, entered in Chapter 100, rather than as a direct reimbursement to the UK Treasury. This way Parliament was able to block the refund until it gained satisfaction; in particular, it got the chance to monitor the way the money was spent.

Usually, however, the entry of appropriations in Chapter 100 is used as a discreet way of bargaining with the Commission, in order to get assurances on the use of particular budget lines and the implementation of programmes. For 1989, for example, the Commission requested a substantial increase in the number of staff to enable it to fulfil its obligations under the Single Act. Parliament did not wish to be rushed into a decision and wanted to know more on the way in which the staff would be recruited. Hence it entered the appropriations in Chapter 100, only releasing them in the course of the year when it was satisfied with the information it received. Similarly, for 1990, the Parliament entered an amount in Chapter 100 for financing the European Environment Agency. This was a supplementary weapon in the argument about the role of the Agency. Parliament wanted the Agency not only to have an information-gathering role, but also a right of investigation in the Member States to verify compliance with Community law. With the appropriations in Chapter 100, the Parliament could block their release if the shape of the Agency as determined by the Council did not satisfy it.

It is worth underlining that not all items entered in Chapter 100 are there expressly to enable the Parliament to exert pressure. The majority of the 15 such items in the 1990 budget were included without controversy in the budgetary procedure. Where, in particular, the legislative base for expenditure has not yet been agreed, it is accepted practice that the related appropriations be entered in Chapter 100, only to be released when the legislation is passed. However, the obligation to go before the Parliament when the release is requested does oblige the Commission to justify its request and permits the Parliament to scrutinize carefully such requests for further expenditure.

Parliament as a litigant

The European Parliament may, in certain circumstances, turn to the Court of Justice to protect its rights in the Community framework or to ensure the correct application of the Treaties. It may also be proceeded against itself.

Before direct elections, the European Parliament was a particularly reluctant litigant, participating in proceedings before the Court of Justice only once in the period 1952–1979, and that at the request of the Court, in a case which turned on the duration of Parliament's annual session. Shortly after the first direct elections, Parliament exercised for the first time the right of intervention it enjoys, in common with the other Community institutions, by virtue of Article 37 of the Statute of the Court of Justice, in proceedings against the Council, instituted by two manufacturers of isoglucose (described in Chapter 11).

Three years later, Parliament made legal history again by taking the first inter-institutional action under Article 175 EEC against the Council for its failure to adopt a common transport policy. The result was a legal victory for Parliament, and though the Community is still some way from the achievement of such a policy, progress in that direction has resumed. A second case was initiated in respect of Council's failure to adopt a draft budget for 1988 (see Chapter 12).

On a number of occasions, proceedings have also been brought against the Parliament in the Court by Member States, political parties and the Council. The first two actions, which were brought by the Grand Duchy of Luxembourg and concern the seat and the working place of Parliament, were based on Article 38 of the ECSC Treaty which expressly provides that the High Authority (Commission) or a Member State can apply to have an act of the Assembly declared void for lack of competence or infringement of an essential procedural requirement. In the first decision, the Court upheld the validity of Parliament's resolution, though establishing certain limits on Parliament's powers in this sensitive area. In the second case

Parliament was held to have overstepped these limits and its resolution was declared void.

These decisions did not deal with the question of whether proceedings could be brought against Parliament under the more broadly based Article 173 EEC which only expressly identifies the Council and Commission as defendants. In its judgement of April 23, 1986, however, the Court answered this question in the affirmative in an action taken by the French Ecologist Party, contesting certain decisions of Parliament's Bureau and Enlarged Bureau on the distribution of information campaign funds for the second direct elections in 1984. Six weeks later, an action against Parliament by the Council, also based on 173 EEC, was admitted by the Court and was successful. In this latter case,the declaration by the President of the Parliament that the 1986 budget had been adopted was struck down and the two arms of the budgetary authority were instructed to complete the Treaty procedure, leading to the adoption of a new budget in June 1986.

Not disheartened by these reversals — the one was a mildly embarrassing judicial intervention in a highly political area, the other merely symptomatic of an entrenched inter-institutional conflict — Parliament took the view in its resolution of Oct. 9, 1986, that , as the Treaty had established a complete system of legal remedies and procedures to enable the Court to review the legality of measures of the institutions, Article 173 should be interpreted so as to permit Parliament to take proceedings for annulment under this provision. A first such action was commenced on Oct. 2, 1987, where Parliament attacked the validity of the Council's comitology decision (see above). Another was on the adoption of a directive based on an incorrect legal base (see above) that avoided the co-operation procedure.

In the first of these cases, the Court ruled that Parliament did not have the right to bring cases for annulment under Article 173 of the Treaty, as it is not specifically mentioned in that article. In view of the Court's previous ruling that Parliament can be proceeded *against* under the same article, the ruling caused much surprise in legal circles. Until it was partly reversed in the second case, it left Parliament in the curious position of:

- being able to bring cases for failure to act;
- being able to be proceeded against itself;
- being able to intervene in cases brought by others;
- but *not* being able to bring cases for annulment itself, even when its own prerogatives have not been respected.

The Court hinted that it was up to the Commission, as guardian of the Treaties, to defend Parliament's rights, but this was clearly unrealistic if the two institutions are on different sides of the argument, and this no doubt led to The Court's change of mind.

Parliament's Rules of Procedure now contain a new section on super-visory powers which should be mentioned in this context. Rule 54 deals with the consequences of the Council failing to act following Parliamentary approval of its common position, and provides for the possibility of action against the Council in the Court of Justice under Article 175 of the EEC Treaty. Rule 55 deals with proceedings before the Court of Justice in cases where Parliament's rights have not been fully respected in the preparation of Community legislation.

Another indirect way in which Parliament contributes to the correct application of Community Law is by drawing to the attention of the Commission any infringements (such as non-application or incorrect application of directives) by Member States. Under the treaties, it is up to the Commission to initiate infringement proceedings against Member States (664 in 1989) and, if the situation is not brought to line, to bring cases before the Court of Justice (97 cases in 1989) most of which are settled before a Court ruling is given. These procedures are essential in ensuring the homogeneity and predominance of Community law in the Member States. The difficulty for the Commission is in finding out about infringements — it has, after all, no police force or inspectorate at its disposal and has a relatively small staff. It has to rely on complaints from the public. In this respect, Parliament, through its members receiving complaints from constituents and from the petitions it receives, is furnishing an increasing number of complaints to the Commission. The importance of this phenomenon has been highlighted in the Commission's Annual Reports on the application of Community Law. On occasion, Parliament itself may highlight problems of application of Community law, by investigating and drawing up a report. A good example was the Collins report on water quality standards which caused quite a stir in the UK where Community directives were not complied with.

Reports from the other institutions to Parliament

The treaties originally provided for an annual report of activities to be submitted by the Commission to Parliament for debate. This has now been complemented by further reporting mechanisms for the Commission, as well as ones for the Council, the Foreign Ministers meeting in political co-operation and the European Council. These reports provide an essential raw material for political activities: formal, public, quotable information.

The Commission now submits the following written reports to Parliament:

- its annual general report
- an annual report on the application of Community law'
- an annual report on competition policy;
- six-monthly reports on how the Commission has responded to Parliament's "own-initiative" resolutions and requests for action;
- monthly reports (printed as an annex to the "Hansard") on how the Commission has responded to Parliament's amendments to legislative proposals;
- monthly reports on the implementation of the budget (brought about since 1988 as part of Parliament's pressure to limit agricultural spending, but also useful generally);
- monthly reports known as "early warning" reports on agricultural spending designed to indicate whether such spending is likely to remain within the budgetary limits laid down;
- annual report on implementation of the 1992 internal market

programme (showing the latest state of play in the challenge of getting the necessary legislation — almost 300 items — adopted in time);
- annual report on the agricultural situation in the Community;
- annual report on social developments within the Community;
- annual report on regional policy within the Community.

As well as these regular reports, the Commission produces ad hoc reports on particular subjects in response to Parliament's requests. The Commission also makes declarations or statements to Parliament in plenary and in committee.

Council Presidents present their "programme" to Parliament at the beginning of each six-month presidency, and report on their achievements at the end of each presidency. There are thus four annual debates on Council reports to Parliament. This practice developed in the 1970s and was formalized by the Member States in the "Solemn Declaration on European Union" adopted in Stuttgart in 1983. The Presidents-in-Office also report in their capacity of presidents of European Political Co-operation, on which they also submit an annual communication to Parliament. Over the last few years, it has also become the practice for the Foreign Ministers to present an annual written report on their activities concerning human rights. They also submit, upon request, a written response to Parliament's foreign policy resolutions.

The European Council of heads of government presents an annual written report on "progress towards European Union". The Prime Minister or President holding the chairmanship reports to Parliament in a plenary debate twice a year (normally after each European Council or "summit"). This practice was inaugurated by Margaret Thatcher in 1981, and formalized in the 1983 Solemn Declaration.

Parliamentary questions

Written and oral questions are an opportunity to obtain precise information on particular points or to force a policy statement to be made. The Treaty itself provided for written and oral questions to the Commission. Council agreed to answer questions as well, an arrangement formalized in 1973. In 1976, in the Paris summit, the heads of government agreed to extend this to the Foreign Ministers meeting in political co-operation. The Solemn Declaration on European Union of 1983 further encoded these practices.

Parliament has in fact developed four different procedures to take advantage of its right to put questions:

(1) *Written questions* may be tabled by any member. The question and the replies are published in the Official Journal. In principle, the Commission has a month and Council two months to reply, and questions not yet answered by the deadline are listed in the Official Journal as well, no doubt to embarrass the institution concerned.

(2) *Oral questions without debate* may also be tabled by any member. These are not to be confused with questions at question-time (see below). Those selected by Parliament's Enlarged Bureau are notified to the

Commission one week in advance of the session in which a reply is requested, those to the Council five weeks. They allow a certain in-depth inquiry into an issue, as the author of the question may speak first for 10 minutes and the institution replying may be given up to half a day on the agenda to reply. The author may ask supplementary questions.

(3) *Oral question with debate* may be tabled only by a committee, a Political Group or seven members. These two are filtered by the Enlarged Bureau though each Political Group is entitled to one per session. They differ from oral questions without debate in that the reply is followed by a debate in which a number of speakers may take part (maximum five minutes each) and the debate may be followed by the adoption of a resolution. A Political Group, a committee or 23 members may propose such a resolution, which is put to the vote at the next voting-time if the House agrees during the debate to do so.

(4) *Questions at question-time* is a procedure introduced in 1973. Any member may table questions, and the President of Parliament decides on their admissibility and on the order in which they are taken. Answers are given during 90 minute periods set aside for this purpose known as "question time". One such period at each part-session is for the Commission, and one for the President-in-Office of Council and EPC. Each member may only table one question to each per month. The author may ask a supplementary question following the reply, and extra supplementaries may be taken from other members. Questions not reached are answered in writing. If a reply gives cause to particular consternation, the President may decide, on a proposal of a Political Group or seven members, to hold a debate of not more than one hour on the matter, though this is very unusual. Questions at question time never have the cut and thrust of the Westminster highlights of the Leader of the Opposition questioning the Prime Minister. It is comparable to Westminster question time for departmental ministers — not so exciting in the media term, but a useful vehicle none the less.

Generally, questions (of all categories) put to the Commission are more rewarding than those to the Council. Commission answers are given by the responsible Commissioner, who has his departmental services to help prepare him. Council answers are given by the President-in-Office, who is not a specialist, and anyway cannot easily take positions on behalf of an organ that represents the Member States. His initial draft replies are, indeed, prepared by the Council secretariat and circulated to all the Permanent Representatives of the Member States for comments or objections (hence the longer deadlines for Council replies). Council is not the executive branch and frequently answers that it has not considered a particular issue as it has not received a Commission proposal on it.

Far more questions are tabled to the Commission than to Council, and the divergence is growing. On the other hand, questions on foreign policy matters to EPC *have* grown, as here the Presidency does play a role in carrying out policies, whereas the Commission role here is smaller. The statistics are also interesting in that they show how much more use has

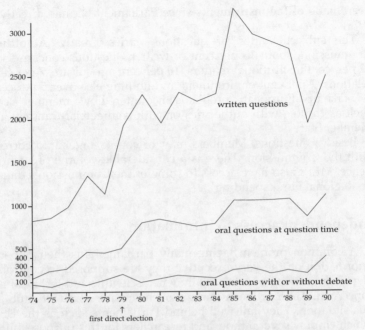

Figure 4 : *Parliamentary questions by type*

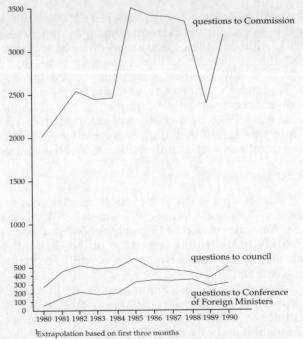

Figure 5 : *Parliamentary questions by destination*

been made of the instruments since Parliament became directly elected in 1979.

The subject matter of questions varies greatly. According to the Commission, about 13 per cent of written questions concern social affairs, 12 per cent institutional matters, 10 per cent agriculture, 7 per cent external relations, 7 per cent environment and nothing else over 5 per cent. Quite a few take up "European" problems encountered by a member's constituents such as trouble with authorities or with commercial transactions in other Member States.

Besides questions, Members may, of course, enter into correspondence with the Commission. There is a considerable volume of such correspondence. MEPs also have access to some of the Commission's databases (e.g. on Regional Fund spending).

Independent access to information

A common problem facing many parliaments is their dependence for information on the very executive they are supposed to control. This problem is a growing one, especially when scientific and technical matters are concerned. The European Parliament has made some attempts to remedy this situation. They fall well behind Parliaments such as the US Congress which employ several thousand researchers for this purpose, but are ahead of some national parliaments in Europe.

Research and Studies Department

As mentioned in Chapter 10, Parliament's DG IV includes some 30 researchers able to produce background briefings and notes on a broad range of issues. Although they specialize in different subjects, they would not easily be able to match the Commission in terms of providing an alternative, but equally detailed, viewpoint on controversial complex subjects. The Research Department also exchanges research papers with the secretariats of national parliaments, providing an additional source of information. In early 1990, a programme of studies requested by the committee chairmen was agreed including items that would be sub-contracted to external organizations such as universities, research institutes, etc.

The STOA experiment

Parliament has set up a small unit in its secretariat known as the office for "Scientific and Technical Options Assessment" (STOA). It was initially created in 1987 for a trial period of 18 months and then made permanent. It is administratively linked to the secretariat of the Committee on Energy and Research, and is supervised by a panel of MEPs, currently chaired by Rolf Linkohr (German SPD).

STOA is designed to help the committees of the European Parliament, which increasingly find themselves having to take positions on matters with a scientific or technological component and having to turn for technical information and advice to the very experts who helped to draft the proposals in the first place. It is only an attempt to respond to the rise in public interest in the social and cultural consequences of the growth of scientific knowledge and the application of new technologies. This phenomenon, now so widely recognized, has a special relevance for the work of Parliamentary representatives.

STOA will therefore have a vocation similar to that of the Office of Technology Assessment (OTA) attached to the US Congress in Washington. However, the European Parliament does not have the financial and personnel resources to set up an operation on the same scale as OTA, which has an annual budget of some $15 million, and an in-house staff of more than 100 qualified researchers. Parliament's strategy is to try to turn some of these apparent disadvantages to its advantage — at least to the extent that the need to turn to outside bodies and individuals for opinions, information and advice will guarantee that its technology assessment activities remain outward-looking. The goal is to create and maintain the widest possible network of contacts with university departments, research institutes, industrial laboratories and others with a contribution to make. Consultation takes the form of commissions for studies, which are remunerated, and invitations to submit evidence, which are not remunerated. In addition, STOA "Fellows" are recruited to work with the STOA team for six-month periods.

Three projects were selected for the experimental phase of STOA: an examination of the European Fusion Research Programme, an examination of the possible impact of de-regulation in telecommunications, and an examination of the problems associated with cross-border chemicals pollution. A conference organized in the context of the first of these projects caused a major stir in nuclear fusion circles and may have helped force a reassessment of the whole policy.

It is anticipated that STOA will give Parliament access to a broader and more varied range of expertise than has been available in the past.

Other external inputs

Parliament and its members may turn to other external sources through public hearings in Parliamentary committees, contacts with lobbyists on different sides of an argument and, occasionally, through contracts with experts. Some of the possibilities are explored more fully in the next chapter.

Overall assessment

Parliament's powers of scrutiny and control (or "oversight" as the Americans call it) have, like its legislative and budgetary powers, developed both by treaty change (notably the 1975 budget treaty granting Parliament the right of discharge) and by agreements reached with the other institutions. In this field of activity, the European Parliament's powers are of a similar order to those common in most national parliaments: access to information, right to debate it in public, right to ask questions, various instruments to exercise pressure or even block the executive and ultimately a right of censure that is not normally exercised but the existence of which helps exert pressure. Where its powers are weaker than most national parliaments is in the appointment of the executive, and the Community's executive is anyway weaker than most national governments.

14. A forum and channel for communication

Parliaments generally have an important function to play as a platform and forum, and as articulator and transmitter of ideas. For some national parliaments, indeed, this role has become their primary role as they rarely amend or reject governments' legislative proposals, but they do provide the theatre in which governments' policies are discussed. This is sometimes done with much drama, but the bulk of this work is carried out in a less spectacular way, which nonetheless helps shape political debate and sets the political agenda in a general sense.

The role of a parliament as a forum naturally overlaps with its other roles. Parliaments are naturally "forums" when they are debating proposed legislation, when questions are being asked to the Executive, and when they are deciding on priorities for the budget. In this chapter, we shall therefore concentrate on examining some of the specific instruments that the European Parliament has established to enhance its role as a forum other than those that fall primarily under its legislative, budgetary and control functions and which have already been described.

Of course, the European Parliament suffers from a number of handicaps in its role as a forum, despite the reference to it in the Single European Act as "an indispensable means of expression" for the "democratic peoples of Europe". It is not, as national parliaments are in many countries, the "meeting place" of the country, the centre of national debate and the hub of public life. It is often perceived as remote and its multilingual character does not provide much opportunity for cut and thrust or drama in its debates. Media coverage, although growing (see Table 12 and Figures 7, 8 and 9 at the end of this chapter) is difficult for most local, regional and even national newspapers and this is accentuated by the fact that plenary sessions are held away from Brussels where the European press corps is based. It operates in the context of an institutional system which is not widely understood.

Only one sixth as many members of the public in the UK could identify correctly the name of their MEP as could do the same for their Westminster MP in a poll conducted in 1988 (though this proportion may have gone up with the 1989 elections). Not all Members think that the relative lack of public interest is important. David Curry, former MEP and now a Westminster MP said in an interview with EP news: "I don't think there is any foreseeable chance of (the public) becoming passionately interested in internal market, external trade or all the things that are life and blood to European Members. My recommendation is to stop worrying about it, get on with the job and recognize that 100 years ago just about the only issue which would get a full house in the House of Commons was motions to do with the status of the Church of England."

On the other hand, the European Parliament does have some advantages. Unlike many national parliaments, it is fully master in its own house: it adopts its own rules of procedure and its own agenda, it organizes itself autonomously and votes its own internal budget. Many national parliaments, perhaps surprisingly, do not have this level of autonomy or have surrendered it in practice to the government, even for something as basic as adopting the agenda. The European Parliament, however, can raise issues in the way it likes and when it likes, no matter how embarrassing it may be for the other institutions, or for particular governments.

Its role as a forum is also distinctive by the simple virtue of the fact that it brings together politicians from 12 different countries, with different political experiences. This has a tremendous potential for enriching debates and allowing members to compare and contrast different ways of dealing with similar problems in different countries. As we have seen, many members have had government experience, and this too can contribute to debates which, whilst not always spectacular, nonetheless contribute to the shaping of ideas in the Community framework.

It is also important to remember that Parliament is not always an adversarial forum in that its members are not rigidly divided into govern- ment supporters and opposition, and they frequently seek to build a common perspective to defend as Parliament. Issue-by-issue coalition building is the key, rather than entrenched confrontation.

The European Parliament has developed a number of instruments and mechanisms for maximizing its role as a forum or at least, as an articulator and transmitter of ideas and as a channel of communication. We shall now examine these major instruments.

Major debates

The European Parliament allocates a considerable amount of parlia- mentary time to the debates that are introduced by the Presidents of the European Council and of the Commission reporting on the results of "summit" meetings, major Commission statements, the presentation of the Commission's annual work programme and annual report, and the debates on the Council President's presentations at the beginning and end of each Presidency. These are all set-piece debates covering the major issues facing the Community at the time. The Political Groups put considerable effort into preparing these debates, and each one normally tables a resolution to wind up the debate. As Parliament normally only adopts one such resolu- tion, there is much detailed negotiation among the Political Groups to arrive at a text capable of having majority support. Once adopted, this text represents Parliament's initial reaction to the issues raised.

It is also interesting to note that the main speakers in such debates tend to be the chairmen of the various Political Groups and those MEPs who have formerly occupied prominent positions in national government. Media coverage of such debates is also higher than average, in particular, perhaps, in some Member States.

Topical and urgent debates

As described in Chapter 8, Parliament sets aside three hours per part-session for debates on topical and urgent subjects in the news. One of the five subjects chosen is invariably human rights (see sub-section below) and one is frequently natural disasters enabling Parliament to call for aid to be sent by the Commission to the areas affected. The Commission reports back at the next session as to how it has complied with Parliament's wishes. The other three subjects chosen most commonly relate to foreign affairs, thus allowing the Parliament to take a position on the latest events in, say, South Africa, Nicaragua, or the Middle East. Parliament can thus add its voice to those taking positions on these matters. Judging by the number of diplomats who attend such debates when their country's interests are at stake, and the number of national parliaments and governments who react to such resolutions, they do not go unnoticed. Clearly, Parliament's opinion is likely to carry more clout when it concerns countries that might be affected by Parliament's powers to, for instance, block the renewal of a protocol under the assent procedure or cut off funds under the budgetary procedure.

Urgency debates can often deal with issues that are internal to the Community and sometimes, though unusually, internal to one Member State. Thus, Parliament's recent debate and resolution on the ambulance dispute in the United Kingdom, whilst not very popular with the British government, nonetheless attracted attention in the UK in particular in view of the speakers from other countries professing support for the ambulance drivers and the NHS.

Other resolutions adopted at the Parliament's own initiative

Subjects that are not so pressing as those mentioned in the previous sections can be raised in other ways. As seen in Chapters 7 and 8, Rule 63 Motions for Resolutions tabled by individual members or "own initiative" reports by parliamentary committees can lead to Parliament adopting non-legislative resolutions. As was described in Chapter 11, these mechanisms are often used as ways of initiating new Community action. They can equally be used as part of Parliament's "forum" role to debate common problems facing the Member States of the Community, or to discuss external problems (foreign policy, human eights, etc). Thus, for example, Parliament drew up a major report on Northern Ireland in the early 1980s which helped pave the way to the Anglo-Irish Agreement. The British government at that time was strongly opposed to Parliament drafting such a report, but was powerless to stop it. MEPs argued that as the European Parliament contained members from Ireland, Northern Ireland and Great Britain, it was uniquely placed to make a constructive contribution and it was quite legitimate to investigate whether Community funds spent in Northern Ireland were being used equitably and were helping make progress or not.

More commonly, such reports deal with major policy questions facing the Community, or with overall assessment of the impact of Community policies on particular economic sectors or regions. Many such resolutions are in response to Commission memoranda or white papers.

Rule 63 Motions for Resolution tabled by individual members only occasionally give rise to a report from a parliamentary committee, but are nonetheless an important mechanism allowing individual MEPs to raise issues. Such motions are translated into all the Community languages and distributed and are therefore quite useful, even if no follow-up takes place within Parliament, for the individual MEP concerned to demonstrate his/her activities on behalf of constituents, to place a viewpoint on record, to draw attention to a particular problem or to contribute to discussions in other frameworks.

Another mechanism allowing MEPs to raise issues is Rule 65 Written Declarations. If signed by a majority of Members of the European Parliament they are forwarded to the institutions named therein, without debate in committee or plenary. Few such declarations are signed by the requisite number of members but again, even those tabled without further action can serve the same purposes as those mentioned above.

It is noticeable that there has been a major increase in the use of such mechanisms by MEPs following direct elections and the creation of a full-time Parliament. There has been a slight levelling-off or decline of the most recent period, no doubt resulting from greater concentration on legislative powers following the entry into force of the Single Act.

Finally, it should be mentioned that resolutions winding up debates on more routine statements by other institutions, or in the context of an oral question with debate, also enable Parliament to take a position on a wide variety of issues.

Hearings

Hearings are a common feature of most of the world's parliaments: some 63 parliaments even have the power to summon witnesses in the manner of a court. In the Community, nine national parliaments have such a power and all 12 can invite voluntary experts to present evidence to a parliamentary committee, though some make more use of this tool than others. Hearings provide an opportunity to seek independent expertise and advice; to enter into a dialogue with interested parties; to attract media attention to a particular issue and to obtain endorsement from third parties (such as public figures, other institutions or academic bodies) of particular viewpoints.

It is therefore not surprising that the European Parliament has made increasing use of this instrument, which can help it in a variety of ways, including scrutiny or gaining information on complex legislative proposals, although up to now most hearings have been in the context of own initiative reports rather than a legislative procedure. Committees are empowered to hold hearings by Rule 124(3) of Parliament's Rules, with the permission of the Enlarged Bureau. In practice, committees invite outside experts without reference to the Bureau if no expenses are incurred, but request the Bureau's permission beforehand if there are expenses.

Table 9: *Hearings in European Parliamentary Committees*

Year	Total Hearings	By Standing Committee[2]	By Inquiry Committee	No. of different Standing Committees holding hearings
1974	3	3	0	–
1975	1	1	0	–
1976	6	6	0	–
1977	1	1	0	–
1978	3	3	0	–
1979[1]	0	0	0	–
first direct elections				
1980	19	18	1	6
1981	16	16	0	9
1982	23	23	0	8
1983	19	17	2	8
1984	11	10	1	6
1985	20	13	3	10
1986	23	18	5	11
1987	13	10	3	6
1988	31	21	10	12
1989	12	10	2	6

[1] Election year: numbers inevitably lower due to impossibility of forward planning
[2] Hearings by a sub-committee attributed to main committee

Few hearings were held by committees in the European Parliament prior to its transformation into an elected body in 1979. Since then, its committees have shown considerable interest in using this tool as illustrated in Table 9.

Table 10: *Standing Committees most frequently holding hearings since 1979*

Transport	32	Agriculture	8
Economic and Monetary Affairs	18	External Economic Relations (REX)	8
Youth/Education/Culture/Info.	17	Development	8
Social Affairs & Employment	12	Political Affairs	7
Regional Affairs	11	Environmental/Consumer Protection	7

The statistics in Tables 9 and 10 can only be considered to be approximate, as the criteria used by various committees to define what is a "hearing" are not identical.

In general, experts present their evidence orally at meetings and are then subject to questioning by members. Most committees ask the experts concerned also to present their evidence in writing, preferably in advance. Hearings are almost always conducted in the context of drafting a report, either on behalf of a standing committee or a committee of inquiry.

The selection of experts is carried out by procedures determined within each committee. In some committees it is left to the chairman, in others the Bureau and others select at a meeting of co-ordinators from all the Political Groups. Some committees take a final vote in the full meeting. The response of invited experts has generally been good, given that there is no obligation to attend. There appears to be a widespread interest in being able to present evidence to the European Parliament.

Most committees follow a format in which the expert makes an official statement which is followed by questions from MEPs. The rapporteur is normally given a predominant role in this. The anglo-saxon tradition of "cross-examination" of the witness is slowly beginning to develop. The other institutions attend hearings in the same way as they attend the normal course of committee business. The Commission is frequently called upon to react to views expressed by expert witnesses. Most committees publish at least a summary of the results of their hearings in the relevant report or in a specific committee document for this purpose. It is unusual to have an *in extenso* report in the style of the House of Lords, or the US Congress, the main constraint being the multilingual nature of Parliament's hearings which normally precludes the preparation of verbatim reports on cost grounds. Sometimes a brochure or booklet has been produced, but this has been unusual except for committees of inquiry owing to the length of time required for translation and printing. Distribution of the reports of a hearing is thus usually the same as distribution of the report concerned. Where appropriate, the Parliament's information office in each national capital distributes them to appropriate bodies (national parliaments, universities, organizations, libraries, research institutes etc.).

Some hearings bring together virtually the whole range of companies, trade unions and consumers concerned with a particular industry. Thus, a public hearing on civil aviation was held by the transport committee in November 1989 bringing together most of Europe's airlines, trade unions, consumer organizations, etc., to discuss the proposed second phase of liberalization in air transport in the run up to the single market of 1992. Others may be more "horizontal", such as a hearing in 1989 on fraud which led to the issue being discussed by the European Council and to subsequent tightening of regulations for CAP refunds.

Press and television coverage has been extremely variable. Some hearings have had considerable impact, even appearing on television news in Member States. In one case, the comments made by one witness (a leading industrialist) led to a strike the following day in a British car factory. However, most receive far less publicity and coverage than those held by the US Congress. Publicity is anyway not always among the objectives of holding a hearing, and this sort of impact varies not only with the subject and the desire of the committee to seek publicity or not, but also with such factors as the notoriety of expert witnesses, and timing.

Committees of inquiry

Committees of inquiry whose structure and working methods are described in Chapter 7 enable in-depth investigation of a particular issue. They also put the public spotlight on the issue concerned and in that sense are useful not only for placing issues on the political agenda but also for enhancing Parliament's scrutiny and control.

Parliament first started to make systematic use of this Parliamentary instrument soon after the first direct elections in 1979. It established a committee of inquiry into the situation of women in Europe. This committee led to the establishment of a permanent committee on womens' affairs. This is the only instance of an inquiry committee being converted into a permanent committee.

Apart from this case, the following committees have been set up:

– Committee of inquiry into the treatment of toxic and dangerous substances by the European Community and its Member States (1983–84): this committee examined the procedures applicable for handling these substances, and in particular where trans-frontier shipment of dangerous waste was concerned, in the light notably of the scandal surrounding the waste from the Seveso accident. Its report stimulated new legislation in this field. This committee also set the precedent of all national governments except one agreeing to send officials to testify before the committee, despite the lack of any legal requirement to do so.

– Committee of inquiry into the rise of fascism and racism in Europe: this was set up following the 1984 European elections and the entry into the Parliament of sufficient members to form the "European Right" Group led by Jean-Marie Le Pen. The other Political Groups wished to make a political point in reaction to this. The report drawn up represented a systematic study of these phenomena in the different Member States, examining the links between the extreme right groups across Europe. It is thus a useful reference tool for people working against racism in the Member States. Its work led to the adoption by Council, Commission, Parliament and the representatives of the Member States of the Joint Declaration against racism and xenophobia on June 11, 1986. This Declaration, known as the Evregenis Declaration after the Chairman of Parliament's committee of inquiry who died just before its adoption, was a solemn affirmation of the determination of the signatories to work against racism and all forms of intolerance.

– Committee of inquiry into the drugs problem: this compared the methods used by the different Member States to deal with this problem and examined the problem of extradition of drug traffickers. It also looked at the problems facing developing countries where drugs are produced. It stimulated the interest of Member States to co-operate in this field, albeit largely outside the EC framework. It held an exhibition on drugs which received many visitors and was subsequently mounted elsewhere.

– Committee of inquiry on agricultural stocks: this committee investigated the causes and ramifications of agricultural stocks at a time when a debate on the reform of the CAP was at a crucial juncture. Its conclusions contributed to shaping the reformed CAP and the de-stocking policy.

– Committee of inquiry on the handling of nuclear materials: this committee investigated the Mol/Transnuclear scandal. Its investigations concluded that Community officials were not involved in the scandal, but that there were lacunae in Community regulations pertaining to the transfrontier shipment of nuclear waste. The Commission undertook to bring forward new legislative proposals as a result. This committee of inquiry initially had some difficulties in obtaining the testimony of some officials from the Belgian government. As a result, the problem of inquiry committees was discussed in Council which adopted a statement emphasizing that, while there was no *obligation* on national authorities to attend EP hearings or inquiries, they were invited to do so on a voluntary basis, bearing in mind the duty of mutual obligation between the Member States and the Community institutions enshrined in the Treaties. Invitations to national authorities from the European Parliament could be sent through Council.

- Committee of inquiry on hormones in meat: this investigated another important aspects of Community policy and one which had recently sparked off a "trade war" with the USA. It endorsed the continuation of the Community's restrictive policy on this matter.
- Committee of inquiry on the application of the joint declaration against racism and fascism: this committee, currently under way, is a follow-up to the previous committee of inquiry on the same subject attempting to investigate what progress has been made five years on.

Interparliamentary delegations

Interparliamentary delegations (whose structures and composition are described in Chapter 7) are the means by which the European Parliament may discuss foreign policy or trade issues directly with parliamentarians from third countries. Most meet with their counterparts once or twice a year.

Discussions at such meetings normally concentrate on mutual briefings on recent developments in the countries concerned, discussion of bilateral issues and on common problems, including world affairs. Any follow-up must be made in the respective parliaments. Thus, the US Congress followed up requests by Parliament's delegation to scrap US visa requirements for citizens of EC countries (none of which required visas for US citizens). An interesting initiative whose follow-up was not ultimately successful was the so-called "Lange-Gibbons Code", a code of conduct for multinational companies drawn up by the US Congress and European Parliament delegations.

Delegations are also an instrument for Parliament to keep abreast of developments in between delegation visits. Individual delegations frequently meet in Brussels and Strasbourg, on the fringe of sessions or other meetings, to be briefed by the Ambassador to the Community of the country concerned, and/or by Commissioners responsible for relations with those countries. On occasion, delegations may meet to hear a visiting VIP from the country concerned. Individual delegation members may also slot into other informal networks. For instance, British delegation members are now invited to Foreign Office functions held for visiting diplomats and dignitaries.

The chairmen of these delegations, having particular responsibilities concerning a particular country, naturally serve as a link person with representatives of that country, not only from the national parliaments and governments, or ambassador in Brussels, but also with other bodies or interest groups who make contact with that chairman.

Ad hoc delegations

Besides the permanent interparliamentary delegations, Parliament on occasion establishes ad hoc delegations to third countries for particular purposes, such as to observe elections in, for instance, Nicaragua, Chile, and Namibia. The European Parliament, as an international parliament, is a popular body for providing a team to be included among the international observers in elections where such observers are deemed to be useful.

Parliament may also send ad hoc delegations for its own reasons, to present Parliament's views or to undertake fact-finding activities. Such delegations may well be quite small, consisting of a single member (possibly a rapporteur on the subject) and an official. For instance, Parliament monitored in this way the application for the food aid programme which it had got off the ground using its budgetary powers. Such delegations require approval by the Bureau.

On occasion, parliamentary delegations have participated in international conferences. For instance, Parliament sent a delegation (including the chairmen of its human rights' sub-committee) to the CSCE Review Conference in Vienna in 1987. The delegation held talks with the ambassadors of the Twelve, the Commission representative, the US, Soviet, Polish, East German, Romanian and Czechoslovak delegation leaders. It was able to discuss, *inter alia*, individual human rights' cases and also participated in the plenary session as part of the EPC President's delegation (Denmark). This development illustrated how attitudes to parliamentary involvement have evolved, as it had proved impossible for Parliament to participate in the previous CSCE review conference four years earlier in Madrid. There may well be scope for further parliamentary participation in international conferences in which the Community participates, as the Commission President Jacques Delors made an undertaking to this effect before Parliament in February 1990.

Parliament also sends two Members as observers to the WEU Assembly and maintain contacts with the parliamentary assembly of the Council of Europe (which include periodic meetings between delegations of the respective bureau and co-operation between parliamentary committees). There are no official links between the European Parliament and NATO, but a European Parliament representative — generally the chairman of the subcommittee on disarmament — attends the annual session of the North Atlantic Assembly and subsequently reports to the political affairs committee. There are also regular meetings between delegations of the European Parliament and of the committee of Members of Parliament of the EFTA countries.

The President of the European Parliament may also make official visits to third countries. These generally have a protocol side (audience with Head of State, participation in ceremonies) and a functional side (meetings with Head of Government, Foreign Ministers, Trade Minister etc.). In some countries these may be an opportunity to make the European Parliament better known to a wider public. Such visits generally receive considerable press coverage in the country concerned.

Visits to the Parliament

The Parliament also receives many visitors, particularly during sessions. Only Heads of State, or Heads of Government from Community countries, may address the plenary session. The Parliament has been addressed in this way by the Head of State of every Member State of the European Community except the United Kingdom and Luxembourg, though the latter did address the joint parliamentary assembly with the ACP countries. Heads of Government, of course, address the Parliament as Presidents-in-office of the European Council, though extra visits sometimes take place. For instance, Chancellor Kohl and President Mitterrand both participated in a parliamentary debate on events in Eastern Europe in November 1989.

Foreign Heads of State also use the Parliament as a platform to address the Community. President Reagan of the USA, Pope Jean Paul II, President Alfonsin of Argentina, President Herzog of Israel, King Hussein of Jordan, President Sadat of Egypt have all been among those to address the Parliament in such a way.

Some Heads of Government of third countries of Foreign Ministers have visited the Parliament in Brussels rather than in Strasbourg. On such occasions, a special joint meeting of the political affairs committee, the REX committee, the Enlarged Bureau of Parliament and the interparliamentary delegation for the country concerned may be held. This was the case, for instance, for the visits of Prime Minister Mazowiecki of Poland and Foreign Minister Shevardnadze of the Soviet Union.

Besides persons holding public office, the European Parliament is visited, notably during sessions, by a constant stream of visitors who do not necessarily address any particular organ of Parliament, but carry out a series of meetings with Political Group leaders, committee chairmen etc. They include, typically, spokesmen for political parties in national parliaments, industrialists, trade unionists, ambassadors from third countries, and even media personalities (usually on behalf of various public interest campaigns).

Besides visitors coming to do business with members, the general public may also, of course, visit Parliament and sit in the public gallery. In view of the wide geographical spread of the European electorate, Parliament makes a particular efforts to help visitors who have come so far. Visitors' groups may apply for a special subsidy, and a programme of meetings with members and staff is arranged. Such groups may be, for instance, constituency party sections, universities, polytechnics, professional associations, trade unions, etc. The number of visitors coming to Parliament sessions has increased enormously over the years (from 36,000 in 1979 to 117,000 in 1988, though just over half come from Germany and France).

Another special group of visitors to Parliament's sessions are lobbyists, but their activity is of a different nature and merits a separate section.

Lobbyists

Brussels is becoming increasingly like Washington in the variety of lobbyists based there, and some of them are specialists in following the European Parliament, attending most or all of Parliament's sessions in Strasbourg and also those committee meetings in Brussels which are open to the public (an increasing number of committees, Environment, Economic etc., have opened their doors). Listening to lobbyists on various of sides of a particular issue can be an important source of information for MEPs.

Besides the regular lobbying there are also individual lobbying campaigns on particular issues, such as tobacco excise harmonization, where a major campaign was launched against the Commission's proposals. The Commission's proposals for a block exemption for beer supply agreements (notably the tied house system in the United Kingdom) is another example, where the British brewers and British publicans, and consumer organizations such as CAMRA, were all lobbying in Brussels and Strasbourg. Most well-known of all, perhaps, was the multinational's lobby against the so-called Vredeling proposals from the Commission on employee information and consultation in multinational companies.

Since access to the Parliament is rather open and since Parliament has not established a registry of lobbyists, it is practically impossible to measure the increase in lobbying activity since 1979. Nevertheless, it is clear to all involved that it has increased greatly.

During sessions, some 200 passes are issued every day to visitors other than members of the public in visitors' groups, staff of other institutions, and member's personal assistants. Of these 200, it is estimated that some 150 per day are lobbyists.

Lobbying takes many forms, from briefings in Strasbourg hotels for 100 or more members down to lobbying of individual MEPs in their constituencies. Their influence is also hard to measure, although it is often apparent in the tenor of amendments to committee reports and Commission proposals, in Rule 63 resolutions, or in written or oral questions. Some lobbyists, such as the animal welfare lobbyist who has been active in Strasbourg for years, have had a very high profile.

Contact channels to the other institutions

Besides the formal appearance of Commissioners and Council Presidents in plenary and in front of parliamentary committees, a number of other methods of pursuing dialogue with the other institutions have grown up over the years, and new techniques continue to be explored.

The most publicly apparent is, perhaps, the attendance of the President of the European Parliament at the meetings of the European Council of Heads of Government. The President does not attend the whole of the European Council meetings, but presents Parliament's views on the issues to be discussed at the opening of the meeting. This is a relatively recent development, started during Lord Plumb's presidency of Parliament in 1988.

The President of the European Parliament is also invited, on occasion, to attend particular meetings of the Council, especially informal meetings of the Foreign Ministers where major issues facing the Community are discussed without a formal agenda.

More regular are the monthly meetings (usually in Strasbourg during sessions) of the Presidents of the Commission, Parliament and Council. These are used as an opportunity to explore solutions to a whole range of problems where the three institutions are in disagreement. When it comes to budgetary disagreements, these meetings are known as the "tripartite dialogue" (or, familiarly the "trialogue"), and have been formalized in the Joint Declaration on the budgetary procedure of June 1982. According to this agreement, it is up to the three Presidents to propose solutions to classify budgetary expenditure and to consider any unresolved problems in order to prepare joint proposals for a solution to be submitted to the institutions.

The President of Parliament, although formally responsible for its external relations, does not have the monopoly on channels of communication. There have, on occasion, been meetings between the Council, (Foreign Ministers) and the entire Enlarged Bureau of Parliament. More common are meetings between Political Group chairmen and Commissioners. Commissioners also are invited to attend certain meetings of Political Groups with which they have links.

Committee chairmen are normally in close contact with the Commissioners responsible for their area and meet regularly. An active committee chairman will also maintain close contact with the minister responsible for chairing Council meetings in his/her area. Recently, committee chairmen have been invited on occasion to relevant meetings of Council, but it is more common for the Chairman to meet just the President of Council before Council meetings.

Contacts also exist at staff level. Compared to the more intense level of contact between Commission and Council staff, who are based in the same town, Parliament is at a disadvantage here. Regular and easy contact, reinforced by informal contact and social conversations outside the office, plays an important role in facilitating communication between institutions. The recent transfer of some categories of Parliament staff from Luxembourg has certainly been a help. But, as the head of the Commission's legal Service has gone on record to say: "There is no doubt that, as is shown by the situation of the governments and the parliaments in all our Member States, only a geographical re-grouping of the two branches of the legislative authority (Council and Parliament) and the executive (Commission) will contribute decisively to an improvement in inter-institutional relations."

Notwithstanding the limitations of informal contacts, the Commission has set up a comprehensive internal structure for maintaining contacts with Parliament. Each Commissioner has a parliamentary attache among the members of his private office (Cabinet), acting as a permanent link-man with Parliament and its organs. These parliamentary attaches, together with members of the Commission's legal service and general secretariat, constitute the Commission's "Parliamentary Affairs Group" which meets every week to examine all aspects of relations with the Parliament and reports directly to the College of Commissioners, enabling them to react quickly if there is a risk of political difficulties with Parliament. In addition, each Commission department (DG) has a co-ordinator responsible for parliamentary affairs. These co-ordinators maintain permanent contact between their department and the relevant parliamentary committee on the one hand and their Commissioner's parliamentary attache on the other.

As a result of this structure, most Commission departments are quite well informed as to parliamentary opinions and the state of play in Parliament. It is also relatively easy for meetings to be arranged between MEPs and individual officials within the Commission. The Commission has a relatively open bureaucracy and this structure ensures that MEPs can take full advantage of that openness. The Secretary-General of the Commission, indeed, stated on BBC Radio 4 recently that some 40 per cent of his time was spent on issues concerned with the European Parliament, as opposed to 5 per cent when he was first in the Commission (before direct elections).

Finally, a word about Parliament sessions in Strasbourg. These are an opportunity for an intense round of contacts as MEPs are joined by the entire Commission (which holds its weekly meetings in Strasbourg during plenary sessions), Ministers of the Council, and so on. This relatively open week-long "conclave" enables MEPs to "collar" Commissioners away from their civil servants. All concerned are also virtually obliged to socialize as none of them are rushing home straight after work, all being "away from home" in a congress atmosphere. As a result, plenaries are the Community's information market where it is possible to get a picture of the latest state of play on any issue.

Contact channels to national parliaments

Prior to direct elections, every MEP was, of course, also a member of his national parliament. Since then, the dual mandate has declined from about one fifth of MEPs immediately after the first elections in 1979 to 34 (6.5 per cent) in January 1990: 18 Italian, seven French, six UK (four Lords), two Irish and one Dane. New structures have had to be put in place, or old ones developed, in order to ensure that contacts are maintained with national parliaments.

The most intense contacts are probably those that are not established on a formal parliament-to-parliament basis, but are maintained through individual MEPs as members of their own political parties. There is no doubt that this is the most frequent form of contact, and, as we have seen, the party Groups in the Parliament have also established a variety of links with their corresponding national parties.

A number of more formalized parliament-to-parliament contacts exist. There is a bi-annual meeting of the President of the European Parliament with the Presidents or speakers of the national parliaments of the Member States, which provides an opportunity to review the network of relations among parliaments and to suggest improvements.

This meeting alternates with the bi-annual meeting of the President of the European Parliament and the Parliamentary Assembly of the Council of

Europe with the Presidents of national parliaments from all Council of Europe Member States (currently 23). This "big" conference has been held on a regular basis since 1976, whereas the "small" conference began only in 1981. These meetings are an opportunity to review links and structures of co-operation.

Current political issues are more a matter for contacts between the European Parliament's committees and corresponding committees in national parliaments. Almost all the European Parliament's committees have relations with national parliamentary bodies. These generally take the form of meetings with small delegations, or sometimes a whole committee of a national parliament visiting Brussels or Strasbourg. Due to timetable and cost constraints, contacts tend to be sporadic, though the Economic Committee did organize a series of meetings with all national parliamentary committees on fiscal harmonization, and the Transport Committee has done likewise on various issues. The "market committee" of the Danish *Folketing* has been a particularly frequent visitor.

Besides committee-to-committee contact, national parliaments often send delegations to the European Parliament during plenary sessions in Strasbourg in order to have a series of meetings with different committees, Group chairmen, etc. Over the last five years, there have been, on average, just over six such visits per annum. Conversely, the European Parliament sends occasional delegations to meet national parliamentary committees and MEPs are often invited to give evidence in hearings in national parliaments.

Most national parliaments have set up specialist committees or other organs to deal with European affairs. Their powers vary greatly. The House of Commons committee, for instance, may do little more than examine Community documents and recommend that some of them should be subject to debate on the floor of the House. The Danish *Folketing*'s committee, on the other hand, normally has a discussion with Danish ministers prior to Council meetings and virtually mandates the minister as to what position to take (though this power has largely arisen due to the long period of minority government in Denmark). Many of these committees invite MEPs to give evidence formally or informally. In three cases, the committees are actually composed on a parity basis of national MPs and MEPs from the country concerned. This is the case in Belgium, Greece and in the Federal Republic of Germany.

In 1989, following a suggestion by Laurent Fabius (who is both an MEP and President of a national parliament, the French *Assemblée Nationale*), it was agreed to have a meeting of the organs in national parliament responsible for European affairs (see Table 7). This was held in Paris in autumn 1989 and it was agreed to meet again in Cork in May 1990 (i.e. in the countries holding the Presidency of Council). The European Parliament also attends (and provides the technical facilities, such as interpretation).

Almost all the national parliaments have also altered their administrative structure and set up liaison offices with the European Parliament. For its part, the European Parliament has a division responsible for relations with national parliaments which maintains contact with these bodies. Officials from almost all the national parliaments attend each session of the European Parliament.

Table 11: *List of specialist bodies within the parliaments of Member States*

BELGIUM	Adviescomité voor Europese aangelegenheden/Comité d'Avis chargé de Questions européennes (*Kamer van Volksvertegenwoordigers/Chambre des Représentants*)
DENMARK	Markedsudvalget (*Folketing*)
GERMANY	Unterausschuss des Auswärtigen Ausschusses für Fragen der Europäischen Gemeinschaften (*Bundestag*) Ausschuss für Fragen der Europäischen Gemeinschaften (*Bundesrat*)
GREECE	Committee On European Community Affairs
SPAIN	Comisión Mixta para Las Comunídades Europeas (*Congreso de los Diputados/Senado*)
FRANCE	Délégation de L'Assembleé Nationale (et du Sénat) pour les Communautés européennes (*Assemblée Nationale/Séna*t)
IRELAND	Joint Committee on the secondary legislation of the European Communities (*Dail Eireann/Séanad Eireann*)
ITALY	Commissione Affari Esteri e Communitari (*Camera dei Deputati*) Giunta per gli Affari delle Comunità europee (*Senato della Republica*)
LUXEMBOURG	—
NETHERLANDS	Vaste Commissie voor EG-Zaken (*Tweede Kamer*) Vaste Commissie voor Europese Samenwerkingsorganisaties (*Eerste Kamer*)
PORTUGAL	Comissão do Assuntos Europeus (*Assembleia da República*)
UNITED KINGDOM	Select Committee on European legislation (House of Commons) Select Committee on the European Communities (House of Lords)

In September 1977, the European Parliament, the Parliamentary Assembly of the Council of Europe and the national parliaments set up a joint "European Centre for Parliamentary Research and Documentation". The aims of the centre are to promote the exchange of information among parliaments, to prevent duplication of what is often costly research, and to establish co-operation for documentation purposes between parliamentary libraries and research departments (including mutual access to databases). The centre is administered jointly by the Parliamentary Assembly and the European Parliament, though the latter in fact provides most of the administrative back-up. The centre comes under the authority of the Conference of Presidents (see above) to which the Presidents of the European Parliament and the Parliamentary Assembly jointly present a report and an action programme. The centre has set up seven different working parties composed of officials from the different parliaments in order to work on improved co-operation among Parliament libraries, data processing departments, researchers etc. It publishes a newsletter between four and six times a year which provides information on activities in various parliaments, extensive lists of documentation and studies available upon request from each parliament, and continually updates a directory of who is responsible for what in each parliament.

Contacts with individual governments

As well as national parliaments, national governments are represented at Parliament sessions and, frequently, committees, quite apart from their contacts via Council. This is normally done through the Permanent Representations of Member States in Brussels. For the UK, for instance, three of their officials travel to Strasbourg for each session when they are usually joined by another official from the Foreign Office headquarters in London. British Ministers also attend almost every session.

Officials from the permanent representations similarly attend the more important committee meetings, where they may sit in the seats reserved for Council.

These officials report back to their ministries on what is happening in Parliament within hours or even minutes of events. They are also able to brief MEPs, especially of their own nationality, on particular concerns of their government. MEPs frequently contact them for information or to ask for their own views to be passed on.

Contacts also take place in national capitals. Heads of government or foreign ministers may meet MEPs formally or informally. In some Member States, such as Italy, these contacts are regular and may involve all the MEPs from that country having a working session with the Prime Minister.

The President of the European Parliament also makes an official visit to each Member State during his or her term of office, which is normally used to meet the head of state and government and relevant ministers. The President also normally visits the Member State holding the Presidency of Council at the beginning (or even just before) its term of office.

Activities in the field of human rights

This deserves a special mention as the European Parliament has put some effort into being a channel through which human rights cases can be raised. Besides dealing with general human rights issues, it is one of the few parliaments which carries out case-work on individual human rights violations. It has set up an administrative unit with a staff of six to help carry out these activities.

Parliament has a number of ways of dealing with human rights issues. Discreet approaches, frequently the most effective way to help in individual cases, can be made by the President of Parliament with ambassadors or visiting dignitaries from third countries. The President may also send messages to the governments of countries concerned. Interparliamentary delegations can also be used as vehicle for raising particular cases discreetly, as can ACP Assembly meetings. A special mechanism for discussing human rights issues was set up in the ACP – EEC Assembly framework in 1986, overcoming a previous reluctance of the ACP countries to discuss these matters.

In cases where public action is thought to be more appropriate, a similar variety of instruments can be used. The President can make public statements, delegations may make public pronouncements and, above all, Parliament itself may adopt a resolution. This is most frequently done in the human rights section of topical and urgent debates.

Human rights resolutions follow a particular procedure, being referred first to the human rights sub-committee of the Political Affairs Committee which, with the assistance of the human rights unit, ascertains the most urgent cases and attempts, often at short notice, to verify the facts surrounding each case. This latter task is not always easy, though the human rights unit is in close contact with organizations such as Amnesty International. Besides resolutions, MEPs may address parliamentary questions, notably to the Foreign Ministers and the Commission.

The human rights sub-committee also prepares for Parliament an annual report on the situation of human rights across the world. This usually gives rise to a major debate and intense lobbying by representatives of the countries most criticized.

Parliament has also been successful in encouraging the other institutions to take up human rights matters. Since 1986, the Foreign Ministers have agreed to transmit to Parliament an annual memorandum on the activities of the Twelve in the field of human rights in the course of the previous year. In the 1989 report, they stated that "resolutions of the Parliament make an important contribution to the development of the Twelve policies on human rights", and that they "would continue to draw inspiration from the European Parliament". In 1987, the ministers of the Twelve established within EPC a working group on human rights, and the Member States of the Community now try to act as a unit in organs such as the United Nations' Human Rights Commission.

Similarly, the Commission, in response to parliamentary pressure, has set up a human rights database. It also administers a budget line created by

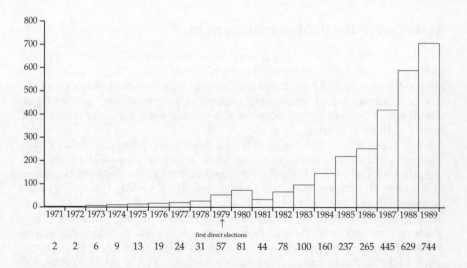

first direct elections

| 2 | 2 | 6 | 9 | 13 | 19 | 24 | 31 | 57 | 81 | 44 | 78 | 100 | 160 | 237 | 265 | 445 | 629 | 744 |

Figure 6: *Number of petitions received by the European Parliament*

the European Parliament entitled "Human Rights Foundation" intended to give support to human rights organizations. The Commission has its own diplomatic network of delegates in many third countries (89 at present), and these delegates participate in the regular consultation meetings between Community ambassadors.

Petitions

Every citizen of the European Community has "the right, individually or jointly with others to address written requests or complaints (petitions) to the European Parliament" (Rule 128 of Parliament's Rules of Procedure). This right was first introduced into Parliament's Rules in 1953. It is the only rule which confers rights on persons other than MEPs. Little use was made of this right until the mid-1970s when the number began to rise. It has risen substantially since direct elections were introduced in 1979 (see Figure 6).

The conditions for their admissibility are straightforward. They are deemed admissible if they are formally in order (are signed by a petitioner who indicates his name, occupation, nationality and address) and if they fall within the sphere of activities of the Community (concept usually interpreted liberally). Since 1987, they have been dealt with by a special committee which Parliament set up for this purpose (having previously been dealt with initially by the Legal Affairs Committee and subsequently by the committee on Rules of Procedure and Petitions). This committee can draw up the report on matters referred to it, organize hearings, send MEPs to investigate on the spot, or request information or action from the Commission and to a certain extent, as we shall see, Member States.

Most petitions fall into one of two categories. Some express views on a particular issue (most frequently environmental matters, human rights, foreign policy matters, animal protection and European Union). Such petitions frequently have a very large number of signatories. Generally, the petitions committee forwards the petition to the parliamentary committee responsible for the subject in question, and informs the first signatory of the petition of any recent Parliament standpoints on the issue.

The other common type of petition is for the redress of a particular grievance. Such petitions are usually signed by individuals. They mostly concern matters such as disputes with customs authorities at internal Community frontiers, eligibility for social security benefits in other Member States, problems with importing and registering motor vehicles from another Member State, access to employment in the public sector, civil law, taxation and residence permits. In such cases the committee frequently turns to the Commission for help in clarifying whether there may have been a violation of Community Law, in taking the matter up with the Member State and, if necessary, beginning infringement proceedings, possibly leading to a Court case.

As is the experience of petition committees in national parliaments, or ombudsmen, in many cases little can be done to help the petitioner. Nevertheless, the European Parliament can claim some important successes in helping individual petitioners to overcome certain problems (e.g. disentangling pension problems when they have moved from one country to another), in causing the Commission to bring infringement proceedings against Member States (e.g. on taxation of imported vehicles), in persuading Member States to change administrative practices (e.g. Germany modified from one year to three years the deadline for foreigners to change their driving licence) and in helping to obtain refunds in cases of double taxation.

One particularly delicate problem for the Parliament was in knowing exactly what rights it had to approach Member States for in information or assistance. Here, it has made progress on two fronts. Firstly, on April 12, 1989, the Presidents of the Parliament, Commission and Council signed a solemn declaration concerning the rights of European citizens to petition the European Parliament and encouraging Member States to give "as clear and swift replies as possible to those questions which the Commission might decide, after due examination, to forward to the Member States concerned". They pointed to the principle enshrined, in particular, in Article 5 of the EEC Treaty, requiring the Member States and Community institutions to "co-operate wholeheartedly in applying the treaties." Secondly, the Petitions Committee has established links with equivalent committees in national parliaments.

The Petitions Committee prepares an annual report on its work which is submitted to the European Parliament for debate in plenary.

Prizes

The European Parliament awards a certain number of prizes. These awards are an opportunity to express certain values and positions and to attract media attention to a particular person or issue.

The most well known prize is the Sakharov prize for freedom of thought. Winners so far have included Nelson Mandela and Alexander Dubcek. The latter was able to receive his prize in person and address the Parliament in the immediate aftermath of the Czechoslovak revolution of 1989 and the former was able to address Parliament after his release from prison in 1990. Another important prize is the annual Prix Europa, which is a competition for the best non-fictional television programme in Europe. There may also be one-off prizes such as when Parliament decides to award a prize for the best initiative taken in the course of the European Year of the Environment.

Conferences, symposia and exhibitions

The European Parliament or its committees on occasion sponsor conferences that bring together decision-takers or holders of office concerned with a particular issue. In recent years there have been, for instance, conferences on energy and on technological research. In February 1988, Parliament took the initiative of organizing the world food conference with experts from around the globe to examine how to transform short-term food aid policies into a long-term strategy to overcome rural poverty in the Third World.

Similarly, exhibitions are sometimes organized under Parliament's auspices. At almost every plenary session, at least two exhibitions are authorized on Parliament's premises. Occasionally, an organ of Parliament itself may organize an exhibition, such as recent ones on the drug problem, the life of Jean Monnet (on the hundredth anniversary of his birth), etc.

Miscellaneous

This chapter has described only some of the essential mechanisms through which Parliament acts as a forum or a channel of communication. It would be incomplete without referring the reader back to sections on Political Groups and on intergroups (Chapters 5 and 9), both of which play an important role in this respect. Some mention should also be made of the following:

- Opinion polls: Parliament can ask the Commission's "Euro-barometer" survey to ask particular questions, usually to illustrate public support for its positions. Thus, 57 per cent of those polled in March/April 1988 were in favour of the European Parliament drafting a new constitution for European Union, as compared to 15 per cent opposed to this.
- Publications: Parliamentary reports are, naturally, printed and distributed to the relevant authorities. On occasion, special reports and studies are drawn up in the form of printed brochures for wider distribution. They have not yet reached the status of the House of Lords reports, being constrained by financial limitations and the multilingual nature of Parliament. Brochures and pamphlets are also available explaining Parliament's mechanisms and activities. Political Groups

Parliament's information services produce a monthly newspaper which reports on the topics dealt with the plenary sessions. Circulation of the various language versions totals over two million copies per issue.
- National information offices: Parliament maintains a small office in each national capital. These are used not only to maintain links with national authorities, but also provide information for the general public. Any interested citizen can turn to them for information. They are most frequently in contact with the media, professional organizations, politicians and diplomats.
- External meetings: each Parliamentary committee may meet once a year away from the working places, usually in a national capital. Such meetings are normally used for contacts with members of the government and national parliament and other figures in the country concerned.

Overall assessment

Having examined this diverse list of instruments available to Parliament to enhance its role as a forum and channel of communication, it is perhaps worth dwelling for a moment on the purposes which these serve. It is possible to discern three directions in which Parliament serves as a transmitter and articulator of ideas.

First, and most obviously, MEPs transmit concerns "upwards". Parliament is a platform where MEPs, often in response to worries voiced in their constituencies or by national political parties, articulate concerns, express viewpoints, communicate reactions and take initiatives. Issues raised may be directed to Community institutions where the EC has a particular role to play, or outside the Community when dealing with foreign policy issues or human rights.

The second, and most distinctive direction, is, "sideways". Parliament is an arena for exchanging experiences and transmitting ideas from one national political culture to another. Parliament is a meeting place for members of political parties facing similar problems, for political activists dealing with similar issues in different countries, and, often, for members having faced similar governmental difficulties. National experiences can be compared. MEPs come into more regular contact with politicians in other countries than almost any other national politicians.

Third, and perhaps not always consciously, MEPs have a role to play "downwards" in explaining the European Community to a wider public. They do this within their constituencies (where many for them have circular newsletters reporting back to party members, local industrialists and/or trade unionists, local government and others). They spend considerable time explaining their actions and therefore the Community to the local media. Last, but by no means least, they are inevitably caught up in explaining Community issues, and frequently justifying Community policies, within their national political party. Over the years, these activities must surely have an effect in gradually changing perceptions on Europe and stimulating a greater awareness of what is happening in the Community.

Table 12: Media coverage of the European Parliament

	1979	1980	1981	1982	1983	1984	1985[1]	1986	1987	1988	1989[3]
Average number of journalists attending sessions[2]	130	116	109	106	117	156	134	146	137	172	192
Number of TV reports of sessions	n.a.	347	216	182	392	394	413[4]	488	576	676	792
Number of hrs of TV reports of sessions	57h 10	52h 30	28h	25h 34	46h 15	58h 15	39h 41	58h 24	58h 34	79h 15	96h 50
Number of radio reports of sessions using EP studio/radio circuits (most do not)	n.a.	767	597	528	596	547	619	644	674	790	792

[1] All figures for 1985 exclude the month of May (President Reagan's visit) which had an exceptional high media coverage

[2] Excluding journalists coming as a group (e.g. specialized press for a particular debate)

[3] Only 11 sessions in 1989 due to elections

[4] A 9-minute TV commemoration of Robert Schuman compiled by EP services was also transmitted by several stations. It is not included in these figures

Source: DG III

Note: All these figures represent only those journalists/stations accredited during sessions of Parliament or using its facilities. They do not include productions in Member States nor coverage of EP activities between sessions (committees,hearing, etc.). For radio figures, particular caution is urged, as they do not include telephone circuits, now widely used by radio reporters. The figure must therefore be considered as indicative of trends rather than precise statistics.

Trend: All figures were in decline until 1982, since when they have recovered, especially for TV coverage which is higher than ever.

247

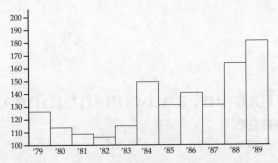

Figure 7: *Average number of journalists attending sessions each month*

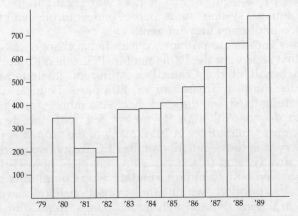

Figure 8: *Number of TV reports on sessions*

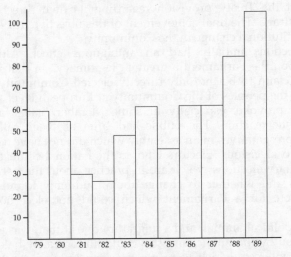

Figure 9: *Number of hours of TV reports on sessions*

15. Parliament and constitutional change

One of the features that distinguishes the European Parliament from most national parliaments is that it does not regard itself as part of a finished institutional system, but as part of one requiring evolution or even transformation into something different.

Parliament's vocation to promote constitutional change was emphasized in the very first session of the Parliament in 1952 when Konrad Adenauer, speaking on behalf of the Council of Ministers, invited the European Parliament to draft a Treaty for a European Political Community. Parliament, designated as the "ad hoc Assembly" for this purpose, proceeded to do so. Although its project fell with the demise of the European Defense Community in 1954, many of the proposals prepared by Parliament served in the negotiation of the EEC Treaty two years later.

We have already seen in the preceding chapters how Parliament has continually pressed both to improve and develop Community policies and to improve its position within the institutional framework of the Community, achieving this through undertakings from Council and from the Commission, through interpretation of the Treaties, through inter-institutional agreements supplementing the Treaties and even through Treaty amendments. Parliament also had to press constantly for the implementation of the Treaty provision regarding its own direct election by universal suffrage. The final achievement of this objective in 1979 was itself a major constitutional change in the Community.

Direct elections initially had an ambiguous effect. Although they conferred upon the Parliament a greater "legitimacy" in that its Members could justly claim to be the only directly elected Community institution, representing the peoples of the Community at European level, on the other hand it did provoke, especially in some Member States, a somewhat negative public reaction. The public had, after all, been called upon to choose its representatives in an assembly which did not have a decisive say in Community decisions. Electors who, in the national context, were used to Parliamentary elections which are in practice about the performance of governments and whether to change them, suddenly found themselves having to vote for a Parliament which could not elect nor change a government.

This new political animal, and a migratory one at that, was all too easily misunderstood by the public, and this could all too easily be exploited by those vested interests which were not keen on seeing a strong European Parliament.

Nevertheless, direct elections were a step forward. In transforming the Parliament into a full-time body it created a new class of politicians in Europe. Within almost every significant political party, there was now a small but not insignificant number of politicians whose career depended on making something of the European dimension. As we saw in the previous chapter they acted as vital go-betweens in explaining the Community and its potential to national parties and in bringing national parties further into European discussions. This was a painstaking process. Nevertheless, it slowly helped to reshape attitudes. Nowhere has this been more apparent than in the several political parties from various Member States whose MEPs — or some of whose MEPs — were initially elected to the European Parliament on an anti-Community platform, but who, over the years, have changed their position.

Besides these general processes of reshaping attitudes, the European Parliament has also set out since direct elections to propose specific institutional changes. These changes have generally promoted three distinct but related objectives.

First, Parliament has sought to strengthen the competences and responsibilities of the European Community itself. Parliament has tended to argue that powers should be attributed to the Community on the basis of the "Principle of Subsidiarity", that is to say that it should exercise those responsibilities — and *only* those responsibilities — that can be carried out more effectively by common policies at Community level than by the Member States acting separately. It is a measure of how far Parliament has managed to shape the political debate that this rather ungainly expression — Principle of Subsidiarity — has become part of the political vocabulary, as it was a term virtually unknown in the English language until the early 1980s.

Second, Parliament has argued that those responsibilities that are exercised at Community level should be carried out more effectively than at present. Here Parliament has been particularly critical of the practice of unanimity in the Council of Ministers, arguing that, where it has been agreed to run a policy jointly, it makes no sense to give a blocking power to each of the component states of the Community. The unanimity rule has been described as "dictatorship of the minority". Parliament has also pleaded for a stronger role to be given to the Commission in carrying out policies once they have been agreed, as we saw in Chapter 13 on scrutiny and control.

Third, Parliament has pleaded for better democratic control and accountability at Community level. Those responsibilities which national parliaments, in ratifying the Treaties, have transferred to the Community should not be exercised by Council (i.e. national ministers) alone. The loss of Parliamentary powers at the national level should be compensated by an increase in Parliamentary power at European level. Council is also the only legislature in Western Europe to adopt legislation behind closed doors. Parliament has generally sought to have a power of co-decision with Council on Community legislation so that Council's decisions would only enter into force with the explicit approval of a vote in an elected assembly. Co-decision would not allow Parliament to impose legislation on the

Members States which their representatives in Council did not want. It would, however, require Council to ensure that it had the agreement of the representatives that the electorate has chosen directly at that level, for any legislation which it desires. This is, after all, the norm in democracies.

The most important of Parliament's initiatives in seeking to promote these objectives was its proposal in 1984 for a new Treaty on European Union. In this initiative, Parliament was encouraged by Altiero Spinelli MEP, one of the founders of the federalist movement at the end of the Second World War, former resistance leader, former member of the Commission and elected to Parliament as an independent ally of the Italian Communists. Spinelli, with colleagues of other Political Groups in the "Crocodile Club" (see Chapter 9) first persuaded Parliament to set up a special committee on Institutional Affairs in 1982 for this purpose.

He was to become the general rapporteur of the committee, leading a team of six co-rapporteurs covering different sectors and representing the main Political Groups. The committee held public hearings and its drafts were circulated via party political networks. By September 1983, Parliament was able to approve a lengthy resolution specifying the contents that such a new treaty should have. The committee, with the assistance of a team of legal experts, then transformed this into a draft treaty which was adopted on the Feb. 14, 1984 by a vote of 237 to 31.

This huge majority reflected the careful work of compromise and consensus building that had taken place among the main Groups. Spinelli's whole approach had been based on thrashing out a political compromise among the main political forces in Europe on the grounds that this was more likely to lead to genuine progress than the traditional method of preparing treaties by working parties of officials from foreign ministries.

Adopting a draft treaty was one thing: gaining support for it was another. Parliament pursued four main channels in trying to build up support. These were:

– directly to governments, both individually and collectively in the European Council;
– through national political parties who had to take a position on the issue in their policy statements and manifestos for the 1984 European election, and which would have to bear in mind how their MEPs had voted;
– through national parliaments who were invited to support the initiative and to each of which the European Parliament sent delegations to explain and seek support;
– through interest groups, non-governmental organizations and academia by supporting and responding to the considerable interest stimulated in these circles by the draft treaty.

Generally positive reactions were immediately forthcoming from Heads of State or Government in Italy, the Netherlands, Belgium and Germany. By far the most significant reaction, however, was that of President Mitterrand, speaking as President of the European Council to the European Parliament on May 24. In a major turning point in French attitudes towards European integration, his speech culminated in an expression of support for the draft treaty, stating that "France, ladies and gentlemen, is available for such an enterprise. I on its behalf state its willingness to examine and defend your project, the inspiration behind which it approves. I therefore suggest that preparatory consultations leading up to a conference of the Member States concerned be started up". This speech placed the draft treaty firmly on the political agenda. It is not without significance that he had been visited a couple of weeks before by Spinelli and Piet Dankert, President of the European Parliament.

At the subsequent Fontainebleau European Council, it was agreed to set up an ad hoc committee of personal representatives of the Heads of State or Governments, modelled on the Spaak Committee which had paved the way to the negotiation of the EEC Treaty in the 1950s. The committee was instructed to put forward proposals on institutional matters to the European Council.

Some heads of government nominated MEPs or former MEPs to represent them on the committee. These included Enrico Ferri, former chairman of Parliament's Committee on Institutional Affairs, and Fernand Herman, still a member. The committee also had meetings with the President of Parliament (then Pierre Pflimlin) and Spinelli.

The work of the ad hoc committee finally led to the adoption of a report which agreed with Parliament on the need for a new treaty establishing European Union. It recommended that this treaty be based on the existing Communities, the Stuttgart Solemn Declaration, and be "guided by the spirit and the method of the draft treaty voted by the European Parliament", As regards the substance of this treaty, there were striking similarities between the proposals of the ad hoc committee and the European Parliament's draft treaty. However, three members of the ad hoc committee — the representatives of the UK, Denmark, and Greece — were in a minority and stated publicly that they did not accept the main conclusions of the committee's report.

The report was considered at the meeting of the European Council in Milan in June 1985. By then, several national parliaments had lent their support to the draft treaty. In Italy and Belgium, the parliaments had adopted resolutions calling for the draft treaty to be ratified as such. In Germany, the Netherlands and in the French Parliament's responsible organs, more general support was forthcoming, urging their respective governments to open negotiations on the basis of the draft treaty. Even in Member States not noted for their enthusiasm, the proposals were taken seriously. Thus, the House of Lords set up a special sub-committee to consider the issue, which had held public hearings including one with Spinelli.

The Milan European Council decided by a majority vote to convene an intergovernmental conference to revise the existing treaties in accordance with the procedures set out in Article 236 of the EEC Treaty (requiring, ultimately, unanimous support from the Member States for any Treaty changes). During the autumn of 1985, the Member States pursued negotiations which eventually led to the Single European Act. The three recalcitrant states were, in the end, willing to go along with the process of Treaty reform, but were only willing to accept limited changes.

During the course of the negotiations, Parliament monitored the work of the intergovernmental conference carefully. Its President and Altiero Spinelli were invited to two of the ministerial level meetings of the conference, but mainly informal contacts were used. The intergovernmental conference had agreed to submit the results of its work to the European Parliament, and this was done in January 1986, prior to the signature of the text by the Member States. Indeed, Italy had indicated that it would not ratify the Act if the European Parliament rejected it. Parliament, although considering the results to be insufficient, nevertheless accepted them. The Single European Act was signed in February 1986. After national ratification (involving referenda in Denmark and Ireland) it came into force in June 1987.

The whole draft treaty episode illustrates that, whilst Parliament is clearly not able to secure all its wishes, it is nonetheless able to act as a catalyst and to stimulate change. Parliament embarked on the draft treaty exercise at a time of crisis in the Community, when confidence in its future was at an all-time low. Summits had broken down on the issue of budgetary contributions of Member States, the European economy was in a period of "Eurosclerosis" and few thought that there was any realistic chance of amending the Treaties. Yet, in thrashing out an agreement among the Political Groups in the Parliament and pressing for support at various levels, Parliament was able to create a sufficient political momentum for at least some national governments to press its case, and a majority to accept that there was a case to look at. Of course, the bottom line of unanimity among the Member States meant that there were limits as to what could be achieved, but the momentum was sufficient to enable a compromise package to get through.

Since the adoption of the Single European Act, Parliament has again returned to the issue of constitutional change. It has in particular taken the view that the consequences of the single market, notably in the monetary sector, require further treaty amendments. It has also pressed for a strengthening of foreign policy co-operation and the Community's instruments of external relations. It has drawn attention to the discrepancies now existing in the Treaties between the areas where majority voting applies and those where unanimity is still the norm. It has pointed to the inconsistencies in its own powers.

The Member States have now agreed to call a new intergovernmental conference starting towards the end of 1990 on reforming the treaties in the field of economic and monetary union. Parliament has welcomed this, but called for the agenda of the conference to be enlarged to other matters as well, notably a strengthening of Community responsibilities in the environmental and social sector, bringing EPC more into the Community framework, institutional changes (more majority voting in Council, a stronger Commission whose President should be elected by Parliament, co-decision on legislation), and adoption of a list of Fundamental Rights. A report by Parliament's Vice-President, David Martin, to this effect was adopted in March 1990 by an even broader majority than that supporting the draft treaty in that it won the support of some parties that had abstained or voted against the draft treaty six years earlier, not least the British Labour delegation.

By the end of March 1990 the Commission, the Italian Parliament, the Belgian government, the German government and President Mitterrand all took positions supporting a widening of the agenda. By mid-1990 all Member States agreed to convene a second intergovernmental conference on political union. Furthermore, the Commission and the Council agreed to participate in a preparatory conference hosted by Parliament and bringing together representatives of the Council (including all Member States), the Commission and Parliament before the start of the intergovernmental conferences. Thus, Parliament is again playing an important role in seeking constitutional change. It remains to be seen what will be the outcome of this particular round of treaty amendment, but another incremental step forward for the Community, and for Parliament within it is not unlikely. In the next chapter, we examine some possible paths for the future development of the European Parliament's powers.

IV: CONCLUSION

16. Perspectives for the future

And what of that future for the Parliament? This book has concentrated on the way in which the institution has developed, in its structure, operation and powers, in the 10-year period between the first direct elections in June 1979 and the third such elections in June 1989. It has shown that there has been major change, far beyond anything that took place in the much longer period of 27 years before 1979 when the Parliament was a nominated body. Will the next years be equally important? And if so, in what direction are they likely to take the Parliament?

Much will depend on the way in which the Community as a whole develops. As the 1990s begin, it faces a challenging period, both internally and externally. Internally, the move towards Economic and Monetary Union raises big questions about the extent to which individual Member States will be willing to go in pooling sovereignty. If they do decide to move decisively in this direction, they will then have to decide whether they are prepared to accept that democratic control should be exercised beyond the national level. An issue to watch out for in this respect is that of a European Central Bank. If such a bank is established, as seems rather likely, on what model will it be based? Will it be allowed the kind of independence that the German Bundesbank has traditionally been thought to enjoy? Or will its decision be subject to a control beyond that exercised by the Economics and Finance Ministers of the Member States, with the Parliament given the chance to call it to account in a way that no single national Parliament in the Community could effectively do?

The external dimension of the Community is also generating major challenges and anxieties. The dramatic changes in Eastern Europe and the debate in other European states about what relationship to develop with the Community is encouraging some to think again in terms of a looser association of states than that provided by the existing EC structure. The purely practical difficulties of integrating ever more states into the Community are daunting and provide the ammunition for some to argue that the supranational element should be downgraded. This debate extends far beyond the Parliament itself but the Parliament will certainly be involved. The assent procedure under Article 238 of the Treaty does not simply give the opportunity to say yes or no to prospective members or associates of the Community, it also provides the means to influence the terms under which negotiations are concluded. Moreover, it provides a precedent for extending the involvement of the parliament to other forms of agreement, other than full membership, which are under discussion in relation to Eastern Europe.

The changes affecting the Community as a whole will therefore have a knock-on effect on the Parliament. The nature of Parliament's response cannot be predicted with any certainty, but one can identify two distinct but not necessarily incompatible strategies for change. The first of these is based on the assumption that the mutual independence of Council, Commission and Parliament will be maintained but the Parliament will seek to improve its position, in the adoption of Community legislation and the budget. Under these circumstances, the Parliament will seek above all co-decision including a stronger conciliation procedure, a broader budgetary role, better scrutiny of secondary legislation, the right to go to Court for annulment, and a formal right to initiate legislative proposals.

The second strategy would see Parliament claiming a wider "gubernatorial" role, something which would have a more fundamental effect on the existing instituitional balance, in particular with regard to relations between the Parliament and the Commission. On this basis, the Commission would not only be appointed by the Parliament but would reflect the political balance in the Parliament. It would effectively become the executive arm of a Parliament whose role would be to govern rather than simply to influence the decisions of the governors. The first elements of such strategy are the appointment of the President of the Commission, vote of confidence in the whole Commission and the vetting of appointments.

Such rights would place considerable pressure on the Parliament to find and sustain the necessary majorities but would have as its consequence that Commission proposals could be expected to correspond to a political prog-ramme upon which the electorate had been consulted. It might therefore play an important part in underlining the democratic legitimacy of the institution. However, some would claim that the European Parliament would run the risk of being dominated by the executive, through the majority coalition that elected it, in the same way that some national Parliaments are.

Let us briefly consider the elements of each of these two strategies. The points raised are not all new ones but they are brought together here to provide a checklist against which future developments can be set.

Improving the existing institutional structure: a first strategy.

If we take first the strategy designed to improve the existing institutional structure, maintaining the strict independence of each institution but modifying their powers, then of particular importance is the legislative area, given that a growing volume of legislation is being adopted at Community level. This may or may not reach the level of 80 per cent of economic and social legislation predicted by President Delors but it will nevertheless comprise a significant area of public policy making. A single market is inexorably leading to common rules in areas as diverse as consumer protection, banking law, environmental standards, technical norms. etc. It is strange to suppose that this legislation could be adopted without adequate democratic scrutiny.

The main demand of the European Parliament: co-decision on legislation

As indicated in Chapter 11, Community legislation is a particularly entrenched form of legislation. Once adopted it cannot be modified by any national Parliament and it overrides national legislation, even that which is adopted subsequently. Modification of Community legislation requires going through the full Community procedure and ending with a qualified majority or unanimity in the Council. In other words, if a national parliament does not like existing Community provisions, it can do nothing to modify them without the co-operation of the Commission and the bulk (if not all) of the national governments. For these reasons, effective democratic scrutiny *prior to the adoption* of Community legislation is essential.

The European Parliament argues that Community legislation should only come into force with the explicit approval both of Council representing national governments and the European Parliament representing the electorate as a whole. This is a already the case in a limited number of fields (enlargement of the Community, Association agreements, minor revisions to the ECSC Treaty and, partially, to the budget). For ordinary Community legislation, however, this is not the case although the co-operation procedure has been a step forward in so far as Council can only overrule parliamentary rejection of a text in second reading if it acts unanimously within three months.

Co-decision would not enable the European Parliament to impose legislation which the Member States cannot accept, as Council's consent would continue to be required. It would, however, ensure that legislative acts are subject to the sanction of a public vote in a democratically elected assembly: this is after all the norm in democracies.

Attempts to control Council by means of an increase in the powers of national Parliaments are not a sufficient solution. There is certainly a case to improve national parliamentary scrutiny, but it must be remembered that national Parliaments exercise their control merely over one individual Member of Council (who can be outvoted). Such control is important, but it surely must be complemented by scrutiny over Council as a whole by the European Parliament.

A simple form of co-decision could be achieved without Treaty amendment if the Council undertook not to adopt acts which have been explicitly rejected by the European Parliament, or if the Commission undertook to withdraw any such proposals. If this is considered to be too big a step, it could initially apply only where Parliament rejects a text in the second reading of the co-operation procedure.

Extension of the Conciliation Procedure

The conciliation procedure, whereby a delegation from Parliament meets Council in order to seek compromises, presently applies only to legislation with budgetary consequences. Its extension to all important areas of legislation is highly desirable, especially if seen in conjunction with an extension of Parliament's legislative powers. A proposal to this effect has been blocked in Council by Denmark alone. Its approval could be taken by a majority vote in Council.

It is also possible to envisage a sort of "simplified conciliation", through regular meetings of the President-in-Office of the Council and the relevant committee chairman before each Council meeting. Committee chairmen could be invited to attend Council meetings, as has happened on a number of occasions. These changes would not require Treaty amendment.

A wider budgetary role

Particularly in the context of the discussions on Economic and Monetary Union, there will be a debate as to whether the existing budgetary provisions in force since 1975 correspond to the higher level of integration implicit in such a Union. One can cite two areas where reform might be sought. First, it is often commented that the present arrangements give the Parliament the right to increase expenditure within certain limits, but without being responsible for determining the type of revenue needed to cover that expenditure. It is a situation which has sometimes been referred to as the "luxury of revenue irresponsibility". One way of changing this situation would be to involve the Parliament in the process of determining the volume and type of revenue provided to the Community. In particular, if a new source of Community revenue were decided upon — examples such as a tax on energy imports are often cited — then the level of that taxation could be decided upon jointly between the Council and the Parliament at Community level, rather than through Council and national procedures. This would certainly constitute a challenge to concepts of national sovereignty but it should not be seen as entirely revolutionary. The Commission already has the right to impose a levy on coal and steel producers within the context of the Coal and Steel Community (ECSC). Moreover, it can vary the level of that levy rate, only having to consult the Council and the Parliament. It has therefore broad discretion in this area. The question of whether such rights should be extended to the budgetary authority of the Community will certainly become more hotly debated in the coming years.

Second, there is the question of the widening of the Parliament's powers in relation to expenditure. In particular, will it be necessary to maintain the existing distinction between compulsory and non-compulsory expenditure? The distinction is basically a political one which cordons off agricultural expenditure from the scope of Parliament's control. However, the example of the inter-institutional agreement of 1988, which has laid down ceilings for expenditure in different categories of the budget, opens up the possibility that an arrangement could be found whereby the budget would be determined for the coming years on the basis of such a framework and without reference to any distinction between compulsory and non-compulsory expenditure. This might mean that the contents of the different categories of expenditure would be subject to slightly different rules, but these would, nonetheless, be decided upon jointly by the two arms of the budgetary authority. Such changes can certainly not take place without a modification of the existing Treaty articles, in particular Article 203, and although the obstacles to such change are certainly great, the pressure to change will also grow in the coming years.

Scrutiny of implementing decisions

Several hundred implementing decisions are taken every year by the Commission which is empowered to do so by a variety of existing Community acts. Usually these decisions are subject to the approval of committees of national civil servants which have the power to refer the decision to Council. The Commission has undertaken to inform the European Parliament of all draft implementing decisions that it transmits to such committees, but Parliament has no power to reject them. As these decisions can sometimes concern important matters and as they are not necessarily subject to scrutiny even by national ministers, there is a good case for increasing the European Parliament's powers of control in this area. One possibility, modelled on House of Commons procedure, would be for such proposals to "lie on the table" for an appointed time during which MEPs could take them up. If the Parliament does not reject the proposal by this deadline it can stand.

Such procedures should ultimately be incorporated in a Treaty revision, but could initially be carried out informally by agreement amongst the Institutions.

Right to go to Court

Following the Court's ruling in the "Comitology" case discussed in Chapter 13, Parliament is in the curious position of being able to go to the Court for failure to act, being able to intervene in cases brought by others, being able to be proceeded against itself, but not able itself to bring cases for annulment. Unless the Court revises its position, a Treaty amendment would be desirable to eliminate this anomaly.

Right of Initiative

With few exceptions under the Treaty, the Commission has a monopoly of legislative initiative. Parliament frequently comes up with suggestions through its "own-initiative" reports, and the Commission often responds with formal proposals. The Commission summarizes its response in six-monthly reports to Parliament. However, to give Parliament a formal right of legislative initiative (say by a qualified majority), a Treaty amendment would be required.

Changing the Community's institutional structure: a second strategy

All the issues raised above have been based on the assumption that the existing institutional structure should stay unchanged. The second strategy referred to earlier is much more overtly designed to *change* the institutional structure of the Community, although individual elements of the strategy could be implemented without such a change being brought about. Its basic aim would effectively be to give Parliament a bigger role in appointing Members of other institutions, notably the Commission, without necessarily changing their formal powers. This would make them more directly dependent on Parliament, or, to be more precise, a parliamentary majority.

Appointment of the President of the Commission

Under present practice, the Commission President is appointed by the European Council after consulting the Enlarged Bureau of the European Parliament. An initial extension of powers could take place by allowing Parliament to elect the President of the Commission, leaving the appointment of the rest of the team to be made as now by national governments.

The President of the Commission does not follow a pattern of rotation of Members States so no Member State would be losing its "turn" if such a proposal were accepted. Such a change would not even require Treaty amendment if Member States simply undertook to appoint the candidate elected by Parliament.

More radically, Parliament could select a whole team of Commissioners, whose political composition would reflect that of the Parliament as a whole. This could help to combat the argument that the Commission is an unelected bureaucracy with no clear political direction, but would at the same time undermine the existing separation of powers between the Community institutions.

Vote of confidence in the Commission as a whole

Since 1981, the European Parliament has held a debate and a vote of confidence on incoming Commissions. (Parliament, of course, already has the power to dismiss the Commission). A new Commission presents itself and its programme to Parliament as soon as it takes office and since 1985 incoming Commissions have delayed their oath-taking ceremony at the Court of Justice until after they have received the confidence of Parliament. This practice could be formalized in the Treaties.

Vetting of appointments

Appointments to important positions in Community institutions are made by the Member States, by Council or by the Commission. Such appointments could be vetted by the European Parliament, possibly with public hearings of the individuals concerned by the appropriate parliamentary committee, as in the US Congress. If not satisfied, Parliament could reject proposed appointments.

One could envisage such procedures being followed for instance, for:

- Members of the Court of Justice
- Members of the Court of Auditors (on which Parliament is already consulted)
- the Director of the European Investment Bank
- Heads of the Community's Missions in Third Countries
- the Governor of the Central Bank, if it is set up.

Such procedures would ultimately have to be incorporated in a Treaty revision but could initially be carried out informally by agreement amongst the Institutions. The case of nominations to the Court of Auditors at the end of 1989, referred to earlier, shows the potential for influence over appointments without formal changes in the existing structure of powers. However, use of such influence on a wider scale will almost certainly require Treaty revision.

These ideas can only give a flavour of the kind of change that the Parliament itself is likely to seek. No doubt there will be others which the authors have not considered. The tantalizing question that arises is that of the success of whatever kind of strategy prevails. At this stage it must be pure speculation to suggest what the Parliament will look like on the eve of the 21st century after the fifth direct elections in 1999. Even to hazard a guess at the number of members or its place of work would be a rash enterprise.

However, one can comment on the basis of what has occurred over the last 10 years. The impact of the Parliament over that period is very hard to measure. It is certainly not sufficient to quantify precisely the number of amendments that the Council has accepted, the hours of media coverage in 1989 as compared with 1979 or the increase in the volume of visits by foreign statesmen. What one can say is that the development of the Community as a whole in the last decade has certainly benefited the Parliament. It has acquired a broader institutional role in an environment where the commitment to a single market and the consequences arising out of it have generated a greater recognition of the need for, if not the inevitability of, a more developed European tier of government.

The next 10 years will involve the same linkage between the role of the Parliament and that of the Community. If the Community does acquire a much wider role and develops into some kind of European Union, it is hard to imagine that the Parliament's powers will not be modified as part of the change. The precise form of that change can only be dimly discerned. Will it involve the Parliament becoming an equal chamber with Council of a two-house legislature? Will the relations with national parliaments be intensified, by, for example, joint committees? Will the pressure for a uniform electoral procedure have to be acceded to? These are the kinds of issues that will have to be addressed by the Parliament itself and by the Member States, starting with the two intergovernmental conferences (on EMU and political union) due in December 1990.. For both, it will be a question of determining the form and content of democratic control at the European level; for neither side will the transition be easy. The Member States will be obliged to review long-cherished nostra as to how such control should be exercised: the Parliament will be in a much more exposed position, where it will be observed more closely, lobbied more determinedly and criticized more forcefully. However, if the Community has a democratic future, the Parliament will certainly have a vital role to play in it.

V: APPENDICES

APPENDIX ONE

EUROPEAN PARLIAMENT ELECTIONS

The following tables show results of elections to the European Parliament in alphabetical order by country. (Figures obtained from the European Parliament's Summary of Results.)

Belgium

Party		Votes	1989 %	1989 Seats	1984 %	1984 Seats	1979 %	1979 Seats
Socialist Party (Soc)	Flanders	733,247		3		4	12.8	3
	Wallonia	854,148	26.9	5	30.4	5	10.6	4
Christian People's Party (EPP)	Flanders	1,247,090	29.2	5	27.4	4	29.5	7
Social Christian Party	Wallonia	476,802		2		2	8.2	3
Reform and Freedom Party (LDR)	Flanders	625,566	17.8	2	18.0	2	9.4	2
Freedom and Progress Party	Wallonia	423,511		2		3	6.9	2
People's Union, Flanders (RBW)		318,146	5.4	1	8.5	2	6.0	1
Vlaams Blok		241,117	4.1	1	1.3	—	0.7	—
Agalev (RBW)	Flanders	446,524		1	4.3	1	1.4	—
Ecologists	Wallonia	371,053	13.9	2	3.9	1	2.0	—
Walloon Rally		85,870	1.5	—	2.5	—	7.6	2
Others		76,211	1.2	—	3.7	—	4.9	—
TOTAL		5,899,285	100	24	100	24	100	24

Denmark

Party	Votes	1989 %	1989 Seats	1984 %	1984 Seats	1979 %	1979 Seats
Social Democratic Party (Soc)	417,076	23.3	4	19.5	3	21.9	3
Peoples' Movement against the EC (RBW)[1]	338,953	18.9	4	20.8	4	21.0	4
Liberal Party (LDR) (Venstre)	297,565	16.6	3	12.5	2	14.5	3
Conservative Peoples' Party (ED)	238,760	13.3	2	20.8	4	14.1	2
Centre Democrats (EPP)	142,190	8.0	2	6.6	1	6.2	1
Socialist Peoples' Party (Com)[2]	162,902	9.1	1	9.2	1[2]	4.7	1
Progress Party (EDA)	93,985	5.3	—	3.5	—	5.8	1
Others	97,964	5.5	—	2.1	—	11.9	—
TOTAL	1,789,395	100	16	100	16	100	16

[1] includes Greens

[2] the Socialist Peoples' Party were allocated a second seat when Greenland left the EC on Jan 1, 1985

France

Party	Votes	1989 %	1989 Seats	1984 %	1984 Seats	1979 %	1979 Seats
Union UDF-RPR (EPP/Lib/EDA) (Giscard D'Estaing list)	5,241,354	28.88	26	(43.02 (	41[1]))	16.3	15
Centre Party (EPP/Lib) (Simone Veil list)	1,528,931	8.42	7	(	)	27.6	25
Socialist Party (Soc)	4,284,734	23.61	22	20.75	20	23.5	22
National Front (ER)	2,128,589	11.73	10	10.95	10	1.3	—
Green Party	1,922,353	10.59	9	3.37	—	4.4	—
Communist Party (Com)	1,399,939	7.71	7	11.20	10	20.5	19
Others	1,639,688	9.06	—	10.65	—	6.3	
TOTAL	18,145,588	100	81	100	81	100	81

[1] there was one single right/centre list in 1984 and two in 1979

Germany

Party	Votes	1989 %	1989 Seats	1984 %	1984 Seats	1979 %	1979 Seats
Christian Democratic Union	8,332,846	29.5	25	37.5	34	39.1	34
Christian Social Union (EPP)	2,326,277	8.2	7	8.5	7	10.1	8
Social Democrat Party (Soc)	10,525,728	37.3	31	37.4	33	40.8	35
Greens (RBW)	2,382,102	8.4	8	8.2	7	3.2	—
Republicans	2,008,629	7.1	6	—	—	—	—
Free Democrat Party (Lib)	1,576,715	5.6	4	4.8	—	6.0	—
Others	1,054,393	3.7		3.6	—	0.8	—
TOTAL	28,206,690	99.9	81	100	81	100	81

Greece

Party	Votes	1989 %	1989 Seats	1984 %	1984 Seats	1981 %	1981 Seats
New Democracy (EPP)	2,647,215	40.45	10	38.05	9	31.34	8
Socialist Party (Soc) (PASOK)	2,352,271	35.94	9	41.58	10	40.12	10
Communist Alliance–SAP (Com)	936,175	14.30	4	11.64	3	12.84	3
Other Left alliance (Com)			—	3.42	1	5.29	1
Centre/Right Alliance–DIANA	89,469	1.37	1	—	—	—	—
EPEN (ER)	75,877	1.16	—	2.29	1	—	—
Others	443,662	6.78	—	3.02	—	11.41	—
TOTAL	6,544,669	100	24	100	24	100	24

Ireland

Party	1989 First Preference Votes	%	Seats	1984 %	Seats	1979 %	Seats
Fianna Fail (EDA)	514,537	31.5	6	39.2	8	34.7	5
Fine Gael (EPP)	353,094	21.6	4	32.2	6	33.1	4
Progressive Democrats (Lib)	194,059	11.9	1	—	—		
Independents (1 Lib)	193,823	11.9	2	10.1	1	14.1	2
Labour Party (Soc)	155,782	9.5	1	8.4	—	14.5	4
Workers' Party	123,265	7.5	1	4.3	—	3.3	—
Green Alliance	61,041	3.8	—	0.5	—	—	—
Sinn Fein	37,127	2.3	—	4.9	—	—	—
Other	—	—	—	0.5	—	0.27	—
TOTAL	1,632,728	100	15	100	15	100	15

Italy

Party	1989 Votes	%	Seats	1984 %	Seats	1979 %	Seats
Christian Democrats (EPP)	11,460,702	32.9	26	33.0	26	36.4	29
Communist Party (Com)	9,602,618	27.6	22	33.3	27	29.6	24
Socialist Party (Soc)	5,154,515	14.8	12	11.2	9	11.0	9
Green Parties (RBW)	2,148,723	6.2	5	—	—	—	—
Centre Parties (LDR/Ind)	1,533,053	4.4	4				
–Radical Party (Ind)				3.4	3	3.7	3
–Liberal Party (Lib)				(6.1)	5	3.5	3
–Republican Party (Lib)				( )		2.6	2
Italian Social Movement (ER)	1,922,761	5.5	4	6.5	5	5.4	4
Social Democrat Party (Soc)	946,856	2.7	2	3.5	3	4.3	4
Lombardy Regional Party	636,546	1.8	2	—	—	—	—
Proletarian Democracy (RBW)	450,058	1.3	1	1.4	1	0.7	1
De-criminalize Drug Offences Movement	429,554	1.2	1	—	—	—	—
Sardinian Action Party (RBW)	208,775	0.6	1	0.5	1	—	—
South Tyrol People's Party (EPP)	172,488	0.5	1	0.6	1	0.6	1
Others	162,479	0.5	—	0.5	—	0.9	—
TOTAL	34,829,128	100	81	100	81	100	81

Luxembourg

Party	1989 Votes	1989 %	1989 Seats	1984 %	1984 Seats	1979 %	1979 Seats
Christian Social People's Party (EPP)	346,621	34.87	3	34.9	3	36.1	3
Luxembourg Socialist Workers' Party (Soc)	252,920	25.45	2	29.9	2	21.6	1
Democratic Party (Lib)	198,254	19.95	1	22.1	1	28.1	2
Others	196,156	19.73	—	13.1	—	14.2	—
TOTAL	993,951	100	6	100	6	100	6

[1] each voter has six votes

Netherlands

Party	1989 Votes	1989 %	1989 Seats	1984 %	1984 Seats	1979 %	1979 Seats
Christian Democrats (EPP)	1,813,935	34.6	10	30.02	8	35.6	10
Labour Party (Soc)	1,609,408	30.7	8	33.72	9	30.4	9
Freedom & Democracy Party (LDR)	714,721	13.6	3	18.93	5	16.2	4
Green Progressive Alliance (RBW)	365,527	7.0	2	5.60	2	—	—
Coalition of Protestants (Ind)	309,059	5.9	1	5.21	1	—	—
Democrats '66	311,973	6.0	1	2.28	—	9.0	2
Others	117,260	2.2	—	4.26	—	8.8	—
TOTAL	5,241,883	100	25	100	25	100	25

Portugal

Party	Votes	1989 %	1989 Seats	1987 %	1987 Seats
Social Democrat Party (LDR)	1,356,889	32.70	9	37.42	10
Socialist Party (Soc)	1,183,415	28.52	8	22.46	6
Party of the Social Democratic Centre (EPP)	586,337	14.13	3	15.4	4
United Democratic Alliance (Com/RBW)[1]	597,404	14.40	4	11.51	3
Democratic Renewal Party (EDA)	—	—	—	4.43	1
Others (incl. invalid votes)	425,022	10.25	—	8.73	—
TOTAL	4,149,067	100	24	100	24

[1] includes one Green candidate

Spain

Party	Votes	1989 %	1989 Seats	1987 %	1987 Seats
Socialist (Soc)	6,275,554	40.2	27	39.1	28
Popular Party (EPP)[1]	3,395,015	21.7	15	24.6	17
Social Democrat Centre Party (Ind)	1,133,929	7.2	5	10.26	7
Izquierda Unida (Com)	961,742	6.2	4	5.24	3
Convergencia Unió (EPP & LDR)	666,602	4.3	2	4.41	3
Supporters of the election of Ruiz-Mateos (Financier)	608,560	3.9	2	—	—
Andalucia (Regional party)	295,047	1.88	1	—	—
Nationalist Coalition (Regional Parties)	303,038	1.94	1	—	—
Izquierda de los Pueblos (Regional Left Party)	290,286	1.85	1	—	—
Basque Party (Ind)	269,089	1.72	1	1.88	1
European People's Coalition (Regional Party)(RBW)	238,909	1.53	1	1.7	1
Others	1,220,251	7.8	—	12.75	—
TOTAL		100	60	100	60

[1] the Popular Alliance Party, previously with the European Democrats, has now joined the EPP

United Kingdom (for Northern Ireland see below)

Party	Votes	1989 %	Seats	1984 %	Seats	1979 %	Seats
Lab (Soc)	6,153,604	38.88	45	34.76	32	31.6	17
Con (ED)	5,224,037	33.00	32	38.76	45	48.4	60
Green Party	2,299,274	14.52	—	0.55	—	—	—
SLD	986,292	6.23	—				
–SDP/Lib All				18.51	—	—	—
–Liberal						12.6	1
SNP (EDA)	406,686	2.57	1	1.65	1	1.9	1
Plaid Cymru	115,062	0.73	—	0.74	—	0.6	—
SDP	75,886	0.48	—				
DUP (Ind)	160,110	1.01	1	1.64	1	1.3	1
SDLP (SOC)	136,335	0.86	1	1.08	1	1.1	1
OUP	118,785	0.75	1	1.05	1	0.9	1
Others	152,983	0.97	—	1.25	—	1.6	—
TOTAL	15,829,054	100	81	100	81	100	81

Northern Ireland

Name and Party	First preference votes	%	Seats
Paisley, Ian (Democratic Unionist Party)	160,110	29.94	1
Hume, John (Social Democratic and Labour Party)	136,335	25.49	1
Nicholson, Jim (Official Unionist Party)	118,785	22.21	1
Morrison, Danny (Sinn Fein)	48,914	9.15	
Alderdice, John (Alliance)	27,905	5.22	
Kennedy, Lawrence (North Down Conservative Association)	25,789	4.83	
Samuel, M.H. (Green Party)	6,569	1.23	
Lynch, S. (Workers' Party)	5,590	1.04	
Langhammer, Mark (Labour Representation in Northern Ireland)	3,540	0.66	
Caul, B. (Labour 87)	1,274	0.24	
TOTAL	534,811	100	3

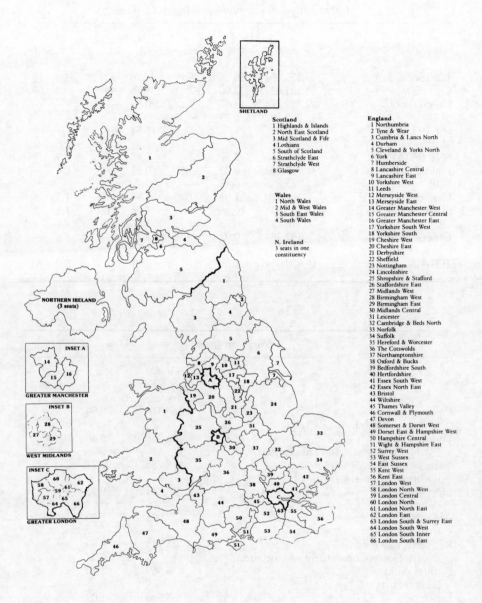

SHETLAND

Scotland
1 Highlands & Islands
2 North East Scotland
3 Mid Scotland & Fife
4 Lothians
5 South of Scotland
6 Strathclyde East
7 Strathclyde West
8 Glasgow

Wales
1 North Wales
2 Mid & West Wales
3 South East Wales
4 South Wales

N. Ireland
3 seats in one
constituency

England
1 Northumbria
2 Tyne & Wear
3 Cumbria & Lancs North
4 Durham
5 Cleveland & Yorks North
6 York
7 Humberside
8 Lancashire Central
9 Lancashire East
10 Yorkshire West
11 Leeds
12 Merseyside West
13 Merseyside East
14 Greater Manchester West
15 Greater Manchester Central
16 Greater Manchester East
17 Yorkshire South West
18 Yorkshire South
19 Cheshire West
20 Cheshire East
21 Derbyshire
22 Sheffield
23 Nottingham
24 Lincolnshire
25 Shropshire & Stafford
26 Staffordshire East
27 Midlands West
28 Birmingham West
29 Birmingham East
30 Midlands Central
31 Leicester
32 Cambridge & Beds North
33 Norfolk
34 Suffolk
35 Hereford & Worcester
36 The Cotswolds
37 Northamptonshire
38 Oxford & Bucks
39 Bedfordshire South
40 Hertfordshire
41 Essex South West
42 Essex North East
43 Bristol
44 Wiltshire
45 Thames Valley
46 Cornwall & Plymouth
47 Devon
48 Somerset & Dorset West
49 Dorset East & Hampshire West
50 Hampshire Central
51 Wight & Hampshire East
52 Surrey West
53 West Sussex
54 East Sussex
55 Kent West
56 Kent East
57 London West
58 London North West
59 London Central
60 London North
61 London North East
62 London East
63 London South & Surrey East
64 London South West
65 London South Inner
66 London South East

NORTHERN IRELAND
(3 seats)

INSET A
GREATER MANCHESTER

INSET B
WEST MIDLANDS

INSET C
GREATER LONDON

Figure 10: *United Kingdom Constituencies for the*
European Parliament.

APPENDIX TWO

CONTACT DETAILS OF PARLIAMENT OFFICES

The following is a list of addresses and telephone numbers of the European Parliament's main offices in Luxembourg, Brussels and Strasbourg, and of its information office in each Member State.

European Parliament

Plateau de Kirchberg, L-2929 Luxembourg, Tel: 430 01

89–91 rue Belliard, 1040 Bruxelles, Tel: 2/234 2111
Belliardstraat 89–91, 1040 Brussel

Bat I.P.E., BP 1024, F-67070 Strasbourg Cedex, Tel: 88 37 40 01

Information Offices

ATHENS
2, Vassilissis Sophias Avenue, 10674 Athens, Tel: 1/723 34 21

BONN
Bonn-Center, Bundeskanzlerplatz, 5300 Bonn 1, Tel: 228/22 30 91

BRUSSELS
89-91 rue Belliard, 1040 Bruxelles, Tel: 2/234 21 11

BRUSSELS
Belliardstraat 89–91, 1040 Brussel, Tel: 2/234 21 11

THE HAGUE
Korte Vijverberg 6, 2513 Ab Den Haag, Tel: 70/62 49 41

DUBLIN
43, Molesworth Street, Dublin 2, Tel: 1/71 91 00

COPENHAGEN
Borsen DK-1217, Kbenhavn K, Tel: 33/14 33 77

LISBON
Centro Europeu Jean Monnet
Largo Jean Monnet 1–6°, 1200 Lisboa, Tel: 1/57 80 31; 1/57 82 98

LONDON
2 Queen Anne's Gate, London SW1H 9AA, Tel: (71)222 0411

LUXEMBOURG
1, rue du Fort Thüngen, 2929 Luxembourg, Tel: 43 00 25 97

MADRID
Fernan Flor 4, 28014 Madrid, Tel: (1)429 33 52

PARIS
288, Bld St Germain, 75007 Paris, Tel: (1)40 63 40 00

ROME
Via IV Novembre 149, 00187 Roma, Tel: 6/679 06 18; 6/679 05 07

STRASBOURG
Boite Postale 1024, 67070 Strasbourg Cedex, Tel: 88 37 40 01

APPENDIX THREE

WHO ARE THE MEPs?

The following is a list of names of MEPs divided by country and by national party, as at March 1990.
Further biographical details on each MEP are available from the European Parliament (Elections 1989, Biographical Notes on 518 Members of the European Parliament).

BELGIUM

Wallonia (11)

Socialist Party (Parti Socialiste) (5)
Desama, Claude; Di Rupo, Elio; Dury, Raymonde; Glinne, Ernest; Happart, José

Social Christian Party (Christian Democrats) (Parti Social Chrétien) (2)
Deprez, Gérard; Herman, Fernand

Reform and Freedom Party (Liberals) (Parti Reformateur Liberal) (2)
De Donnea, François-Xavier; Defraigne, Jean

Ecolo (Greens) (Ecolo - Verts) (2)
Ernst de la Graete, Brigitte; Lannoye, Paul

Flanders (13)

Christian People's Party (Christian Democrats) (Christelijke Volkspartij) (5)
Chanterie, Raf; Hermans, An; Marck, Pol; Pinxten, Karel; Tindemans, Leo

Socialist Party (Socialistische Partij) (3)
Galle, Marc; Van Hemeldonck, Marijke; Van Outrive, Lode

Freedom and Progress Party (Liberals) (Partij voor Vrijheid en Vooruitgang) (2)
De Clercq, Willy; De Gucht, Karel

Agalev (Greens) (1)
Staes, Paul

People's Union (Volksunie) (1)
Vandemeulebroucke, Jaak

Vlaams Blok (1)
Dillen, Karel

DENMARK

Social Democratic Party (Socialdemokratiet) (4)
Blak, Freddy; Christiansen, Ejner Hovgaard; Jensen; Ronn, Joanna

The People's Movement against the EC (Folkebevaegelsen mod EF) (4)
Bjornvig, Birgit; Bonde, Jens-Peter; Christensen, Ib; Sandbaek, Ulla

Liberal Party (Venstre) (3)
Kofoed, Niels Anker; Nielsen, Tove; Pedersen, Klaus Riskaer

Conservative Peoples' Party (Det Konservative Folkeparti) (2)
Jepsen, Marie; Rovsing, Christian

Centre Democracy (Centrum-Demokraterne) (2)
Christensen, Frode Nor; Jacobsen, Erhard

Socialist Peoples' Party (Socialistisk Folkeparti) (1)
Iversen, John

FRANCE

Union UDF-RPR (Union pour la Démocratie Française/Rassemblement pour la République) (26)
Alliot-Marie, Michèle (RPR); Baur, Charles (UDF-PSD); Briant, Yvon (CNI); Chabert, Henry (RPR); de la Malène, Christian (RPR); Galland, Yves (Radical); Giscard d'Estaing, Valéry (UDF); Guillaume, François; Hersant, Robert (UDF); Lacaze, Jeannou; Lamassoure, Alain (UDF); Lataillade, Pierre (RPR); Lauga, Louis; Malhuret, Alain (PR); Marleix, Alain (RPR); Martin, Simone (PR); de Montesquiou Fezensac, Aymeri; Musso, François; Nordmann, Jean-Thomas (UFD-Rad); Pasty, Jean-Claude (RPR); Pompidou, Alain (RPR); Raffarin, Jean-Pierre; Reymann, Marc (CDS); Ukeiwe, Dick (RPR); Vernier, Jacques (RPR); Verwaerde, Yves (PR)

Socialist Party (Parti Socialiste) (22)
Alexandre, Jean-Marie; Benoit, Jean-Paul; Bombard, Alain; Buron, Martine; Caudron, Gérard; Cheysson, Claude; Cot, Jean-Pierre; Denys, Marie-José; Fabius, Laurent; Fuchs, Gérard; Gallo, Max; Hervé, Michel; Hory, Jean-François; Mebrak-Zaidi, Nora; Pery, Nicole; Rosmini, Frédéric; Saby, Henry; Sainjon, André; Schwartzenberg, Léon; Thareau, Bernard; Trautmann, Catherine; Vayssade, Marie-Claude

National Front (Front National) (10)
Antony, Bernard; Blot, Yvan; Ceyrac, Pierre; Gollnisch, Bruno; Le Chevallier, Jean-Marie; Lehideux, Martine; Le Pen, Jean-Marie; Martinez, Jean-Claude; Megret, Bruno; Tauran, Jacques

The Greens (Les Verts) (9)
Anger, Didier; Aulas, Marie-Christine; Cochet, Yves; Fernex, Solange; Joanny-Schlecht, Claire; Monnier-Besombes, Gérard; Simeoni, Max;

Tazdait, Djida; Waechter, Antoine

Centre (Centre des Démocrates Sociaux) (7)
Bernard-Reymond, Pierre; Borloo, Jean-Louis; Bourlanges, Jean-Louis; Douste-Blazy, Philippe; Fontaine, Nicole; Veil, Simone; Zeller, Adrien

Communist Party (Parti Communiste Français) (7)
Ainardi, Sylviane; Elmalan, Mireille; Gremetz, Maxime; Herzog, Philippe; Mayer, Sylvie; Piquet, René; Wurtz, Francis

FEDERAL REPUBLIC OF GERMANY

Christian Democrats (Christlich Demokratische Union) (25)
Alber, Siegbert; Böge, Reimer; Braun-Moser, Ursula; Brok, Elmar; Florenz, Karl-Heinz; Funk, Honor; Hoppenstedt, Karsten; Keppelhoff-Wiechert, Hedwig; Klepsch, Egon; Langes, Horst; Lemmer, Gerd Ludwig; Lenz, Marlene; Luster, Rudolf; Malangre, Kurt; Menrad, Winfried; Merz, Friedrich; Münch, Werner; Pack, Doris; Perschau, Hartmut; Poettering, Hans-Gert; Quisthoudt-Rowohl, Godelieve; Rinsche, Gunter; Saelzer, Bernhard; Theato, Diemut; Wogau, Karl von

CSU (Christlich-Soziale Union) (7)
Bocklet, Reinhold; Friedrich, Ingo; Habsburg, Otto; Müller, Gerd; Pirkl, Fritz; Schleicher, Ursula; Stauffenberg, Franz Ludwig Graf von

SPD (Sozialdemokratische Partei Deutschland) (31)
Görlach, Willi; Gröner, Lieselotte; Hänsch, Klaus; Hoff, Magdalene; Junker, Karin; Köhler, Heinz; Linkohr, Rolf; Lüttge, Gunter; Maibaum, Gepa; Mihr, Karl-Heinz; Onur, Leyla; Peter, Helwin; Peters, Hans; Randzio-Plath, Christa; Rogalla, Dieter; Roth-Behrendt, Dagmar; Rothe, Mechtild; Rothley, Willi; Sakellariou, Jannis; Salisch, Heinke; Samland, Detlev; Schinzel, Dieter; Schmid, Gerhard; Schmidbauer, Barbara; Simons, Barbara; Topmann, Gunter; Vittinghoff, Kurt; von der Vring, Thomas; Walter, Gerd; Weber Beate; Wettig, Klaus

The Greens and Allies (Die Grünen) (8)
Breyer, Hiltrud; Cramon Daiber, Birgit; Graefe zu Baringdorf, Friedrich-Wilhelm; Partsch, Karl; Piermont, Dorothee; Quistorp, Eva; Roth, Claudia; Telkämper, Wilfried

Republicans (Die Republikaner) (6)
Grund, Johanna; Köhler, Peter; Neubauer, Harald; Schlee, Emil; Schodruch, Hans Gunter; Schönhuber, Franz

Liberals (Freie Demokratische Partie) (4)
Alemann Von, Mechtild; Holzfuss, Martin; Vohrer, Manfred; Wechmar, Freiherr Von Rudiger

GREECE

New Democracy (Nea Dimokratia) (10)
Anastasopoulos, Georgios; Christodoulou, Efthymios; Giannakou-Koutsikou, Marietta; Lagakos, Efstathios; Lambrias, Panayotis; Pezmazoglou, Ioannis; Pierros, Filippos; Saridakis, Georgios; Sarlis, Pavlos; Stavrou, Konstantinos

Socialist Party (PASOK) (Panellinio Socialistiko Kinima) (9)
Avgerinos, Paraskevas; Kostopoulos, Sotiris; Livanos,Dionysis; Pagoropoulos, Dimitrios; Papoutsis, Christos; Romeos, Georgios; Roumeliotis, Panayotis; Stamoulis, Ioannis; Tsimas, Kostas

Communist Alliance (SAP) (Synaspismos tis Aristeras kai tis Proodou) (4)
Alavanos, Alexandros; Desyllas, Dimitrios; Ephremidis, Vassilis; Papagiannakis, Michalis

Centre/Right (DIANA) (Dimokratiki Ananeossi) (1)
Nianias, Dimitrios

IRELAND

Fianna Fáil (6)
Andrews, Niall; Fitzgerald, Gene; Fitzsimons, Jim; Killilea, Mark; Lalor, Paddy; Lane, Paddy

Fine Gael (4)
Banotti, Mary; Cooney, Paddy; Cushnahan, John; McCartin, Joe

Independent (2)
Blaney, Neil T.; Maher, T. J.

Labour Party (1)
Desmond, Barry

Progressive Democrats (1)
Cox, Pat

Workers' Party (1)
De Rossa, Proinsias

ITALY

Christian Democrats (Democrazia Cristiana) (26)
Bindi, Rosy; Bonetti, Andrea; Borgo, Franco; Casini, Carlo; Cassanmagnago–Cerretti, Luisa; Chiabrando, Mauro; Colombo, Emilio; Contu, Felice; De Vitto, Lorenzo; Fantini, Antonio; Forlani, Arnaldo; Formigoni, Roberto; Forte, Mario; Gaibisso, Gerardo; Gallenzi, Giulio Cesare; Goria, Giovanni; Guidolin, Francesco; Iodice, Antonio; Lima, Salvatore; Lo Giudice, Mario; Michelini, Alberto; Mottola, Giuseppe; Pisoni, Ferrucio; Pisoni, Nino; Ruffini, Mario; Sboarina, Gabriele

Communist Party (Partito Comunista Italiano) (22)
Barzanti, Roberto; Bontempi, Rinaldo; Ceci, Adriana; Castellina, Luciana; Catasta, Anna; Colajanni, Luigi; De Giovanni, Biagio; De Piccoli, Cesare; Duverger, Maurice; Fantuzzi, Giulio; Imbeni, Renzo; Napoletano, Pasqualina; Napolitano, Giorgio; Occhetto, Achille; Porrazzini, Giacomo; Raggio, Andrea; Rossetti, Giorgio; Regge, Tullio; Speciale, Roberto; Trivelli, Renzo; Valent, Dacia; Vecchi, Luciano

Socialist Party (Partito Socialista Italiano) (12)
Baget Bozzo, Gianni; Bettiza, Enzo; Carniti, Pierre; Craxi, Bettino; Ferrara, Giuliano; Iacono, Franco; La Pergola, Antonio; Lagorio, Lelio; Laroni, Nereo; Magnani Noya, Maria; Mattina, Enzo; Vertemati, Luigi

Italian Social Movement (Movimento Sociale Italiano) (4)
Fini, Gianfranco; Mazzone, Antonio; Muscardini, Cristiana; Rauti, Pino

Centre Parties (Republicans, Liberals, Radicals) (Polo Laico — Liberali, Repubblicani, Federalisti) (4)
Gawronski, Jas; La Malfa, Giorgio; Pannella, Marco; Visentini, Bruno

Greens (Verdi) (3)
Amendola, Gianfranco; Falqui, Enrico; Langer, Alexander

Other Greens (Verdi Arcobaleno) (2)
Aglietta, Maria Adelaide; Bettini, Virginio

Social Democrat Party (Partito Socialista Democratico Italiano) (2)
Cariglia, Antonio; Ferri, Enrico

Lombardy Regional Party (Lega Lombarda) (2)
Moretti, Luigi; Speroni, Francesco

Proletarian Democracy (Democrazia Proletaria) (1)
Melandri, Eugenio

De-criminalise drug offences movement (Lega antiproibizionisti droga) (1)
Taradash, Marco

Sardinian Action Party (Partito Sardo d'Azione - Unione Valdostana) (1)
Melis, Mario

South Tyrol People's Party (Südtiroler Volkspartei) (1)
Dalsass, Joachim

LUXEMBOURG

Christian Social Party (Christian Democrats) (Parti Chrétien Social) (3)
Estgen, Nicolas; Lulling, Astrid; Reding, Viviane

Socialist Workers' Party (Parti Ouvrier Socialiste Luxembourgeois) (2)
Fayot, Ben; Krieps, Robert

Democratic Party (Demokratesch Partei) (1)
Flesch, Colette

NETHERLANDS

Christian Democrats (Christen Demokratisch Appel) (10)
Beumer, Bouke, Cornelissen, Pam; Janssen van Raay, Jim; Pronk, Bartho; Oomen-Ruijten, Ria; Oostlander, Arie; Peijs, Karla; Penders, Jean; Sonneveld, Jan; Verhagen, Maxime

Labour Party (Partij van de Arbeid) (8)
Brink, van den, Mathilde; Goedmakers, Annemarie; Metten, Alman; Muntingh, Hemmo; Van Putten, Maartje; Van Velzen, Wim; Visser, Ben; Woltjer Eisso

Liberal Party (Volkspartij voor Vrijheid en Demokratie) (3)
Larive, Jessica; Vries, Gijs de; Wijsenbeek, Florus

Greens (Regenboog Groen) (2)
Van Dijk, Nel; Verbeek, Herman

Coalition of Protestants (1)
Van der Waal, Leen

Democrats '66 (1)
Bertens, Jan-Willem

PORTUGAL

Social Democrat Party (Partido Social Democrata) (9)
Amaral, Rui; Capucho, António; Garcia, Vasco; Lopes Porto, Manuel; Marques Mendes, António; Mendes Bota, José; Pereira, Virgílio; Pimenta, Carlos; Salema, Margarida

Socialist Party (Partido Socialista) (8)
Belo, Maria; Canavarro, Pedro Manuel; Coimbra Martins, António; Cravinho, João; Cunha Oliveira, Artur; Gomes, Fernando; Marinho, Luís; Torres Couto, José Manuel

Communist and Allies (Coligação Democrática Unitaria) (4)
Barros Moura, José; Carvalhas, Carlos; Miranda da Silva, Joaquim; Santos, Maria

Centre Party (Partido do Centro Democrático Social) (3)
Beiroco, Luis; Carvalho Cardoso, José; Lucas Pires, Francisco

SPAIN

Socialist Party (Partido Socialista Obrero Español) (27)
Alvarez De Paz, José; Arbeloa Muru, Victor Manuel; Baron Crespo, Enrique; Bofill Abeilhe, Pedro; Bru Puron, Carlos; Cabezon Alonso, Jesùs;

De La Camara Martinez, Juan; Cano Pinto, Eusebio; Colino Salamanca, Juan Luis; Colom i Naval, Joan; Diez de Rivera Icaza, Carmen; Dührkop Dührkop, Barbara; Garcia Arias, Ludvina; Izquierdo Rojo, Maria; Medina Ortega, Manuel;Miranda de Lage, Ana; Moran Lopez, Fernando; Oliva Garcia, Francisco; Planas Puchades, Luis; Pons Grau, Josep Enric; Ramirez Heredia, Juan de Dios; Rubert de Ventos, Xavier; Sanz Fernandez F., Javier; Sapena Granell, Enrique; Sierra Bardaji, Mateos; Vasquez Fouz, José; Verde i Aldea, Josep

Popular Party (Partido Popular) (15)
Arias Canete, Miguel; Cabanillas Gallas, Pìo; Escuder Croft, Arturo Juan; Fernandez Albor, Gerardo; Garcia Amigo, Manuel;Gil Robles, José Maria; Llorca Vilaplana, Carmen; Navarro Velasco, Antonio; Oreja Aguirre, Marcelino; Ortiz Climent, Leopoldo; Robles Piquer, Carlos; Romera i Alcazar, Domenec; Siso Cruellas, Joaquim; Suarez Gonzalez, Fernando; Valverde Lopez, José

Social Democrat Centre (Centro Democratico y Social) (5)
Calvo Ortega, Rafael; Escudero, José Antonio; Morodo Leoncio, Raùl; Punset i Casals, Eduardo; Ruiz-Jimenez, Guadalupe

Communist and Allies (Izquierda Unida) (4)
Domingo Segarra, Teresa; Gutierrez Diaz, Antoni; Perez Royo, Fernando; Puerta Gutierrez, Alonso

Convergence and Union (Convergència i Unió) (2)
Ferrer i Casals, Concepcio; Gasoliba i Bohm, Carles

Group for the election of José Maria Ruiz-Mateos (Agrupación de electores José Maria Ruiz-Mateos) (2)
Perreau de Pinninck Domenech, Carlos; Ruiz-Mateos, José Maria

European People's Coalition (Regional Party) (Coalición por la Europa de los Pueblos) (1)
Garaikoetxea Urriza, Carlos

Herri Batasuna (1)
Montero Zabala, José Maria

Andalucia Regional Party (Partido Andalucista) (1)
Pacheco Herrera, Pedro

National Coalition (Coalición Nacionalista) (1)
Gangoiti Llaguno, Jon

Izquierda de los Pueblos (1)
Bandres Molet, Juan Maria

UNITED KINGDOM

Labour (45)
Adam, Gordon; Balfe, Richard; Barton, Roger; Bird, John; Bowe, David; Buchan, Janey; Coates, Ken; Collins, Ken; Crampton, Peter; Crawley, Christine; David, Wayne; Donnelly, Alan; Elliott, Michael; Falconer, Alex; Ford, Glyn; Green, Pauline; Harrison, Lyndon; Hindley, Michael; Hoon, Geoffrey; Hughes, Stephen; Lomas, Alf; McGowan, Michael; McCubbin, Henry; McMahon, Hugh; Martin, David; Megahy, Tom; Morris, David; Newens, Stan; Newman, Eddie; Oddy, Christine; Pollack, Anita; Read, Mel; Seal, Barry; Simpson, Brian; Smith, Alex; Smith, Llewellyn; Stevenson, George; Stewart, Ken; Titley, Gary; Tomlinson, John; Tongue, Carole; West, Norman; White, Ian; Wilson, Anthony; Wynn, Terence

Conservatives (32)
Beazley, Christopher; Beazley, Peter; Bethell, The Lord; Cassidy, Bryan; Catherwood, Sir Fred; Daly, Margaret; Elles, James; Howell, Paul; Inglewood, Lord; Jackson, Caroline; Jackson, Sir Christopher; Kellett-Bowman, Edward; McIntosh, Anne; McMillan-Scott, Edward; Moorhouse, James; Newton Dunn, Bill; O'Hagan, The Lord; Patterson, Ben; Plumb, Lord, of Coleshill; Prag, Derek; Price, Peter; Prout, Sir Christopher; Rawlings, Patricia; Scott-Hopkins, Sir James; Seligman, Madron; Simmonds, Richard; Simpson, Anthony; Spencer, Tom; Stevens, John; Stewart-Clark, Sir Jack; Turner, Amedee; Welsh, Michael

Scottish National Party (1)
Ewing, Winifred

Social Democratic and Labour Party (1)
Hume, John

Democratic Unionist Party (1)
Paisley, The Rev Ian

Official Unionist Party (1)
Nicholson, Jim

SELECT BIBLIOGRAPHY

The reader will find below a selected series of books and articles on the Parliament. The majority were written in the second half of the 1980s but the authors have also included a number of works from earlier years as well as a few not in English which they considered to be of particular interest.

The material is divided into six sections based on the framework provided by the Directorate-General for Research of the Parliament in its comprehensive bibliography.

General

ARGUS and MINOS, *Le Parlement européen: cinq ans pour une revanche* Bruxelles: Rossel, 1984, 172 pp.

BIEBER, Roland, "Achievements of the European Parliament 1979–1984", *Common Market Law Review*, Vol. 21, No. 2, June 1984, pp. 283–304

BIEBER, Roland, "Legal Developments in the European Parliament", *Yearbook of European Law*, 1984, Oxford 1985, pp. 341–359

BIEBER, Roland, "Legal Developments in the European Parliament", *Yearbook of European Law*, 1985, Oxford 1986, pp. 341–363

BIEBER, Roland, "Legal Developments in the European Parliament", *Yearbook of European Law*, Vol. 6, 1986, Oxford 1987, pp. 357–378

BIEBER, Roland, BRADLEY, Kieran St. C., "Legal Developments in the European Parliament", *Yearbook of European Law*, Vol. 7, 1987, Oxford 1988, pp. 285–308

BIEBER, R.; PANTALIS, J.; SCHOO, J., "Implications of the Single Act for the European Parliament", *Common Market Law Review*, No. 4, Winter 1986, pp. 767–792

BOGDANOR, Vernon, "The Future of the European Community: Two Models of Democracy; The Abnormal Situation of the European Parliament, Separation and Interdependence of Powers", *Government and Opposition*, No. 2, Spring 1986, pp. 161–176

BOURGUIGNON, R.; WITTKE, E.; GRABITZ, O.; SCHMUCK, E.A., "Five Years of the Directly Elected European Parliament: Performance and Prospects", *Journal of Common Market Studies*, No. 1, September 1985, pp. 39–59

BRADLEY, K., "Legal Developments in the European Parliament", *Yearbook of European Law*, Vol. 8, 1988, Oxford 1989

BRADLEY, Kieran St. C., "Maintaining the Balance: the Role of the Court of Justice in defining the Institutional Position of the European Parliament", *Common Market Law Review*, 1987, pp. 41–64

COCKS, Barnett, *The European Parliament, Structure, Procedure and Practice*, London: HMSO, 1973, 336 pp.

COLLOQUE, Actes du, *Le Parlement européen à la vieille de la deuxième élection au suffrage universel direct: bilan et perspectives; The European Parliament on the eve of the second direct election: Balance Sheet and Prospects*, Colloque organizé par le Collège d'Europe et l'Institut for Europäische Politik, Bruges, 16–18 juin 1983, Bruges: De Temple, 1984, 845 pp.

DEHOUSSE, Renaud, "1992 and Beyond: the Institutional Dimension of the Internal

Market Programme (Role of the European Parliament and Delegation of Powers)", *Legal Issues of European Integration*, No. 1, 1989, pp. 109–136

EARNSHAW, David J., The European Parliament's Quest for a Single Seat, *Revue d'intégration européenne*, No. 1, automne 1984, pp. 77–93

EUROPEAN PARLIAMENT, The, *Forging ahead, European Parliament 1952–1988, 36 Years*, Directorate-General for Research, Luxembourg, Office for Official Publications, Third Edition 1989, 222 pp.

KIRCHNER, Emil Joseph, *The European Parliament: Performance and Prospects*, Aldershot: Gower Publications, 1984, 170 pp.

LODGE, Juliet, "The European parliament in Election Year", *European Access*, No. 2, April 1989, pp. 10–13

LODGE, Juliet, The Single European Act. A Threat to the National Parliament of Europe? *The Parliamentarian*, No. 1, January 1987, pp. 21–24

PALMER, Michael, *The European Parliament, what it is, what it does, how it works*, Oxford, Permagon Press, 1981, 235 pp.

PLUMB, Henry, "Building a Democratic Community: the Role of the European Parliament", *The World Today*, No. 7, July 1989, pp. 112–117

ROBINSON, Ann; BRAY, Caroline, *The Public Image of the European Parliament*, Studies in European Politics, No. 10, London: Policy Studies Institute, 1986, 77 pp.

ROBINSON, Ann: WEBB Adrian, *The European Parliament in the EC Policy Process*, Report of a Conference held at Wiston House, Sussex, October 12–14, 1984, Studies in European Politics, No. 9, London: Policy Studies Institute, 1985, 61 pp.

SCHMUCK, Otto and WESSELS, Wolfgang (eds.), *Das Europäische Parliament im dynamischen Intergrationsprozess: auf der Suche nach einem Zeitgemässen Leitbild*, Instut für Europaische politik (EP) and Trans European Policy Studies Association (TEPSA), Europa Union Verlag, 1989

SHONFIELD, Andrew, *Europe: Journey to an Unknown Destination*, London: Penguin 1972, 96 pp.

VEDEL, Georges, *Report of the Working Party examining the Problem of the Enlargement of the Powers of the European Parliament* ("Vedel Report"), Bulletin of the European Communities Supplement 4/72, 89 pp.

VEDEL, Georges, *The Role of the parliamentary Institution in European Integration* (Symposium on European Integration and the future of parliaments in Europe), Luxembourg 1975, pp. 236–244)

VINCI, Enrico, *Il Parlamento Europeo* (Pianeta Europa), Firenze: Le Monnier, 1980, 73 pp.

WOOD, Alan (ed.), *TIMES GUIDE to the European Parliament 1989*, London: Times Books 1989, 288 pp.

Powers

BIEBER, Roland, "Legislative Procedure for the Establishment of the Single Market", *Common Market Law Review*, 1988 pp. 711–724

BRADLEY, Kieran St. Clair, "The Variable Evolution of the Standing of the European Parliament in Proceedings before the Court of Justice", *Yearbook of European Law*, No. 8, 1988, Oxford 1989, pp. 27–57

BULMER, Simon; WESSELS, Wolfgang, "The European Council and the European Parliament", *The European Council: Decision–making in European Politics*, 1987, pp. 113–118

CARDOZO, R.; CORBETT, R., "The Crocodile Initiative", *European Union: The Community in Search of a Future*, edited by Juliet Lodge, Macmillan 1985

CORBETT, R.; NICKEL, D., "The draft Treaty establishing the European Union", *The Yearbook of European Law* 1984

CORBETT, Richard, "The 1985 Intergovernmental Conference and the Single

European Act", *An Ever Closer Union*, Roy Pryce (ed.) of the Trans-European Political Studies Association, TEPSA, Croom Helm, 1986

CORBETT, Richard; JACOBS, Francis, Paper submitted to TEPSA/Symposium "Beyond Traditional Parliamentarism: The European Parliament in the Community System", Strasbourg, 17–18 November 1988: Luxembourg, TEPSA, July 1988, 44 pp.

CORBETT, Richard, "Testing the New Procedures: the European Parliament's First Experiences with its new 'Single Act' Powers", *Journal of Common Market Studies*, No. 4, June 1989, pp. 359–372

FITZMAURICE, John, "An analysis of the European Community's co-operation procedure", *Journal of Common Market Studies*, No. 4, June 1988, pp. 389–400

LEONARD, Dick, "The Single Act and the Parliament: Shifts in the Balance of Power", *European Trends, the Economist Intelligence Unit*, No. 4, 1988, pp. 57–63

LODGE, Juliet, "The Single European Act and the new legislative co-operation procedure: a critical analysis", *Revue d'Intégration Européenne*, no. 1, 1987, pp. 5–28

LODGE, Juliet, "The European Parliament — from "Assembly" to co-legislature: changing the institutional dynamics", *The European Community and the challenge of the Future*, ed. J. Lodge, London 1989, pp. 58–79

NICKEL, Dietmar, "Le Projet de traité instituant l'Union Européenne élaboré par le Parlement Européen"), *Cahiers de droit européen*, No. 5–6, 1984, pp. 511–542

NICOLL, William, "From Rejection to Repudiation: EC Budgetary Affairs in 1985", *Journal of Common Market Studies*, No. 1, 1986, pp. 31–49

SHACKLETON, M., *Financing the European Community*, London, Pinter for Royal Institute of International Affairs, 1990, 101 pp.

VAN HAMME, Alain, "The European Parliament and the Co-operation Procedure", *Studia Diplomatica*, No. 3, 1988, pp. 291–314

WALLACE, Helen, "A European Budget made in Strasbourg and unmade in Luxembourg", *Yearbook of European Law*, Vol. 6, 1986, Oxford 1987, pp. 263–282

WELLER, Joseph, "Institutional and Jurisdictional Questions: European Pride and Prejudice — Parliament v. Council", *European Law Review*, No. 5, October 1989, pp. 334–346

Members

HOLLAND, Martin, *Candidates for Europe, the British Experience*, Aldershot: Gower Publications, 1986, 210 pp.

SCHOLL, Edward L., "The electoral System and Constituency-oriented Activity in the European Parliament", *International Studies Quarterly*, No. 3, September 1986, pp. 315–332

VALLANCE, Elizabeth; DAVIES, Elizabeth, *Women of Europe, Women MEPs and Equality Policy*, Cambridge: University Press, 1986, 180 pp.

VALLANCE, Elizabeth, "Do Women make a difference? The Impact of Women MEPs on Community Equality Policy", *Women, Equality and Europe*, ed. M. Buckley and M. Anderson, London 1988, pp. 126–141

Sessions and activities

BOUMANS, Etienne; NORBART, Monica, "The European Parliament and Human Rights", *Netherlands Quarterly of Human Rights*, No. 1, 1989, pp. 36–56

LAKE, Gordon, "The STOA Experiment in the European Parliament: the Fusion Project", *Energy Policy*, No. 3, June 1989, pp. 284–288

PENDERS, Jean J. M., "The European Parliament and European Political Co-operation", *Irish Studies in International Affairs*, No. 4, 1988, pp. 41–48

PONIATOWSKI, M., "Europe's Technological Challenge: a View from the European

Parliament", *Science and Public Policy*, No. 6, December 1988, pp. 383–393

SCOTT, Dermot, "The European Parliament and European Security: some Pointers for Ireland", *Administration*, No. 1, 1985, pp. 86–115

ZAHORKA, Hans-Jurgen, "The European Parliament and the EC–EFTA Relationship", *EFTA-Bulletin*, No. 2, April-June 1988, pp. 10–13

Direct elections

ADONIS, Andrew, "Great Britain (the 1989 European Election)", *Electoral Studies*, No. 3, December 1989, pp. 262–269 — this volume contains contributions from all the countries of the Community

BOGDANOR, Vernon, "Direct Elections, Representative Democracy and European Integration", *Electoral Studies*, No. 3, December 1989, pp. 205–216

BOGDANOR, Vernon, "The June 1989 European Elections and the Institutions of the Community", *Government and Opposition*, No. 2, Spring 1989, pp. 199–214

BUTLER, David; JOWETT, Paul, *Party Strategies in Britain. A Study of the 1984 European Elections*, Hampshire: Macmillan Press, 1985, 171 pp.

CURTICE, John, "The 1989 European Election: Protest or Green Tide", *Electoral Studies*, No. 3, December 1989, pp. 217–230

EUROPEAN PARLIAMENT, The, *Towards a uniform procedure for direct elections*, with contributions by Roland Bieber and Howard C. Yourow. With articles by Ch. Sasse, D. A. Brew, J. Georgel (Publications of the European University Institute, 11), Florence: European University Institute 1981, 449 pp.

JACKSON, Robert; FITZMAURICE, John, *The European Parliament — a guide to direct elections*, London: Penguin, 1979, 95 pp.

JOWETT, Paul, "The Second European Elections: 14–17 June 1984", *West European Politics*, No. 1, January 1985, pp. 109–112

MINOR, Jacqueline, "Further skirmishes on election spending", Case 221/86R, Group of European Right v. European Parliament, *European Law Review*, 1987, pp. 191–195

NORTHAWL, Rod; CORBETT, Richard, *Electing Europe's first Parliament* (Fabian Tract 449), London, Fabian Society, 1977; 28 pp.

PRIDHAM, Geoffrey, "European Elections, Political Parties and Trends of Internalization in Community Affairs", *Journal of Common Market Studies*, No. 4, June 1986, pp. 279–296

REIF, Karlheinz, *Ten European Elections, Campaigns and Results of the 1979/81 First Direct Elections to the European Parliament*, Aldershot: Gower Publications, 1985, 223 pp.

RÜDIG, Wolfgang, "The Greens in Europe: ecological Parties and the European Elections of 1984", *Parliamentary Affairs*, No. 1, Winter 1985, pp. 56–72

SCHOLL, Edward L., "The Electoral System and Constituency-oriented activity in the European Parliament", *International Studies Quarterly*, No. 3, September 1986, pp. 315–332

SVENNEVIG, Michael; GUNTER, Barrie, "Television coverage of the 1984 European Parliamentary Elections", *Parliamentary Affairs*, No. 2, April 1986, pp. 165–178

Political Groups

FEATHERSTONE, Kevin, *Socialist Parties and European Integration, a comparative history* Manchester: Manchester University Press, 1988, 366 pp.

Federalism in the European Parliament; "The Convergence of the British and European Conservative Traditions", *Burgess, M., Federalism and European Union*, London/New York, 1989, pp. 147–162

HAYWOOD, Elizabeth Z., "The French Socialists and European Institutional Reform", *Revue d'Intégration Européenne*, No. 2–3, 1989, pp. 121–149

JACOBS, Francis B., *Western European Political Parties: A Comprehensive Guide*, Longman 1989

MARTIN, David, *Bringing common sense to the Common Market: a left agenda for Europe* (Fabian Tract 525), London: Fabian Society, 1988, 28 pp.

REIF, Karlheinz; NIEDERMAYER, Oskar, "The European Parliament and the Political Parties", *Revue d'Intégration européenne*, No. 2–3, Hiver 1986 - Printemps 1987, pp. 157–172

SELECT BIBLIOGRAPHY

GENERAL INDEX

NAMES INDEX

The following part of the index contains all those people who are cited in the text. It does not contain the names of those who are mentioned as office holders or in lists included in the individual chapters or appendices.